Black Atlantic Writers
OF THE EIGHTEENTH CENTURY

Black Atlantic Writers
OF THE EIGHTEENTH CENTURY

*Living the New Exodus in
England and the Americas*

EDITED BY
Adam Potkay and Sandra Burr

ST. MARTIN'S PRESS
NEW YORK

BLACK ATLANTIC WRITERS OF THE EIGHTEENTH CENTURY.
© Adam Potkay and Sandra Burr 1995

First published in the United States of America in 1995

ISBN 0-312-12133-4 (cloth)
ISBN 0-312-12518-6 (paperback)

Library of Congress Cataloging-in-Publication Data

Black Atlantic writers of the eighteenth century : living the new
    exodus in England and the Americas / edited by Adam Potkay and
    Sandra Burr with an introduction by Adam Potkay.
        p.   cm.
    Contents: Introduction — Ukawsaw Gronniosaw — John Marrant —
Quobna Ottobah Cugoano — Olaudah Equiano.
    Includes bibliographical references (p.).
    ISBN 0-312-12133-4 (hard cover)
    1. English prose literature—18th century. 2. Africans—England-
-History—18th century—Sources. 3. Blacks—England—History—18th
century—Sources. 4. Afro-Americans—History—18th century-
-Sources. 5. English prose literature—Black authors. 6. Africans-
-Great Britain—Biography. 7. Blacks—Great Britain—Biography.
8. Afro-Americans—Biography. 9. Autobiography. I. Potkay, Adam,
1961- . II Burr, Sandra.
PR1297.B57 1995
818'.108080896073—dc20   94-36117
                                                          CIP

First Edition April 1995:
10 9 8 7 6 5 4 3 2 1

Interior Design by Digital Type & Design

Contents

ACKNOWLEDGMENTS

FOR THEIR HELPFUL ADVICE AND INSPIRATION during the compilation of this volume, we gratefully thank Michael Blum, Chris Bongie, Stephen Constantelos, Stephen R. Hawkins, Robert Maccubbin, Jamie Quatro, and Patricia Wesp. Our thanks extend as well to Chandos Brown, and to David Hindman of the Wesleyan Foundation, for their comments on early versions of the introduction. Robert J. Fehrenbach's bibliographical expertise and common sense have proved invaluable.

For access to texts and key historical materials, we thank Dr. Laura V. Monti, the Keeper of Rare Books and Manuscripts, Boston Public Library; Margaret Cook, Curator of Manuscripts and Rare Books, and Carol S. Linton and her Interlibrary Loan staff, Earl Gregg Swem Library, The College of William and Mary; the staff of The Mariners' Museum Research Library and Archives, Newport News, Virginia; and Betty Odabashian, Schomburg Center for Research in Black Culture, New York.

For assistance with Masonic materials, we are deeply grateful to Mr. Raymond Coleman of the Prince Hall Grand Lodge of Free and Accepted Masons, Boston; and to Cynthia W. Alcorn and Michael S. Kaulback of The Samuel Crocker Lawrence Library, The Museum of the Grand Lodge of Massachusetts—the two friendliest librarians we have ever met. We also thank The College of William and Mary for providing the research grant that allowed Sandra Burr to travel to Boston.

Thanks go to Michelle Jarrett and Sonya Willie for typing portions of the manuscript.

Our editors at St. Martin's, Laura Heymann and Jennifer Farthing, were remarkably committed to this volume, inspiring us with their consistent and enthusiastic support throughout the preparation of the manuscript.

Finally, Sandra would like to thank Donald S. Burr (Boston's Super Sleuth) and Liliana Krysiak, whose assistance and inexhaustible good cheer considerably brightened the days of a visitor far from home. Equally important were the love and encouragement of Kathleen and Bob Bergmann—and the sheer cussedness of David F. Morrill.

Adam would like especially to thank Monica Brzezinski Potkay, with whom he co-teaches "The Bible as Literature" at The College of William and Mary. Without her influence and her expertise, this book would never have been conceived.

ADAM POTKAY
SANDRA BURR
Williamsburg, Virginia

About This Edition

THROUGH OUR SCHOLARLY APPARATUS, we offer a panoramic view of the eighteenth-century world inhabited by Gronniosaw, Marrant, Cugoano, and Equiano. We have aimed at giving the modern reader a vivid sense of the various *contexts* necessary for understanding the stories of their lives: for their lives are illuminated by, and in turn cast light upon, the history of the slave trade and of the cultures of blacks in Africa, the Americas, and Europe; of the Great Awakening and of Freemasonry; of Nova Scotia and of New Jersey; of the naval campaigns of Britain and of printing in Bath. When we began this project, relatively little was known about the personal lives of these four men. What information existed was widely dispersed, some of it having found its way into contemporary scholarship, though much of it to be found only in dusty volumes. To consolidate and to extend what was known of these men, we looked closely at their texts, of course, but also to eighteenth- and nineteenth-century newspapers, magazines, pamphlets, books, and financial ledgers and to secondary sources on an array of subjects from Igbo customs to Whitefield's travels. While we have pieced together many of the details of the lives of these black Atlantic authors, much remains unknown about them. We hope our edition will provide a foundation for the work of future scholars.

Our edition is intended primarily for the student of history and literature, though we hope to have produced a volume that may be read with pleasure by the general audience. Original biographical research, bibliographical notes, and fully annotated texts should also make this book of interest to more advanced scholars of eighteenth-century and black Atlantic studies. For each of the four authors included in this volume we have supplied an introduction consisting of a short biographical essay followed by a bibliographical note that canvasses the printing history, insofar as it is known, of that author's work or works. Notes are placed at the end of each individual work.

The works of Olaudah Equiano and Quobna Ottobah Cugoano have been abridged due to constraints of space. We have reproduced over half of Equiano's *Narrative*, omitting portions of Equiano's life as a mariner and entrepreneur, and maintaining in full what we perceive as the central unifying theme of his autobiography: his account of his spiritual and intellectual development. We have included brief narrative summaries where Equiano's text has been omitted. With Cugoano's essay *Thoughts and Sentiments*, we have tried to capture the main points of his argument against slavery; we have also provided brief summaries of those portions of his argument that we have not reproduced. Where we have deleted text from the original source the break is marked as (✳✳✳); the end of an editorial insertion is marked by (————); whereas the end of a section in the original text is denoted by (✠✠✠). Our narrative summaries appear in the same typeface and style as that used on this page and in each of the "About . . ." sections introducing the individual writers.

We present a "diplomatic reprint" of the five eighteenth-century texts in this volume. Unlike facsimile reprints, which are exact duplicates of original texts taken from either the original plates or photographic negatives, diplomatic reprints reproduce only the style and general format of the original text. Capitalization, punctuation, spelling, and italics are retained, while the original pagination is reset to the page specifications of the modern publisher. We have introduced minor changes to allow for ease of reading, changing the eighteenth-century *f* to the modern *s*; deleting line-by-line quotation marks from the texts and from all verse quotations; omitting the tag words set flush right under the last printed line of each page (a device used by eighteenth-century printers to indicate the first printed word of the following page); and changing footnotes to endnotes. In those few instances in which the original typesetting contained misprinted words or a lack of punctuation that *obscured* the meaning of a sentence, we have inserted either letters or appropriate punctuation marks in square brackets ([ ]) for the sake of clarity; we have retained all other misprinted words and original punctuation.

In Equiano's *Narrative,* constraints of space have necessitated cutting all front and back matter; the miscellaneous verses located between chapters 10 and 11; and the lengthy chapter titles. The Roman numeral subheads within each chapter have been removed as well in accordance with the style of this volume.

For specific bibliographical information on each text, please refer to the notes that follow our biographical sketches of each author.

ABBREVIATED TITLES OF BIBLIOGRAPHICAL SOURCES

THE FOLLOWING PRINTED OR ON-LINE SOURCES were consulted for the publishing histories provided in this volume. Please note that we use these abbreviations solely within the confines of our bibliographical notes.

AC Angelo Costanzo, *Surprizing Narrative: Olaudah Equiano and the Beginnings of Black Autobiography* (Westport, CT: Greenwood Press, 1987).

AY *Narratives of Captivity among the Indians of North America: A List of Books and Manuscripts on This Subject in the Edward E. Ayer Collection of the Newberry Library* (Chicago: Newberry Library; rpt. Detroit: Gale Research, 1974).

BM *British Museum General Catalogue of Printed Books.*

CA *[Collection of African-American Writings, 1760-1840]* (Nendeln, [Liechtenstein]: Kraus Reprint, 1972).

G Wilcomb E. Washburn, ed., *The Garland Library of Narratives of North American Indian Captivities,* vol. 17 (New York: Garland, 1978).

J Janheinz Jahn, *A Bibliography of Neo-African Literature from Africa, America, and the Caribbean* (New York: Frederick A. Praeger, 1965).

JD Janheinz Jahn and Claus Peter Dressler, *Bibliography of Creative African Writing* (Millwood, NY: Kraus-Thomson Organization, 1975).

NUC *National Union Catalog.*

OCLC On-line Catalog of the Library of Congress.

P Dorothy Porter, "Early American Negro Writings: A Bibliographical Study," *Papers of the Bibliographical Society of America* 39 (October 1945): 192-268.

PE Dorothy Porter, ed., *Early Negro Writing 1760-1837* (Boston: Beacon Press, 1971).

S Ralph R. Shaw and Richard H. Shoemaker, comps., *American Bibliography: A Preliminary Checklist for 1809* (New York: Scarecrow Press, 1961).

V Richard VanDerBeets, ed., *Held Captive by Indians: Selected Narratives 1642-1836* (Knoxville: University of Tennessee Press, 1973).

W D'Alté A. Welch, *A Bibliography of American Children's Books Printed Prior to 1821* ([n.p.]: American Antiquarian Society and Barre Publishers, 1972).

We have used *OCLC* to designate only those imprints found in the database but not replicated in printed sources. We have used *AC* only in reference to two uncommon entries not confirmed in traditional bibliographical sources.

In preparing the texts for this volume, we have compared the major imprints of each author's work or works. Our textual comparisons have thus been extensive but not exhaustive. Glosses on significant variations are included to stimulate further study into matters literary, historical, and bibliographical.

Black Atlantic Writers
OF THE EIGHTEENTH CENTURY

INTRODUCTION

This edition brings together for the first time works by four black writers who published between 1770 and 1793: Ukawsaw Gronniosaw, John Marrant, Quobna Ottobah Cugoano, and Olaudah Equiano. Crisscrossing the Atlantic Ocean from West Africa to the West Indies, from the American mainland to the British Isles, these men share not only a dramatic story of captivity and liberation, wayfaring and adventure, but also the Christian faith that allows them to tell the story of their physical deliverance as an allegory of spiritual salvation. Freedom from bondage—both the shackle of chains and, as they came to understand it, the prison of sin—is the theme, petition, and prophecy of these works.

Those who are familiar with nineteenth-century African-American slave narratives may be surprised by the relatively muted depiction of slave life found in the following works. In these eighteenth-century black narratives, we sometimes hear the voice of moral indignation that reaches its peak of eloquence in the late antebellum period with the autobiographies of Frederick Douglass and Harriet Jacobs. However, the atrocities of slavery tend to be noted less often by eighteenth-century blacks: the writers here, from Gronniosaw to Equiano, show less interest than Douglass in "detailing bloody deeds."[1] It is a matter of conjecture as to whether this is because eighteenth-century slaveowners tended to be less brutal or because the decorum of late eighteenth-century writing required greater circumspection in representing violence, particularly that of an interracial variety. It may have been such decorum—as embodied, perhaps, in William Aldridge, who wrote down and published Marrant's *Narrative*—that prevented the inclusion of a graphic scene of slave whipping in all but one imprint of that work. It is difficult to determine the degree to which the conventions and the politics of representation have sifted or indeed stifled the outrage of the earliest black writers and the range of their testimony.[2]

The indignant voice, when it does appear, is but one of the strains we hear in the following pages, as it is balanced, and at times more than balanced, against other voices or moods. One such voice is that of the matter-of-fact celebrator of worldly business and adventure—a buoyant voice more akin to Robinson Crusoe's than to the Spanish picaro's, to which the slave's narrative is sometimes compared.[3] In their breezy narrations of lives undertaken with gusto, Gronniosaw and his successors situate themselves in the Atlantic world during a period that Donald Greene has aptly dubbed "the age of exuberance."[4] The aplomb of these works is truly remarkable, given the potentially crushing experience of enslavement and alienation that these men shared. The very descent into the hell of colonial slave life appears but an episode in the epic series of open-air adventures, professions, and avocations that the eighteenth-century black writers recount. They serve, variously, as wartime sailors, merchant mariners, tradesmen, explorers (Equiano, for one, saw the Arctic Ocean), carpenters, barbers, butlers, musicians, teachers, preachers, and, of course, writers.

As protean as their professional identities were, their "national" characters were still more fluid, for in their repeated sailings across the Atlantic, they led lives that were neither simply African nor American, West Indian nor British, but in succession all of these, and ultimately all of these at once. In effect, their autobiographies lay the foundation for "the transcultural, international formation" that Paul Gilroy usefully calls "the black Atlantic world," the hybrid sphere of black culture in which ideas and activities, thinkers and activists, circulate among Africa, America, the Caribbean, and Europe.[5] However, as they themselves were but forerunners of a black Atlantic, these men lived most of their adult lives in white communities; even their time aboard ship, after the initial and horrific experience of the middle passage, was spent alongside predominately white crews. The exception to this rule is John Marrant—the only writer in the present volume born in America—whom we typically see in relation to various black communities: the free blacks and plantation slaves of Charleston and its environs; the blacks transplanted by the British to Nova Scotia after the Revolutionary War; Prince Hall's first black Masonic lodge in 1780s Boston. The works of the other (African-born) writers are touched, despite details of family, activism, camaraderie, or transcendence, by a quiet sense of loneliness. Cugoano, for example, longed to return to his African home. Even Ignatius Sancho, surely the most "bourgeois" of England's black men of letters—married, fairly comfortable, and an acquaintance of no less famous an author than Laurence Sterne—voiced disquiet, observing, "I am only a lodger [in England]—and hardly that."[6]

Sancho may have felt at times a mere lodger, Gronniosaw a "poor pilgrim," Marrant a wayfarer, Cugoano an African in a land not his own, but each demonstrated a tremendous power to adapt to his new surroundings. And each found some balm for his loneliness in a cosmopolitan ideal of Christian community. Poised against an apparent appetite for life in the here and now is the religious voice assumed by the black writers—an otherworldly chant in praise of Christian truths. Equiano speaks for this entire fraternity of black writers when he exclaims, at the climax of his spiritual autobiography, "Now the Ethiopian was willing to be saved by Jesus Christ, the sinner's only surety, and also to rely on none other person or thing for salvation" (*Narrative*, ch. 10).

The Christian idiom of the pioneer black writers suggests at times—and especially in Equiano—the syncretic presence of distinctly African ideas. For example, as Paul Edwards and Rosalind Shaw have argued, the mature Equiano's belief in divine providence is rooted in the Igbo conception of *chi*, "an entity sometimes described as a 'personal god' responsible for the individual's destiny." In the Igbo world view as described by Herbert Cole and Chike Aniakor, an individual's personal *chi* is part of a larger, universal "Great Chi" or "Chi Na Eke"; this dual conception of a god at once universal and personal is, again, in keeping with the Christian belief adopted by Equiano.[7] Similarly, if we accept the view that Brodie Cruickshank offers of Fanti culture, then Cugoano spent his formative years believing in one supreme god and a constellation of tribal or personal gods; divine soul possession; predestination; and an afterlife "beyond space and time"—beliefs that find an echo in Christianity.[8]

The correspondences between Christianity and some African religions evident from these examples suggest that conversion for Equiano and his fellow writers was less jarring than we might at first imagine. Indeed, these writers tended to think of conversion not as something that obliterated their African identity but as an experience that complemented and fulfilled their earlier selves. Cugoano is firm on this point: "Christianity does not require that we should be deprived of our own personal name, or the name of our ancestors; but it may very fitly add another name unto us, Christian, or one anointed" (p. 149 of this volume). Surely it was evangelicalism that gave these Africans an English voice; but, conversely, these voices gave evangelicalism a new resonance, by making it clear that each Christian self is rooted in cultural pasts that cannot and ought not be forgotten. For many Africans, the past is—paradoxically to Western thought—always present through the community's embrace of abiding ancestral spirits and through the unmediated presence of the ever-creating godhead to every individual within the community. For many Africans, these beliefs became, within the context of Christianity, a sense that one can talk to as well as walk with Jesus—a black Christian experience that is, as Harold Bloom maintains, of seminal importance to white evangelicals. In religion as in so much else, the races of the Atlantic world have insensibly shaped each other's characters, if not their very beings. Kwame Anthony Appiah asserts that we are all already influenced by each other in a complex, interdependent world that is ill-served, finally, by the manufacture of Otherness.[9]

Still, although contact or influence between blacks and whites was prevalent throughout the eighteenth-century Atlantic world, a certain degree of *sympathy* between the races was much more likely to be found in England than in America. Baptized and literate blacks from Gronniosaw to the early nineteenth-century writer John Jea felt that the urban centers of England offered a relatively safe and humane haven in comparison to any place to be found in America (excepting perhaps Philadelphia), before or after its war of independence. Their reasons were many. For runaway slaves who sought refuge in England from the property claims of their masters, Lord Mansfield's judgment in the Somerset case of 1772 provided some, if not complete or consistent, legal protection. (The freedom of James Somerset, a black slave who had escaped from his master while in England, was defended at the bar by Granville Sharp, who argued that slaves were free the moment they stepped on English soil. Mansfield, Lord Chief Justice of England, found in favor of Somerset, though the shuffling language of his ruling offered no decisive precedent for future cases.)

While their legal status remained uncertain, London's free blacks could still expect spiritual encouragement as well as some material assistance from men such as Granville Sharp and Thomas Clarkson, both of whom became founding members of the Society for the Abolition of the Slave Trade in May 1787. (Britain's role in the slave trade was eventually ended by an act of Parliament in 1807, though the emancipation of British West Indian slaves did not occur until 1833–38.) Black Methodists such as John Marrant could find a patron in Selina Hastings, the Countess of Huntingdon, and her circle; for instance, Selina's friend and cousin Walter Shirley wrote the preface to Gronniosaw's *Narrative*. Indeed, the general climate among the "polite" classes in England was such that in 1771 Samuel Johnson could, provocatively but not perversely, offer his famous toast: "Here's to the next insurrection of the negroes in the West Indies."[10] Among the lower classes, where historical evidence of opinion is always harder to find, some degree of interracial harmony may be inferred from the high incidence of marriage between white women and black men

(Britain's black population of ten to twenty thousand was predominately male).[11] Thus, Gronniosaw and Equiano—and, insofar as we can determine, Cugoano—married white Englishwomen.[12]

Whatever else it might mean, becoming English meant, for the writers included in this volume, gaining admittance to the Church of England—even if, once admitted, denominational differences might cease to matter. Equiano was baptized in the Anglican church in 1759 (*Narrative*, ch. 4); and although his actual conversion experience in 1774 revolved around his fellowship in the Congregationalist establishment of Westminster Chapel (*Narrative*, ch. 10), he could nonetheless proudly assert to Governor Macnamara in 1779 that he "was a protestant of the church of England, agreeable to the thirty-nine articles of that church" (*Narrative*, ch. 12, not reprinted in this volume). It is important to remember that in the eighteenth century the Anglican establishment embraced a wide variety of communicants, from those attracted to polite high-churchmen such as Sterne, to those moved by evangelical field preachers such as—first and foremost—the Reverend George Whitefield. Neither Whitefield nor John Wesley—the original Methodists—ever broke from the Church that ordained them. The relation of Methodism to the established Church was attenuated by the death of Whitefield in 1770; by the reluctant secession of the Countess of Huntingdon's "Connexion" (or religious society) between 1781 and 1783; by the splintering off of American Methodism in 1784; and, finally, by the death of Wesley in 1791. Still, during most of the period in which Gronniosaw, Marrant, Cugoano, and Equiano lived and composed, Methodism remained a movement and society within the Church of England, and—most significantly, for our purposes—it generally stood fast in its opposition to slavery and in its acceptance of black participants.

Methodism's openness to blacks was in keeping with its broad agenda: Methodists were eager to unite all races and classes of people, and all denominations of Christians, in an experience of the "new birth" in Jesus Christ. Whitefield explained the idea of the new birth concisely in a sermon on Jeremiah 18:1-6:

> This "marred clay," I mean these depraved natures of ours, must necessarily undergo a universal moral change. . . . This moral change is what some call repentance, some conversion, some regeneration . . . our Lord calls it a "new birth, or being born again, or born from above." . . . Some indeed content themselves with a figurative interpretation [of these expressions]; but unless they are made to experience the power and efficacy thereof, by a solid, living experience in their own souls, all their learning,

all their labored criticisms, will not exempt them from real damnation. Christ hath said it, and Christ will stand, "Unless a man," learned or unlearned, high or low, though he be a master of Israel as Nicodemus was, unless he "be born again, he cannot see, he cannot enter into, the kingdom of God" [John 3:3].[13]

Both Whitefield and Wesley agreed that the new birth must be a sudden and vividly conscious experience; it must strike the convert just as the light overcame Paul on the road to Damascus (Acts 9).

It was to this message of the new birth that many blacks in the Atlantic world responded—at least those who recorded their experience. Typical is the black Methodist preacher Boston King, who recalled his conversion crisis in his *Memoirs* (1798), expressly written for the Wesleyan *Methodist Magazine:*

> The first Sunday in March, as I was going to the preaching, and was engaged in prayer and meditation, I thought I heard a voice saying to me, "Peace be unto thee!" I stopped, and looked round about, to see if any one was near me. But finding myself alone, I went forward a little way, when the same words were again powerfully applied to my heart, which removed the burden of misery from it; and while I sat under the sermon, I was more abundantly blessed. Yet in the afternoon, doubts and fears again arose in my mind. Next morning I resolved like Jacob, not to let the Lord go till he blessed me indeed. As soon as my wife went out, I locked the door, and determined not to rise from my knees until the Lord fully revealed his pardoning love. I continued in prayer about half an hour, when the Lord again spoke to my heart, "Peace be unto thee." All my doubts and fears vanished away: I saw, by faith, heaven opened to my view; and Christ and his holy angels rejoicing over me. I was now enabled to believe in the name of Jesus, and my Soul was dissolved into love. . . . I could truly say, I was now become a new creature.[14]

According to Walter F. Pitts, an account such as this from the early black diaspora suggests the proximity between Christian conversion and the West African religious tradition of ecstatic soul possession.[15]

While the new birth was central to the beliefs of all Methodists and, more generally, all evangelicals, black writers tended to follow Whitefield's teaching rather than Wesley's on the one important topic on which the two men differed doctrinally: the question of free will. Whitefield believed that men and women do not have the willpower to choose whether or not to pursue a good and holy life, but that God had predestined some people, the "elect," to eternal salvation, and all others, the "reprobate," to eternal damnation. As Whitefield wrote to Wesley in a letter dated 24 December 1740:

> I frankly acknowledge, I believe the doctrine of reprobation, in this view, that God intends to give saving grace, through Jesus Christ, only to a certain number, and that the rest of mankind, after the fall of Adam, being justly left of God to continue in sin, will at last suffer that eternal death, which is its proper wages.[16]

The doctrine of God's election and reprobation—traceable to Paul in Romans 8:28-9:18 and to the writings of St. Augustine—was elaborated on during the Reformation by the French theologian John Calvin; largely through the influence of Calvin's writings, it was incorporated into the seventeenth of the Thirty-Nine Articles of the Church of England. The Anglican orthodoxy of his own position is what Whitefield urged against Wesley. Wesley, for his part, maintained a countervailing doctrine of universal redemption: the notion that salvation was within reach of all people and that individuals could actively prepare themselves, through prevenient grace, for repentance and the holy life.[17]

Among Wesley's objections to Calvinist doctrine, the most pointed perhaps is this: If some are infallibly saved and some inexorably damned, what is the use of preaching? Indeed, what is the use of religion of any sort? Preaching can have no influence upon individuals whose lives are foreordained; thus, as Wesley wrote in his sermon "Free Grace," "our preaching is vain, and your hearing also vain." Whitefield's response to Wesley, while not necessarily persuasive, is certainly agile:

> Since we know not who are elect, and who reprobate, we are to preach promiscuously to all. For the word may be useful, even to the non-elect, in restraining them from wickedness and sin. However, it is enough to excite to the utmost diligence in preaching and hearing, when we consider that by these means, some, even as many as the Lord hath ordained to eternal life, shall certainly be quickened and enabled to believe. And who, that attends, especially with reverence and care, can tell but he may be found of that happy number?

That Whitefield ends with a question is significant, for part of Calvinism's appeal to Whitefield was precisely the uncertainty it entailed. Whitefield hoped that the state of not knowing where one stood in the divine dispensation would inspire his listeners with salutary fear and trembling, a painstaking self-examination, and, ideally, the self-renunciation requisite to an acceptance of God's amazing grace. Whitefield says as much when he adds,

> What if the doctrine of election and reprobation does put some upon doubting? So does that of regeneration. But, is not this doubting a good means to put them upon searching and striving; and that striving, a good means to make their calling and election sure?

Am I or am I not of the elect? This is the question that haunts all Puritan spiritual autobiographies. The basic drama we find in the spiritual lives of Gronniosaw, Marrant, and Equiano—uncertainty, despair, quickening, and regeneration—reflects not only Whitefield's influence, but that of the Puritan world of letters that Whitefield inherited: from Baxter's *A Call to the Unconverted* (1658) to Bunyan's *Holy War* (1682); from Mary Rowlandson's *The Soveraignty & Goodness of God* (1682) to James Janeway's *A Token for Mariners* (pre-1708). These narratives of "surprising conversion"—whether they are cast as sailors' tales, accounts of Indian captivity, or allegorical romances—all tend to express a Calvinist world view of election and grace; of saints and sinners; of the just workings of providence through human misery and delight. Gronniosaw, Marrant, Cugoano, and Equiano all subscribed to this Calvinist world view; and indeed it is the shared faith of these men that lends coherence to the present volume.[18]

Whitefield himself—as a preacher and as a man—is a crucial presence in early black Atlantic autobiography. All but Cugoano heard or professed to have heard Whitefield's eloquence and testified to its power to captivate and convert an audience. Gronniosaw claimed to have known Whitefield "very well," both as a preacher and as a personal friend of his master, "Mr. Freelandhouse" (Theodorus Jacobus Frelinghuysen, a seminal figure in colonial America's Great Awakening); it is to Whitefield that he turned upon arriving in London. Marrant attributed his spectacular conversion to a providential meeting with Whitefield, whom he had gone to see expressly to deride:

> I was pushing the people to make room, . . . just as Mr Whitefield was naming his text, and looking round, as I thought, directly upon me, and pointing with his finger, he uttered these words, "PREPARE TO MEET THY GOD O ISRAEL." The Lord accompanied the word with such power, that I was struck to the ground, and lay both speechless and senseless near half an hour. (p. 78 of this volume)

Finally, Equiano presents himself as hearing Whitefield preach in Philadelphia in early 1766:

> When I got into the church I saw this pious man exhorting the people with the greatest fervour and earnestness, and sweating as much as ever I did while in slavery on Montserrat-beach. I was very much struck and impressed with this; I thought it strange I had never seen divines exert themselves in this manner before; and was no longer at a loss to account for the thin congregations they preached to. (*Narrative*, ch. 7)

As a matter of factual record, Equiano could not have seen Whitefield when and where he said he did, because the preacher was in England between July 1765 and September 1768; thus Equiano either makes a mistake in his chronology, or his vision of Whitefield presents "truth" rather than "fact." By Equiano's time, the appearance of Whitefield, as character and as symbol, had become an important motif of black autobiography.

Converted through Whitefield's oratory, many blacks began to testify and to preach themselves, among them Gronniosaw and Marrant. Winthrop D. Jordan remarks of this phenomenon: "The equalitarian implications in Protestant Christianity have never been more apparent; if it was difficult for Negroes to become men of affairs in this world, it became increasingly easy, after the Great Awakening, for them to become men of God."[19] The Christian community offered some measure of dignity and status to dislocated blacks. Phillis Wheatley observed precisely this in her well-known poem, "On the Death of the Reverend George Whitefield" (1770); here, she presents the preacher offering his benediction and promise:

> Take HIM ye *Africans* he longs for you;
> Impartial SAVIOUR, is his title due:
> If you will chuse to walk in grace's road,
> You shall be sons, and kings, and priests to GOD.[20]

Wheatley's uncertain syntax in this last line—shall Africans be "kings . . . to God," or shall they simply be "kings"?—reflects the pressing ambiguity of Whitefield's own message. Some whites indeed feared that the spiritual enfranchisement of blacks might translate all too easily into expectations of political power. Whitefield's message of spiritual liberation from the bondage of "these depraved natures of ours" sounded to some like a call for liberation, pure and simple, and at least one critic consequently blamed Whitefield's influence for the so-called "Negro Plot" of 1741, an alleged conspiracy to raze the town of New York and murder its white citizens.[21]

The ambiguity between spiritual and political liberation inheres, in part, in the very idiom of Christian soteriology. Since the gospel writers first presented Jesus as a new and greater Moses,[22] Christian salvation has routinely been allegorized as freedom from Egyptian captivity. As Whitefield put it,

> Let us consider ourselves . . . as persons travelling to a long eternity; as rescued by the free grace of God, in some measure, from our natural Egyptian bondage, and marching under the conduct of our spiritual Joshua, through the wilderness of this world, to the land of our heavenly Canaan.[23]

The themes of Exodus—freedom from the land of enslavement and pilgrimage through the wilderness—had a special significance to Whitefield and Wesley because they were traveling preachers. As Isabel Rivers notes, "in the majority of Puritan narratives (*Pilgrim's Progress* is the archetype) pilgrimage is a metaphor for the human condition, and the narrator is allegorically, not literally, a pilgrim. Methodist autobiographies, however, are based on actual itinerancy."[24] Pilgrimage well described the life of the Methodist preacher: Wesley himself, setting a pattern for his lay preachers, traveled 4,000 to 5,000 miles a year. So intent was the Countess of Huntingdon on maintaining the itinerant ideal among the clergy and laymen who preached throughout her chapels that she refused to grant any congregation's petition for the permanent assignment of one preacher, a policy that eventually caused William Aldridge, John Marrant's amanuensis/editor, to leave her Connexion in 1776.

Marrant himself, freeborn in New York, tells a story that is closer to those of other Methodist preachers than it is to the slave narratives of Gronniosaw and Equiano. Marrant's life roughly conforms to the pattern of Methodist autobiography, as described by Rivers:

> [The preacher] experiences conversion and the call to preach, gives up his trade, leaves behind his wife and children and takes to the road, is harassed by justices and the clergy, attacked by mobs, sometimes imprisoned or threatened with impressment, and constantly faces the temptation to give up this arduous life and return to his home, his family, his trade. In resisting temptation he learns the symbolic nature of his experience: his sufferings are providential. In recording this experience, he encourages others to imitate him, just as he himself is supported by a literary tradition.[25]

The path that Marrant takes is through the wilderness of the Georgia and South Carolina woods, and his imprisonment is rather more dramatic than that of most converts, as he is seized not by civic authorities but by Cherokees. Marrant's deliverance from his death sentence is rather more spectacular than one might expect; according to his account, he converts the Cherokee king's daughter and then the king himself, upon which "the poor condemned prisoner had perfect liberty, and was treated like a prince." (As the London *Monthly Review* of November 1785 archly noted, Marrant's narrative has "a little touch of the MIRACULOUS.")[26] After proselytizing among several Native American nations, however, Marrant desires to revisit his home, and like the biblical Joseph he is reunited with a family that thought him dead. As a Methodist preacher, however—not to mention as a black in the Revolutionary era—his destiny lies in no settled home, but in constant wayfaring. Thus we see Marrant sailing the American seas with the British fleet, lodging with a merchant in London, and being ordained a minister at Bath; we hear him delivering a sermon to the African Lodge of Freemasons in Boston over a year after having preached throughout Nova Scotia. Adorn it as he might, his is by any account a biblically inspired life of wonders, a new exodus through the New World.

But while Marrant's narration of his captivity and deliverance may seem too orchestrated to modern readers, not so the tales of bondage and escape told by the African-born writers. In the lives of Gronniosaw, Cugoano, and Equiano we find the most moving engagement with the narrative pattern of Exodus. Each of these men knew slavery in the British colonies; each experienced liberation from real chains, as well as the Christian conversion that frees the believer from the "Egyptian bondage" of sin; each set out on a literal as well as an allegorical pilgrimage through the wilderness of the world. All three men lived the new exodus and lived to tell it.

Equiano is the most explicit and systematic in conjuring the parallels between his life's journey and the career of the Israelites. As Equiano represents it, the "progress" of his life consists of three stages.[27] The first stage comprises his boyhood within his native Igbo (or "Eboe") culture, in the section of West Africa that is now Nigeria.[28] To the mature Equiano, Igbo society resembles nothing so much as the society of the patriarchs. Through much of chapter 1 of the *Narrative*, Equiano elaborates on "the strong analogy, which . . . appears to prevail in the manners and customs of my countrymen and those of the Jews, before they reached the Land of Promise, and particularly the Patriarchs, while they were yet in that pastoral state which is described in Genesis—an analogy which alone would induce me to think that the one people had sprung from the other."

Equiano ventures the hypothesis that Africans are lineally descended from Abraham and his wife Keturah (Genesis 25:1-4).

Polemically, Equiano's Igbo/Hebrew analogy serves to discredit two myths about the black race that were current in the eighteenth century. First, it runs contrary to the common (though fantastic) taunt that blacks are the cursed descendants of Ham who are ordained to serve God's chosen people—here, white Europeans—as slaves.[29] According to Equiano's account, the Igbo people are the immediate heirs of Abraham and bear no relation to the Hamitic line. While Equiano thus removes from blacks the appellation "the sons of Ham," other writers note that the epithet, properly understood, carries with it no blame. While Cugoano accepts the Hamitic origin of African peoples, he aptly rebuffs the notion that Ham's line is cursed, noting that Noah's curse falls only on Ham's son Canaan, the eponymous ancestor of the Canaanite tribes eventually subjugated by the Israelites. Cugoano then addresses a related point of confusion: Namely, that blacks were also dubbed "the sons of Cain," an embarrassment that presumably originates in a popular mistaking of "Cham"—a variant English spelling of Ham—for "Cain." Cugoano simply notes that according to biblical history blacks could not be of the lineage of Cain since "the whole posterity of Cain were destroyed in the universal deluge" that only Noah and his family survived (p. 141 of this volume).

Equiano's analogy between the Igbos and the patriarchal Hebrews, aside from figuring in these (now seemingly arcane) biblical-historical polemics, also serves to correct his age's opposite and equally unreal view of Africa not as a damned but as an Edenic state. The "Rousseauist" image of an African paradise was made popular by certain passages of Michel Adanson's *A Voyage to Senegal,* published in French in 1757 and translated into English two years later. According to Adanson's best known description:

> Which way soever I turned my eyes on this pleasant spot, I beheld a perfect image of pure nature: an agreeable solitude, bounded on every side by a charming landskip; the rural situation of cottages in the midst of trees; the ease and indolence of the Negroes, reclined under the shade of their spreading foliage; the simplicity of their dress and manners; the whole revived in my mind, the idea of our first parents, and I seemed to contemplate the world in its primeval state.[30]

Equiano's *Narrative* intends at its outset to dispel the fallacy that his fellow Africans are mere primitives, lacking not only culture but the very need for it. Equiano would show that his kinsfolk derive from the Hebrew patriarchs and still embody their distinguishing characteristics: organization under paternal chiefs and judges; a legal system that enshrines the law of retaliation ("an eye for an eye"); cleanliness codes and circumcision.

While the patriarchal state of Igbo/Hebrew culture thus represents the first stage of Equiano's own life, his second stage is enslavement—an event that corresponds, of course, to the captivity of Israel in Egypt, the bondage of the house of Jacob among a people of strange language. Equiano was kidnapped at the age of eleven and sojourned among diverse African tribes on his way to the coast, where he was ultimately loaded upon a slave ship bound for Barbados. From the West Indies he was shipped to a Virginia plantation, where he labored outdoors. Here, as Equiano writes, "I was called JACOB" (Narrative, ch. 3). It is a specially apt name, for Jacob, as "Israel," is the eponymous patriarch who descends into Egypt. Equiano's subsequent bondage on the island of Montserrat further supports his identification with the Israelite after whom he had been named.

The third and final stage of Equiano's life is freedom from captivity, a literal freedom that serves as well to anticipate and to allegorize spiritual deliverance from innate depravity. Equiano's freedom from literal bondage came at the price of forty pounds; freedom from his "natural Egyptian bondage" arrived with the assurance of his salvation, a revelation that attends his reading of the fourth chapter of Acts, twelfth verse: "Neither is there salvation in any other: for there is none other name under heaven given among men whereby we must be saved, but only Jesus Christ" (Narrative, ch. 10). The centrality of this verse from Acts is commemorated in the original frontispiece engraving of Equiano's Narrative, in which Equiano, in elegant European dress, holds a Bible open to a page on which Acts 4:12 is boldly printed. Equiano's portrait shows that he writes from the perspective of Christianity; and from this vantage, he reads and renders his own life—and perhaps, by extension, the life of the black race—as mirroring the movement of biblical history from the Old Testament to the New. Having been born among the patriarchs, Equiano ends up among the apostles.

The book of Acts to which Equiano appealed was of special importance to many blacks and their white abolitionist friends for its strong message of Christian universalism. As Equiano declares at the end of his first chapter, God "hath made of one blood all nations of men for to dwell on all the face of the earth" (Acts 17:26). Furthermore, Acts recounts the conversion of an Ethiopian (8:26-40); thus Whitefield encouraged his black listeners, "in Jesus Christ there is neither male nor female, bond nor free. . . . Did you never read of the eunuch belonging to the queen of Candace? a negro, like yourselves."[31] The universal Christian community that transcends caste distinctions of race was indeed the motivating ideal of the abolitionist societies that emerged in the later eighteenth century, first in Philadelphia (1775), and next in London (1787). It is this vision, surely, that lies behind the seal of the British Abolitionist Society, adopted on 16 October 1787 and later impressed on the title page of Equiano's *Narrative*: the image of a chained black man, kneeling in supplication, and crested by the motto "Am I Not A Man And A Brother?" And it is this fraternal ideal that served, too, as the measure by which so many "nominal Christians" were judged and found wanting. Thus Equiano's brilliant fifth chapter and Cugoano's mesmerizing last sentence—perfect instances of what Wilson Jeremiah Moses calls "the black jeremiad"—denounce white slaveholding society by foretelling the disastrous consequences of social relations founded on brute violence rather than fraternal love.[32]

Historically, Christian brotherhood did not always go hand in hand with abolitionism: even St. Paul, returning the runaway slave Onesimus to his master Philemon with the exhortation to treat him "no longer as a slave but more than a slave, a beloved brother" (Philemon 1:16, RSV), neither overtly condemns slavery nor predicts its end. In his acceptance—if not approval—of slavery, Paul follows the Torah teaching that as a Pharisee he had been taught to revere (Exodus 21:2-6) as well as a custom in the Greco-Roman world in which he claimed citizenship.[33] But eighteenth-century abolitionists were determined, in a way that earlier Christian writers had not been, to apply the idea of equality before God to actual social practice. Especially from the 1770s onwards, more and more British commoners came to believe that to eliminate slavery was to bring the city of man into closer conformity with the city of God. And in both Houses of Parliament, as Linda Colley notes, growing numbers responded to William Wilberforce's argument "that anti-slavery was a necessary act of national atonement."[34]

Colley proceeds to note, however, that not all opposition to slavery was based on religious argument: "Other politicians, including William Pitt the Younger, shared Adam Smith's opinion that slavery was the most uneconomic form of labour as well as a blight on humanity." In *The Wealth of Nations* (1776), Smith had argued that the slave laborer would necessarily be inefficient, because he or she was deprived of the chief incentive to work—the prospect of acquiring property. The abolition of slavery was thus, according to the more advanced political economy of the day, a sure way to add to the wealth of nations. Cugoano and Equiano shared Smith's belief that a world crisscrossed by peaceful trade would be more advantageous to all than a world given to slave routes; they subscribed, moreover, to the age's typically buoyant faith in the compatibility of international commerce and Christian values. We must read Equiano's closing exhortation to his European readers in light of this faith—a passage, now apt to seem curious, in which he observes that Africans are not only men and therefore brothers, but men and therefore potential *buyers* (see pp. 248-50 of this volume). Just as Equiano accepts the Christian tenet that all souls have similar needs, so he appears to accept the economic notion that all people are driven by similar material needs and that these needs will expand to include a theoretically limitless number of commodities. In an ever-increasing spiral of needs lies the present and future peace and glory of the world.[35] Though by the late twentieth century many of us have soured on the idea of boundless—and boundary-less—commercial progress, we ought still to recognize that in its first flush it was a genuinely utopian, even a millenarian, idea. Equiano foretells a peaceable kingdom of rational and industrious beings, unequal, perhaps, in wealth, but equal before the providence of God and the possibilities of the market.[36]

While eighteenth-century black English writers sought a union between Christian egalitarianism and friendly capitalism, a number of blacks in America found that such a union was already enshrined as an ideal in the institution of Freemasonry. Starting in Boston in the 1770s, American blacks became Masons, doing so in ways that reflected their own heritage and their own needs. The attraction of Freemasonry to these men may be explained in part by their African heritage: as John Thornton notes, "[Western and Central] African societies functioned something like Masonic lodges, in which members were initiated into organizations whose formal purposes were social, religious, and charitable."[37] But the attraction of Freemasonry to many blacks doubtlessly lay not only in its organization, but in its distinctive message. Masonic sermons drew upon the same vocabulary of Christian brotherhood that animated evangelical abolitionism; and both Masons and evangelicals sought to enact that brotherhood in political and economic as well as spiritual terms, on earth as well as before heaven. This congruence may be partly explained in terms of actual membership: among the corps of eighteenth-century Masons were numbered more evangelical Christians than has sometimes been noted. In the black community, the inaugural members of the African Lodges of Boston (started in 1776, chartered September 1784) and Philadelphia (chartered March 1797) included the Methodist preachers Prince Hall, Richard Allen, Absalom Jones, and Peter Mantore; Marrant, another Methodist, addressed his fellow Freemasons of the Boston Lodge in his *Sermon* of 1789.[38]

Just as many black evangelicals embraced Christianity on their own behalf, so too did they make Freemasonry their own. Witness the ode, "MASONRY," that appeared in the *Massachusetts Centinel* for Saturday, 5 May 1787:

> THRO'OUT the globe's extensive round,
>   The fire of love extends,
> Which glows in true masonick hearts—
>   That family of friends!
> Ev'n AFRIC's SONS—ill-fated race!
>   Now feel its genial heat;
> With charter'd rights, from England's Duke,
>   THE SABLE LODGES MEET.
> No more shall COLOURS disagree;
>   But hearts with hands unite;
> For in the wond'rous mystery,
>   There's neither BLACK nor WHITE.
> And lest a BLEACHED BROTHER shou'd,
>   In scorn turn up his nose—
> Know, that a PRINCE* may favours take,
>   From Dukes, nor honour lose.

*A PRINCE—Master of the African Lodge—H-ll is only an American addition to his name.

"England's Duke" is Henry Frederick, the Duke of Cumberland and Grand Master of the Mother Grand Lodge of England, who granted the charter to the first African Lodge; the "Prince" is Prince Hall, the Master of that Lodge. Other key elements of the poem, however, are far less certain. The "fire of love" and "the wond'rous mystery" could as easily refer to Christian conversion, or the Christian community, as to Masonic ritual and fellowship. The poem shows, indeed, how difficult it is to disentangle talk about Masonry from Christian talk. It shows, too, how "blackness" and "whiteness" are melded in a similar manner, each making sense only in relation to the other, like the two sides of a coin. Thus the phrase "bleached brother," as evidence of a black perspective, challenges any who would forget that Christianity, Masonry, and the Atlantic world are black as well as white—and that they are, upon reflection, neither.

NOTES

1. Frederick Douglass, *Narrative of the Life of Frederick Douglass, an American Slave. Written by Himself* in *The Classic Slave Narratives*, ed. Henry Louis Gates, Jr. (New York: Penguin, Mentor, 1987), p. 270.

2. William L. Andrews, in his essay "The First Fifty Years of the Slave Narrative, 1760-1810" (*The Art of Slave Narrative: Original Essays in Criticism and Theory*, ed. John Sekora and Darwin T. Turner [Macomb: Western Illinois University, 1982], pp. 6-24), analyzes the complex relationship between black first-person narrator and white amanuensis-editor, contending that "even the most well-meaning of editorial collaborators arrogated to themselves decisions regarding the institutional frameworks and ethical meanings" of the "brute facts" of the narrator's life (p. 7).

3. See, for example, Charles H. Nichols, "The Slave Narrators and the Picaresque Mode: Archetypes for Modern Black Personae," in *The Slave's Narrative*, ed. Charles T. Davis and Henry Louis Gates (New York: Oxford University Press, 1985), pp. 283-97.

4. Donald Greene, *The Age of Exuberance: Backgrounds to Eighteenth-Century English Literature* (New York: Random House, 1970).

5. Paul Gilroy, *The Black Atlantic: Modernity and Double Consciousness* (Cambridge, MA: Harvard University Press, 1993), pp. 4, 12.

6. *Letters of the Late Ignatius Sancho*, ed. Paul Edwards (London: Dawsons of Pall Mall, 1968), p. 214.

7. Paul Edwards and Rosalind Shaw, "The Invisible Chi in Equiano's *Interesting Narrative*," *Journal of Religion in Africa* 19, no. 2 (1989): 146-56; Herbert Cole and Chike Aniakor, *Igbo Arts: Community and Cosmos* (Los Angeles: UCLA Museum of Cultural History, 1984), pp. 10, 15.

8. Brodie Cruickshank, *Eighteen Years on the Gold Coast of Africa including an account of the native tribes, and their intercourse with the Europeans*, 2nd ed., 2 vols. (1853; rpt. New York: Barnes & Noble, 1966), vol. 1, p. 19; vol. 2, pp. 127-29.

9. Kwame Anthony Appiah, *In My Father's House: Africa in the Philosophy of Culture* (New York: Oxford University Press, 1992), p. 72; Harold Bloom, *The American Religion: The Emergence of the Post-Christian Nation* (New York: Simon & Schuster, Touchstone, 1992), pp. 237-55.

10. James Boswell, *Life of Johnson*, ed. R. W. Chapman, intro. by Pat Rogers (Oxford: Oxford University Press, 1980), p. 876. Boswell, who records the toast, heartily disapproved of it, no less, presumably, than did a good part of Johnson's company, "very grave men at Oxford."

11. Britain's blacks constituted a very small percentage of the nation's population; in 1781, England alone had seven million inhabitants. On black population and interracial marriages, see Folarin Shyllon, *Black People in Britain 1555-1833* (London: Oxford University Press, 1977), pp. 101-02, 109-77; Paul Edwards and James Walvin, *Black Personalities in the Era of the Slave Trade* (Baton Rouge: Louisiana State University Press, 1983), pp. 19-22; Peter Fryer, *Staying Power: The History of Black People in Britain* (London: Pluto Press, 1984), pp. 68, 235.

12. Most of what we know of Cugoano comes from Henri Grégoire, *An Enquiry concerning the Intellectual and Moral Faculties, and Literature of Negroes; Followed with an Account of the Life and Works of Fifteen Negroes & Mulattoes,*

Distinguished in Science, Literature and the Arts (Paris, 1808; Eng. trans. D. B. Warden [Brooklyn, NY: Printed by Thomas Kirk, 1810]), pp. 188-96.

13. George Whitefield, "The Potter and the Clay," in *Sermons on Important Subjects* (London: William Tegg, n.d.), p. 180.

14. *The Methodist Magazine* (April 1798), p. 160. King's *Memoirs* appeared in four monthly installments, from March to June. King is a fascinating figure in his own right: born in slavery in South Carolina around 1760, he escaped from his master and joined the British army at the outset of the Revolutionary War. After the American victory, he, along with the other blacks who had "taken refuge in the British lines," was declared free by Royal Proclamation and conveyed by the British fleet to Nova Scotia; in 1792, he formed part of the expedition to settle Sierra Leone. King wrote his *Memoirs* in 1796 during a sojourn in England, when it was again possible to retain optimism for what had been an ill-fated Sierra Leone colony. King's experiences roughly parallel those found in "An Account of the Life of Mr. David George, from Sierra Leone in Africa," *The Baptist Annual Register* (1793), pp. 473-84.

15. Walter F. Pitts, *Old Ship of Zion: The Afro-Baptist Ritual in the African Diaspora* (New York: Oxford University Press, 1993); see especially pp. 36-39, 92, 129.

16. This and the following two quotations are from Whitefield's "A Letter to the Rev. Mr. John Wesley," reprinted in George Whitefield, *Journals,* ed. Iaian Murray et al. (London: Banner of Trust, 1960), pp. 575-76. On Whitefield, Wesley, and the varieties of early modern evangelicalism, see D. W. Bebbington, *Evangelicalism in Modern Britain: A History from the 1730s to the 1980s* (London: Unwin Hyman, 1989), pp. 1-74.

17. Wesley's position was called "Arminianism," after Jacobus Arminius, an early seventeenth-century Dutch divine who countered John Calvin; hence Wesley's monthly digest of devotional and theological literature was during his lifetime titled *The Arminian Magazine.* In 1798, its title was changed to *The Methodist Magazine.*

18. Of course, our principle of selection in the present volume serves to exclude eighteenth-century black writers less centrally concerned with the drama of the Christian life: most notably Ignatius Sancho (1729-1780), the "polite" (that is, not zealous) Christian and friend of Sterne, but also figures such as Briton Hammon (fl. before 1747-after 1760?) and Venture Smith (1729-1805). On the development of the black spiritual autobiography after Equiano, see *Black Itinerants of the Gospel: The Narratives of John Jea and George White,* ed. Graham Russell Hodges (Madison, WI: Madison House, 1993).

19. Winthrop D. Jordan, *White Over Black: American Attitudes towards the Negro, 1550-1812* (Chapel Hill: University of North Carolina Press, 1968), p. 213.

20. Quoted from the original 1770 version of "An Elegiac Poem, on the Death of that celebrated Divine . . . the late Reverend, and pious George Whitefield," as printed in *The Poems of Phillis Wheatley,* ed. Julian D. Mason, Jr. (Chapel Hill: University of North Carolina Press, 1966), p. 69.

21. Jordan, *White Over Black*, p. 181. If Whitefield was often depicted in his own day as a leveller, more recent commentators have dwelt on his unwillingness to take a stand against the institution of slavery per se. Indeed, although Whitefield proved a friend to unfortunates, he nonetheless petitioned the trustees of Georgia to admit slavery into the colony (which before 1750 had permitted neither slavery nor liquor), largely because he felt his orphanage there could not be maintained without slaves. Whitefield rationalized his position on biblical grounds by noting that "*Abraham's* money" had purchased slaves (Genesis 17:12-13). See Stuart C. Henry, *George Whitefield: Wayfaring Witness* (Nashville: Abingdon Press, 1957), pp. 115-17; see also, Stephen J. Stein, "George Whitefield on Slavery: Some New Evidence," *Church History* 42, no. 2 (1973): 243-57.

22. See, in particular, Matthew 2:13-15; 5-7; 17.

23. George Whitefield, "The Necessity and Benefits of Religious Society," in *Sermons*, p. 111.

24. Isabel Rivers, "'Strangers and Pilgrims': Sources and Patterns of Methodist Narrative," in *Augustan Worlds*, ed. J. C. Hillson et al. (New York: Barnes & Noble, 1978), p. 189.

25. Ibid., p. 197.

26. *The Monthly Review; or, Literary Journal* 73 (November 1785): 399.

27. I more thoroughly examine Equiano's *Narrative* and its legacy to contemporary black writing in my essay, "Olaudah Equiano and the Art of Spiritual Autobiography," *Eighteenth-Century Studies* 27, no. 4 (Summer 1994): 677-92.

28. James Africanus Beale Horton noted that the orthographic variations between "Eboes, Iboes, Igboes, and Egboes" derive from local differences in pronunciation among the various peoples of Igboland. See *West African Countries and Peoples* (London, 1868; rpt. Edinburgh: Edinburgh University Press, 1969), p. 154.

29. The story of Noah's curse on Canaan, the son of Ham, appears in Genesis 9. In certain nonbiblical Jewish stories from the early common era, black skin itself is presented as a curse placed on Ham's progeny; some of these stories entered into Christendom during the Renaissance. See St. Clair Drake, *Black Folk Here and There: An Essay in History and Anthropology*, 2 vols. (Los Angeles: University of California Center for Afro-American Studies, 1990), vol. 2, pp. 13-23, 275-79.

30. Michel Adanson, *A Voyage to Senegal, the Isle of Goree, and the River Gambia* (London, 1759), p. 54. This passage from Adanson was quoted and greatly popularized in the Quaker Anthony Benezet's *Historical Account of Guinea* (Philadelphia, 1771), pp. 15-16; it also supplies a footnote to Thomas Day's well-known poem, *The Dying Negro* (1773; new ed. London, 1793).

31. George Whitefield, "The Lord Our Righteousness," in *Sermons*, p. 197.

32. Wilson Jeremiah Moses, *Black Messiahs and Uncle Toms: Social and Literary Manipulations of a Religious Myth* (University Park: Pennsylvania State University Press, 1982), pp. 32-33; see also Theophus Smith, *Conjuring*

Culture: Biblical Formations of Black America (New York: Oxford University Press, 1994), pp. 90-95.

33. According to Aristotle, slavery is the just consequence of either natural inferiority or conquest in war (*Politics* I, 5-6): this "classical" view of slavery persisted in the writings of More, Hobbes, Locke, and many proslavery writers of the early modern period. On the classical view and its eclipse, see Wylie Sypher, *Guinea's Captive Kings: British Anti-Slavery Literature of the Eighteenth Century* (Chapel Hill: University of North Carolina Press, 1942), pp. 76-83.

34. Linda Colley, *Britons: Forging the Nation 1707-1837* (New Haven: Yale University Press, 1992), p. 358. The following quotation appears on the same page.

35. It is with some reason that I write that Equiano "appears" to believe in the ideals of international commerce. The paean to "commercial intercourse" that ends the *Narrative* first appeared in nearly identical form as a letter to Lord Hawkesbury, President of Council for Trade and Plantations, dated 13 March 1788 (reprinted in Shyllon, *Black People in Britain,* pp. 254-55); in incorporating that letter into his book, however, Equiano deleted, among others, one provocative line, printed here in italics. Speaking of the "endless Field of Commerce" to be opened by the end of slavery, Equiano originally wrote: "the Abolition of Slavery would be in reality an universal Good, *and for which a partial Ill must be supported.*"

36. The economic ideals of Equiano's age are well expressed by the title character of Caryl Phillips's historical novel, *Cambridge* (New York: Knopf, 1992); Cambridge, a black evangelical preacher in the early nineteenth century, declares at the outset of his narrative: "The Lord intended commerce to enable man to develop the friendly bent of his social affections. Finding his brothers in scattered locales it was hoped that man might forge the sweet blessed security of peace and friendship, while diffusing the goods and commodities of his native land. Such enterprise, with Christian religion as its true companion, would be of profound benefit to any shore fortunate enough to be rewarded with the arrival of traders with soldier-like fortitude, and honest values" (p. 134).

37. John Thornton, in *Africans in the Americas: A History of the Black Diaspora*, ed. Michael L. Conniff and Thomas J. Davis (New York: St. Martin's Press, 1994), p. 57.

38. On black Freemasonry, see William H. Grimshaw, *Official History of Freemasonry Among the Colored People in North America* (1903; rpt. New York: Negro Universities Press, 1969); Donn A. Cass, *Negro Freemasonry and Segregation* (Chicago: Ezra A. Cook, 1957).

UKAWSAW
GRONNIOSAW

ABOUT

UKAWSAW GRONNIOSAW

LIFE

Ukawsaw Gronniosaw was born some time between 1710 and 1714 in Borno (also known as Bornu) in the northeastern tip of modern-day Nigeria. As an adolescent, Gronniosaw felt alienated from most of his family and was thus enchanted with a merchant-cum-slave trader's tempting suggestion that they travel together to the Gold Coast, where he could fraternize with boys his own age and witness the strange phenomena of the white presence there. His sojourn soon became a journey of terror, however, in which he narrowly escaped abandonment in the wild and decapitation by a Gold Coast king before being sold into slavery. It was a bitter fate, but one that the traumatized fifteen-year-old preferred to remaining among unscrupulous traders.

As a domestic slave to a wealthy Dutch family in New York City, Gronniosaw attracted the attention of the Dutch Reformed minister Theodorus Jacobus Frelinghuysen ("Mr. Freelandhouse"), who became his next master around 1730. Gronniosaw thereupon moved to New Jersey's Raritan Valley, where he labored outdoors, learned to read Dutch, and witnessed the birth of the Great Awakening. After listening to many of Frelinghuysen's prayers and sermons, Gronniosaw experienced a heartfelt conversion to Christianity. These events appear to happen rather quickly in the *Narrative*, but they actually took place over a period of roughly eighteen years. Frelinghuysen died shortly after Gronniosaw's conversion (ca. 1747/48), but not before freeing the faithful slave who had remained at his bedside. Gronniosaw's simple description of this event is quite extraordinary because it is the sole extant record of Frelinghuysen's death, filling a centuries-old gap in the information available on the minister's personal life.

As a freeman, Gronniosaw stayed with different members of the Frelinghuysen family until a series of untimely deaths in the family forced him to fend for himself in the New York-New Jersey area (ca. 1759). At this time his movements become easier for us to trace. Forced by debt to serve as cook aboard a privateer, he took part in the licensed piracy that pervaded the naval theatre during the Seven Years' War (1756-1763). Once free of debt and of all ties to the American colonies he fulfilled his yearning to go to England by enlisting in the British 28th regiment, thereby allowing the British government to subsidize his trip. His journey was indirect, however, for on the way he took part in the victorious British sieges of the French island of Martinique (early 1762), and the Spanish stronghold at Havana (summer 1762). He finally reached Portsmouth, England, later in the year.

Gronniosaw may have stayed only briefly in Portsmouth before going to visit George Whitefield in London; if so, then his trip to Holland in 1762 may have been with Whitefield. While in Amsterdam Gronniosaw met with Dutch Reformed ministers and worked for approximately one year with a Dutch family. By 1763 or so, he had returned to England to marry Betty, a weaver he had met in London; before the wedding, he was baptized by the eminent Baptist theologian Dr. Andrew Gifford.

The Gronniosaws weathered much hardship during widespread postwar unemployment. The weaving trade of southeastern England was particularly hard hit, and so the growing family traveled north from London to Colchester to Norwich in search of secure employment. They suffered long periods of starvation and deprivation between—and sometimes during—the jobs they procured. Yet Gronniosaw clung tenaciously to his faith, which gave him strength to prevail despite desperate circumstances. By the *Narrative*'s end, he has moved his family west to the midland town of Kidderminster, the birthplace of Puritan clergyman Richard Baxter (1615-1691) and a town considered by many a wellspring of faith. In history's last glimpse of the Gronniosaws, they are assured of being neither more nor less than "poor pilgrims . . . traveling through many difficulties towards our heavenly home." It was some time after this that Gronniosaw recounted his life's story to the "young Lady of the town of Leominster" who wrote it down and, in making it available for publication, hoped to assist Gronniosaw's impoverished family with the profits from its sale.

BIBLIOGRAPHICAL NOTE

The printing history of Gronniosaw's *Narrative* is extremely complicated and made even more difficult by inconsistent records in key references.

Since some of the "editions" may represent conflations or multiple copies of one issue, we list here, in chronological order by year of publication, names and dates of imprints and the sources in which they are found to provide both an overall view for readers and a general reference for scholars interested in pursuing more detailed information. Imprints that claim to be a particular edition are grouped together; English language imprints, listed alphabetically by place of publication, are followed by foreign language imprints. When several sources appear to cite the same imprint or "edition," the most authoritative sources are listed first. Parenthetical information is taken from title pages and from sources. Asterisks mark those works we have seen.

Bath: S. Hazard, [1770?] . . . . *BM, P, J, JD*
n.p., [16.] purported 2nd ed. . . . . *NUC*
[Bath? 1770?] purported 2nd ed. . . . . *NUC*
[n.p., n.d.] purported 2nd ed. . . . . *P*
*Newport, RI: S. Southwick, 1774
    (rpt. of Bath ed.) . . . . *NUC, P, J, JD*
Aberhonddu, [Wales]: W. Williams,
    1779 (Welsh trans.) . . . . *BM, NUC, P*
n.p., [178-?] . . . . *NUC*
*Bath: W. Gye and T. Mills, [1780?] . . . . *BM, P, J, JD*
Bath, [1780?] . . . . *NUC*
Providence: Bennett Wheeler, 1781 . . . . *P*
Clonmel, [Ireland]: Thomas Lord, 1786 . . . . *NUC*
Dublin: B. Dugdale, 1790 . . . . *BM, NUC, P, J, JD*
American Moral and Sentimental Magazine
    (serial, New York, 3 July-25 September 1797) . . . . . *AC*
Leeds: W. Nicholson, [1800?] . . . . *BM, J, JD*
[1800?] . . . . *BM*
[n.p., 1800?] . . . . *NUC*
*Salem, [NY]: Dodd & Rumsey, 1809 . . . . *S, W*
Catskill, [NY]: Printed at the Eagle Office,
    1810 . . . . *NUC, P, J, JD*
Leeds: Printed by Davies and Co., 1810 . . . . *NUC*
Leeds: Davies & Booth, 1811 . . . . *BM, P, J, JD*
Leeds: Davies and Booth, 1814 . . . . *NUC, P*
Halifax: Nicholsons and Walker, [1820?] . . . . *NUC*
*Nendeln, [Liechtenstein]: Kraus, 1972
    (rpt. of London: R. Groombridge; Manchester:
    J. Gadsby; Glasgow: David Robertson, 1840) . . . . . . *CA*

A key text that has languished in obscurity is the Salem imprint of 1809: *The Black Prince; Being a Narrative of the Most Remarkable occurrences and* strange Vicissitudes, exhibited in the Life and Experience of James Albert Ukawsaw Gronniosaw, An African Prince, as was related by himself. This 1809 imprint is the only one we have seen that identifies Hannah More (1745-1833), the religious author and social reformist in England, as Gronniosaw's amanuensis, the "young Lady of the town of Leominster."[1]

Scholars tend to be familiar with Gronniosaw's work through the 1972 Kraus reprint of the 1840 imprint. Henry Louis Gates, Jr., and the team of Paul Edwards and David Dabydeen rely heavily on this version; Edwards and Dabydeen assert that it is "the only conveniently available full text" and that it "differs slightly but insignificantly, from earlier editions."[2] The text for our diplomatic reprint, however, is the 1774 imprint, which is earlier and more complete. It appears, in fact, to be a reprint of one of the initial editions—perhaps the first—of Gronniosaw's Narrative. Moreover, its 1774 imprint date may be closer in time to the original publication date of the Narrative than the "[1770?]" speculatively assigned the work in the holdings listed, particularly, BM, P, J, and JD. There are two reasons for this supposition. First, it was in 1774 that Bath printer and publisher Samuel Hazard acquired the business of T. Mills, a fellow Bath publisher and bookseller. Since Mills published an edition of the Narrative with printer W. Gye around 1780, Mills may have procured contractual rights to the Narrative that Hazard was enabled to share only after he commenced a business relationship with Mills in 1774. Second, Walter Shirley must have written the Narrative's preface in 1774, the year he preached—and probably met Gronniosaw—at the new Huntingdonian chapel in Kidderminster.

Throughout our reprint we provide textual glosses of the most important variations among four major imprints of the Narrative: Newport, 1774; Bath: W. Gye and T. Mills, [1780?]; Salem, 1809; and Nendeln, 1972, the reprint of 1840.

NOTES

1. The Black Prince is not listed under its title, nor is it cited under "Hannah More," her pseudonym "Will Chip," "Ukawsaw Gronniosaw," or "James Albert" (Gronniosaw's English name) in BM, NUC, P, J, or JD. See instead S and W.
2. See Henry Louis Gates, Jr., The Signifying Monkey: A Theory of African-American Literary Criticism (New York: Oxford University Press, 1988), p. 273, n. 4; and Paul Edwards and David Dabydeen, eds., Black Writers in Britain 1760-1890 (Edinburgh: Edinburgh University Press, 1991), p. 8.

A Narrative of the Most Remarkable Particulars in the Life of James Albert Ukawsaw Gronniosaw, An African Prince, Written by Himself [1]

THE PREFACE To the READER.

*T*HIS *account of the life and spiritual experience of* James Albert, *was taken from his own mouth, and committed to paper by the elegant pen of a young* Lady[2] *of the town of* Leominster, *for her own private satisfaction, and without any intention, at first, that it should be made public. But she has now been prevailed on to commit it to the press, both with a view to serve* Albert *and his distressed family, who have the sole profits arising from the sale of it; and likewise, as it is apprehended, this little history contains matter well worthy the notice and attention of every Christian reader.[3]*

Perhaps we have here, in some degree, a solution of that question that has perplex'd the minds of so many serious persons, viz. In what manner will God deal with those benighted parts of the world where the gospel of Jesus Christ hath never reached? Now, it appears, from the experience of this remarkable person, that God does not save without the knowledge of the truth; but, with respect to those whom he hath foreknown, though born under every outward disadvantage, and in the regions of the grossest darkness and ignorance, he most amazingly acts upon, and influences, their minds, and in the course of wisely and most wonderfully appointed providence, he brings them to the means of spiritual information, gradually opens to their view the light of his truth, and gives them full possession and enjoyment of the inestimable blessings of his gospel. Who can doubt but that the suggestion so forcibly press'd upon the mind of Albert *(when a boy) that there was a Being superior to the sun, moon, and stars (the objects of African idolatry) came from the Father of lights, and was, with respect to him, the first fruit of the display of gospel glory? His long and perilous journey to the coast of* Guinea,[4] *where he was sold for a slave, and so brought into a Christian land; shall we consider this as the alone effect of a curious and inquisitive disposition? Shall we, in accounting for it refer to nothing higher than mere chance & accidental circumstances? Whatever Infidels & Deists may think, I trust the Christian reader will easily discern an all wise and omnipotent appointment and direction in these movements. He belonged to the Redeemer of lost sinners; he was the purchase of his cross; and therefore the Lord undertook to bring him by a way he knew not, out of darkness into his marvellous light,[5] that he might lead him to a saving heart-acquaintance and union with the triune God in Christ, reconciling the world unto himself; and not imputing their trespasses.[6] As his call was very extraordinary, so there are certain particulars exceedingly remarkable in his experience. God has put singular honor upon him in the exercise of his faith and patience, which, in the most distressing and pitiable trials and calamities, have been found to the praise and glory of God. How deeply must it affect a tender heart, not only to be reduc'd to the last extremity himself, but to have his wife and children perishing for want before his eyes! Yet his faith did not fail him; he put his trust in the Lord, and he was delivered. And, at this instant, though born in an exalted station of life, and now under the Pressure of various afflicting Providences, I am persuaded (for I know the man) he would rather embrace the dunghill,[7] having Christ in his heart, than give up his spiritual possessions and enjoyment, to fill the throne of Princes. It perhaps may not be amiss to observe, that* James Albert *left his native country (as near as I can guess from certain circumstances) when he was about* 15 *years old. He now appears to be turn'd of* 60; *has a good natural understanding; is well acquainted with the scriptures, and the things of God; has an amiable and tender disposition; and his character can be well attested not only at* Kidderminster, *the place of his residence, but likewise by many creditable persons in* London *and other places. Reader, recommending this* Narrative *to your perusal, and him who is the subject of it, to your charitable regard,*

I am your faithful and obedient servant,
For Christ's sake,
W. SHIRLEY.[8]

✠ ✠ ✠

An Account of James Albert, &c.

I WAS born in the city of *Baurnou,*[9] my mother was the eldest daughter of the reigning King there. I was the youngest of six children, and particularly loved by my mother, and my grand-father almost doated on me.

I had, from my infancy, a curious turn of mind; was more grave and reserved, in my disposition, than either of my brothers and sisters, I often teazed them with questions they could not answer; for which reason they disliked me, as they supposed that I was either foolish or insane. 'Twas certain that I was, at times, very unhappy in myself: It being strongly impressed on my mind that there was some GREAT MAN of power which resided above the sun, moon and stars, the objects of our worship. — My dear, indulgent mother would bear more with me than any of my friends beside. — I often raised my hand to heaven, and asked her who lived there? Was much dissatisfied when she told me the sun, moon and stars, being persuaded, in my own mind, that there must be some SUPERIOR POWER. — I was frequently lost in wonder at the works of the creation: Was afraid, and uneasy, and restless, but could not tell for what. I wanted to be informed of things that no person could tell me; and was always dissatisfied. — These wonderful impressions began in my childhood, and followed me continually till I left my parents, which affords me matter of admiration and thankfulness.

To this moment I grew more and more uneasy every day, insomuch that one Saturday (which is the day on which we kept our sabbath) I laboured under anxieties and fears that cannot be expressed; and, what is more extraordinary, I could not give a reason for it. — — I rose, as our custom is, about three o'clock (as we are obliged to be at our place of worship an hour before the sun rise) we say nothing in our worship, but continue on our knees with our hands held up, observing a strict silence till the sun is at a certain height, which I suppose to be about 10 or 11 o'clock in *England*: When, at a certain sign made by the Priest, we get up (our duty being over) and disperse to our different houses. — Our place of meeting is under a large palm tree; we divide ourselves into many congregations; as it is impossible for the same tree to cover the inhabitants of the whole city, though they are extremely large, high and majestic; the beauty and usefulness of them are not to be described; they supply the inhabitants of the country with meat, drink and clothes;[10] the body of the palm tree is very large; at a certain season of the year they tap it, and bring vessels to receive the wine, of which they draw great quantities, the quality of which is very delicious: The leaves of this tree are of a silky nature; they are large and soft; when they are dried and pulled to pieces, it has much the same appearance as the English flax, and the inhabitants of BOURNOU manufacture it for clothing, &c. This tree likewise produces a plant, or substance, which has the appearance of a cabbage, and very like it, in taste almost the same: It grows between the branches.

Also the palm tree produces a nut, something like a cocoa, which contains a kernel, in which is a large quantity of milk, very pleasant to the taste: The shell is of a hard substance, and of a very beautiful appearance, and serves for basons, bowls, &c.

I hope this digression will be forgiven. — I was going to observe, that after the duty of our sabbath was over (on the day in which I was more distressed and afflicted than ever) we were all on our way home as usual, when a remarkable black cloud arose and covered the sun; then followed very heavy rain and thunder, more dreadful than ever I had heard: The heavens roared, and the earth trembled at it: I was highly affected and cast down; insomuch that I wept sadly, and could not follow my relations & friends home. — I was obliged to stop, and felt as if my legs were tied, they seemed to shake under me: So I stood still, being in great fear of the MAN of POWER, that I was persuaded, in myself, lived above. One of my young companions (who entertained a particular friendship for me, and I for him) came back to see for me: He asked me why I stood still in such very hard rain? I only said to him that my legs were weak, and I could not come faster: He was much affected to see me cry, and took me by the hand, and said he would lead me home, which he did. My mother was greatly alarmed at my tarrying out in such terrible weather; she asked me many questions, such as what I did so for? And if I was well? My dear mother, says I, pray tell me who is the GREAT MAN of POWER that makes the thunder? She said, there was no power but the sun, moon and stars; that they made all our country. — — I then inquired how all our people came? She answered me, from one another; and so carried me to many generations back. — Then says I, who made the *first man?* And who made the first cow, and the first lion, and where does the fly come from, as no one can make him? My mother seemed in great trouble; she was apprehensive that my senses were impaired, or that I was foolish. My father came in, and seeing her in grief asked the cause, but when she related our conversation to him he was exceedingly angry with me, and told me he would punish me severely if ever I was so troublesome again; so that I resolved never to say any thing more to him. But I grew very unhappy in myself; my relations and acquaintance endeavoured, by all the means they could think on, to divert me, by taking me to ride upon goats (which is much the custom of our country) and to shoot with a bow and arrow; but I experienced no satisfaction at all in any of these things; nor could I be easy by any means whatever: My parents were very unhappy to see me so dejected and melancholy.

About this time there came a merchant from the *Gold Coast* (the third city in GUINEA) he traded with the inhabitants of our country in ivory, &c. he took great notice of my unhappy situation, and inquired into the cause; he expressed vast concern for me, and said, if my parents would part with me for a little while, and let him take me home with him, it would be of more service to me than any thing they could do for me. — He told me that if I would go with him I should see houses with wings to them walk upon the water, and should also see the white folks; and that he had many sons of my age, which should be my companions; and he added to all this that he would bring me safe back again soon. — I was highly pleased with the account of this strange place, and was very desirous of going. — I seemed sensible of a secret impulse upon my mind, which I could not resist, that seemed to tell me I must go. When my dear mother saw that I was willing to leave them, she spoke to my father and grandfather and the rest of my relations, who all agreed that I should accompany the merchant to the Gold Coast. I was the more willing as my brothers and sisters despised me, and looked on me with contempt on the account of my unhappy disposition; and even my servants slighted me, and disregarded all I said to them. I had one sister who was always exceeding fond of me, and I loved her entirely; her name was LOGWY, she was quite white, and fair, with fine light hair, though my father and mother were black.[11] — I was truly concerned to leave my beloved sister, and she cry'd most sadly to part with me, wringing her hands, and discovered every sign of grief that can be imagined.[12] Indeed if I could have known when I left my friends and country that I should never return to them again my misery on that occasion would have been inexpressible. All my relations were sorry to part with me; my dear mother came with me upon a camel more than three hundred miles, the first of our journey lay chiefly through woods: At night we secured ourselves from the wild beasts by making fires all around us; we and our camels kept within the circle, or we must have been torn to pieces by the lions, and other wild creatures, that roared terribly as soon as night came on, and continued to do so till morning. — There can be little said in favour of the country through which we passed; only a valley of marble that we came through which is unspeakably beautiful. — On each side of this valley are exceedingly high and almost inaccessible mountains — Some of these pieces of marble are of prodigious length and breadth but of different sizes and colour, and shaped in a variety of forms, in a wonderful manner. — It is most of it veined with gold mixed with striking and beautiful colours; so that when the sun darts upon it, it is as pleasing a sight as can be imagined. — — The merchant that brought me from BOURNOU was in partnership with another gentleman who accompanied us; he was very unwilling that he should take me from home, as, he said, he foresaw many difficulties that would attend my going with them. — He endeavoured to prevail on the merchant to throw me into a very deep pit that was in the valley, but he refused to listen to him, and said, he was resolved to take care of me: But the other was greatly dissatisfied; and when we came to a river, which we were obliged to pass through, he purposed throwing me in and drowning me; but the merchant would not consent to it, so that I was preserved.

We travel'd till about four o'clock every day, and then began to make preparations for night, by cutting down large quantities of wood, to make fires to preserve us from the wild beasts. — I had a very unhappy and discontented journey, being in continual fear that the people I was with would murder me. I often reflected with extreme regret on the kind friends I had left, and the idea of my dear mother frequently drew tears from my eyes. I cannot recollect how long we were in going from *Bournou* to the *Gold Coast;* but as there is no shipping nearer to *Bournou* than that city, it was tedious in travelling so far by land, being upwards of a thousand miles. — I was heartily rejoiced when we arrived at the end of our journey: I now vainly imagined that all my troubles and inquietudes would terminate here; but could I have looked into futurity, I should have perceived that I had much more to suffer than I had before experienced, and that they had as yet but barely commenced.

I was now more than a thousand miles from home, without a friend or any means to procure one. Soon after I came to the merchant's house I heard the drums beat remarkably loud, and the trumpets blow — the persons accustom'd to this employ, are oblig'd to go upon a very high structure appointed for that purpose, that the sound might be heard at a great distance: They are higher than the steeples are in *England.* I was mightily pleased with sounds so entirely new to me, and was very inquisitive to know the cause of this rejoicing, and asked many questions concerning it; I was answered that it was meant as a compliment to me, because I was grandson to the King of *Bournou.*

This account gave me a secret pleasure; but I was not suffered long to enjoy this satisfaction, for, in the evening of the same day, two of the merchant's sons (boys about my own age) came running to me, and told me, that the next day I was to die, for the King intended to behead me. — I reply'd, that I was sure it could not be true, for that I came there to play with them, and to see houses walk upon the water, with wings to them, and the white folks; but I was soon informed that their King imagined I was sent by my father as a spy, and would make such discoveries, at my return home, that would enable them to make war with the greater advantage to ourselves; and for these reasons he had resolved I should never return to my native country. — When I heard this, I suffered misery that cannot be described. — I wished, a thousand times, that I had never left my friends and country. — But still the Almighty was pleased to work miracles for me.

The morning I was to die, I was washed and all my gold ornaments made bright and shining, and then carried to the palace, where the King was to behead me himself (as is the custom of the place). — He was seated upon a throne at the top of an exceeding large yard, or court, which you must go through to enter the palace, it is as wide and spacious as a large field in *England*. — I had a lane of life-guards to go through. — I guessed it to be about three hundred paces.

I was conducted by my friend, the merchant, about half way up; then he durst proceed no further: I went up to the King alone — I went with an undaunted courage, and it pleased God to melt the heart of the King, who sat with his scymitar in his hand ready to behead me; yet, being himself so affected, he dropped it out of his hand, and took me upon his knee and wept over me. I put my right hand round his neck, and prest him to my heart. — He set me down and blest me; and added that he would not kill me, and that I should not go home, but be sold for a slave, so then I was conducted back again to the merchant's house.

The next day he took me on board a French brig;[13] the Captain did not chuse to buy me: He said I was too small; so the merchant took me home with him again.

The partner, whom I have spoken of as my enemy, was very angry to see me return, and again purposed putting an end to my life; for he represented to the other, that I should bring them into troubles and difficulties, and that I was so little that no person would buy me.

The merchant's resolution began to waver, and I was indeed afraid that I should be put to death: But however he said he would try me once more.

A few days after a *Dutch* ship came into the harbour, and they carried me on board, in hopes that the Captain would purchase me. — As they went, I heard them agree, that, if they could not sell me *then*, they would throw me overboard. — I was in extreme agonies when I heard this; and as soon as ever I saw the *Dutch* Captain, I ran to him, and put my arms round him, and said, "Father save me." (for I knew that if he did not buy me I should be treated very ill, or, possibly murdered) And though he did not understand my language, yet it pleased the Almighty to influence him in my behalf, and he bought me *for two yards of check,* which is of more value *there,* than in *England.*[14]

When I left my dear mother I had a large quantity of gold about me, as is the custom of our country, it was made into rings, and they were linked into one another, and formed into a kind of chain, and so put round my neck, and arms and legs, and a large piece hanging at one ear almost in the shape of a pear. I found all this troublesome, and was glad when my new master took it from me.—I was now washed, & clothed in the *Dutch* or *English* manner.—My master grew very fond of me, and I loved him exceedingly. I watched every look, was always ready when he wanted me, and endeavoured to convince him, by every action, that my only pleasure was to serve him well.—I have since thought that he must have been a serious man. His actions corresponded very well with such a character.—He used to read prayers in public to the ship's crew every sabbath day; and when first I saw him read, I was never so surprised in my whole life as when I saw the book talk to my master; for I thought it did, as I observed him to look upon it, and move his lips.—I wished it would do so to me.—As soon as my master had done reading I follow'd him to the place where he put the book, being mightily delighted with it, and when nobody saw me, I open'd it and put my ear down close upon it, in great hope that it would say something to me; but was very sorry and greatly disappointed when I found it would not speak, this thought immediately presented itself to me, that every body and every thing despised me because I was black.[15]

I was exceedingly sea-sick at first; but when I became more accustom'd to the sea, it wore off.—My master's ship was bound for *Barbados.*[16] When we came there, he thought fit to speak of me to several gentlemen of his acquaintance, and one of them exprest a particular desire to see me.—He had a great mind to buy me; but the Captain could not immediately be prevail'd on to part with me; but however, as the gentleman seemed very solicitous, he at length let me go, and I was sold for fifty dollars (*four and six penny pieces in English.*) My new master's name was *Vanhorn,* a young gentleman; his home was in *New-England,* in the city of *New-York;* to which place he took me with him. He dress'd me in his livery,[17] & was very good to me. My chief business was to wait at table, and tea, & clean knives, & I had a very easy place; but the servants used to curse & swear surprizingly; which I learnt faster than any thing, 'twas almost the first English I could speak. If any of them affronted me, I was sure to call upon God to damn them immediately; but I was broke

of it all at once, occasioned by the correction of an old black servant that
lived in the family. — One day I had just clean'd the knives for dinner,
when one of the maids took one to cut bread and butter with; I was very
angry with her, and called upon God to damn her; when this old black
man told me I must not say so: I ask'd him why? He replied there was
a wicked man, call'd the Devil, that liv'd in hell, and would take all that
said these words and put them in the fire and burn them. — This terrified me greatly, and I was entirely broke of swearing. Soon after this, as
I was placing the china for tea, my mistress came into the room just as
the maid had been cleaning it; the girl had unfortunately sprinkled the
wainscot[18] with the mop; at which my mistress was angry; the girl very
foolishly answered her again, which made her worse, and she called
upon God to damn her. — I was vastly concern'd to hear this, as she was
a fine young lady, and very good to me, insomuch that I could not help
speaking to her: Madam, says I, you must not say so: Why, says she?
Because there is a black man, call'd the Devil,[19] that lives in hell, and he
will put you in the fire and burn you, and I shall be very sorry for that.
Who told you this, replied my lady? Old Ned, says I. Very well was all
her answer; but she told my master of it, who ordered that old Ned
should be tied up and whipp'd, and was never suffered to come into the
kitchen, with the rest of the servants, afterwards. — My mistress was not
angry with me, but rather diverted at my simplicity, and, by way of talk,
she repeated what I had said to many of her acquaintance that visited
her; among the rest, *Freelandhouse*,[20] a very gracious, good minister,
heard it, and he took a great deal of notice of me, and desired my master to part with me to him. He would not hear of it at first, but, being
greatly persuaded, he let me go; and Mr. *Freelandhouse* gave £.50 for
me. — He took me home with him, and made me kneel down, and put my
two hands together, and prayed for me, and every night and morning he
did the same. — I could not make out what it was for, nor the meaning
of it, nor what they spoke to when they talked — I thought it comical, but
I liked it very well. — After I had been a little while with my new master I grew more familiar, and asked him the meaning of prayer: (I could
hardly speak *English* to be understood)[21] he took great pains with me,
and made me understand that he pray'd to God, who liv'd in Heaven;
that he was my father and *best* friend. — I told him that this must be a
mistake; that *my* father lived at *Bournou*, and I wanted very much to see
him, and likewise my dear mother, and sister, and I wished he would be
so good as to send me home to them; and I added, all I could think of to
induce him to convey me back, I appeared in great trouble, and my good

master was so much affected that the tears run down his face. He told me that God was a great and good Spirit, that he created all the world, and every person and thing in it, *Ethiopia*, *Africa* and *America*, and every where. I was delighted when I heard this: There, says I, I always thought so when I lived at home! Now, if I had wings like an eagle,[22] I would fly to tell my dear mother that God is greater than the sun, moon and stars; and that they were made by him.

I was exceedingly pleas'd with this information of my master's, because it corresponded so well with my own opinion; I thought now if I could but get home, I should be wiser than all my country-folks, my grandfather, or father, or mother, or any of them. — But though I was somewhat enlightened, by this information of my master's, yet I had no other knowledge of God than that he was a good Spirit, and created every body, and every thing. — I never was sensible, in myself, nor had any one ever told me, that he would punish the wicked, and love the just. I was only glad that I had been told there was a God, because I had always thought so.

My dear kind master grew very fond of me, as was his lady;[23] she put me to school, but I was uneasy at that, and did not like to go; but my master and mistress requested me to learn in the gentlest terms, and persuaded me to attend my school without any anger at all; that, at last, I came to like it better, and learnt to read pretty well. My schoolmaster was a good man, his name was *Vanosdore*,[24] and very indulgent to me. — I was in this state when, one Sunday, I heard my master preach from these words out of the *Revelations*, chap. i. v. 7. *"Behold, He cometh in the clouds and every eye shall see him and they that pierc'd Him."* These words affected me excessively; I was in great agonies because I thought my master directed them to me only; and, I fancied, that he observed me with unusual earnestness — I was farther confirm'd in this belief as I looked round the church, and could see no one person beside myself in such grief and distress as I was; I began to think that my master hated me, and was very desirous to go home, to my own country; for I thought that if God did come (as he said) He would be sure to be most angry with me, as I did not know what He was, nor had ever heard of him before.

I went home in great trouble, but said nothing to any body. — I was somewhat afraid of my master; I thought he disliked me. — The next text I heard him preach from was, *Heb.* xii. 14. *"Follow peace with all men, and holiness, without which no man shall see the LORD."* He preached the law so severely, that it made me tremble. — He said, that GOD would judge the whole world;[25] *Ethiopia*, *Asia*, and *Africa*, and every where. — I was now excessively perplexed, and undetermined what to do; as I had now reason to believe that my situation would be equally bad to go as to stay. — I kept these thoughts to myself, and said nothing to any person whatever.

I should have complained to my good mistress of this great trouble of mind, but she had been a little strange to me for several days before this happened, occasioned by a story told of me by one of the maids. The servants were all jealous, and envied me the regard, and favour shewn me by my master and mistress; and the Devil being always ready, and diligent in wickedness, had influenced this girl to make a lie on me. — This happened about hay harvest, and one day, when I was unloading the wagon to put the hay into the barn, she watched an opportunity, in my absence, to take the fork out of the stick,[26] and hide it: When I came again to my work, and could not find it, I was a good deal vexed, but I concluded it was dropt somewhere among the hay; so I went and bought another with my own money: When the girl saw that I had another, she was so malicious that she told my mistress I was very unfaithful, and not the person she took me for; and that she knew, I had, without my master's permission, ordered many things in his name, that he must pay for; and as a proof of my carelessness produced the fork she had taken out of the stick, and said, she had found it out of doors — My Lady, not knowing the truth of these things, was a little shy to me, till she mentioned it, and then I soon cleared myself, and convinced her that these accusations were false.

I continued in a most unhappy state for many days. My good mistress insisted on knowing what was the matter. When I made known my situation, she gave me John Bunyan on the holy war, to read; I found his experience similar to my own, which gave me reason to suppose he must be a bad man; as I was convinced of my own corrupt nature, and the misery of my own heart: And as he acknowledged that he was likewise in the same condition, I experienced no relief at all in reading his work, but rather the reverse. — I took the book to my lady, and informed her I did not like it at all, it was concerning a wicked man as bad as myself; and I did not chuse to read it, and I desired her to give me another, wrote by a better man, that was holy, and without sin. — She assured me that John Bunyan was a good man, but she could not convince me; I thought him to be too much like myself to be upright, as his experience seemed to answer with my own.[27]

I am very sensible that nothing but the great power and unspeakable mercies of the Lord could relieve my soul from the heavy burden it laboured under at that time. — A few days after my master gave me

Baxter's *call to the unconverted*.[28] This was no relief to me neither; on the contrary it occasioned as much distress in me as the other had before done, *as it* invited all to come to *Christ;* and I found myself so wicked and miserable that I could not come —. This consideration threw me into agonies that cannot be described; insomuch that I even attempted to put an end to my life—I took one of the large case-knives, and went into the stable with an intent to destroy myself; and as I endeavoured with all my strength to force the knife into my side, it bent double. I was instantly struck with horror at the thought of my own rashness, and my conscience told me that had I succeeded in this attempt I should probably have gone to hell.

I could find no relief, nor the least shadow of comfort; the extreme distress of my mind so affected my health that I continued very ill for three days, and nights; and would admit of no means to be taken for my recovery, though my lady was very kind, and sent many things to me; but I rejected every means of relief and wished to die—I would not go into my own bed, but lay in the stable upon straw—I felt all the horrors of a troubled conscience, so hard to be born, and saw all the vengeance of God ready to overtake me—I was sensible that there was no way for me to be saved unless I came to *Christ*, and I could not come to Him: I thought that it was impossible He should receive such a sinner as me.

The last night that I continued in this place, in the midst of my distress these words were brought home upon my mind, *"Behold the Lamb of God,"*[29] I was something comforted at this, and began to grow easier and wished for day that I might find these words in my bible—I rose very early the following morning, and went to my school-master, Mr. Vanosdore, and communicated the situation of my mind to him; he was greatly rejoiced to find me inquiring the way to Zion, and blessed the Lord who had worked so wonderfully for me a poor heathen.—I was more familiar with this good gentleman than with my master, or any other person; and found my self more at liberty to talk to him: He encouraged me greatly, and prayed with me frequently, and I was always benefited by his discourse.

About a quarter of a mile from my master's house stood a large, remarkably fine oak-tree, in the midst of a wood; I often used to be employed there in cutting down trees, (a work I was very fond of) I seldom failed going to this place every day; sometimes twice a day if I could be spared. It was the highest pleasure I ever experienced to sit under this oak; for there I used to pour out all my complaints to the LORD: And when I had any particular grievance I used to go there, and talk to the tree, and tell my sorrows, as if it had been to a friend.

Here I often lamented my own wicked heart, and undone state; and found more comfort and consolation than I ever was sensible of before. — Whenever I was treated with ridicule or contempt, I used to come here and find peace. I now began to relish the book my master gave me, Baxter's *call to the unconverted,* and took great delight in it.[30] I was always glad to be employed in cutting wood, 'twas a great part of my business, and I followed it with delight, as I was than quite alone and my heart lifted up to GOD, and I was enabled to pray continually;[31] and blessed for ever be his holy name, he faithfully answered my prayers. I can never be thankful enough to Almighty GOD for the many comfortable opportunities I experienced there.

It is possible the circumstance I am going to relate will not gain credit with many; but this I know, that the joy and comfort it conveyed to me, cannot be expressed, and only conceived by those who have experienced the like.

I was one day in a most delightful frame of mind; my heart so overflowed with love and gratitude to the author of all my comforts: — I was so drawn out of myself, and so fill'd and awed by the presence of God, that I saw (or thought I saw) light inexpressible dart down from heaven upon me, and shone around me for the space of a minute. — I continued on my knees, and joy unspeakable took possession of my soul. — The peace and serenity which filled my mind after this was wonderful, and cannot be told. — I would not have changed situations, or been any one but myself for the whole world. I blest God for my poverty, that I had no worldly riches or grandeur to draw my heart from him.[32] I wished at that time, if it had been possible for me, to have continued on that spot forever. I felt an unwillingness in myself to have any thing more to do with the world, or to mix with society again. I seemed to possess a full assurance that my sins were forgiven me. I went home all my way rejoicing, and this text of scripture came full upon my mind. *"And I will make an everlasting covenant with them, that I will not turn away from them, to do them good; but I will put my fear in their hearts that they shall not depart from me."*[33] The first opportunity that presented itself, I went to my old schoolmaster, and made known to him the happy state of my soul who joined with me in praise to God for his mercy to me the vilest of sinners. — I was now perfectly easy and had hardly a wish to make beyond what I possessed, when my temporal comforts were all blasted by the death of my dear and worthy master Mr. *Freelandhouse,* who was taken from this world rather suddenly: He had but a short illness, and died of a fever.[34] I held his hand in mine when he departed;[35] he told me he had given me my freedom. I was at liberty to go where I would.—He added that he had always prayed for me and hoped I should be kept unto the end. My master left me by his will ten pounds, and my freedom.

I found that if he had lived twas his intention to take me with him to Holland, as he had often mentioned me to some friends of his there that were desirous to see me; but I chose to continue with my mistress who was as good to me as if she had been my mother.

The loss of Mr. *Freelandhouse* distressed me greatly, but I was rendered still more unhappy by the clouded and perplexed situation of my mind; the great enemy of my soul being ready to torment me, would present my own misery to me in such striking light, and distress me with doubts, fears, and such a deep sense of my own unworthiness, that after all the comfort and encouragement I had received, I was often tempted to believe I should be a cast-away[36] at last.—The more I saw of the beauty and glory of God, the more I was humbled under a sense of my own vileness. I often repaired to my old place of prayer; I seldom came away without consolation. One day this scripture was wonderfully apply'd to my mind, *And ye are complete in him which is the head of all principalities and power*[37]—The Lord was pleased to comfort me by the application of many gracious promises at times when I was ready to sink under my troubles. *Wherefore he is able also to save them to the uttermost that come unto God by him, seeing he ever liveth to make intercession for them,*[38] Heb. x. xiv. *For by one offering he hath perfected forever them that are sanctified.*[39]

My kind, indulgent mistress liv'd but two years after my master. Her death was a great affliction to me. She left five sons, all gracious young men, and ministers of the gospel.—I continued with them all, one after another, till they died; they lived but four years after their parents.[40] When it pleased God to take them to himself. I was left quite destitute, without a friend in the world. But I, who had so often experienced the goodness of God, trusted in him to do what he pleased with me.—In this helpless condition I went in the wood to prayer as usual; and though the snow was a considerable height, I was not sensible of cold, or any other inconveniency.—At times, indeed, when I saw the world frowning round me, I was tempted to think that the LORD had forsaken me. I found great relief from the contemplation of these words in Isai. xlix. 16. *Behold I have graven thee on the palms of my hands; thy walls are continually before me.* And very many comfortable promises were sweetly applied to me. The 89th Psal. and 34th ver. *My covenant will I not break, nor alter the thing that is gone out of my lips.* Heb. xvi. 17, 18. Phil. i. 6. and several more.[41]

As I had now lost all my dear and valued friends,[42] every place in the world was alike to me. I had for a great while entertained a desire to come to *England.* — I imagined that all the inhabitants of this island were *holy;* because all those that had visited my master from thence were good (Mr. Whitefield[43] was his particular friend) and the authors of the books that had been given me were all English. — But, above all places in the world, I wish'd to see Kidderminster, for I could not but think that on the spot where Mr. Baxter had lived, and preach'd, the people must be all *righteous.*[44]

The situation of my affairs required that I should tarry a little longer in *New York,* as I was something in debt, and was embarrassed how to pay it. About this time a young gentleman that was a particular acquaintance of my young master's,[45] pretended to be a friend to me, and promis'd to pay my debts, which was three pounds; and he assured me he would never expect the money again. — But, in less than a month, he came and demanded it; and when I assured him I had nothing to pay, he threatened to sell me.[46] — Though I knew he had no right to do that, yet, as I had no friend in the world to go to, it alarm'd me greatly. — At length he purpos'd my going a privateering,[47] that I might, by these means, be enabled to pay him, to which I agreed. — Our Captain's name was — — — — — —. I went in character of cook to him. — Near St. *Domingo*[48] we came up to five French ships, merchantmen. — We had a very smart engagement, that continued from eight in the morning till three in the afternoon; when victory declared on our side. — Soon after this we were met by three English ships which join'd us, and that encouraged us to attack a fleet of 36 ships.[49] — We boarded the three first, and then followed the others, and had the same success with twelve; but the rest escaped us. — There was a great deal of blood shed, and I was near death several times, but the LORD preserv'd me.

I met with many enemies, and much persecution, among the sailors; one of them was particularly unkind to me, and studied ways to vex and teaze me. I can't help mentioning one circumstance that hurt me more than all the rest, which was, that he snatched a book out of my hand, that I was very fond of, and used frequently to amuse myself with, & threw it into the sea.[50] — But, what is remarkable, he was the first that was killed in our engagement. — I don't pretend to say that this happened because he was not my friend; but I thought 'twas a very awful providence, to see how the enemies of the LORD are cut off.[51]

Our Captain was a cruel, hard-hearted man. I was excessively sorry for the prisoners we took in general: But the pitiable case of one young gentleman grieved me to the heart. — He appeared very amiable; was strikingly handsome. — Our Captain took four thousand pounds from him; but that did not satisfy him, as he imagined he was possessed of more, and had somewhere concealed it, so that the Captain threatened him with death, at which he appeared in the deepest distress, and took the buckles out of his shoes, and untied his hair, which was very fine, and long; and in which several very valuable rings were fastened. He came into the cabin to me, and in the most obliging terms imaginable asked for something to eat and drink; which when I gave him he was so thankful and pretty in his manner that my heart bled for him; and I heartily wished that I could have spoken in any language in which the ship's crew would not have understood me; that I might have let him know his danger;[52] for I heard the Captain say he was resolved upon his death; and he put his barbarous design into execution, for he took him on shore with one of the sailors, and there they shot him.

This circumstance affected me exceedingly. I could not put him out of my mind a long while. — When we returned to *New York* the Captain divided the prize-money among us,[53] that we had taken. When I was called upon to receive my part, I waited upon Mr. — — —, (the gentleman that paid my debt and was the occasion of my going abroad) to know if he chose to go with me to receive my money, or if I should bring him what I owed. — He chose to go with me; and when the Captain laid my money on the table ('twas an hundred and thirty-five pounds) I desired Mr. — — — to take what I was indebted to him; and he swept it all into his handkerchief, and would never be prevailed on to give a farthing of money, nor any thing at all beside. — And he likewise secured a hogshead of sugar[54] which was my due from the same ship. The Captain was very angry with him for this piece of cruelty to me, as was every other person that heard it. — But I have reason to believe (as he was one of the principal merchants in the city) that he transacted business for him and on that account did not chuse to quarrel with him.

At this time a very worthy gentleman, a wine merchant, his name *Dunscum*, took me under his protection, and would have recovered my money for me if I had chose it; but I told him to let it alone; that I would rather be quiet. — I believed that it would not prosper with him, and so it happened, for by a series of losses and misfortunes he became poor, and was soon after drowned, as he was on a party of pleasure. — The vessel was driven out to sea, and struck against a rock by which means every soul perished.

I was very much distressed when I heard it, and felt greatly for his family who were reduced to very low circumstances. —I never knew how to set a proper value on money, if I had but a little meat and drink to supply the present necessaries of life, I never wished for more; and when I had any I always gave it if ever I saw an object in distress. If it was not for my dear wife and children I should pay as little regard to money now as I did at any time. —I continued some time with Mr. *Dunscum* as his servant; he was very kind to me. —But I had a vast inclination to visit *England*, and wished continually that it would please providence to make a clear way for me to see this island. I entertained a notion that if I could get to *England* I should never more experience either cruelty or ingratitude, so that I was very desirous to get among Christians. I knew Mr. *Whitefield* very well. —I had heard him preach often at *New-York*. In this disposition I listed in the twenty-eight regiment of foot, who were designed for *Martinico* in the late war.[55] —We went in Admiral Pocock's fleet from *New York* to *Barbados;* from thence to *Martinico*.[56] —When that was taken we proceeded to the *Havanna*, and took that place likewise. —There I got discharged.[57]

I was then worth about thirty pounds, but I never regarded money in the least, nor would I tarry to receive my prize-money lest I should lose my chance of going to *England*. —I went with the *Spanish* prisoners to *Spain;* and came to *Old England* with the English prisoners.[58] —I cannot describe my joy when we were within sight of *Portsmouth*.[59] But I was astonished when we landed to hear the inhabitants of that place curse and swear, and otherwise profane. I expected to find nothing but goodness, gentleness and meekness in this Christian land, I then suffered great perplexities of mind.

I inquired if any serious Christian people resided there, the woman I made this inquiry of, answered me in the affirmative; and added that she was one of them. —I was heartily glad to hear her say so. I thought I could give her my whole heart: She kept a public house. I deposited with her all the money that I had not an immediate occasion for; as I thought it would be safer with her. —It was 25 guineas,[60] but 6 of them I desired her to lay out to the best advantage, to buy me some shirts, hat, and some other necessaries. I made her a present of a very handsome large looking-glass, that I brought with me from Martinico, in order to recompence her for the trouble I had given her. I must do this woman the justice to acknowledge that she did lay out some little for my use, but the 19 guineas, and part of the 6, with my watch, she would not return, and denied that I ever gave it her.

I soon perceived that I was got among bad people, who defrauded me of my money and watch; and that all my promis'd happiness was blasted, I had no friend but GOD, and I prayed to him earnestly. I could scarcely believe it possible that the place where so many eminent Christians had lived and preached could abound with so much wickedness and deceit. I thought it worse than *Sodom* (considering the great advantages they have) I cry'd like a child, and that almost continually: At length GOD heard my prayers and raised me a friend indeed.

This publican[61] had a brother who lived on *Portsmouth* common, his wife was a serious good woman. When she heard of the treatment I had met with, she came and inquired into my real situation, and was greatly troubled at the ill usage I had received, and took me home to her own house. — I began now to rejoice, and my prayer was turned into praise. She made use of all the arguments in her power to prevail on her who had wronged me, to return my watch and money, but it was to no purpose, as she had given me no receipt, and I had nothing to show for it, I could not demand it. — My good friend was excessively angry with her, and obliged her to give me back four guineas, which she said she gave me out of charity: Though in fact it was my own, and much more. She would have employed some rougher means to oblige her to give up my money,[62] but I would not suffer her, let it go, says I, "My GOD is in heaven." Still I did not mind my loss in the least; all that grieved me was, that I had been disappointed in finding some Christian friends, with whom I hoped to enjoy a little sweet and comfortable society.

I thought the best method that I could take now, was to go to *London*, and find out Mr. *Whitefield*, who was the only living soul I knew in *England*, and get him to direct me to some way or other to procure a living without being troublesome to any person. — I took leave of my Christian friend at *Portsmouth*, and went in the stage to *London*. — A creditable tradesman in the city, who went up with me in the stage, offered to show me the way to Mr. *Whitefield*'s tabernacle.[63] Knowing that I was a perfect stranger, I thought it very kind, and accepted his offer; but he obliged me to give him half-a-crown for going with me, and likewise insisted on my giving him five shillings more for conducting me to Dr. *Gifford*'s meeting.[64]

I began now to entertain a very different idea of the inhabitants of *England* than what I had figured to myself before I came among them. — Mr. *Whitefield* received me very friendly, was heartily glad to see me, and directed me to a proper place to board and lodge in Petticoat-lane, till he could think of some way to settle me in, and paid for my lodging, and all my expences. The morning after I came to my new lodging, as I was at breakfast with the gentlewoman of the house, I heard the noise of some looms over our heads: I inquired what it was; she told me a person was weaving silk. — I expressed a great desire to see it, and asked if I might: She told me she would go up with me: She was sure I should be very welcome. She was as good as her word, and as soon as we entered the room, the person that was weaving looked about, and smiled upon us, and I loved her from that moment. She asked me many questions, and I in turn talked a great deal to her. I found she was a member of Mr. *Allen*'s meeting,[65] and I began to entertain a good opinion of her, though I was almost afraid to indulge this inclination, least she should prove like all the rest I had met with at *Portsmouth* &c. and which had almost given me a dislike to all white women. — But after a short acquaintance I had the happiness to find she was very different, and quite sincere, and I was not without hope that she entertained some esteem for me. We often went together to hear Dr. *Gifford*, and as I had always a propensity to relieve every object in distress as far as I was able, I used to give to all that complained to me; sometimes half a guinea at a time, as I did not understand the real value of it. — This gracious, good woman took great pains to correct and advise me in that and many other respects.

After I had been in *London* about six weeks I was recommended to the notice of some of my late master Mr. *Freelandhouse*'s acquaintance, who had heard him speak frequently of me. I was much persuaded by them to go to *Holland*. My master lived there before he bought me, and used to speak of me so respectfully among his friends there, that it raised in them a curiosity to see me; particularly the gentlemen engaged in the ministry, who expressed a desire to hear my experience and examine me.[66] I found that it was my good old master's design that I should have gone if he had lived; for which reason I resolved upon going to *Holland*, and informed my dear friend Mr. *Whitefield* of my intention; he was much averse to my going at first, but after I gave him my reasons appeared very well satisfied. I likewise informed my *Betty* (the good woman that I have mentioned above) of my determination to go to *Holland*, and I told her that I believed she was to be my wife: That if it was the LORD's will I desired it, but not else. — She made me very little answer, but has since told me, she did not think it at that time.

I embarked at tower-wharf at four o'clock in the morning, and arrived at *Amsterdam* the next day by three o'clock in the afternoon. I had several letters of recommendation to my old master's friends, who received me very graciously. Indeed, one of the chief ministers was particularly good to me, he kept me at his house a long while, and took great plea-sure in asking questions, which I answered with delight, being always ready to say, "*Come unto me all ye that fear GOD, and I will tell what he hath done for my soul.*"[67] I cannot but admire the footsteps of *Providence;* aston-ished that I should be so wonderfully preserved! Though the grandson of a King, I have wanted bread, and should have been glad of the hard-est crust I saw. I who, at home, was surrounded and guarded by slaves, so that no indifferent person might approach me, and clothed with gold, have been inhumanly threatened with death; and frequently wanted clothing to defend me from the inclemency of the weather; yet I never murmured, nor was I discontented. — I am willing, and even desirous, to be counted as nothing, a stranger in the world,[68] and a pilgrim here; for "*I know that my* REDEEMER *liveth,*"[69] and I'm thankful for every trial and trouble that I've met with, as I am not without hope that they have been all sanctified to me.

The Calvinist ministers desired to hear my experience from myself, which proposal I was very well pleased with: So I stood before 48 min-isters every Thursday for seven weeks together,[70] and they were all very well satisfied, and persuaded I was what I pretended to be. — They wrote down my experience as I spoke it; and the Lord almighty was with me at that time in a remarkable manner, and gave me words, and enabled me to answer them; so great was his mercy to take me in hand a poor blind Heathen.

At this time a very rich merchant at *Amsterdam* offered to take me into his family, in the capacity of his butler, and I very willingly accepted it. — He was a gracious, worthy gentleman, and very good to me. — He treated me more like a friend than a servant. — I tarried there a twelve-month, but was not thoroughly contented, I wanted to see my wife (that is now) and for that reason I wished to return to *England.* I wrote to her once in my absence, but she did not answer my letter; and I must acknowledge if she had, it would have given me a less opinion of her. — My master and mistress persuaded me not to leave them, and likewise their two sons, who entertained a good opinion of me; and if I had found my Betty married, on my arrival in *England,* I should have returned to them again immediately.

My lady proposed my marrying her maid; she was an agreeable young woman, had saved a good deal of money, but I could not fancy her, though she was willing to accept of me, but I told her my inclina-tions were engaged in *England,* and I could think of no other person. — On my return home I found my Betty disengaged. — She had refused several offers in my absence, and told her sister that she thought if ever she married I was to be her husband.

Soon after I came home I waited on Dr. Gifford, who took me into his family, and was exceedingly good to me. The character of this pious, worthy gentleman is well known; my praise can be of no use or signification at all.[71] — I hope I shall ever gratefully remember the many favours I have received from him. Soon after I came to Dr. Gifford, I expressed a desire to be admitted into their church, and set down with them; they told me I must first be baptized; so I gave in my experience before the church, with which they were very well satisfied, and I was baptized by Dr. Gifford, with some others. I then made known my intentions of being married; but I found there were many objections against it, because the person I had fixed on was poor. She was a widow, her husband had left her in debt, and with a child, so that they persuaded me against it out of real regard to me. But I had promised, and was resolved to have her; as I knew her to be a gracious woman, her poverty was no objection to me, as they had nothing else to say against her. When my friends found that they could not alter my opinion, respecting her, they wrote Mr. Allen, the minister she attended, to persuade her to leave me; but he replied that he would not interfere at all, that we might do as we would. I was resolved that all my wife's little debts should be paid before we were married; so that I sold almost every thing I had, and with all the money I could raise, cleared all that she owed; and I never did any thing with a better will in all my life, because I firmly believed that we should be very happy together, and so it proved, for she was given me from the Lord. And I have found her a blessed partner, and we have never repented, though we have gone through many great troubles and difficulties.

My wife got a very good living by weaving, and could do extremely well; but just at that time there was great disturbance among the weavers, so that I was afraid to let my wife work, least they should insist on my joining the rioters, which I could not think of, and, possibly, if I had refused to do so they would have knock'd me on the head.[72] So that by these means my wife could get no employ, neither had I work enough to maintain my family. We had not yet been married a year before all these misfortunes overtook us.

Just at this time a gentleman, that seemed much concerned for us, advised me to go into *Essex* with him, and promised to get me employed. I accepted his kind proposal, and he spoke to a friend of his, a Quaker, a gentleman of large fortune, who resided a little way out of the town

of *Colchester,* his name was *Handbarrar,* he ordered his steward to set me
to work.

There were several employed in the same way with myself. I was very
thankful and contented though my wages were but small. I was allowed
but eight pence a day, and found myself; but after I had been in this situation for a fortnight, my master, being told that a Black was at work
for him, had an inclination to see me. He was pleased to talk to me for
some time, and at last inquired what wages I had; when I told him, he
declared it was too little, and immediately ordered his steward to let me
have eighteen pence a day, which he constantly gave me after; and I then
did extremely well.

I did not bring my wife with me: I came first alone, and it was my
design, if things answered according to our wishes, to send for her. I was
now thinking to desire her to come to me, when I received a letter to
inform me she was just brought to bed,[73] and in want of many necessaries. This news was a great trial to me, and a fresh affliction: But my
God, *faithful and abundant in mercy,*[74] forsook me not in this trouble. As I
could not read English,[75] I was obliged to apply to some one to read the
letter I received, relative to my wife. I was directed by the good providence of God to a worthy young gentleman, a Quaker, and friend of my
master. — I desired he would take the trouble to read my letter for me,
which he readily complied with, and was greatly moved and affected at
the contents; insomuch that he said he would undertake to make a gathering for me, which he did and was the first to contribute to it himself.
The money was sent that evening to London, by a person who happened
to be going there; nor was this all the goodness that I experienced from
these kind friends, for as soon as my wife came about and was fit to
travel, they sent for her to me, and were at the whole expence of her
coming; so evidently has the love and mercy of God appeared through
every trouble that ever I experienced.

We went on very cordially all the summer. We lived in a little cottage
near Mr. *Handbarrar's* house; but when the winter came on I was discharged, as he had no further occasion for me. And now the prospect
began to darken upon us again. We tho't it most adviseable to move our
habitation a little nearer to the town, as the house we lived in was very
cold and wet, and ready to tumble down.

The boundless goodness of God to me has been so very great, that,
with the most humble gratitude, I desire to prostrate myself before him;
for I have been wonderfully supported in every affliction. — — My God
never left me. I perceived light *still,* thro' the thickest darkness.[76]

My dear wife and I were now both unemployed, we could get nothing to do. The winter proved remarkably severe, and we were reduced to the greatest distress imaginable. — I was always very shy of asking for any thing; I could never beg; neither did I chuse to make known our wants to any person, for fear of offending, as we were entire strangers; but our last bit of bread was gone, and I was obliged to think of something to do for our support. I did not mind for myself at all; but to see my dear wife and children in want, pierc'd me to the heart. — I now blam'd myself for bringing her from London, as doubtless had we continued there we might have found friends to keep us from starving. The snow was remarkably deep; so that we could see no prospect of being relieved. In this melancholy situation, not knowing what step to pursue, I resolved to make my case known to a gentleman's gardiner that lived near us, and entreat him to employ me; but when I came to him my courage fail'd me, and I was ashamed to make known our real situation. — I endeavoured all I could to prevail on him to set me to work, but to no purpose; he assured me it was not in his power: But just as I was about to leave him, he asked me if I would accept of some carrots? I took them with great thankfulness, and carried them home; he gave me four, they were very large and fine. — We had nothing to make fire with, so consequently could not boil them; but was glad to have them to eat raw. Our youngest child was quite an infant; so that my wife was obliged to chew it, and fed her in that manner for several days. We allowed ourselves but one every day, lest they should not last till we could get some other supply. I was unwilling to eat at all myself; nor would I take any the last day that we continued in this situation, as I could not bear the thought that my dear wife and children would be in want of every means of support. We lived in this manner till our carrots were all gone: Then my wife began to lament because of our poor babes; but I comforted her all I could; still hoping, and believing, that my God would not let us die; but that it would please him to relieve us, which he did by almost a miracle.

We went to bed, as usual, before it was quite dark (as we had neither fire nor candle) but had not been there long before some person knocked at the door, and inquired if *James Albert* lived there? I answer'd in the affirmative, and rose immediately; as soon as I opened the door I found it was the servant of an eminent attorney who resided at *Colchester.* He asked me how it was with me? If I was not almost starved? I burst out a crying, and told him I was indeed. He said his master suppos'd so, and that he wanted to speak with me, and I must return with him. This gentleman's name was *Daniel,* he was a sincere, good Christian. He used to stand and talk with me frequently, when I work'd in the road for Mr. *Handbarrar,* and would have employed me himself if I had wanted work.[77] — When I came to his house he told me that he had thought a good deal about me of late, and was apprehensive that I must be in want, and could not be satisfied till he sent to inquire after me. I made known my distress to him, at which he was greatly affected; and generously gave me a guinea; and promised to be kind to me in future. I could not help exclaiming, *O the boundless mercies of my God!* I prayed unto him, and he has heard me; I trusted in him, and he has preserv'd me: Where shall I begin to praise him? Or how shall I love him enough?

I went immediately and bought some bread and cheese and coal and carried them home. My dear wife was rejoiced to see me return with something to eat. She instantly got up and dressed our babies, while I made a fire; and the first nobility in the land never made a more comfortable meal. We did not forget to thank the Lord for all his goodness to us. Soon after this, as the spring came on, Mr. *Peter Daniel* employed me in pulling down a house, and rebuilding it. I had then very good work, and full employ: He sent for my wife and children to *Colchester,* and provided us a house, where we lived very comfortably. I hope I shall always gratefully acknowledge his kindness to myself and family. I worked at this house for more than a year, till it was finished; and after that I was employed by several successively, and was never so happy as when I had something to do; but perceiving the winter coming on, and work rather slack, I was apprehensive that we should again be in want, or become troublesome to our friends.[78]

I had at this time an offer made me of going to *Norwich,* and having constant employ. My wife seemed pleased with this proposal, as she supposed she might get work there in the weaving manufactory, being the business which she was brought up to, & more likely to succeed there than any other place; and we thought as we had an opportunity of moving to a town where we could both be employed, it was most adviseable to do so; and that probably we might settle there for our lives. When this step was resolved on, I went first alone to see how it would answer; which I very much repented after, for it was not in my power immediately to send my wife any supply, as I fell into the hands of a master that was neither kind nor considerate; and she was reduced to great distress, so that she was obliged to sell the few goods that we had, and when I sent for her was under the disagreeable necessity of parting with our bed.

When she came to *Norwich* I hired a room ready furnished. — I experienced a great deal of difference in the carriage of my master from what I had been accustomed to from some of my other masters. He was very irregular in his payments to me. — My wife hired a loom and wove all the leisure time she had and we began to do very well, till we were overtaken by fresh misfortunes. Our three poor children fell ill of the small pox; this was a great trial to us; but still I was persuaded in myself we should not be forsaken. — And I did all in my power to keep my dear partner's spirits from sinking. Her whole attention now was taken up with the children, as she could mind nothing else, and all I could get was but little to support a family in such a situation, beside paying for the hire of our room, which I was obliged to omit doing for several weeks: But the woman to whom we were indebted would not excuse us, though I promised she should have the very first money we could get after my children came about, but she would not be satisfied, and had the cruelty to threaten us that if we did not pay her immediately, she would turn us all into the street.[79]

The apprehension of this plunged me in the deepest distress, considering the situation of my poor babies: If they had been in health I should have been less sensible of this misfortune. But my God, *still faithful to his promise,* raised me a friend. Mr. *Henry Gurdney,* a Quaker, a gracious gentleman[80] heard of our distress, he sent a servant of his own to the woman we hired the room of, paid our rent, and bought all the goods, with my wife's loom, and gave it us all.

Some other gentlemen, hearing of his design, were pleased to assist him in these generous acts, for which we never can be thankful enough; after this my children soon came about; we began to do pretty well again; my dear wife worked hard and constant when she could get work, but it was upon a disagreeable footing, as her employ was so uncertain, sometimes she could get nothing to do, and at other times when the weavers of *Norwich* had orders from *London,* they were so excessively hurried, that the people they employed were often obliged to work on the Sabbath-day: But this my wife would never do, and it was matter of uneasiness to us that we could not get our living in a regular manner, though we were both diligent, industrious, and willing to work.[81] I was far from being happy in my master, he did not use me well. I could scarcely ever get my money from him; but I continued patient till it pleased GOD to alter my situation.

My worthy friend Mr. *Gurdney* advised me to follow the employ of chopping chaff,[82] and bought me an instrument for that purpose. There were but few people in the town that made this their business beside myself; so that I did very well indeed and we became easy and happy. — But we did not continue long in this comfortable state. Many of the inferior people were envious and ill-natur'd, and set up the same employ, and worked under price on purpose to get my business from me, and they succeeded so well that I could hardly get any thing to do, and became again unfortunate: Nor did this misfortune come alone, for just at this time we lost one of our little girls, who died of a fever; this circumstance occasioned us new troubles, for the Baptist minister refused to bury her because we were not their members. The parson of the parish denied us because she had never been baptized. I applied to the Quakers, but met with no success; this was one of the greatest trials I ever met with, as we did not know what to do with our poor baby[83] — At length I resolved to dig a grave in the garden behind the house, and bury her there; when the parson of the parish sent for me to tell me he would bury the child, but did not chuse to read the burial service over her. I told him I did not mind whether he would or not, as the child could not hear it.[84]

We met with a great deal of ill treatment after this, and found it very difficult to live. — We could scarcely get work to do, and were obliged to pawn our clothes. We were ready to sink under our troubles. — When I proposed to my wife to go to *Kidderminster*, and try if we could do there. I had always an inclination for that place, and now more than ever, as I had heard Mr. *Fawcet*[85] mentioned in the most respectful manner, as a pious worthy gentleman, and I had seen his name in a favourite book of mine, Baxter's *Saints everlasting rest;* and as the manufactory of *Kidderminster* seemed to promise my wife some employment, she readily came into my way of thinking.[86]

I left her once more, and set out for *Kidderminster* in order to judge if the situation would suit us. — As soon as I came there I waited immediately on Mr. *Fawcet,* who was pleased to receive me very kindly and recommended me to Mr. *Watson,* who employed me in twisting silk and worsted together. I continued here about a fortnight, and when I thought it would answer our expectation, I returned to *Norwich* to fetch my wife; she was then near her time, and too much indisposed. So we were obliged to tarry until she was brought to bed, and as soon as she could conveniently travel we came to *Kidderminster,* but we brought nothing with us, as we were obliged to sell all we had to pay our debts, and the expences of my wife's illness, &c.

Such is our situation at present. — My wife, by hard labor at the loom, does every thing that can be expected from her towards the maintenance of our family; and God is pleased to incline the hearts of his people at times to yield us their charitable assistance; being myself through age and infirmity able to contribute but little to their support. As pilgrims, and very poor pilgrims we are traveling through many difficulties towards our heavenly home, and waiting patiently for his glorious call, when the Lord shall deliver us out of the evils of this present world,[87] and bring us to the everlasting glories of the world to come. — —To HIM be praise for ever and ever. AMEN.

NOTES

1. "Written by Himself" appears only in the title of the 1774 imprint. Typically, the title of the *Narrative* ends with the phrase "as Related by Himself," although in the Catskill, New York, imprint of 1810 it reads "as Dictated by Himself."

2. A footnote indicated here in the 1809 imprint reads: "Supposed to be Miss HANNAH MORE." More (1745-1833) was a poet, playwright, and religious writer deeply concerned with humanitarian issues. She worked for the abolition of slavery and the slave trade with Sir Charles Middleton and the Thornton family's Clapham sect; her name is on the subscription list for the first edition of Equiano's *Narrative*, as are theirs.

3. The 1809 imprint does not contain the rest of this preface. The 1840 imprint reprints an abbreviated version, omitting from the second paragraph the text "Perhaps we have here, . . . not imputing their trespasses."

4. In the eighteenth century, the name "Guinea" referred to the vast stretch of West African coast from the river Senegal down to the kingdom of Angola. Gronniosaw calls the Gold Coast a "city" in Guinea (pp. 31, 32 of this volume), perhaps to correct the common notion that "Guinea" and "the Gold Coast" denoted the same area. The Gold Coast, however, is a discrete area within Guinea, named for the rich deposits of gold that Portuguese traders found there in the fifteenth century. It encompasses the coastal strip between Benyori and the Volta River, as well as the regions immediately north of that area, in what is now modern Ghana.

5. Isaiah 42:16.

6. See Matthew 6:15, part of the Lord's Prayer. The second paragraph in the 1840 preface begins with the sentence immediately following this phrase.

7. See Psalms 113:7-8.

8. "W. Shirley" is the Reverend Walter Shirley (1726-1786), first cousin and right-hand man of Selina, the Countess of Huntingdon (to whom Gronniosaw dedicates his narrative). Gronniosaw and Shirley probably met through the Connexion. In 1774, at the invitation of the Reverend Benjamin Fawcett (see note 85 below), the Countess sent her preachers and several students from Trevecca (the Countess's religious college in Wales) to open a chapel in Kidderminster, Gronniosaw's last known residence. Shirley, one of the Connexion's busiest itinerant preachers, often preached there and doubtless joined Gronniosaw in

fellowship. Once aware of Gronniosaw's desperate financial situation, Shirley, himself a published author of a successful volume of sermons, may have suggested that a book might raise revenue. If so, the first edition of the *Narrative* could have been published in 1774.

9. Borno (also known as Bornu) is now a state in the northeastern corner of Nigeria, within which lie Lake Chad and the plains of Bornu. According to Richard Lobban in *Africans in the Americas: A History of the Black Diaspora* (ed. Michael L. Conniff and Thomas J. Davis [New York: St. Martin's Press, 1994]), Borno was "organized at least twelve hundred years ago. As it began to control the trade of the central Sahel, [it] took on aspects of other empires in the region, especially Ghana, Mali, and Songhai. Bornu imposed taxes on both east-west and north-south routes, the north-south routes extending to modern Tunisia and Libya. Bornu's King Houme converted to Islam in 1086, and at its peak four hundred years later, Bornu controlled the region from the Hausa and Fulani city-states in northern Nigeria to the Sudan" (p. 27). Gronniosaw's "Baurnou" appears to be a residual spelling of the earlier placename "Baranu," for Bar-anu, place of the Baran or Barbars, who are numbered among the area's early founders.

Missing from this sentence in the imprints of 1774 and [1780?]—yet present in the 1809 and 1840 imprints—is an additional reference to Gronniosaw's birthplace: his mother is "the eldest daughter of the reigning king of Zaara, of which Bournou is the chief city."

10. Gronniosaw's note: "It is a generally received opinion, in *England*, that the natives of *Africa* go entirely unclothed; but this supposition is very unjust: They have a kind of dress so as to appear decent, though it is very slight and thin." The "Bornou" entry in *A Compendious Geographical Dictionary, Containing A Concise Description of the Most Remarkable Places, Ancient and Modern, in Europe, Asia, Africa & America, Interspersed with Historical Anecdotes* (London: Printed for W. Peacock, 1795) exemplifies the narrow attitude that Gronniosaw combats: "Bornou, a kingdom of Negroland, in Africa. The inhabitants of this kingdom go almost naked, and have their women in common" (unpaginated).

11. Logwy was probably an albino. John Matthews mentions that he saw "several white negroes in different parts of Africa of a milky, or chalky whiteness, and white wool" (*A Voyage to the River Sierra-Leone* [London, 1788; rpt. London: Frank Cass, 1966], p. 95). John Adams corroborates Matthews's observation in his *Sketches Taken during Ten Voyages to Africa, Between the Years 1786 and 1800* (n.d.; rpt. New York: Johnson Reprint, 1970): "That *lusus naturæ*, the white negro, born of black parents, is to be seen in almost every populous town" (p. 70). The color and texture of Logwy's "fine light hair," though perhaps not typical, were certainly not unheard of. In *A Voyage to Senegal, the Isle of Goree, and the River Gambia* (London, 1759), Michel Adanson observes that the curly black hair of the Senegal natives was "downy, and extremely fine" (p. 38).

12. Logwy's deep grief at her brother's departure may signal more than a typical reaction of a loving sister; Gronniosaw may well have been the only person who ever "loved her entirely," despite her appearance, because albinos were often looked down upon by their own people. Equiano recalls having seen in Africa "three

negro children, who were tawny, and another quite white, who were universally regarded as deformed by myself and the natives in general, as far as related to their complexions" (p. 172 of this volume). Similarly, Adams notes that albinos were subject to their family and friends' opinion that "they are unfortunately by this malady degraded" (*Sketches,* p. 70). Gronniosaw's closeness to his albino sister may have contributed to his unpopularity with his other siblings and his family's servants.

13. Originally, "brig" was short for "brigantine," the two-masted vessel that marauding bands of pirates, or brigands, commonly used on the seas. Eventually the brig evolved into a new kind of ship popular with merchants for coastal trading voyages.

14. Different fabrics were regular mediums of exchange throughout West Africa. In the eighteenth century, "check" (or "cheque," as it is spelled in the 1809 imprint) was a cheap material woven in a checkerboard design.

15. This scene is the earliest known example in the black English literary tradition of what Henry Louis Gates, Jr., terms the "trope" of the talking book. The topos reappears in Marrant, Cugoano, Equiano, and, in the nineteenth century, John Jea. See chapter 4 in Gates, *The Signifying Monkey: A Theory of African-American Literary Criticism* (New York: Oxford University Press, 1988).

16. Gates avers that Fort Elmina is the most "probable" place from which the Dutch ship captain sailed with Gronniosaw for Barbados and the colony of New York (*The Signifying Monkey,* p. 140). Elmina, formerly the first Portuguese stronghold in West Africa's Gold Coast, had long been a Dutch town and fortification by the eighteenth century; today it is located in Ghana.

17. Vanhorn (or Van Horne, as it is spelled in the 1809 imprint) is here following a fashion popular throughout Europe and the American colonies. In seventeenth- and eighteenth-century England, for example, it was a general practice among the nobility to outfit black boys in rich, brilliantly hued costumes, or "livery," patterned after each family's coat of arms. As domestic servants at the table, or as dazzling adornments on the owner's arm on strolls through St. James's Park, these boys symbolized the wealth and the imperial pretentions of England's most prominent social order.

18. A wainscot is the lining—usually made of tile, marble, or wood paneling—that covers the bottom three or four feet of an interior wall.

19. As Peter Fryer notes in *Staying Power: The History of Black People in Britain* (London: Pluto Press, 1984), "The very words 'black' and 'white' were heavily charged with meaning long before the English met people whose skins were black" (p. 135). To the English, blackness had long signified both the foul (death, evil, hell) and the fascinating (sin, danger, bad magic); alternatively, whiteness connoted the mundane (innocuous lies) and the immaculate (purity, innocence, beauty). Yet these very categories were handy gestalts for racist stereotyping. In the early seventeenth century, concomitant with the increased publication of European travel literature about Africa, Africans began to be associated in the European imagination with devils or the forces of Satan: For example, in John Bunyan's *The Holy War* (1682), the character Diabolus, who besieges the

allegorical city of Mansoul, is identified as a black African—"king of the blacks, or negroes." Gronniosaw writes that he was presented a copy of *The Holy War* by Mrs. Frelinghuysen, note 23 below.

20. Mr. Freelandhouse is Theodorus Jacobus Frelinghuysen (1691-1747/48?), an evangelical Dutch Reformed pastor in New Jersey's Raritan Valley from 1720 to the late 1740s. Frank Lambert agrees with this identification of Freelandhouse; see his article "'I Saw the Book Talk': Slave Readings of the First Great Awakening," *Journal of Negro History* 77, no. 4 (Fall 1992): 187. Frelinghuysen, along with Presbyterian Gilbert Tennent and Methodist George Whitefield, is credited with sparking the Great Awakening in colonial America. Tennent, newly ordained in the fall of 1726, often turned to Frelinghuysen for advice and fellowship; the two occasionally shared church services. Tennent, in turn, greatly influenced George Whitefield; it was through Tennent that Whitefield met Frelinghuysen. On Tuesday, 20 November 1739, Whitefield recorded in his *Journal* upon first meeting the Dutch pastor that he found him "a worthy old soldier of Jesus Christ."

21. It is unclear why Gronniosaw, who after his stint in the Vanhorn household would have been well acquainted with the Dutch language, should attempt to speak in English with the primarily Dutch-speaking Frelinghuysen.

22. See Isaiah 40:31.

23. Mrs. Freelandhouse was Eva Terhune Frelinghuysen (1708-ca. 1749/50?), the youngest of seventeen children born to Albert Terhune, a wealthy and respected farmer in Flatbush, Long Island. By 1720, both parents had died, leaving the Terhune children in the care of Bernard Freeman, Dutch Reformed minister and good friend of Frelinghuysen. The two men promptly married the two youngest Terhune daughters; twelve-year-old Eva became Mrs. Frelinghuysen, while fourteen-year-old Annetje was wed to Freeman.

24. Gronniosaw must be referring to Peter Van Arsdalen, one of the two "helpers" in Frelinghuysen's North Branch church. Abraham Messler records that Frelinghuysen, in typically unorthodox fashion, "appointed from among the most gifted and experienced of his male members certain individuals whom he called 'helpers,' whose office was to expound the Scriptures in the meetings for prayer and conduct them with order, visit and converse with the anxious and inquiring, and to catechise the youth" (*Forty Years at Raritan: Eight Memorial Sermons, with Notes for a History of the Reformed Dutch Churches in Somerset County, N.J.* [New York: A. Lloyd, 1873], p. 27). Van Arsdalen would have been the proper teacher for Gronniosaw, whose spiritual development in the Protestant religion would have required special nurturing. Thus when the young African finds himself "inquiring the way to Zion" he seeks out Van Arsdalen, who, exempt from the exorbitant pressures and responsibilities of a Dutch Reformed pastor in the American colonies, had sufficient time to befriend and counsel him. Frelinghuysen himself would have been tremendously busy as the pastor to several congregations in an area encompassing approximately 250 square miles. Those churches were Three Mile Run (in the New Brunswick area), Six Mile Run (now in Franklin Park), North Branch (now called Readington in Readington),

Raritan (now First Raritan in Somerville), and Millstone (now Harlingen in Belle Mead).

25. See Micah 4:3. The members of the Dutch Reformed congregation were well used to Frelinghuysen's expositions on fallen humanity. According to Messler, the pastor's public discourses "laid open the depravity and selfishness of the human heart, showed its entire alienation from God, and insisted upon the absolute necessity that it should be regenerated" (*Forty Years,* p. 30).

26. Gronniosaw may mean that he stuck the pitchfork into a pile or bundle of cut hay, from which the maid plucked and then absconded with the tool.

27. For Bunyan's *Holy War,* see note 19. It is unclear whose "experience" Gronniosaw identifies with here: he may be comparing his "own corrupt nature" with that of Diabolus, the devil figure in *The Holy War;* alternatively, he may be referring to the life of Bunyan himself, as represented in Bunyan's spiritual autobiography *Grace Abounding to the Chief of Sinners* (1666), or some condensation of that work. On the other hand, his allusions to "a bad man" and "a wicked man as bad as myself" may be to Bunyan's *The Life and Death of Mr. Badman, Presented to the World in a Familiar Dialogue between Mr. Wiseman and Mr. Attentive* (1680). All three of these texts were available in Dutch translations at this time. Gronniosaw, unfortunately, does not supply sufficient context to clarify his conversation with Mrs. Frelinghuysen.

28. Here Gronniosaw refers to Richard Baxter's *A Call to the Unconverted* (1658). According to Isabel Rivers, it was "the most popular conversion treatise of the 17th century." See her "Dissenting and Methodist Books of Practical Divinity" in *Books and Their Readers in Eighteenth-Century England* (New York: St. Martin's Press, 1982), p. 139. Richard Baxter (1615-1691) was an eminent Presbyterian minister and prodigious theological author who preached in Kidderminster from 1641 to 1660.

29. John 1:29.

30. The 1840 imprint, which generally tones down Gronniosaw's evangelicalism, omits this sentence: "I now began to relish the book my master gave me, Baxter's *call to the unconverted,* and took great delight in it." See notes 44 and 87 below.

31. I Thessalonians 5:17.

32. See I Timothy 6:9-10 and Matthew 19:21-24.

33. Jeremiah 32:40.

34. Gronniosaw's account is the sole extant record of the circumstances surrounding Frelinghuysen's death. According to James Tanis, the pastor suffered throughout his life from "intermittent poor health, due to a series of mild psychoses," which Frelinghuysen himself likened to Paul's "thorn in the flesh" (*Dutch Calvinistic Pietism in the Middle Colonies: A Study in the Life and Theology of Theodorus Jacobus Frelinghuysen* [The Hague: Martinus Nijhoff, 1967], p. 63). It is possible that the illness and fever Gronniosaw mentions stemmed from this proclivity. In the eighteenth century, however, "fever" was a general term that connoted a wide range of illnesses from dysentery to pneumonia to a variety of viral diseases.

The exact date of Frelinghuysen's death also continues to be a mystery. Messler first postulates that "it must have been previous to April 26th, 1748, since the

Elder Hendrick Fisher reported to the Coetus in New-York at that date the vacancy of the church at New-Brunswick" (*Forty Years,* p. 174). Yet thirty-six pages later, he avers that the pastor "must have died previous to September 27th, 1748" because upon that date Fisher requested John Leydt to become the new minister of New Brunswick and Six Mile Run (p. 211). Tanis agrees with Messler's first estimation, fixing the date of Frelinghuysen's death during the autumn of 1747 or the winter of 1747/48 (pp. 89-90).

35. The phrase "my dear and worthy master" is in neither the 1809 nor the 1840 imprint; the latter also excludes the clause "I held his hand in mine when he departed." Sentences and words have also been recast, sometimes subtly, to smooth over prose too coarsely colloquial for an increasingly refined middle-class taste. For example, the sentence "He had but a short illness, and died of a fever" becomes "He died of a fever, after a very short illness."

36. See I Corinthians 9:27.

37. Colossians 2:10. Gronniosaw's text is only slightly different than the King James Version.

38. This quotation is from Hebrews 7:25.

39. This quotation is from Hebrews 10:14. The 1809 and 1840 imprints omit the scriptural reference preceding this verse.

40. The date and circumstances of Eva Frelinghuysen's death are lost to history except for this information in Gronniosaw's *Narrative.* If Eva's husband died in 1747/48 (see note 34 above), by Gronniosaw's reckoning Eva would have died circa 1749/50. Missing as well are records about Frelinghuysen family life and the childhood years of the seven Frelinghuysen offspring—Theodore, John, Jacobus, Ferdinandus, Henricus, Anna, and Margarette. Six of them were dead, or missing and presumed dead, by 1759. Jacobus and Ferdinandus died together of smallpox in 1753 on their return voyage to America after their respective ordinations in Holland. John, minister of Harlingen, Neshanic, Readington, and Raritan churches in New Jersey, suffered a sudden death in 1754. Henricus was a student preacher for three years, then died of smallpox two weeks after his ordination in 1757; the end of that year saw Margarette's death as well. Theodore, the pastor at Albany for fifteen years, sailed from New York for Holland on 10 October 1759 to raise money for an American Dutch Reformed academy and was never heard from again (see Messler, *Forty Years,* pp. 181-84). It is unclear why Gronniosaw states that Frelinghuysen's five sons died "four years after their parents" when the brothers are documented as having died over a six-year period. *Four* sons, however, die within four years of *each other,* but not within four years of Eva. Only three of her children are dead approximately four years after her. Gronniosaw may simply have miscalculated his timeline.

41. In the 1840 imprint, "mouth" replaces "lips," the word used in the King James Version. Furthermore, the scriptural references succeeding this sentence are deleted in this imprint, as well as in that of 1809.
        Readers familiar with the Bible may be puzzled with Gronniosaw's reference to "Heb. xvi. 17, 18"—that is, Hebrews 16:17, 18—because the book of Hebrews

has only thirteen chapters. Gronniosaw may have quoted the number incorrectly, and/or the printer may have inadvertently made an error in transcription. The scripture that Gronniosaw alludes to is probably Hebrews 6:17, 18, which neatly fits into his theme of God's "comfortable promises": "Wherein God, willing more abundantly to shew unto the heirs of promise the immutability of his counsel, confirmed it by an oath: / That by two immutable things [God's promise and his oath], in which it was impossible for God to lie, we might have a strong consolation, who have fled for refuge to lay hold upon the hope set before us."

42. Not every Frelinghuysen was dead, or believed dead, by 1759. Anna Frelinghuysen had married Reverend William Jackson and was living in Bergen, New Jersey. John's widow, Dinah Van Bergh Frelinghuysen, had remarried and continued to live in the same house because her second husband, Jacob Rutzen Hardenbergh, had taken over her first husband's ministries at North Branch, Neshanic, Millstone, and Raritan. Presumably circumstances precluded Gronniosaw from living with either family.

43. On Whitefield, see the introduction to this volume.

44. The last sentence in this paragraph is not in the 1840 imprint.

45. In the [1780?], 1809, and 1840 imprints the text is slightly different. The young "gentleman" who pretends to be Gronniosaw's friend is described in these imprints as "a particular acquaintance of one of my young master's [or masters]." Although the difference is subtle, the resulting change in meaning is not. Here Gronniosaw seems to be referring to a current master, even though he received his freedom; in the other three imprints, he appears to be referring to a man who used to be a good friend of one of the five Frelinghuysen brothers.

46. Not protected by any legislation, free blacks could be and often were re-enslaved. Olaudah Equiano is particularly eloquent about the dangers attendant upon "free" black life (see pp. 229-234 of this volume).

47. Privateering was a lucrative business in times of war. Individuals could license their privately owned ships with a government, which in turn granted those ships the right to attack and seize enemy trade vessels in the name of that government. The government and the captors would then share the value of the booty, or "prizes." In agreements with the British Crown, the captors snared a hefty 90 percent; the Crown, the remaining 10 percent. The word "privateer" refers to both the licensed ship and it crew members. See also note 98 in the Equiano section of this volume.

England was at war with France and her allies at this time; the conflict would later be known as the Seven Years' War (1756-1763). War was formally declared between England and France in the late spring of 1756 and between England and Spain in January 1762, although hostilities between England and her enemies had erupted before official measures were taken. Gronniosaw probably was a privateer at some point between 1759 and 1761.

48. St. Domingo is the island of Hispaniola in the West Indies, currently occupied in the west by the Republic of Haiti and in the center and east by the Dominican Republic. In Gronniosaw's time, a French and a Spanish colony inhabited the island; the French was named Saint Domingue; the Spanish, Santo Domingo.

St. Domingo was also a Spanish town on the southeastern shore. The French colony, also known as "the Pearl of the Antilles," housed one of two French naval bases in the Caribbean. The other was in Martinique (see notes 55 and 56 below).

49. The 1809 imprint reads "39 ships."

50. The text in the 1840 imprint reads as follows: "I was reading a book that I was very fond of, and which I frequently amused myself with, when this person snatched it out of my hand, and threw it into the sea."

51. Incidents in which persecutors of innocent Christians meet their death through God's intervention are a commonplace in conversion narratives. See also Gronniosaw, p. 42, and Marrant, pp. 91-92.

52. The syntax is recast in the 1840 imprint: "I heartily wished that I could have spoken in some language which the crew did not understand, so that I might have let him know his danger."

53. See note 98 in the Equiano section of this volume.

54. The sugar trade was a booming industry in the West Indies during the eighteenth century and beyond; British, French, and Dutch land owners were eager to profit from the Atlantic world's newfound pleasure in sweetened tea and, later, coffee. More than 75 percent of all Africans enslaved in the Americas were purchased to support the sugar and tobacco trades among the Caribbean islands and coastal Brazil.

55. The British attacked the French island of Martinique in early 1762, eager to seize one of the enemy's richest trade colonies. British troops landed at St. Anne's Bay on 10 January; by 5 February the French had surrendered the garrison and the citadel of Fort Royal. With the fall of Martinique came the fall of French power in the Caribbean for the war's duration. As a member of the 28th foot regiment, Gronniosaw was one of 7,000 men in twelve military units traveling from North America with Commander in Chief Major-General the Hon. Robert Monckton to join the other 6,965 men who comprised the British land forces at the siege of Martinique. Monckton's fleet traveled via Barbados, where it resupplied in December 1761.

56. Admiral Sir George Pocock (1706-1792) was a distinguished and experienced naval commander in the British fleet at this time, but he was not involved in the siege of Martinique; Rear-Admiral G. B. Rodney commanded the 11,000-man fleet there, with the assistance of Commodore Sir James Douglas. Pocock did command the fleet at Havana, leaving England on 5 March 1762; the fleet stopped at Martinique on 26 April. Gronniosaw would not have seen Admiral Pocock's fleet before his arrival in Martinique. On 6 May Gronniosaw must have been part of the unit that accompanied the fleet to Cuba.

57. At this time the port and fortress of Havana—often called "the Havannah" in eighteenth- and nineteenth-century documents—was Spain's richest and strongest possession in the Americas. It was responsible for protecting the linchpin of the Spanish economy: the plunder-laden ships that annually sailed from the Americas to Spain. The British stormed Fort Moro on 30 July 1762. Gronniosaw, a member of the ten-company 28th regiment captained by Townshend, saw battle as part of Brigadier-General Walsh's second brigade. By

12 August, the Spanish had capitulated and agreed to surrender formally at noon three days later. With this victory the British seized over one hundred merchant ships and hobbled Spain's finances.

Commodore Augustus Keppel was second in command of the naval forces at Havana. Previous to this expedition, he had fought with Olaudah Equiano at Belle Isle (see pp. 202, 204-5 of this volume).

58. Gronniosaw's trajectory from Havana to Old Spain to England with different groups of war prisoners accords with formal military procedure. The nineteenth article in the Articles of Capitulation signed at Havana in August 1762 states that "all prisoners made on both sides, since the 6th of June, when the English squadron appeared before the harbour, shall be returned reciprocally, and without any ransom, within the term of two months, . . . or before, if they can." See Robert Beatson, *Naval and Military Memoirs of Great Britain 1727 to 1783*, 6 vols. (London: Printed for Longman, Hurst, Rees and Orme et al.; Edinburgh: A. Constable and Co.; Aberdeen: A. Brown, 1804), vol. 3, pp. 401-2.

59. Portsmouth was a major naval base and port of call in eighteenth-century Britain. Olaudah Equiano as well as Gronniosaw passed through the town as members of His Majesty's Navy, mingling easily with the other sailors, both black and white, who frequented the area. This high concentration of soldiers attracted hordes of prostitutes and press gangs, whose oftentimes nefarious business dealings lent Portsmouth a reputation for violent crime. The African-American Methodist preacher John Jea (b. 1773) settled here to proselytize among these "fleshpots of Egypt" and in so doing followed in the footsteps of George Whitefield and John Wesley, who had preached in Portsmouth throughout the latter half of the eighteenth century. See also note 62 below.

60. For information on the guinea, see note 101 in the Equiano section of this volume.

61. Gronniosaw mentions earlier that this woman runs a public house, or tavern; thus she is called a publican.

62. The 1840 imprint considerably softens Gronniosaw's brief but evocative portrait of the publican's sister-in-law, who, well used to the gritty realities confronting Portsmouth's itinerant population (see note 59 above), appears ready to hire local toughs to reclaim Gronniosaw's money. By 1840, she merely "would have employed other means" to persuade the publican.

63. Whitefield's "New Tabernacle," capable of containing roughly 4,000 people, was built in 1753 in the Moorfields district of London. It was demolished in 1869.

64. Dr. Andrew Gifford (1700-1784) was the Baptist minister of the Eagle Street meeting in London from 1730 until his death fifty-four years later.

65. Gronniosaw must be referring to John Allen (fl. 1764), a rather colorful Calvinist preacher and tract writer who was then minister of the Baptist church on Petticoat Lane, the street in London where Gronniosaw was boarding. Little information exists about him. Allen eventually became the defendant in a protracted forgery suit, and his congregation dismissed him for indecorous behavior some time after 1764.

66. By "examining" him, the Dutch ministers sought to determine the breadth and depth of Gronniosaw's grasp of Protestant theology. The Dutch ministry's interest

in Gronniosaw was by no means exceptional. Earlier in the eighteenth century at least two Africans—Jacobus Elisa Joannes Capitein (1717-1747) and Anton Wilhelm Amo (ca. 1700-after 1743)—had distinguished themselves in Dutch theology. Born in what is now Ghana, Capitein had studied in Holland from 1726 to 1742, the year he graduated from Leyden University and was ordained by the Classis of Amsterdam. His Latin dissertation defended slavery on Biblical grounds, a position that may have influenced his appointment as teacher and pastor to the Dutch-held West African town of Elmina. Disillusioned by the lack of Christian fellowship he found there, Capitein turned to trade and died bankrupt on 1 February 1747. Amo, also a native of Ghana, was born to African parents who had converted to the Dutch Reformed Church. A Dutch preacher sent Amo to Holland with the understanding that he would return to Africa as a pastor and teacher. Studying first in Wolfenbütell—where he was baptized—and then at the University of Halle, Amo graduated in 1729 with a dissertation that, unlike Capitein's, denounced the European enslavement of Africans. Fluent in six languages, he went on to earn his Master of Philosophy degree and to teach at the University of Jena before he returned to the Gold Coast sometime after 1743, where he eventually died.

67. Gronniosaw's text is only slightly different than the King James Version of Psalms 66:16. The 1840 imprint omits this section of the *Narrative* from "and took great pleasure" to "*hath done for my soul.*"

68. See Exodus 2:22 and 18:3.

69. Job 19:25.

70. This portion of the text changes throughout the imprints. In the 1840 imprint, for example, the phrase "which proposal I was very well pleased with: So" is missing. Furthermore, the number of ministers and the day they meet with Gronniosaw tends to change as well. Forty-eight ministers gather on Thursday in our volume, a number that shrinks to thirty-eight in the [1780?] and 1809 imprints. By 1840, however, those thirty-eight ministers are meeting every Tuesday.

71. This sentence concerning Dr. Gifford's character is not included in the 1840 imprint.

72. After the cessation of the Seven Years' War in 1763, demobilization coupled with a slump in foreign trade resulted in widespread unemployment. The Spitalfields (London) weavers were struck especially hard by the reopening of English markets to French silks; rioting among the weavers was common. Gronniosaw is probably alluding here to the riots that culminated in the May 1765 siege of the Duke of Bedford's Bloomsbury Square house. The Spitalfields weavers were also actively involved in the famous Wilkes and Liberty riots in 1768. The weavers of Norwich, where Gronniosaw would later move, rioted to protest their persistently low earning power, which did not increase during the eighteenth century. Especially serious were the Norwich riots of 1720, 1740, 1757, and 1766; on each occasion the local militia had to be called in to calm the crowds.

73. "Brought to bed" was a common eighteenth-century expression for giving birth. In the 1809 imprint the phrase has been replaced with the euphemistic "She had just got to bed and wanted many necessaries."

74. See I Peter 1:3.

75. The word "writing" replaces "English" in the 1809 imprint, a change that drastically alters the meaning of this passage.
76. See, for example, Psalm 18, especially verse 28. The 1840 imprint omits this sentence.
77. Missing from the 1840 imprint is the text from "he was a sincere" to "if I had wanted work."
78. The 1840 imprint deletes two portions of this paragraph: the sentence "I hope I shall always gratefully acknowledge his kindness to myself and family" and the text from "and was never so happy" to "troublesome to our friends."
79. The text from "would not excuse us" to "and had the cruelty to" is not in the 1840 imprint.
80. The clause "If they had been in health I should have been less sensible of this misfortune" and the phrase "a gracious gentleman" are missing from the 1840 imprint.
81. The 1840 imprint deletes the text from "sometimes she could get nothing" to "and willing to work."
82. "Chaff" refers to any grains or grasses cut in the process of threshing, or to any weeds cut to clear or beautify an area. Straw and hay "chaff" were often cut very finely for cattle food.
83. The poignant statement "this was one of the greatest trials I ever met with, as we did not know what to do with our poor baby" was omitted from the 1840 imprint.
84. When Equiano is in Savannah, Georgia, he performs a funeral service for a black child whose mother cannot procure aid from the local white ministry. He echoes Gronniosaw when he assures the mother that "the service over the dead did not affect the soul" (see the end of ch. 8 of his *Narrative*, not reprinted in this volume).
85. Benjamin Fawcett (1715-1780) was a popular dissenting minister who lived and preached in Kidderminster from 1745 until his death. There he published abridgements of many of Richard Baxter's works, among them *Saints' Everlasting Rest*, which was reissued over fifty times by the late nineteenth century. Gronniosaw or his wife Betty may also have been familiar with Fawcett's work *The Religious Weaver: or, Pious Meditations on the Trade of Weaving* (Shrewsbury: J. Eddowes, 1773). See also note 8 above for his connection to the Countess of Huntingdon and Walter Shirley.
86. The 1840 imprint deletes the text from "I had always an inclination" to the end of this paragraph.
87. See Galatians 1:4. Missing from the 1840 imprint are such religious allusions as "and very poor pilgrims" and "towards our heavenly home."

JOHN
MARRANT

ABOUT
JOHN MARRANT

LIFE

On 15 June 1755, John Marrant was born into a free black family in the colony of New York. His was to be a traveling life. He moved three times by his eleventh birthday, living and going to school in Florida and Georgia before heading to Charleston, South Carolina—then the fourth largest city in the American colonies—to live with his older sister and brother-in-law and to look for work. Between the ages of eleven and thirteen he served a music master, who taught him to play the French horn and the violin. During the following year and a half Marrant worked alongside a carpenter by day and played music for the white gentry by night; his career as a musician ended suddenly, however, once he encountered George Whitefield in late 1769 or early 1770 and experienced his Christian rebirth.

For the next two years, Marrant zealously proselytized among the Cherokee, Creek, Choctaw, and Chickasaw tribes, converting a Cherokee chief and his daughter, among others, before returning to his family in about mid-1772. Over the next three years Marrant engaged in Christian fellowship in the Charleston area and witnessed the conversion and death of his seven-and-a-half-year-old neighbor, Mary Scott. He also witnessed a plantation owner and several henchmen brutally whip thirty slaves—both children and adults—for attending the church school that Marrant established among them. Although Marrant as a freeman escaped the bloody fate of the slaves, he did not, shortly thereafter, escape the clutches of the Revolutionary War. He was impressed by the British upon the 14-gun *Scorpion* war sloop during the time that it was stationed in the Carolina waters, 12 November 1775 to 2 October 1776.

Here we lose track of Marrant for the next few years. Presuming that he remained aboard the *Scorpion* when it sailed on 2 October, he would have arrived off the coast of New York seventeen days later. The *Scorpion*, no longer fit for service at sea, apparently remained in New York coastal waters during November and December (perhaps for repairs), while its captain, John Tollemache, left the ship to attend to urgent business in England. Under the command of Lieutenant Samuel Reeve, the *Scorpion* then protected the transport ships stationed in Long Island Sound from January to August of 1777. We then lose sight of the *Scorpion* until late summer 1779, when records show it on the Hudson River in bad disrepair. The Royal Navy sold the sloop in 1780. In that year Marrant took part in the British siege of Charleston (11 February to 12 May). We next see him on 5 August 1781 aboard the warship *Princess Amelia* (84 guns), part of the British fleet fighting a Dutch convoy in the North Sea off Dogger Bank during the Dutch-Anglo war of 1780-1784. The Royal Navy discharged him in 1782, his health too broken to serve.

Between 1782 and 1785 Marrant lived in London with cotton merchant John Marsden, attempting to recover prize money due him from the war. He also spent much time listening to preachers such as the Anglican Reverend William Romaine and the popular Huntingdonian Reverend Thomas Wills. Through his friendship with Wills, Marrant was ordained a minister in the Countess of Huntingdon's Chapel in Bath on 15 May 1785. It was around the time of his ordination that he told the story that William Aldridge, Methodist minister and friend of the Countess, wrote down and published as Marrant's *Narrative*. That same year in Bath, S. Whitchurch published a poem based on incidents from Marrant's life. This work, entitled *The Negro Convert, a Poem; Being the Substance of the Experience of Mr. John Marrant, A Negro, As related by himself, previous to his Ordination, at the Countess of Huntingdon's Chapel in Bath, On Sunday the 15th of May, 1785. Together with a concise Account of the most remarkable Events in his very singular Life,* was "Printed and sold by S. Hazard," undoubtedly the same Samuel Hazard who had published Ukawsaw Gronniosaw's *Narrative* in Bath over a decade earlier.

After preaching in Bristol and in Bath, Marrant sailed for Nova Scotia aboard the *Peggy* on 18 August to preach for the black Loyalists who had fled there at the end of the Revolutionary War. Marrant explains in the *Narrative* that he went at the request of his "brother"—referring either to his brother-in-law with whom he had lived in Charleston or to another family member not previously mentioned or specifically identified. He was accompanied on his voyage to Nova Scotia by a fellow black Huntingdonian, William Furmage.

Landing on 20 November 1785, Marrant soon settled in Birchtown, three miles outside Shelburne, reacquainting himself with old friends and family. Over the next two years he encountered violence and religious factionalism as he preached Calvinistic Methodism to whites, blacks, and native tribes throughout southern Nova Scotia. On 19 December he discovered that prominent Wesleyan layman Philip Marchinton had sent a letter from Halifax to the blacks of Shelburne and Birchtown, warning them of the dire errors of Marrant's teachings. In the spring of 1786 Birchtown's black Wesleyan pastor Moses Wilkinson broke a promise to Marrant and sold government supplies intended for the Huntingdonian parishioners; in July he tried to bar Marrant from the Birchtown meetinghouse in order to admit fellow Wesleyan Freeborn Garrettson, the distinguished American Methodist, who informed the residents that Marrant was a "devil." Despite this opposition, Marrant built a chapel in Birchtown, ordained two black men, Cato Perkins and William Ash, as preachers, taught over one hundred children in the Birchtown school, preached four times a week, and answered other towns' demands for spiritual ministering. Exhausted with this schedule, Marrant relinquished charge of the school by late November of 1786 and focused on his route of itinerant preaching.

By February of 1787 he had succumbed to the smallpox epidemic raging in Shelburne; his illness lingered for over six months, aggravated by incessant preaching under raw conditions. His labors abated only when, wracked by a violent cough, he began to choke on his own blood. Still, the Wesleyan Society class leaders continued to harass Marrant, twice bringing him up on charges in the Shelburne court. Concerning the first case, Marrant merely states in his *Journal* that he was 120 miles away from the scene of the purported crime (whatever it may have been), a statement that his witnesses supported in court. His account of the second case is still more obscure. It seems that he married a woman whom someone later claimed was already married; Marrant denied this claim and once again apparently won the case. It seems likely that Marrant's wife is Mellia Marrant, who is listed in the 1783 New York City Inspection Roll of Negroes as "formerly the property of John Marrant near Santee Carolina" where she "left him at the Siege of Charlestown." The same record of Mellia finds her aboard the *William and Mary,* accompanied by her children Amelia and Ben, headed for Annapolis Royal, Nova Scotia. In Marrant's account of his travels through Nova Scotia, he often mentions one or two boys who accompany him: one of these boys may be his (step)son, Ben.

Throughout his stay in Nova Scotia, Marrant, desperately poor and physically frail, continually wrote to the Countess of Huntingdon for financial assistance. He finally heard that money was available for him in Halifax; yet when he arrived on 17 January 1788, his contact could not be located. Thus ten days later he sailed for Boston, too destitute to remain unassisted in an area sinking into economic depression. Five days later Baptist Reverend Samuel Stillman (one of Boston's twelve delegates to the convention for the ratification of the federal Constitution) introduced Marrant to two black men: Samuel Bean and Prince Hall. Hall, the dynamic leader who championed equal rights and education for Boston's black community, had recently founded the first black Freemason Lodge in the United States. For the next two years Marrant lived alternately with Bean and with Hall. He preached his first sermon to a group of Stillman's friends and associates in a Boston society room; his next sermon was delivered to a packed room on 3 February in "the west end of town"—perhaps an allusion to the African Lodge. Thereafter, in addition to preaching weekly Friday afternoon and Sunday evening sermons to both whites and blacks, he apparently procured a job as a schoolteacher.

On 27 February 1789 a crowd of forty armed men attempted to kill Marrant because their girlfriends, instead of waiting at home for them, had attended his Friday sermon. With the help of a man we presume is Reverend Stillman, he escaped from this savage mob. In March he was initiated into the African lodge; Samuel Bean also became a Freemason that year, perhaps in the same ceremony. At 11:00 A.M. on 24 June the African Lodge members, adorned with their Masonic insignia, proceeded to Boston's South School, where Marrant delivered a sermon celebrating the Festival of St. John the Baptist. They then shared a meal. At the brethrens' request, the sermon was printed. Marrant remained in and around Boston until setting sail for England on 5 February 1790, still poor and baffled by the Countess of Huntingdon's continual lack of response to his letters.

Marrant reached England sometime after 7 March, the last day recorded in his *Journal*. He published his *Journal* in late June or early July; the preface is dated 29 June 1790. His only other published work is a funeral sermon for one John Lock, given while in Nova Scotia and published along with his *Journal* in 1790. Marrant died in April 1791 and is buried in Islington in the Church Street burial grounds.

BIBLIOGRAPHICAL NOTES

The *Narrative*

John Marrant's *Narrative* is one of the earliest narratives in black English literary history. Like its predecessor, *Narrative of the Uncommon Sufferings and Surprizing Deliverance of Briton Hammon, A Negro Man* (Boston, 1760), Marrant's work is usually classified as an Indian captivity narrative; indeed, it was one of the three most popular works of that genre during the eighteenth and nineteenth centuries. Accordingly, the text was frequently amended and republished to meet market demand. The publication history of the *Narrative* is, as a result, somewhat tangled. Volumes listed as "editions" may in fact represent multiple copies of one issue or conflations of variant texts. The text of Marrant's *Narrative* varies from one publication to another; portions of the story and various notes are sometimes reassembled in a seemingly haphazard manner. The following list of imprints and the sources in which they are found illustrates the general scope of the *Narrative*'s printing history and provides a reference for those interested in pursuing the matter. The titles are arranged chronologically by year of publication. Imprints that claim to be a particular edition are grouped together; English language imprints, listed alphabetically by place of publication, are followed by foreign language imprints. When several sources appear to cite the same imprint or "edition," the most authoritative sources are listed first. Parenthetical information is taken from title pages and from sources. Asterisks mark those texts we have seen.

London: Gilbert and Plummer, 1785 . . . . *AY, J*
London, 1785 (2nd ed.) . . . . *BM*
*London: Gilbert and Plummer, 1785 (2nd ed.) . . . . . . *NUC, P, J*
London, 1785 (3rd ed., w/notes) . . . . *BM*
London: Gilbert and Plummer, 1785 (3rd ed., w/notes) . . . . *P, J*
London, 1785 (4th ed., w/additions) . . . . *BM*
London: Gilbert and Plummer, 1785 (4th ed., w/additions) . . . *P, J*
*London: R. Hawes, [1785] (4th ed.,
   printed for the author) . . . . *NUC, P*
[London? 1785?] (5th ed., w/additions) . . . . *NUC, P*
London: Gilbert and Plummer, 1785 (5th ed.,
   w/additions) . . . . *OCLC*
n.p., 1787 . . . . *AY, NUC*
[London], 1787 . . . . *P*
London, 1787 . . . . *J*
London, 1788 (6th ed., w/additions) . . . . *BM*
London: Gilbert and Plummer, 1788 (6th ed.,
   w/additions) . . . . *AY, NUC, P, J*
Dublin: B. Dugdale, 1790 (6th ed., w/additions) . . . . . . *NUC, P*
Dublin: B. Dugdale, 1790 (7th ed., w/additions) . . . . *OCLC*
London: T. Plummer, 1802 (7th ed., w/additions) . . . . *NUC, P, J*
Halifax: J. Nicholson, 1808 . . . . *NUC*

Halifax: J. Nicholson, 1808 (w/*The Female Pilgrim,*
  or, The Travels of Hephizabah [1807]) . . . . *OCLC*
Leeds: Davies & Co., 1810 . . . . *NUC, P, J*
Leeds: Preston and Co., 1810 . . . . *P*
Halifax: J. Nicholson, 1812 . . . . *BM, AY, P*
York: R. and J. Richardson, 1812 . . . . *NUC*
Brighton: T. Sharp, 1813 . . . . *NUC, J*
Brighton: T. Sharp and J. Forbes, 1813 . . . . *P*
Halifax, 1813 . . . . *BM*
Halifax: J. Nicholson, 1813 . . . . *NUC, P, J*
Newry: A. Wilkinson, 1813 . . . . *NUC*
Halifax: J. Nicholson and Co., 1815 . . . . *NUC, P*
*Leeds: Davies and Co., 1815 . . . . *NUC, P*
Carmarthen: Z. B. Morris, 1817 . . . . *NUC*
Caerdydd: Richard Lloyd, 1818 (Welsh trans.) . . . . . *AY, NUC, J*
Yarmouth: J. Barnes, 1824 . . . . *P*
Halifax: J. Nicholson, 1825 . . . . *AY, NUC*
*Brighton: W. Brunton, 1829 . . . . *NUC, P*
Brighton: T. Sharp, 1829 . . . . *J*
Manchester: John Gadsby; London: E. Fowler, 1835 . . *AY, NUC, P*
Manchester: J. Gadsby, 1835 . . . . *NUC*
Manchester: J. Gadsby; London: R. Groombridge, 1837 . . *OCLC*
London: R. Groombridge, 1838 . . . . *NUC*
London: R. Groombridge; Manchester: J. Gadsby, 1838 . . . *NUC*
London, 1850 . . . . *NUC*
London: C. J. Farncombe & Sons, [19—?] . . . . *J*
*London: C. J. Farncombe & Sons, [n.d.] . . . . *NUC*
*Boston: Beacon Press, 1971 (rpt. of London, 1802) . . . . *PE*
*Nendeln, [Liechtenstein]: Kraus, 1972
  (rpt. of London: Gilbert and Plummer, 1785; 2nd ed.) . . . . *CA*
*Knoxville: University of Tennessee Press, 1973
  (rpt. of London, 1788) . . . . *V*
*New York: Garland, 1978 (rpt. of London:
  Gilbert and Plummer, 1785) . . . . *G*

We have chosen the undated "fourth edition" for our diplomatic reprint
because it is, of all the texts we have seen, the most complete; we also
believe it to be unique. The title page of this imprint states that it is
"Enlarged by Mr. MARRANT, and Printed (with Permission) for his Sole
Benefit, WITH NOTES EXPLANATORY"; one R. Hawes of No. 40, Dorset Street,
Spitalfields, prints the story "FOR THE AUTHOR." By contrast, the title pages
of the first six "editions" printed by London's Gilbert and Plummer indicate that William Aldridge, Marrant's amanuensis/editor, had direct con-

trol over Marrant's story because he "ARRANGED, CORRECTED, and PUBLISHED" it to be sold to his parishioners at the Jewry Street Chapel where he was pastor. He did not, however, sell the undated "fourth edition"—a clear indication that he did not take responsibility for its contents. Before Marrant left England for Nova Scotia, he may have asked Aldridge for permission to have a personal edition printed, in which he could freely describe experiences and feelings that Aldridge, sensitive to the sensibilities of the reading public, would not include in his publications. The contents of the undated "fourth edition" bear out this hypothesis, for here Marrant—in a voice apparently untouched by Aldridge's editing—incorporates new information about domestic violence within his family and about Native American resentment over the encroachment of white settlers. Marrant's most striking addition to his story is the portrayal of an insidious plantation mistress and the brutal whipping that is inflicted, on her command, upon the members of a church school that Marrant established—a tale that anticipates the bloody episodes of Frederick Douglass's *Narrative* (1845). Not having seen this material in any other imprint of the *Narrative*, we believe that Marrant's personal edition is singular.

Our diplomatic reprint includes textual notes on the most important substantive variations among seven major imprints: London: Gilbert and Plummer, 1785 (reprinted [rptd.] in *G*); London: Gilbert and Plummer, 1785 (2nd. ed.; original and rptd. in *CA*); London, 1788 (6th ed., w/additions; rptd. in *V*); London: T. Plummer, 1802 (7th ed., w/additions; rptd. in *PE*); Leeds: Davies and Co., 1815; Brighton: W. Brunton, 1829; London: C. J. Farncombe & Sons, [n.d.].

The *Sermon*

In 1789 Thomas and John Fleet printed and sold *A Sermon Preached on the 24th Day of June 1789* at the Bible and Heart on Cornhill Road (now Congress Street) in Boston. Since the Fleets also published the *Charge* that Prince Hall delivered in 1792 in Charlestown, Massachusetts, it is possible that Hall may have been an associate of Thomas Fleet, a longtime white Freemason of high standing; alternatively, the black men who, according to record, worked in the Fleets's shop may have been members of the African Lodge.

The sermon has been published only once since 1789; it was reprinted for private circulation in New York about 1920 by Arthur A. Schomburg, Past Grand Secretary of the Most Worshipful Prince Hall Grand Lodge of New York and associate editor of *Masonic Quarterly Review*. In Schomburg's brief introduction to the *Sermon*, he bids his Masonic brethren "to read with a real sense of joy this curious epistle delivered more than 136 years ago by one of our blood and race."[1]

Marrant undeniably delivered the sermon, but his authorship is questionable. Reverend Jeremy Belknap's inscription on the inside front cover of a printed copy belonging to his friend, St. George Tucker, a judge and a Freemason in Virginia, attributes the *Sermon* to Prince Hall: "Prince Hall claims the whole of this [co]mposition as his own except the [b]eginning + the end." Furthermore, in a letter of 19 September 1789 to his friend Ebenezer Hazard, Belknap admits that although he did not hear the sermon, "those who did say it is much improved since the delivery. This I can easily believe from what I observed myself when I heard him [i.e., Marrant] preach."[2] Since Belknap, a noted historian, was familiar with key personages in Boston's black community—in particular, he 'aided Prince Hall and the African Lodge in petitioning for the freedom of three Boston black freemen who had been kidnapped and sold into slavery in 1788—his opinions demand consideration. Moreover, the rough prose in Marrant's apparently unedited *Journal* contrasts greatly with the polished sentences of the *Sermon*. In sum, then, there is reason to believe that Prince Hall at least edited the *Sermon* before its publication.

NOTES

1. See title page and introduction of sermon reprinted in Flor Piñeiro de Rivera, *Arthur A. Schomburg: A Puerto Rican's Quest for His Black Heritage* (San Juan, Puerto Rico: Centro de Estudios Avanzados De Puerto Rico y el Caribe, 1989), pp. 167-68; the quotation is on p. 168. Note that the Bible and Heart on the title page appears incorrectly as "Binle and Brart." Likewise, the incorporation of "[i.e., 1784]" after the 24 June 1789 date in the sermon's title is a mistake copied from an *NUC* entry of Schomburg's edition.
2. Jeremy Belknap, *The Belknap Papers*, vol. 43, *Collections of the Massachusetts Historical Society*, fifth series, vol. 3 (Boston: Massachusetts Historical Society, 1877), p. 166.

A Narrative of the Lord's Wonderful Dealings with John Marrant, a Black, (Now Going to Preach the Gospel in Nova-Scotia) Born in New-York, in North-America

PREFACE.

READER,

*T*HE following Narrative is as plain and artless, as it is surprising and extraordinary. Plausible reasonings may amuse and delight, but facts, and facts like these, strike, are felt, and go home to the heart. Were the power, grace and providence of God ever more eminently displayed, than in the conversion, success, and deliverances of John Marrant? He and his companion enter the Meeting at Charles-Town[1] together; but the one is taken, and the other is left. He is struck to the ground, shaken over the mouth of hell, snatched as a brand from the burning; he is pardoned and justified; he is washed in the atoning blood and made happy in his God.[2] You soon have another view of him, drinking into his master's cup; he is tried and perplext, opposed and despised; the neighbours hoot at him as he goes along; his mother, sisters, and brother, hate and persecute him; he is friendless and forsaken of all. These uneasy circumstances call forth the corruptions of his nature, and create a momentary debate, whether the pursuit of ease and pleasure was not to be preferred to the practice of religion, which he now found so sharp and severe? The stripling is supported and strengthened. He is persuaded to forsake his family and kindred altogether. He crosses the fence, which marked the boundary between the wilderness and the cultivated country; and prefers the habitations of brutal residence, to the less hospitable dwellings of enmity to God and godliness. He wanders, but Christ is his guide and protector.[3] — Who can view him among the Indian *tribes* without wonder? He arrives among the Cherokees, where gross ignorance wore its rudest forms, and savage despotism exercised its most terrifying *empire. Here the child just turned fourteen, without sling or stone, engages, and with the arrow of prayer pointed with faith, wounded* Goliah, *and conquers the King.*

The untutor'd monarch feels the truth, and worships the God of the Christians; the seeds of the Gospel are disseminated among the Indians *by a youthful hand, and Jesus is received and obeyed.*[4]

The subsequent incidents related in this Narrative are great and affecting; but I must not anticipate the reader's pleasure and profit.

The novelty or magnitude of the facts contained in the following pages, may dispose some readers to question the truth of them. My answer to such is, — 1. I believe it is clear to great numbers, and to some competent judges; that God is with the subject of them; but if he knowingly permitted an untruth to go abroad in the name of God, whilst it is confessed the Lord is with him, would it not follow, that the Almighty gave his sanction to a falsehood? — 2. I have observed him to pay a conscientious regard to his word. — 3. He appeared to me to feel most sensibly, when he related those parts of his Narrative, which describe his happiest moments with God, or the most remarkable interpositions of Divine Providence for him; and I have no reason to believe it was counterfeited.

I have always preserved Mr. Marrant's *ideas, tho' I could not his language; no more alterations, however, have been made, than were thought necessary.*

I now commit the whole to God. — That he may make it generally useful is the prayer of thy ready servant, for Christ's sake.

W. ALDRIDGE.[5]

London,
July 19th, 1785.

✠ ✠ ✠

A NARRATIVE, &c.[6]

I JOHN MARRANT, born June 15th, 1755, in New-York, in North-America, with these gracious dealings of the Lord with me to be published, in hopes they may be useful to others, to encourage the fearful, to confirm the wavering, and to refresh the hearts of true believers. My father died when I was little more than four years of age, and before I was five my mother removed from New-York to St. Augustine,[7] about seven hundred miles from that city. Here I was sent to school, and taught to read and spell; after we had resided here about eighteen months, it was found necessary to remove to Georgia, where we remained;

and I was kept to school until I had attained my eleventh year. The Lord spoke to me in my early days, by these removes, if I could have understood him, and said, "Here we have no continuing city."[8] We left Georgia, and went to Charles-Town, where it was intended I should be put apprentice to some trade. Some time after I had been in Charles-Town, as I was walking one day, I passed by a school, and heard music and dancing, which took my fancy very much, and I felt a strong inclination to learn the music. I went home, and informed my sister, that I had rather learn to play upon music than go to a trade. She told me she could do nothing in it, until she had acquainted my mother with my desire. Accordingly she wrote a letter concerning it to my mother, which when she read, the contents were disapproved of by her, and she came to Charles-Town to prevent it. She persuaded me much against it, but her persuasions were fruitless. Disobedience either to God or man, being one of the fruits of sin,[9] grew out from me in early buds. Finding I was set upon it, and resolved to learn nothing else, she agreed to it, and went with me to speak to the man, and to settle upon the best terms with him she could. He insisted upon twenty pounds currency, which was paid, and I was engaged to stay with him eighteen months, and my mother to find me every thing during that term. The first day I went to him he put the violin into my hand, which pleased me much, and, applying close, I learned very fast, not only to play, but to dance also; so that in six months I was able to play for the whole school. In the evenings after the scholars were dismissed, I used to resort to the bottom of our garden, where it was customary for some musicians to assemble to blow the French-horn. Here my improvement was so rapid, that in a twelvemonth's time I became master both of the violin and of the French-horn, and was much respected by the Gentlemen and Ladies whose children attended the school, as also by my master.[10] This opened to me a large door of vanity and vice, for I was invited to all the balls and assemblies that were held in the town, and met with the general applause of the inhabitants. I was a stranger to want, being supplied with as much money as I had any occasion for; which my sister observing, said, "You have now no need of a trade." I was now in my thirteenth year, devoted to pleasure and drinking in iniquity like water; a slave to every vice suited to my nature and to my years. The time I had engaged to serve my master being expired, he persuaded me to stay with him, and offered me any thing or any money, not to leave him. His intreaties proving ineffectual, I quitted his service, and visited my mother in the country; with her I staid two months, living without God or hope in the world, fishing and hunting on the sabbath-day. Unstable as water, I returned to town, and wished to go to some trade. My sister's husband being informed of my inclination provided me with a master, who was a carpenter in that town,[11] on condition that I should serve him one year and a half on trial, and afterwards be bound, if he approved of me. Accordingly I went, but every evening I was sent for to play on music, somewhere or another; and I often continued out very late, sometimes all night, so as to render me incapable of attending my master's business the next day; yet in this manner I served him a year and four months, and was much approved of by him. He wrote a letter to my mother to come and have me bound, and whilst my mother was weighing the matter in her own mind, the gracious purposes of God, respecting a perishing sinner, were now to be disclosed. One evening I was sent for in a very particular manner to go and play to some Gentlemen, which I agreed to do, and was on my way to fulfil my promise; and passing by a large meeting house I saw many lights in it, and crowds of people going in. I enquired what it meant, and was answered by my companion that a crazy man was hallooing there; this raised my curiosity to go in, that I might hear what he was hallooing about. He persuaded me not to go in, but in vain. He then said, "If you will do one thing I will go in with you." I asked him what that was? He replied, "Blow the French-horn among them." I liked the proposal well enough, but expressed my fears of being beaten for disturbing them; but upon his promising to stand by me and defend me, I agreed. So we went, and with much difficulty got within the doors. I was pushing the people to make room, to get the horn off my shoulder to blow it, just as Mr Whitefield was naming his text,[12] and looking round, as I thought, directly upon me, and pointing with his finger, he uttered these words, "PREPARE TO MEET THY GOD O ISRAEL." The Lord accompanied the word with such power, that I was struck to the ground, and lay both speechless and senseless near half an hour.[13] When I was come a little too, I found two men attending me, and a woman throwing water in my face, and holding a smelling-bottle to my nose; and when something more recovered, every word I heard from the minister was like a parcel of swords thrust in to me, and what added to my distress, I thought I saw the devil on every side of me.[14] I was constrained in the bitterness of my spirit to halloo out in the midst of the congregation, which disturbing them, they took me away; but finding I could neither walk or stand, they carried me as far as the vestry, and there I remained till the service was over. When the people were dismissed Mr. Whitefield came into the vestry, and being told of my condition he came immediately, and the first word he said to me was, "JESUS CHRIST HAS GOT THEE AT LAST." He asked where I lived, intending to come and see me the next day; but recollecting he was to leave the town the next morning, he said he could not come himself, but would send another minister; he desired them to get me home, and then taking his leave of me, I saw him no more. When I reached my sister's house, being carried by two men, she was very uneasy to see me in so distressed a condition. She got me to bed, and sent for a doctor, who came immediately, and after looking at me, he went home, and sent me a bottle of mixture, and desired her to give me a spoonful every two hours; but I could not take any thing the doctor sent, nor indeed keep in bed; this distressed my sister very much, and she cried out, "The lad will surely die." She sent for two other doctors, but no medicine they prescribed could I take. No, no; it may be asked, a wounded spirit who can cure? as well as who can bear? In this distress of soul I continued for three days without any food, only a little water now and then.[15] On the fourth day, the minister[16] Mr. Whitefield had desired to visit me came to see me, and being directed upstairs, when he entered the room, I thought he made my distress much worse. He wanted to take hold of my hand, but I durst not give it to him. He insisted upon taking hold of it, and I then got away from him on the other side of the bed; but being very weak I fell down, and before I could recover he came to me and took me by the hand, and lifted me up, and after a few words desired to go to prayer. So he fell upon his knees, and pulled me down also; after he had spent some time in prayer he rose up, and asked me how I did now; I answered, much worse; he then said, "Come, we will have the old thing over again," and so we kneeled down a second time, and after he had prayed earnestly we got up, and he said again, "How do you do now;" I replied worse and worse, and asked him if he intended to kill me? "No, no, said he, you are worth a thousand dead men, let us try the old thing over again," and so falling upon our knees, he continued in prayer a considerable time, and near the close of his prayer, the Lord was pleased to set my soul at perfect liberty, and being filled with joy I began to praise the Lord immediately;[17] my sorrows were turned into peace, and joy, and love. The minister said, "How is it now?" I answered, all is well, all happy. He then took his leave of me; but called every day for several days afterwards, and the last time he said, "Hold fast that thou hast already obtained, 'till Jesus Christ come."[18] I now read the Scriptures very much. My master sent often to know how I did, and at last came himself, and finding me well, asked me if I would not come to work again? I answered no. He, asked me the reason, but receiving no answer he went away. I continued with my sister about three weeks, during which time she often asked me to play upon the violin for her, which I refused; then she said I was crazy and mad, and so reported it among the neighbours, which opened the mouths of all around against me. I then resolved to go to my mother, which was eighty-four miles from Charles-Town. I was two days on my journey home, and enjoyed much communion with God on the road, and had occasion to mark the gracious interpositions of his kind Providence as I passed along. The third day I arrived at my mother's house, and was well received. At supper they sat down to eat without asking the Lord's blessing, which caused me to burst out into tears. My mother asked me what was the matter? I answered, I wept because they sat down to supper without asking the Lord's blessing. She bid me with much surprise, to ask a blessing. I remained with her fourteen days without interruption; the Lord pitied me, being a young soldier. Soon, however, Satan began to stir up my two sisters and brother, who were then at home with my mother; they called me every name but that which was good. The more they persecuted me, the stronger I grew in grace. At length my mother turned against me also, and the neighbours joined her, and there was not a friend to assist me, or that I could speak to;[19] this made me earnest with God. In these circumstances, being the youngest but one of our family, and young in Christian experience, I was tempted so far as to threaten my life; but reading my Bible one day, and finding that if I did destroy myself I could not come where God was, I betook myself to the fields, and some days staid out from morning to night to avoid the persecutors.[20] I staid one time two days without any food, but seemed to have clearer views into the spiritual things of God.

Not long after this I was sharply tried, and reasoned the matter within myself, whether I should turn to my old courses of sin and vice, or serve and cleave to the Lord; after prayer to God, I was fully persuaded in my mind, that if I turned to my old ways I should perish eternally. Upon this I went home, and finding them all as hardened, or worse than before, and every body saying I was crazy; but a little sister I had, about nine years of age, used to cry when she saw them persecute me, and continuing so about five weeks and three days, I thought it was better for me to die than to live among such people. I rose one morning very early, to get a little quietness and retirement, I went into the woods, and staid till eight o'clock in the morning; upon my return I found them all at breakfast; I passed by them, and went up-stairs without any interruption; I went upon my knees to the Lord, and returned him thanks;

then I took up a small pocket Bible and one of Dr. Watts's hymn books,[21] and passing by them went out without one word spoken by any of us. After spending some time in the fields, I was persuaded to go from home altogether. Accordingly I went over the fence, about half a mile from our house, which divided the inhabited and cultivated parts of the country from the wilderness. I continued travelling in the desart all day without the least inclination of returning back. About evening I began to be surrounded with wolves; I took refuge from them on a tree, and remained there all night. About eight o'clock next morning I descended from the tree, and returned God thanks for the mercies of the night. I went on all this day without any thing to eat or drink.

The third day, taking my Bible out of my pocket, I read and walked for some time, and then being wearied and almost spent, I sat down, and after resting awhile I rose to go forward; but had not gone above a hundred yards when something tripped me up, and I fell down; I prayed to the Lord upon the ground that he would command the wild beasts to devour me, that I might be with him in glory. I made this request to God the third and part of the fourth day.

The fourth day in the morning, descending from my usual lodging, a tree, and having nothing all this time to eat, and but a little water to drink, I was so feeble that I tumbled half way down the tree, not being able to support myself, and lay upon my back on the ground about an hour and a half, praying and crying; after which, getting a little strength, and trying to stand upright to walk, I found myself not able; then I went upon my hands and knees, and so crawled till I reached a tree that was tumbled down, in order to get across it, and there I prayed with my body leaning upon it above an hour, that the Lord would take me to himself. Such nearness to God I then enjoyed, that I willingly resigned myself into his hands.[22] After some time I thought I was strengthened, so I got across the tree without my feet or hands touching the ground;[23] but struggling I fell over on the other side, and then thought the Lord will now answer my prayer, and take me home: But the time was not come. After laying there a little, I rose, and looking about, saw at some distance bunches of grass, called deer-grass; I felt a strong desire to get at it; though I rose, yet it was only on my hands and knees, being so feeble, and in this manner I reached the grass. I was about three-quarters of an hour going in this form twenty yards. When I reached it, I was unable to pull it up, so I bit it off like a horse, and prayed the Lord to bless it to me, and I thought it the best meal I ever had in my life, and I think so still, it was so sweet.[24] I returned my God hearty thanks for it, and then lay down about an hour. Feeling myself very thirsty, I prayed the Lord to provide me with some water. Finding I was something strengthened, I got up, and stood on my feet, and staggered from one tree to another, if they were near each other, otherwise the journey was too long for me. I continued moving so for some time, and at length passing between two trees, I happened to fall upon some bushes, among which were a few large hollow leaves, which had caught and contained the dews of the night, and lying low among the bushes, were not exhaled by the solar rays; this water in the leaves fell upon me as I tumbled down and was lost, I was now tempted to think the Lord had given me water from Heaven, and I had wasted it, I then prayed the Lord to forgive me.[25] What poor unbelieving creatures we are! though we are assured the Lord will supply all our needs. I was presently directed to a puddle of water very muddy, which some wild pigs had just left; I kneeled down, and asked the Lord to bless it to me, so I drank both mud and water mixed together, and being satisfied I returned the Lord thanks, and went on my way rejoicing. This day was much chequered with wants and supplies, with dangers and deliverances. I continued travelling on for nine days, feeding upon grass, and not knowing whither I was going; but the Lord Jesus Christ was very present, and that comforted me through the whole.[26]

The next morning, having quitted my customary lodging, and returned thanks to the Lord for my preservation through the night, reading and travelling on, I passed between two bears, about twenty yards distance from each other. Both sat and looked at me, but I felt very little fear; and after I had passed them, they both went the same way from me without growling, or the least apparent uneasiness. I went and returned God thanks for my escape, who had tamed the wild beasts of the forest, and made them friendly to me: I rose from my knees and walked on, singing hymns of praise to God, about five o'clock in the afternoon, and about fifty-five miles from home, right through the wilderness. As I was going on, and musing upon the goodness of the Lord, an Indian hunter, who stood at some distance, saw me; he hid himself behind a tree; but as I passed along he bolted out, and put his hands on my breast, which surprized me a few moments. He then asked me where I was going? I answered I did not know, but where the Lord was pleased to guide me. Having heard me praising God before I came up to him, he enquired who I was talking to? I told him I was talking to my Lord Jesus; he seemed surprized, and asked me where he was? for he did not see him there. I told him he could not be seen with bodily eyes.

After a little more talk, he insisted upon taking me home; but I refused, and added, that I would die rather than return home. He then asked me if I knew how far I was from home? I answered, I did not know; you are fifty-five miles and a half, says he, from home. He farther asked me how I did to live? I said I was supported by the Lord. He asked me how I slept? I answered, the Lord provided me with a bed every night; he further enquired what preserved me from being devoured by the wild beasts? I replied, the Lord Jesus Christ kept me from them. He stood astonished, and said, you say the Lord Jesus Christ do this, and do that, and do every thing for you, he must be a very fine man, where is he? I replied, he is here present. To this he made me no answer, only said, I know you, and your mother and sister; and upon a little further conversation I found he did know them, having been used in winter to sell skins in our Town.[27] This alarmed me, and I wept for fear he should take me home by force; but when he saw me so affected, he said he would not take me home if I would go with him. I objected against that, for fear he would rob me of my comfort and communion with God: But at last, being much pressed, I consented to go. Our employment for ten weeks and three days was killing deer, and taking off their skins by day, which we afterwards hung on the trees to dry till they were sent for;[28] the means of defence and security against our nocturnal enemies, always took up the evenings: We collected a number of large bushes, and placed them nearly in a circular form, which uniting at the extremity, afforded us both a verdant covering, and a sufficient shelter from the night dews. What moss we could gather was strewed upon the ground, and this composed our bed. A fire was kindled in the front of our temporary lodging-room, and fed with fresh fuel all night, as we slept and watched by turns; and this was our defence from the dreadful animals, whose shining eyes and tremendous roar we often saw and heard during the night.

By constant conversation with the hunter, I acquired a fuller knowledge of the Indian tongue: This, together with the sweet communion I enjoyed with God, I have since considered as a preparation for the great trial I was soon after to pass through.

The hunting season being now at an end, we left the woods, and directed our course towards a large Indian town, belonging to the Cherokee nation; and having reached it, I said to the hunter, they will not suffer me to enter in. He replied, as I was with him, nobody would interrupt me.

There was an Indian fortification all round the town, and a guard placed at each entrance. The hunter passed one of these without molestation, but I was stopped by the guard and examined. They asked me where I came from, and what was my business there? My companion of the woods attempted to speak for me, but was not permitted; he was taken away, and I saw him no more. I was now surrounded by about fifty men, and carried to one of their principal chiefs and Judge to be examined by him. When I came before him, he asked me what was my business there? I told him I came there with a hunter, whom I met with in the woods. He replied, "Did I not know that whoever came there without giving a better account of themselves than I did, was to be put to death?" I said I did not know it. Observing that I answered him so readily in his own language, he asked me where I learnt it? To this I returned no answer, but burst out into a flood of tears, and calling upon my Lord Jesus. At this he stood astonished, and expressed a concern for me, and said I was young. He asked me who my Lord Jesus was? — To this I gave him no answer, but continued praying and weeping. Addressing himself to the officer who stood by him, he said he was sorry; but it was the law. and it must not be broken.[29] I was then ordered to be taken away, and put into a place of confinement. They led me from their court into a low dark place, and thrust me into it, very dreary and dismal; they made fast the door, and set a watch. The judge sent for the executioner, and gave him his warrant for my execution in the afternoon of the next day. The executioner came, and gave me notice of it, which made me very happy, as the near prospect of death made me hope for a speedy deliverance from the body: And truly this dungeon became my chapel, for the Lord Jesus did not leave me in this great trouble, but was very present, so that I continued blessing him, and singing his praises all night without ceasing:[30] The watch hearing the noise, informed the executioner that somebody had been in the dungeon with me all night; upon which he came in to see and to examine, with a great torch lighted in his hand, who it was I had with me; but finding nobody, he turned round, and asked me who it was? I told him it was the Lord Jesus Christ; but he made no answer, turned away, went out, and fastened the door. At the hour appointed for my execution I was taken out, and led to the destined spot, amidst a vast number of people. I praised the Lord all the way we went, and when we arrived at the place I understood the kind of death I was to suffer, yet blessed be God, at that instant none of those things moved me.

When the executioner shewed me a basket of turpentine wood, stuck full of small pieces like skewers; he told me I was to be stripped naked, and laid down on one side by the basket, and these sharp pegs were to be stuck into me, and then set on fire, and when they had burnt to my body,[31] I was to be turned on the other side, and served in the same manner, and then to be taken by four men and thrown into the flame, which was to finish the execution;[32] I burst into tears, and asked what I had done to deserve so cruel a death? To this he gave me no answer. I cried out, Lord, if it be thy will that it should be so, thy will be done:[33] I then asked the executioner to let me go to prayer; he asked me to whom? I answered, to the Lord my God; he seemed surprized, and asked me where he was? I told him he was present; upon which he gave me leave. I desired them all to do as I did, so I fell down upon my knees, and mentioned to the Lord his delivering of the three children in the fiery furnace, and of Daniel in the Lion's den, and had close communion with God. I prayed in English a considerable time, and about the middle of my prayer, the Lord impressed a strong desire upon my mind to turn into their language, and pray in their tongue. I did so, and with remarkable liberty, which wonderfully affected the people. One circumstance was very singular, and strikingly displays the power and grace of God. I believe the executioner was savingly converted to God. He rose from his knees, and embracing me round the middle was unable to speak for about five minutes; the first words he expressed, when he had utterance, were, "No man shall hurt thee till thou hast been to the king."[34]

I was taken away immediately, and as we passed along, and I was reflecting upon the deliverance which the Lord had wrought out for me, and hearing the praises which the executioner was singing to the Lord, I must own I was utterly at a loss to find words to praise him. I broke out in these words, what can't the Lord Jesus do! and what power is like unto his! I will thank thee for what is past, and trust thee for what is to come. I will sing thy praise with my feeble tongue whilst life and breath shall last, and when I fail to sound thy praises here, I hope to sing them round thy throne above: And thus with unspeakable joy, I sung two verses of Dr. Watts's hymns:

> "My God, the spring of all my joys
> The life of my delights;
> The glory of my brightest days,
> And comfort of my nights.
> In darkest shades, if thou appear
> My dawning is begun;
> Thou art my soul's bright morning star,
> And thou my rising sun."[35]

Passing by the judge's door, who had before examined and condemned me, he stopped us, and asked the executioner why he brought
me back? The man fell upon his knees, and begged he would permit me
to be carried before the king, which being granted, I went on, guarded
by two hundred men with bows and arrows. After many windings I
entered the king's outward chamber, and after waiting some time he
came to the door, and his first question was, how came I there? I
answered, I came with a hunter whom I met with in the woods, and who
persuaded me to come there. He then asked me how old I was? I told
him not fifteen. He asked me how I was supported before I met with this
man? I answered, by the Lord Jesus Christ, which seemed to confound
him. He turned round, and asked me if he lived where I came from? I
answered, yes, and here also. He looked about the room, and said he did
not see him; but I told him I felt him. The executioner fell upon his
knees, and intreated the king in my behalf, and told him what he had felt
of the same Lord. At this instant the king's eldest daughter came into the
chamber, a person about nineteen years of age, and stood at my right
hand. I had a Bible in my hand, which she took out of it, and having
opened it, she kissed it, and seemed much delighted with it. When she
had put it into my hand again, the king asked me what it was? And I told
him the name of my God was recorded there; and after several questions,
he bid me read it, which I did, particularly the fifty-third chapter of
Isaiah, in the most solemn manner I was able; and also the twenty-sixth
chapter of Matthew's Gospel;[36] and when I pronounced the name of
Jesus, the particular effect it had upon me was observed by the king.
When I had finished reading, he asked me why I read those names[37] with
so much reverence? I told him, because the Being to whom those names
belonged made heaven and earth, and I and he; this he denied. I then
pointed to the sun, and asked him who made the sun, and moon, and
stars, and preserved them in their regular order; He said there was a
man in their town that did it. I laboured as much as I could to convince
him to the contrary. His daughter took the book out of my hand a second time; she opened it, and kissed it again; her father bid her give it to
me, which she did; but said, with much sorrow, the book would not
speak to her.[38] The executioner then fell upon his knees again, and
begged the king to let me go to prayer, which being granted, we all went
upon our knees, and now the Lord displayed his glorious power. In the
midst of the prayer some of them cried out, particularly the king's
daughter, and the judge who ordered me to be executed, and several
others seemed under deep conviction of sin: This made the king very

angry; he called me a witch, and commanded me to be thrust into the prison, and to be executed the next morning. This was enough to make me think, as old Jacob once did, "All these things are against me;" for I was dragged away, and thrust into the dungeon again with much indignation;[39] but God, who never forsakes his people, was with me. Though I was weak in body, yet I was strong in spirit:[40] The executioner went to the king, and assured him, that if he put me to death, his daughter would never be well. They used the skill of all their doctors that afternoon and night; but physical prescriptions were useless. In the morning the executioner came to me, and, without opening the prison door, called to me, and hearing me answer, said, "Fear not, thy God who delivered thee yesterday, will deliver thee to-day." This comforted me very much, especially to find he could trust the Lord. Soon after I was fetched out; I thought it was to be executed; but they led me away to the king's chamber with much bodily weakness, having been without food two days. When I came into the king's presence, he said to me, with much anger, if I did not make his daughter and that man well, I should be laid down and chopped into pieces before him. I was not afraid, but the Lord tried my faith sharply. The king's daughter and the other person were brought out into the outer chamber, and we went to prayer; but the heavens were locked up to my petitions. I besought the Lord again, but received no answer: I cried again, and he was intreated. He said, "Be it to thee even as thou wilt;"[41] the Lord appeared most lovely and glorious; the king himself was awakened, and the others set at liberty. A great change took place among the people; the king's house became God's house; the soldiers were ordered away, and the poor condemned prisoner had perfect liberty, and was treated like a prince. Now the Lord made all my enemies to become my great friends. I remained nine weeks in the king's palace. praising God day and night: I was never out but three days all the time. I had assumed the habit of the country, and was dressed much like the king, and nothing was too good for me. The king would take off his golden ornaments, his chain and bracelets, like a child, if I objected to them, and lay them aside. Here I learnt to speak their tongue in the highest stile.

I began now to feel an inclination growing upon me to go farther on, but none to return home. The king being acquainted with this, expressed his fears of my being used ill by the next Indian nation, and to prevent it, sent fifty men, and a recommendation to the king, with me. The next nation was called the Creek Indians, at sixty miles distance. Here I was received with kindness, owing to the king's influence, from whom I had parted; here I staid five weeks. I next visited the Catawaw Indians, at about fifty-five miles distance from the others; Lastly, I went among the Housaw Indians,[42] eighty miles distant from the last mentioned; here I staid seven weeks. These nations were then at peace with each other, and I passed among them without danger, being recommended from one to the other. When they recollect, that the white people drove them from the American shores, they are full of resentment.[43] These nations have often united, and murdered all the white people in the back settlements which they could lay hold of, men, women, and children. I had not much reason to believe any of these three nations were savingly wrought upon, and therefore I returned to the Cherokee nation, which took me up eight weeks. I continued with my old friends seven weeks and two days.

I now and then found, that my affections to my family and country were not dead; they were sometimes very sensibly felt, and at last strengthened into an invincible desire of returning home. The king was much against it; but feeling the same strong bias towards my country, after we had asked Divine direction, the king consented, and accompanied me sixty miles with one hundred and forty men. I went to prayer three times before we could part, and then he sent forty men with me a hundred miles farther; I went to prayer, and then took my leave of them, and passed on my way. I had seventy miles now to go to the back settlements of the white people. I was surrounded very soon with wolves again, which made my old lodging both necessary and welcome. However it was not long, for in two days I reached the settlements, and on the third I found a house: It was about dinner-time, and as I was coming to the door the family saw me, were frightened, and ran away. I sat down to dinner alone, and eat very heartily, and, after returning God thanks, I went to see what was become of the family. I found means to lay hold of a girl that stood peeping at me from behind a barn. She fainted away, and it was upwards of an hour before she recovered; it was nine o'clock before I could get them all to venture in, they were so terrified.

My dress was purely in the Indian stile; the skins of wild beasts composed my garments; my head was set out in the savage manner, with a long pendant down my back a sash round my middle, without breeches, and a tomohawk by my side. In about two days they became sociable. Having visited three or four other families at the distance of sixteen or twenty miles, I got them altogether to prayer on the Sabbath days, to the number of seventeen persons. I staid with them six weeks, and they expressed much sorrow when I left them. I was now one hundred and twelve miles from home. On the road I sometimes met with a house, then I was hospitably entertained; and when I met with none, a tree lent me the use of its friendly shelter and protection from the prowling beasts of the woods during the night. The God of mercy and grace supported me thus for eight days, and on the ninth I reached my uncle's house.

The following particulars, relating to the manner in which I was made known to my family, are less interesting; and yet, perhaps, some readers would not forgive their omission: I shall, however, be as brief as I can. I asked my uncle for a lodging, which he refused. I enquired how far the town was off; three quarters of a mile, said he. Do you know Mrs. Marrant and family, and how the children do? was my next question. He said he did, they were all well, but one was lately lost; at this I turned my head and wept. He did not know me, and upon refusing again to lodge me, I departed. When I reached the town it was dark, and passing by a house where one of my old school-fellows lived, I knocked at the door; he came out, and asked me what I wanted? I desired a lodging, which was granted: I went in, but was not known. I asked him if he knew Mrs. Marrant, and how the family were? He said, he had just left them, they were all well; but a young lad, with whom he went to school, who after he had quitted school, went to Charles-Town to learn some trade; but came home crazy, rambled in the woods, and was torn in pieces by the wild beasts.[44] How do you know, said I, that he was killed by wild beasts? I, and his brother, and uncle, and others, said he, went three days into the woods in search of him, and found his carcase torn, and brought it home and buried it.[45] This affected me very much, and I wept; observing it, he said what is the matter? I made no answer. At supper they sat down without craving a blessing, for which I reproved them; this so affected the man, that I believe it ended in a sound conversion. Here is a wild man, says he, come out of the woods, to be a witness for God, and to reprove our ingratitude and stupefaction! After supper I went to prayer, and then to bed. Rising a little before day-light, and praising the Lord, as my custom was, the family were surprised, and got up: I staid with them till nine o'clock, and then went to my mother's house in the next street. The singularity of my dress drew every body's eyes upon me, yet none knew me. I knock'd at my mother's door, my sister opened it, and was startled at my appearance. Having expressed a desire to see Mrs. Marrant, I was answered, she was not very well, and that my business with her could be done by the person at the door, who also attempted to shut me out, which I prevented. My mother being called, I went in, and sat down, a mob of people being round the door. My

mother asked, "what is your business;" only to see you, said I. She said
she was much obliged to me, but did not know me. I asked, how are your
children? how are your two sons? She replied, her daughters were in
good health, of her two sons, one was well, and with her, but the other, —
unable to contain, she burst into a flood of tears, and retired. I was
overcome, and wept much; but nobody knew me.[46] This was an affecting scene! Presently my brother came in: He enquired, who I was, and
what I was? My sister did not know; but being uneasy at my presence,
they were contriving to get me out of the house, which, being over-heard
by me, I resolved not to stir. My youngest sister, eleven years of age,
came in from school, with a book under her arm. I was then sitting in the
parlour, and as she passed by the parlour door, she peep'd in and seeing
a strange person there, she recollected me; she goes into the kitchen, and
tells the servants, her brother was come; but her report finding no credit,
she came and peep'd again, that she might be certain it was me; and then
passing into the next room, through the parlour where I was sitting, she
made a running curtsy, and says to my eldest sister, who was there, it is
my brother John! She called her a foolish girl, and threatened to beat
her: Then she came again and peep'd at me, and being certain she was
not mistaken, she went back, and insisted that it was me: Being then beat
by my sister, she went crying up-stairs to my mother, and told her; but
neither would my mother believe her.[47] At last they said to her, if it be
your brother, go and kiss him, and ask him how he does? She ran and
clasped me round the neck, and, looking me in the face, said, "Are not
you my brother John?" I answered yes, and wept. I was then made
known to all the family, to my friends, and acquaintances, who received
me, and were glad and rejoiced: Thus the dead was brought to life again;
thus the lost was found.[48] I shall now close the Narrative, with only
remarking a few incidents in my life, until my connection with my Right
Honourable Patroness, the Countess of HUNTINGDON.[49]

    I remained with my relations till the commencement of the American
troubles.[50] I used to go and hear the word of God, if any Gospel ministers
came into the country, though at a considerable distance,[51] and thereby got
acquainted with a few poor people, who feared God in Wills' Town, and
Borough Town, Dorchester Town, and other places thereabouts; and in
those places we used to meet and associate together for Christian
Conversation, and at their request I frequently went to prayer with them,
and at times enjoyed much of the Lord's presence among them.[52]

    About this time I went with my brother, who was a house-carpenter,
to repair a plantation belonging to Mr. Jenkins, of Cumbee, about sev-

enty miles from Charles-Town, where after I had done work in the evening, I used to spend my time in reading God's Word, singing Watts's Hymns and in Prayer, the little negro children would often come round the door with their pretty wishful looks, and finding my heart much drawn out in Love to their souls, I one evening called several of them in, and asked them if they could say the Lord's Prayer, &c. finding they were very ignorant, I told them, if they would come every evening I would teach them, which they did, and learned very fast, some of them in about four weeks could say the Lord's Prayer, and good part of the Catechism,[53] after teaching, I used to go to prayer with them before we parted; this continued without interruption for three or four months, in which time, by the children acquainting their parents with it, I soon had my society increased to about thirty persons; and the Lord was pleased often to refresh us with a sense of his love and presence amongst us; one of the negro boys made a very great proficiency in that time, and could exercise in extemporary prayer much to my satisfaction. We are well advised in Ecclesiasticus, chap. ii. *v.* 1. *My Son, if thou come to serve the Lord, prepare thy heart for temptation:* Nor was it long before they were made to pledge our dear Lord in the bitter cup of suffering; for now the old Lion began to roar,[54] their mistress became acquainted with our proceedings, and was full of rage at it, and determined to put a stop to it. She had two of the children brought before her to examine, and made them say the Lord's prayer to her, she then asked who taught them? and they told her the free Carpenter. She also enquired, how many he had instructed, and at what time he taught them; and they told her, it was in the Evening after they had done work. She then stirred up her husband against us, who before had several times come in while I was instructing the children, and did not appear displeased with it: she told him it was the ready way to have all his negroes ruin'd, and made him promise to examine further into the matter, and break up our meeting; which he then very soon did, for a short space; for he, together with his overseer and negro-driver, and some of his neighbours, beset the place wherein we met, while we were at prayers; and as the poor creatures came out they caught them, and tied them together with cords, till the next morning, when all they caught, men, women, and children were strip'd naked and tied, their feet to a stake, their hands to the arm of a tree, and so severely flogg'd that the blood ran from their backs and sides to the floor, to make them promise they would leave off praying, &c. though several of them fainted away with the pain and loss of blood, and lay upon the ground as dead for a considerable time after they were untied. I did not hear that she obtained her end of any of them. She endeavoured to perswade her husband to flog me also, but he told her he did not dare to do it because I was free, and would take the law of him, and make him pay for it; which she told him, she had rather he should run the hazard of, than let me go without the benefit of a good flogging, and was afterwards very angry with him because he was afraid to gratify her. He told me afterwards that I had spoiled all his Negroes, but could not help acknowledging, that they did their tasks sooner than the others who were not instructed, and thereby had time after their tasks were done, to keep their own fields in better order than the others, who used to employ the Sabbath for that purpose, as is the common practice among the Negroes. He then said, I should make them so wise that he should not be able to keep them in subjection. I asked him whether he did not think they had Souls to be saved? He answered, yes. I asked him whether he thought they were in the way to save their Souls whilst they were ignorant of that God who made and preserved them. He made me no answer to that. I then told him that the blood of those poor negroes which he had spilt that morning would be required by God at his hands. He then left me. Soon after, meeting with his wife, I told her the same; but she laught at it, and was only sorry that she had not been able to get me flog'd with them. Finding I could not any longer live peaceably there, I encouraged the poor creatures to call upon God as well as they could, and returned home; where I afterwards heard that their Mistress continued to persecute them for meeting together as often as she discover'd them, and her husband for not being more severe against them; they were then obliged to meet at midnight in different corners of the woods that were about the plantation, and were sure to be flog'd if ever she caught them, they nevertheless continued their meetings though in such imminent danger,[55] and by what I have since heard, I believe it continues to this day, by which it appears that the work was of God; therefore neither the devil nor his servants could overthrow it; and to our faithful Covenant God be all the Glory.

In about two months after I left them, it pleased God to lay his hand upon their Mistress, and she was seized with a very violent fever, which no medicine that they could produce would remove, and in a very few days after she was taken ill, she died in a very dreadful manner, in great anger with her husband, for not preventing their meetings, which she had heard they continued, notwithstanding all her endeavours to stop it. After she was dead, her husband gave them liberty to meet together as before, and used sometimes to attend with them; and I have since heard that it was made very useful to him.

About this time I was an eye-witness of the remarkable conversion of a child seven and a half years old, named Mary Scott, which I shall here mention, in hopes the Lord may make it useful and profitable to my young readers.[56] Her parents lived in the house adjoining to my sister's. One day as I was returning from my work, and passing by the school where she was instructed, I saw the children coming out, and stop'd and looked among them for her, to take her home in my hand; but not seeing her among those that were coming out, I supposed she was gone before, and went on towards home; when passing by the church-yard which was in my way, I saw her very busy walking from one tomb to another, and went to her, and asked her what she was doing there? She told me, that in the lesson she had set her at school that morning, in the Twentieth of the Revelations, she read, "I saw the Dead, small and great, stand before God," &c. and she had been measuring the graves, with a tape she then held in her hand, to see if there were any so small as herself among them; and that she had found six that were shorter. I then said, and what of that? She answered, "I will die, Sir." I told her I knew she would, but hoped she would live till she was grown a woman; but she continued to express her desire to depart, and be with Christ, rather than to live till she was grown up. I then took her by the hand and brought her home with me. After this, she was observed to be always very solid and thoughtful, and that passage appeared always to be fresh upon her mind. I used frequently to be with her when in town, and at her request we often read and prayed together, and she appeared much affected. She never afterwards was seen out at play with other children; but spent her leisure time in reading God's word and prayer. In about four months after this, she was taken ill, and kept her room about three weeks; when first taken, she told me, she should never come down stairs alive. I frequently visited her during her illness, and made light of what she said about her dying so soon; but in the last week of her illness, she said to me in a very solemn manner, "Sir, I shall die before Saturday-night." The Physicians attended her, but she took very few if any medicines, and appeared quite calm and resigned to God's will. On Friday morning, which was the day she died, I visited her, and told her that I hoped she would not die so soon as she said, but she told me that she should certainly die before six o'clock that Evening. About five o'clock I visited her again. She was then sitting in a chair, and reading in her Bible, to all appearance pretty well recovered. After setting with her about a quarter of an hour, she got up, and desired me to go down, and send her mother up with a clean shift for her; which I did; and after a little time, when I went up again, I found her lying on the bed, with her eyes fixed up to heaven; when turning herself and seeing me, she said, "Mr. Marrant, don't you see that pretty town, and those fine people, how they shine like gold? — O how I long to be with my Lord and his redeemed Children in Glory!" and then turning to her parents and two sisters, (who were all present, having by her desire been called to her) she shook hands with them, and bade them farewell; desiring them not to lament for her when she was dead, for she was going to that fine place where God would wipe away all tears from her eyes, and she should sing Hallelujahs to God and to the Lamb for ever and ever,[57] and where she hoped afterwards to meet them; and then turning again to me, she said — "Farewell, and God bless you." and then fell asleep in the arms of Jesus. This afterwards proved the conversion of her mother.

In those troublesome times, I was pressed on board the Scorpion sloop of war, as their musician, as they were told I could play on music.[58] — I continued in his majesty's service six years and eleven months; and with shame confess, that a lamentable stupor crept over all my spiritual vivacity, life and vigour; I got cold and dead. What need, reader, have we to be continually mindful of our Lord's exhortation, *"What I say unto you, I say unto all, Watch."*[59] My gracious God, my dear Father in his dear Son, roused me every now and then by dangers and deliverances. — I was at the siege of Charles-Town,[60] and passed through many dangers. When the town was taken, my old royal benefactor and convert, the king of the Cherokee Indians, riding into the town with general Clinton, saw me, and knew me: He alighted off his horse,[61] and came to me; said he was glad to see me; that his daughter was very happy, and sometimes longed to get out of the body.

Some time after this I was cruising about in the American seas, and cannot help mentioning a singular deliverance I had from the most imminent danger, and the use the Lord made it of to me. We were overtaken by a violent storm; I was washed overboard, and thrown on again; dashed into the sea a second time, and tossed upon deck again. I now fastened a rope round my middle, as a security against being thrown in to the sea again; but, alas! forgot to fasten it to any part of the ship; being carried away the third time by the fury of the waves, when in the sea, I found the rope both useless and an incumbrance. I was in the sea the third time about eight minutes, and several sharks came round me; one of an enormous size, that could easily have taken me into his mouth at once, passed and rubbed against my side. I then cried more earnestly to the Lord than I had done for some time; and he who heard Jonah's prayer, did not shut out mine, for I was thrown aboard again;[62] these were the means the Lord used to revive me, and I began to set out afresh.

I was in the engagement with the Dutch off the Dogger bank,[63] on board the Princess-Amelia, of eighty-four guns.[64] We had a great number killed and wounded; the deck was running with blood; six men were killed and three wounded, stationed at the same gun with me; my head and face were covered with the blood and brains of the slain; I was wounded, but did not fall, till a quarter of an hour before the engagement ended, and was happy in my soul during the whole of it. After being in the hospital three months and sixteen days, I was sent to the West-Indies on board a ship of war, and, after cruising in those seas, we returned home as a convoy. Being taken ill of my old wounds, I was put into the hospital at Plymouth,[65] and had not been there long, when the physician gave it as his opinion, that I should not be capable of serving the king again; I was therefore discharged, and came to London, where I lived with a respectable and pious merchant, near three years,[66] who was unwilling to part with me. During this time, I saw my call to the ministry fuller and clearer; had a feeling concern for the salvation of my countrymen: I carried them constantly in the arms of prayer and faith to the throne of grace, and had continual sorrow in my heart for my brethren, for my kinsmen, according to the flesh.[67] — I wrote a letter to my brother, who returned me an answer, in which he prayed some ministers would come and preach to them, and desired me to shew it to the minister whom I attended. I used to exercise my gifts on a Monday evening in prayer and exhortation, in Spa-fields chapel,[68] and was approved of, and sent down to Bath; where I was ordained, in Lady Huntingdon's Chapel.[69] Her Ladyship having seen the letter from my brother in Nova Scotia, thought Providence called me there: To which place I am now bound, and expect to sail in a few days.

I have now only to intreat the earnest prayers of all my kind Christian friends, that I may be carried safe there; kept humble, made faithful, and successful; that strangers may hear of and run to Christ; that Indian tribes may stretch out their hands to God; that the black nations may be made white in the blood of the Lamb; that vast multitudes of hard tongues, and of a strange speech, may learn the language of Canaan, and sing the song of Moses, and of the Lamb; and, anticipating the glorious prospect, may we all with fervent hearts, and willing tongues, sing Hallelujah; the kingdoms of the world are become the kingdoms of our God, and of his Christ. Amen, and Amen.[70]

Nor can I take my leave of my very dear London Friends without intreating GOD to bless them with every blessing of the upper and nether Springs: — May the good will of Him that dwelt in the bush ever preserve and lead them! is the fervent prayer of their affectionate and grateful Servant in the Gospel,

London, N° 69,
MILE-END ROAD   J. MARRANT.[71]
Aug. 18. 1785.

PSALM CVII.   Dr. WATTS.

1   GIVE Thanks to God; He reigns above;
     Kind are his Thoughts, his Name is Love;
     His Mercy Ages past have known,
     And Ages long to come shall own.

2   Let the Redeemed of the LORD
     The Wonders of his Grace record;
     Isr'el, the Nation whom he chose,
     And rescu'd from their mighty Foes.

3   When GOD's Almighty Arm had broke
     Their Fetters and th' Egyptian Yoke,
     They trac'd the Desert, wand'ring round
     A wild and solitary Ground!

4   There they could find no leading Road,
     Nor City for a fix'd Abode;
     Nor Food, nor Fountain to assuage
     Their burning Thirst, or Hunger's Rage.

5   In their Distress to GOD they cry'd;
     GOD was their Saviour and their Guide;
     He led their March, far wand'ring round,
     'Twas the right Path to Canaan's Ground.

6   Thus when our first Release we gain
     From Sin's old Yoke, and Satan's Chain,
     We have this desert World to pass,
     A dang'rous and a tiresome Place.

7   He feeds and clothes us all the Way,
     He guides our Footsteps lest we stray;

He guards us with a pow'rful Hand,
And brings us to the heav'nly Land.

8   O let the Saints with Joy record
    The Truth and Goodness of the LORD!
    How great his Works! how kind his Ways!
    Let ev'ry Tongue pronounce his Praise.

FINIS.

NOTES

1. Charles-Town is Charleston, South Carolina.
2. The text alludes to Matthew 24:39-41, Amos 4:11, Revelation 1:5, and Romans 5:9, 11.
3. See Psalm 107, and compare with Watts's Psalm 107 at the end of the narrative.
4. Aldridge alludes here to the Parable of the Sower and the Seed (Matthew 13:18-30).
5. William Aldridge (1737-1797), who wrote down and published Marrant's *Narrative*, was the officiating minister of London's Jewry Street Chapel for twenty-one years. At the age of twenty-four he converted to Methodism and entered Trevecca, the Countess of Huntingdon's ministerial college in South Wales, proselytizing throughout Kent as part of his curriculum. After he was ordained he was assigned to the Connexion's Mulberry Gardens Chapel in Wapping and grew so popular that the congregation petitioned for his post to be made permanent. When the Countess refused, Aldridge resigned from the Connexion in 1776 and became the officiating minister at the Calvinistic Methodist Jewry Street Chapel. He remained on friendly terms with the Connexion and the Countess, who occasionally attended his church services. In 1787 he helped to lay the foundation stone for her Swansea Chapel, and when she died in 1791, he gave a funeral sermon for her at Jewry Street.

   Aldridge must have met Marrant through the Connexion. He may have attended Marrant's ordination in 1785, where he would have heard Marrant tell his story.
6. Here Farncombe's London imprint notes: "'The particulars were once related to us by Lady Ann Erskine, who heard them from the lips of Mr. Marrant himself, so that its authenticity cannot be called into question.'—*Gospel Magazine*, April, 1844." Erskine was the Countess of Huntingdon's close associate; she supervised the Huntingdonian Connexion after the Countess's death in 1791. Her name is on the subscription list for Equiano's *Narrative*.
7. Marrant refers to St. Augustine, Florida.
8. Marrant's version of Hebrews 13:14 differs slightly from that in the King James Version.

The Marrant family's move to Georgia around 1761 may have been prompted, in part, by a slight thaw in the colony's attitude toward black freemen. In 1765 Georgia passed legislation encouraging free blacks to immigrate to the colony, which desperately needed a larger population to help stave off the hostile incursions of neighboring Native American tribes.

9. See Proverbs 10:16.

10. Throughout the eighteenth century, black musicians were extremely popular in America and Britain, especially in military bands. These musicians played trumpets, drums, cymbals, tamborines, and other instruments to enthusiastic audiences. Like Marrant, Olaudah Equiano learned to play the French horn (see pp. 234, 235 of this volume). For a good overview of this aspect of black history, see Peter Fryer, *Staying Power: The History of Black People in Britain* (London: Pluto Press, 1984), pp. 79-88.

11. Only this imprint identifies the master as one "who was a carpenter in that town."

12. For George Whitefield, see the introduction to this volume. The text he utters is Amos 4:12.

13. The London imprints of 1788 and 1802 and the Brighton imprint of 1829 also use "near half an hour." The first two London "editions" of 1785, the Leeds imprint of 1815, and Farncombe's London imprint say "for twenty[-]four minutes."

14. See Hebrews 4:12 and Ephesians 6:17.

15. Compare Acts 9:1-20. Saul, after being struck by heavenly light, "was three days without sight, and neither did eat nor drink." On the fourth day he is visited by a disciple named Ananias, who restores his sight and converts him.

16. Marrant's note: "Mr. HART, a Baptist Minister at Charles-Town." This note is also included in the London imprints of 1788 and 1802 and the Brighton imprint of 1829.

17. Compare George Whitefield's account of his own conversion: "I found and felt in myself that I was delivered from the burden that had so heavily oppressed me. . . . I knew what it was truly to rejoice in God my Saviour." See *A Short Account of God's Dealings with the Reverend Mr. George Whitefield* (1740); rptd. in *Journals* (London: Banner of Truth Trust, 1960), p. 58.

18. Compare Revelation 2:25 and 3:11.

19. Matthew 13:57 states that "a prophet is not without honour, save in his own country, and in his own house." Whitefield incorporates this verse into his sermon "The Folly and Danger of Being Not Righteous Enough": "The enemies, the greatest enemies a young convert meets with . . . are those of his own house. They that will be godly, must suffer persecution; so was it in Christ's time, and so was it in the apostle's time, too; for our Lord came not to send peace, but a sword" (*Sermons on Important Subjects* [London: William Tegg, n.d.], p. 118).

20. A young Christian's desperate thoughts of suicide, followed immediately by a revelation that the self-murdered cannot enter Heaven, is a common feature of conversion narratives. See also Gronniosaw, p. 38, and Equiano, p. 243, of this volume.

21. Reverend Isaac Watts (1674-1748), one of the most popular writers of his time, is best known for his *Hymns* and *Psalms of David*, which have been issued in hun-

dreds of editions. According to Walter F. Pitts, Watts's hymnbooks were "a heretical change in Protestant hymnody in the colonies as well as in Britain," where the *Bay Psalm Book* had long reigned supreme. The freedoms he took in crafting loose translations of the Scriptures may have shocked some traditionalists, but his hymns soon became an integral part of revivalism in the Atlantic world. Black slaves greatly appreciated Watts's hymns; indeed, Pitts avers, "So effective a conversion tool was Watts's hymnal that the book was a necessary item in the arsenal of every itinerant preacher who preached to slaves." See Pitts's *Old Ship of Zion: The Afro-Baptist Ritual in the African Diaspora* (New York: Oxford University Press, 1993), pp. 76-77.

22. Marrant's submission to Providence echoes Jesus' advice to his apostles in Matthew 6:25-32. In 6:25 he bids them: "Take no thought for your life, what ye shall eat, or what ye shall drink; nor yet for your body, what ye shall put on. Is not the life more than meat, and the body than raiment?"

23. Although the London imprints of 1788 and 1802 and the Brighton imprint of 1829 also read "feet or hands," the first two London "editions" of 1785, the Leeds imprint of 1815, and Farncombe's London imprint have Marrant crossing the tree without "legs or feet."

24. See Proverbs 27:7. Marrant here reiterates a theme common to Indian captivity narratives; compare Mary Rowlandson, *The Soveraignty and Goodness of God, Together with the Faithfulness of His Promises Displayed; Being a Narrative of the Captivity and Restauration of Mrs. Mary Rowlandson* (1682), in *Held Captive by Indians: Selected Narratives 1642-1836,* ed. Richard VanDerBeets (Knoxville: University of Tennessee Press, 1973), p. 56. Forced to scavenge for food to survive, prisoners would grow so hungry that they eventually ate things they normally considered unusual, or even foul; in their starvation they find these foods supremely savory. Compare with note 39 below.

25. Compare Exodus 15:22-27. Like the people of Israel, Marrant wanders "three days in the wilderness, and [finds] no water" until the fourth day.

26. All other imprints we have seen use "all" in place of "the whole" and, a few lines down, say "no fear" instead of "very little fear."

27. In this imprint, Marrant adds the phrase "having been used in winter to sell skins in our Town." This addition is also incorporated in the London imprints of 1788 and 1802 and the Brighton imprint of 1829.

28. In this imprint, Marrant adds the phrase "which we afterwards hung on the trees to dry till they were sent for." This phrase is included in the 1788 and 1802 London imprints and the 1829 Brighton imprint.

29. The Cherokees, in strictly adhering to the letter of the law, are evidently intended to represent a Christian notion of Old Testament values. This scene in Marrant's *Narrative* is cast as an allegory of Paul's lesson, in Romans 1-8, that under "the law" (that is, the Mosaic Covenant) no one could obtain (eternal) life. For Paul, "life" cannot be merited or earned, but comes only through Christ's free gift of grace. Paul's text is commonly allegorized in medieval and early modern literature; see, for example, Shakespeare's *The Merchant of Venice.*

30. See Thessalonians 5:17.

31. Marrant's note: "These Pegs were to be kindled at the opposite end from the Body." The London imprints of 1788 and 1802 and the Brighton imprint of 1829 include this note.

32. This form of torture and execution was characteristic of the Iroquois and appears throughout Indian captivity narratives.

33. See the Lord's Prayer, Matthew 6:9-13; see also verses 14 and 15. Marrant's trial and his eventual salvation follow a pattern established by Daniel 3 (especially verses 14-30) and 6.

34. Marrant's note: "The Office of Executioner there, in many respects resembles that of a High Sheriff in this country." This imprint is the only one we have seen that includes this note.

35. Watts's Hymn 54, slightly altered.

36. Isaiah 53 describes a servant of the Lord who suffers for his labors; Christians read this chapter as a prophecy of Jesus' career on earth. Matthew 26 chronicles the events that precede Jesus' crucifixion: Jesus prophesies his betrayal by the apostles; the Last Supper takes place; Judas betrays Jesus; and Peter denies Jesus three times.

37. Marrant's note: "Or what those parts were which seemed to affect so much, not knowing what I read, as he did not understand the English language." This note appears in the London imprints of 1788 and 1802 and the Brighton imprint of 1829.

38. On the trope of the talking book, see note 15 in the Gronniosaw section of this volume.

39. See Genesis 42:36. Mary Rowlandson also quotes this passage from Jacob in her *The Soveraignty and Goodness of God,* pp. 49-50. Compare with note 24 above.

40. See 2 Corinthians 12:10. This imprint deletes the next sentence found in the first two London "editions" of 1785: "The Lord works, and who shall let it?"

41. Compare Matthew 26:39.

42. The "Catawaw" are the Choctaw; the "Housaw" are the Chickasaw.

43. In this imprint, Marrant adds the clause "they are full of resentment." This text does not appear in any other imprint we have seen. Moreover, the first two words of the next sentence ("These nations") seem to be unique to this imprint. All other imprints we have seen say "the three first nations."

44. Compare Genesis 37, 39-47. Marrant's story echoes that of Joseph, whom Jacob wrongly thinks has been torn asunder by wild beasts, and who, after his captivity and his eventual rise to power in Egypt, is joyfully reunited with his family.

45. Here Marrant deletes the phrase "and are now in mourning for him," which appears at the end of the sentence in earlier imprints.

46. Marrant's note: "I had been absent from them near twenty-three months."

47. Compare Marrant's description of this scene with the following softened version printed in all other imprints we have seen: "My youngest sister, eleven years of age, came in from school, and knew me the moment she saw me: She goes into the kitchen, and tells the woman her brother was come; but her news finding no credit there she returns, passes through the room where I sat, made a running curtsey, and says to my eldest sister in the next room, it is my brother! She was

then called a foolish girl, and threatened; the child cried, and insisted upon it. She went crying up-stairs to my mother, and told her; but neither would my mother believe her."

48. Marrant alludes to the story of the Prodigal Son, Luke 15:11-32. The father revels over the return of his dissipated but repentant son who "was lost, and is found" (verse 24). Compare the hymn "Amazing Grace," written by John Newton (1725-1807), a curate of Olney who, as a younger man, had commanded a slave ship between 1748 and 1754. After his conversion he studied theology with Whitefield and John Wesley and became a member of the clergy in 1764. He published *Olney Hymns* with William Cowper in 1779, where "Amazing Grace" first appeared.

49. Selina Shirley Hastings, the Countess of Huntingdon (1707-1791), a well-connected member of the British nobility, converted to Methodism in the 1730s. She regularly hosted Methodist meetings in her home for her aristocratic friends, who listened to Whitefield and the Wesley brothers preach. After her husband Theophilus died in 1746, she redoubled her spiritual efforts, appointing Whitefield in 1748 to be her personal chaplain. She channeled her zeal into building her Connexion, a loose consortium of Methodist congregations scattered throughout England and Ireland. She poured thousands of pounds into training and supplying a cadre of itinerant preachers, as well as building or leasing chapels for their use. In 1768 she opened Trevecca, a ministerial college in South Wales, to facilitate the Connexion's growth; by 1780 she had published *A Select Collection of Hymns to be Universally Sung in all the Countess of Huntingdon's Chapels*. Enthusiasm for her Connexion was not universal, however, and the Countess and her followers were forced to secede from the Anglican church and declare themselves dissenters to survive as an organized body. The formal process of secession was effected between 1781 and 1783, the respective dates of the new registration of her chapels and the licensing of her preachers. When the Countess died in 1791, five different preachers throughout England spoke funeral sermons in her honor. The Connexion, willed to four trustees, was placed in the care of the Lady Ann Erskine, the Countess's right-hand woman.

50. Marrant is referring to the American Revolution (1775-1783).

51. At this point, the text of the two 1785 "editions," the 1815 Leeds imprint, and Farncombe's London imprint continues with "and yet, reader, my soul was got into a declining state. Don't forget our Lord's exhortation, 'What I say unto you, I say unto all, Watch.—,'" which is immediately followed by "In those troublesome times, I was pressed on board the Scorpion sloop of war. . . ." Compare this version to that on our p. 94, where Marrant incorporates aspects of this material *after* introducing his descriptions of a cruel slave whipping and young Mary Scott's conversion. See also note 59 below.

52. Here the London imprints of 1788 and 1802 and the Brighton imprint of 1829 include the first excerpt listed in note 51 above. The texts then continue with the paragraph beginning "About this time I was an eye-witness of the remarkable conversion of a child seven and a half years old. . ." (see our p. 93).

Among those "Gospel ministers" with whom Marrant worshipped may have been two black men, Thomas and David, associated with the Methodist movement during this time (that is, the mid-1770s). Thomas, a slave of a Charleston preacher named John Edwards, actively preached in the area. David was a zealous Huntingdonian preacher who, sent from England to the Southern colonies, roused assembled blacks by proclaiming, "the Jews of old treated the Gentiles as Dogs & I am informed the People of this Country use those of my Complection as such." To avoid lynching, David fled secretly to George Whitefield's black orphanage in Georgia and eventually returned to England. David may have been the first to tell Marrant about the Countess of Huntingdon and her Connexion. See pp. 24-25 of Philip D. Morgan, "Black Life in Eighteenth-Century Charleston," bound copy of a colloquium given on 29 February 1984 at The Institute of Early American History and Culture, The College of William and Mary, Williamsburg, VA.

53. Before black slaves could be baptized in the Anglican church, they had to be able to repeat a few key tenets of the faith, including the Lord's Prayer, the Ten Commandments, and the Catechism in the Book of Common Prayer.

54. 1 Peter 5:8 identifies the devil as a roaring lion: "Be sober, be vigilant; because your adversary the devil, as a roaring lion, walketh about, seeking whom he may devour."

55. Throughout the South, black slaves often met clandestinely in the middle of the night, a tradition initiated by their African forebears, who gathered in secret to convey to their American-born children the rituals essential to their cultural heritage.

56. Mary Scott's conversion and death are typical of the examples found within James Janeway's A Token for Children: Being An Exact Account of the Conversion, Holy and Exemplary Lives, and Joyful Deaths, of several young Children (London, 1672). Janeway's "serious," or spiritual, children engage solely in reading the Bible or praying, both secretly and openly; often prophesy their date of death; and quote Scripture from their death bed to their gathered families until they "fall asleep"—that is, die—in the "Faith," "Love," "Bosom," or "Arms" of Jesus.

57. In Revelation, Christ is figured as the Lamb of the New Jerusalem, the "pretty town" that Mary mentions, where all that glitters is gold. See Revelation 21-22.

58. The 14-gun British war sloop Scorpion was stationed off the Carolina coast between 12 November 1775 and 2 October 1776, constantly cruising the waters between Cape Fear River in North Carolina and the Charleston vicinity of South Carolina to "prevent the Colonies having improper Communication with each other, and the Rebels from receiving Supplies of Ammunition." It also provided support for General Henry Clinton's first expedition to Charleston in 1776. Since Vice-Admiral Samuel Graves forbade the sloop "to remain in harbour longer than shall be absolutely necessary to victual and water," Marrant was probably impressed by a small group of seamen on a mission ashore sometime between the dates mentioned above. See Graves's orders to Scorpion captain John Tollemache in Naval Documents of the American Revolution, 9 vols. (Washington, D.C.: Naval Historical Center, Department of the Navy, 1964-1986), vol. 1, pp. 1200-1201.

It is not surprising that Marrant is impressed into the Royal Navy because of his musical skills. According to naval historian N. A. M. Rodger, "music and danc-

ing were a part of life in wardroom and mess throughout the [Royal] Navy. . . .
Some ships had bands of a sort, and privateers, for recruiting purposes, went out
of their way to provide music." See his book *The Wooden World: An Anatomy of
the Georgian Navy* (London: Collins, 1986), p. 44.

59. Mark 13:37. Compare this sentence with the excerpt discussed in note 51.

60. The siege of Charleston (11 February-12 May 1780) was the worst American
defeat of the Revolutionary War. General Henry Clinton (1738?-1795),
Commander in Chief of the British forces based in New York, arrived off the
Carolinas by 1 February with over 7,800 men, a number that had climbed to
14,000 by 11 April. After months of fighting the British successfully seized Ft.
Moultrie on 6 May. American general Benjamin Lincoln (1733-1810) signed the
Articles of Capitulation on 11 May and formally surrendered the next day. The
British, suffering only 255 casualties, took over 5,600 prisoners and seized or
destroyed eight American and several French ships.

61. Marrant's note: "Though it is unusual for Indians to have a horse, yet the king
accompanied the general on the present successful occasion riding on horseback.—If the king wished to serve me, there was no opportunity; the Town being
taken on Friday afternoon, Saturday an express arrived from the commander in
chief at New York, for a large detachment, or the town would fall into the hands
of the Americans, which hurried us away on Sunday morning."

62. See Jonah 2. Imprisoned in the belly of a whale, Jonah entreats the Lord for deliverance and is vomited upon dry land. Marrant's cry to God for help amid perils
at sea echoes numerous cries found in the evangelical "mariner's literature" that
spans from the *Book of Common Prayer* to James Janeway's *A Token for Mariners,
Containing Many Famous and Wonderful Instances of God's Providence in Sea Dangers
and Deliverances, in Mercifully preserving the Lives of his Poor Creatures, when, in
Humane Probability, at the Point of Perishing by Shipwrack, Famine, or other Accidents*
(London, pre-1708) and John Ryther's *A Plat for Mariners; or, The Seamen's
Preacher. Delivered in several Sermons upon Jonah's Voyage* (London, 1672).
According to Ryther, the imperiled cry "speaks the earnestness of [the mariners']
Spirits in calling upon God" (p. 81) and thus reflects their kinship with David,
who in Psalms 130:1 cries to the Lord "out of the depths" of his anguish.

63. Dogger Bank is an extensive sand bank, covered by shallow water, in the central
North Sea between England and Denmark. It has fisheries. See also note 108 in
the Equiano section of this volume.

64. Marrant's note: "This action was on the 5th of August, 1781." On 20 December
1780 Britain declared war against the Netherlands for supplying arms and naval
stores to the American colonies, France, and Spain, and also for collaborating with
the League of Armed Neutrality, an association created by Catherine II of Russia
to protect neutral commerce against blatant British aggression at sea. During the
war Vice-Admiral Hyde Parker (1714-1782) and a dilapidated fleet were assigned
to the North Sea to protect British maritime traffic from the Dutch. While escort-
ing a large convoy of merchant ships across the North Sea, Parker's fleet met a similar Dutch fleet, commanded by Rear-Admiral J. A. Zoutman, off Dogger Bank.
Heavy battle ensued, but nearly four hours of fighting ended in a draw.

On the *Princess Amelia*, 19 men were killed, including the ship's captain and the gunner; Marrant was among the 56 wounded. The ship itself suffered extensive damage to the hull; and its bowsprit and two of its masts were crushed. The other six ships of the line were equally battered. British casualties totaled 104 men killed, 339 men wounded. On the Dutch side, 142 men were killed, and 403 were wounded. For more information on this battle, see Robert Beatson's *Naval and Military Memoirs of Great Britain from 1727 to 1783*, 6 vols. (London: Printed for Longman, Hurst, Rees and Orme et al.; Edinburgh: A. Constable and Co.; Aberdeen: A. Brown, 1804), vol. 6, pp. 315-17.

65. Plymouth is a British port and naval base at the western end of the English Channel in Devon county. In 1758 Equiano was assigned for a brief time to a ship anchored there (see p. 204 of this volume).

66. The London imprints of 1788 and 1802 and the Brighton imprint of 1829 include a footnote here that does not appear in the undated "fourth edition": "About three years; it might be a few weeks over or under." Moreover, they also reproduce two notices—one from Aldridge, the other from the "respectable and pious merchant" John Marsden—not contained in the undated "fourth edition." Although the content of the notices is virtually the same in these imprints, the language of the 1788 version, reproduced here, corresponds most closely with the language of the imprint reprinted in this volume:

> SINCE MR. MARRANT's arrival at Nova-Scotia, several letters have been received from himself by different persons, and some by Mr. ALDRIDGE, the Editor of this Narrative; from which it appears, that Mr. MARRANT has travelled through that province, preaching the Gospel, and not without success; that he has undergone much fatigue, and passed through many dangers; that he has visited the Indians in their Wigwams, who, he relates, were disposed to hear and receive the Gospel.—This is the substance of the letters transmitted by him to the Editor above-mentioned.
>
> [—William Aldridge]

❇ ❇ ❇

> London, August 16, 1785
> MR. *John Marrant liv'd with us about 3 years, which he did with honesty and sobriety—he feared God, and had a desire to save his soul before he ever came to live with us;—he shewed himself to be such while he lived with us, by attending the means of Grace diligently, and by being tender hearted to the poor, by giving them money and victuals if he had left himself none. He left us with no misunderstanding whatever, about April last.*
> *This is nothing but the truth.*
>
> | | (Signed) |
> |------------------------|----------------------|
> | Cotton-Merchant | John Marsden, |
> | No. 38, Dowgate-Hill | H. Marsden. |

67. Here Marrant quotes from Romans 9:2-3, adapted for his own purposes. Upon embarking on his evangelical mission to the newly established black community in Nova Scotia, he no doubt wished to place himself in the spiritual lineage of Paul. A similar quotation from Paul 9:2-3 is used by Jupiter Hammon at the beginning of his last known work, *An Address to the Negroes of the State of New-York* (New York: Printed by Carroll and Patterson, 1787).

68. Spafields Chapel, built next to the Countess of Huntingdon's London home, opened in 1777.

69. Compare the version printed in all other imprints we have seen: "I used to exercise my gifts on a Monday evening in prayer and exhortation, and was approved of, and ordained at Bath." Reverend Thomas Wills, assisted by the eminent Reverend William Romaine (see note 177 in the Equiano section of this volume), ordained Marrant a minister on 15 May 1785 in the Connexion's chapel in Bath. Wills (1740-1802), an extremely popular Methodist preacher, was the curate at Anglican St. Agnes's church in Cornwall before he resigned in 1779 to be the Countess of Huntingdon's chaplain; he left the Connexion in 1788, but thereafter remained friendly with the Countess, preaching one of the five funeral sermons given for her upon her death in 1791.

70. This paragraph alludes to Revelation 7:14, 17:15, 15:3, and 11:15. Revelation 15:3 is the theme of a hymn from the Countess of Huntingdon's hymnbook (1780).

71. Joshua 15:19 speaks of "the upper springs, and the lower springs," which, in verse 20, are "the inheritance of the tribe of the children of Judah." Marrant also refers to Exodus 3, in which Yahweh appears to Moses in the form of a burning bush.

   The last paragraph and Watts's Psalm 107 only appear in the undated "fourth edition." Marrant's address and the date also change here. All other imprints list him at London's "Prescot-street, No. 60, July 18, 1785."

A Sermon Preached on the 24th Day of June 1789,
Being the Festival of Saint John the Baptist,
at the Request of the Right Worshipful the Grand Master
Prince Hall, and the Rest of the Brethren of the
African Lodge of the Honorable Society of
Free and Accepted Masons in Boston

A SERMON.

ROMANS xii. 10.

Be kindly affectioned one to another, with brotherly
love, in honour preferring one another.[1]

In this chapter, from whence my text is taken, we find the Apostle Paul
labouring with the Romans to press on them the great duties of
Brotherly Love.

By an entire submission and conformity to the will of God, whereby
are given to us exceeding great and precious promises, that by these we
might be made partakers of the divine nature, having escaped the corruption that is in the world through lust—That being all members of the
body of Christ with the Church, we ought to apply the gifts we have
received to the advantage of our brethren, those of us especially who are
called to any office in the church, by discharging it with zeal and
integrity and benevolence, which is the most important duty, and com-
prehends all the rest, and particularly the following—which the apostle
here sets down—which are to love one another sincerely, to be ready to
all good offices—to sympathize in the good or evil that befals our

brethren, to comfort and assist those that are in affliction, and to live together in a spirit of humility, peace and unity. Benevolence does yet further oblige christians to love and bless those who hate them and injure them, to endeavour to have peace with all men, to abstain from revenge, and to render them good for evil; these are the most essential duties of the religion we profess; and we deserve the name of christians no further than we sincerely practise them to the glory of God and the good of our own souls and bodies, and the good of all mankind.

But first, my Brethren, let us learn to pray to God through our Lord Jesus Christ for understanding, that we may know ourselves; for without this we can never be fit for the society of man, we must learn to guide ourselves before we can guide others, and when we have done this we shall understand the apostle Romans xii. 16. "Be not wise in your own conceits," for when we get wise in ourselves we are then too wise for God, and consequently not fit for the society of man — I mean the christian part of mankind — Let all my brethren Masons consider what they are called to — May God grant you an humble heart to fear God and love his commandments; then and only then you will in sincerity love your brethren: And you will be enabled, as in the words of my text, to be kindly affectioned one to another, with brotherly love in honour preferring one another. Therefore, with the apostle Paul, I beseech you therefore brethren, by the mercies of God, that ye present your bodies a living sacrifice, holy, acceptable unto God, which is your reasonable service — let love be without dissimulation, abhor that which is evil, cleave to that which is good. These and many other duties are required of us as christians, every one of which are like so many links of a chain, which when joined together make one complete member of Christ; this we profess to believe as Christians and as Masons. — — I shall stop here with the introduction, which brings me to the points I shall endeavour to prove. — —

First, the anciency of Masonry, that being done, will endeavour to prove all other titles we have a just right as Masons to claim — namely, honourable, free and accepted: To do this I must have recourse to the creation of this our world — After the Grand Architect of the Universe[2] had framed the heavens for beauty and delight for the beings he was then about to make, he then called the earth to appear out of darkness, saying, let there be light, and it was so; he also set the sun, moon and stars in the firmament of heaven, for the delight of his creatures — he then created the fishes of the sea, the fowls of the air, then the beasts of the earth after their various kinds, and God blessed them.[3]

Thus all things were in their order prepared for the most excellent accomplished piece of the visible creation, Man. — The forming this most excellent creature Man, was the close of the creation, so it was peculiar to him to have a solemn consultation and decree about his making, and God said, let us make Man.[4] — Seneca says, that man is not a work huddled over in haste, and done without fore-thinking and great consideration, for man is the greatest and most stupendous work of God.[5] — Man hath not only a body in common with all inferior animals, but into his body was infused a soul of a far more noble nature and make — a rational principle to act according to the designs of his creation; that is, to contemplate the works of God, to admire his perfections, to worship him, to live as becomes one who received his excellent being from him, to converse with his fellow creatures that are of his own order, to maintain mutual love and society, and to serve God in consort. Man is a wonderful creature, and not unde[ser]vedly said to be a little world, a world within himself, and containing whatever is found in the Creator.[6] — In him is the spiritual and material nature of God, the reasonableness of Angels, the sensative power of brutes, the vegetative life of plants, and the virtue of all the elements he holds converse with in both worlds. — Thus man is crowned with glory and honour, he is the most remarkable workmanship of God. And is man such a noble creature and made to converse with his fellow men that are of his own order, to maintain mutual love and society, and to serve God in consort with each other? — then what can these God-provoking wretches think, who despise their fellow men, as tho' they were not of the same species with themselves, and would if in their power deprive them of the blessings and comforts of this life, which God in his bountiful goodness, hath freely given to all his creatures to improve and enjoy? Surely such monsters never came out of the hand of God in such a forlorn condition. — — Which brings me to consider the fall of man; and the Lord God took the man and put him into the garden of Eden, to dress it and to keep it, and freely to eat of every tree of the garden; here was his delightful employ and bountiful wages, and but one tree out of all that vast number he was forbidden to eat of. Concerning this garden, there have been different opinions about it by the learned, where it was, but the most of them agree that the four rivers parted or divided the four quarters of the world. The first was Pison, that was it which compasseth the land of Havilah;[7] this river Pison is called by some the Phasis, or Phasi Tigris, it runs (they say) by that Havilah whither the Amalekites fled, see I Sam. xv. 7. and divides it from the country of Susianna, and at last falls into the Persian Gulf, saith Galtruchius[8] and others; but from the opinions of christian writers, who hold, that Havilah is India, and Pison the river Ganges. This was first asserted by Josephus, and from him Eustubius, Jerom,[9] and most of the fathers received it, and not without good reason; for Moses here adds, as a mark to know the place by, that there is gold, and the gold of that land is good; now it is confessed by all, that India is the most noted for gold, and of the best sort. It is added again, a note whereby to discover that place, that there is bdellium and the onyx stone—and India is famous for precious stones and pearls.— The name of the second river is Gihon, the same in it which compasseth the whole land of Ethiopia (or Cush as it is in the original) there is reason to believe that this Gihon is the river of Nile, as the forenamed Josephus and most of the ancient writers of the church hold, and by the help of the river Nile, Paradise did as it were border upon Egypt, which is the principal part of the African Ethiopia, which the ancient writers hold is meant there[.] The name of the third river is Hiddekel, that is it which goeth toward the east of Assyria, ver. 14. That it was a river belonging to Babylon is clear from Dan. x. 4; this is concluded to be the river Tygris, which divides Mesopotamia from Assyria, and goeth along with Euphrates, this being the great middle channel that ran through Edom or Babylon, and may be thought to take its name from its fructifying quality.[10] These are the four grand land marks which the all-wise and gracious God was pleased to draw as the bounds and habitation of all nations which he was about to settle in this world; if so, what nation or people dare, without highly displeasing and provoking that God to pour down his judgments upon them.—I say dare to despise or tyrannize over their lives or liberties, or incroach on their lands, or to inslave their bodies? God hath and ever will visit such a nation or people as this.—Envy and pride are the leading lines to all the miseries that mankind have suffered from the beginning of the world to this present day. What was it but these that turned the devil out of heaven into a hell of misery, but envy and pride?—Was it not the same spirit that moved him to tempt our first parents to sin against so holy and just a God, who had but just (if I may use the expression) turned his back from crowning Adam with honour and glory?—But envy at his prosperity hath taken the crown of glory from his head, and hath made us his posterity miserable.—What was it but this that made Cain murder his brother, whence is it but from these that our modern Cains call us Africans the sons of Cain?[11] (We admit it if you please) and we will find from him and his sons Masonry began, after the fall of his father. Altho' Adam, when placed in the garden, God would not suffer him to be idle and unemployed in that happy state of innocence, but set him to dress and to keep that choice piece of earth; here he was to employ his mind as well as exercise his body; here he was to contemplate and study God's work; here he was to enjoy God, himself and the whole world, to submit himself wholly to his divine conduct, to conform all his actions to the will of his Maker; but by his sudden fall he lost that good will that he owed to his God, and for some time lost the study of God's works; but no doubt he afterwards taught his sons the art of Masonry; for how else could Cain after so much trouble and perplexity have time to study the art of building a city, as he did on the east of Eden, Gen. iv. 17. and without doubt he teached his sons the art, ver. 20, 21. —

But to return, bad as Cain was, yet God took not from him his faculty of studying architecture, arts and sciences — his sons also were endued with the same spirit, and in some convenient place no doubt they met and communed with each other for instruction. It seems that the allwise God put this into the hearts of Cain's family thus to employ themselves, to divert their minds from musing on their father's murder[12] and the woful curse God had pronounced on him, as we don't find any more of Cain's complaints after this.

Similar to this we have in the 6 Gen. 12 & 13, that God saw that all men had corrupted their way, and that their hearts were only evil continually; and 14, 15, 16 verses, the great Architect of the universe gives Noah a compleat plan of the ark and sets him to work, and his sons as assistants, like deputy and two grand wardens. One thing is well known, our enemies themselves being judges, that in whatsoever nation or kingdom in the whole world where Masonry abounds most, there hath been and still are the most peaceable subjects, cheerfully conforming to the laws of that country in which they reside, always willing to submit to their magistrates and rulers, and where Masonry most abounds, arts and sciences, whether mechanical or liberal, all of them have a mighty tendency to the delight and benefit of mankind; therefore we need not question but the allwise God by putting this into our hearts intended, as another end of our creation, that we should not only live happily ourselves, but be likewise mutually assisting to each other. Again, it is not only good and beneficial in a time of peace, in a nation or kingdom, but in a time of war, for that brotherly love that cements us together by the bonds of friendship, no wars or tumults can separate; for in the heat of war if a brother sees another in distress he will relieve him some way or other, and kindly receive him as a brother, prefering him before all others, according to the Apostle's exhortation in my text, as also a similar instance you have I Kings, x. from 31st to 38th verse,[13] where you find Benhadad in great distress, having lost a numerous army in two battles, after his great boasting, and he himself forced to hide himself in a chamber, and sends a message to Ahab king of Israel to request only his life as a captive; but behold the brotherly love of a Mason! no sooner was the message delivered, but he cries out in a rapture — is he alive — he is my brother! Every Mason knows that they were both of the craft, and also the messengers.[14] Thus far may suffice for the anciency of this grand art; as for the honour of it — it is a society which God himself has been pleased to honour ever since he breathed into Adam the breath of life,[15] and hath from generation to generation inspired men with wisdom, and planned out and given directions how they should build, and with what materials. And first, Noah in building the ark wherein he was saved, while God in his justice was pleased to destroy the unbelieving world of mankind. The first thing Noah did upon his landing was to build an altar to offer sacrifice to that great God which had delivered him out of so great a deluge; God accepted the sacrifice and blessed him, and as they journeyed from the east towards the west, they found a plain in the land of Shinar and dwelt there, and his sons.[16]

Nimrod the son of Cush, the son of Ham, first founded the Babylonian monarchy, and kept possession of the plains, and founded the first great empire at Babylon, and became grand master of all Masons, he built many splendid cities in Shinar,[17] and under him flourished those learned Mathematicians, whose successors were styled in the book of Daniel, Magi, or wise men, for their superior knowledge. The migration from Shinar commenced fifty three years after they began to build the tower,[18] and one hundred and fifty four years after the flood, and they went off at various times and travelled east, west, north and south, with their mighty skill, and found the use of it in settling their colonies; and from Shinar the arts were carried to distant parts of the earth, notwithstanding the confusion of languages, which gave rise to Masons faculty and universal practice of conversing without speaking, and of knowing each other by signs and tokens; they settled the dispersion in case any of them should meet in distant parts of the world who had been before in Shinar. Thus the earth was again planted and replenished with Masons the second son of Ham carried into Egypt; there he built the city of Heliopolis — Thebes with an hundred gates[19] — they built also the statue of Sphynx, whose head was 120 feet round, being reckoned the first or earliest of the seven wonders of arts. Shem the second son of Noah remained at Ur of the Chaldees in Shinar, with his father and his great grandson Heber,[20] where they lived in private and died in peace: But Shem's offspring travelled into the south and east of Asia, and their offspring propagated the science and the art as far as China and Japan.

While Noah, Shem and Heber diverted themselves at Ur in mathematical studies, teaching Peleg the father of Rehu, of Sereg, Nachor, and Terah, father of Abram, a learned race of mathematicians and geometricians; thus Abram, born two years after the death of Noah, had learned well the science and the art before the God of glory called him to travel from Ur of the Chaldees, but a famine soon forced him down to Egypt;[21] the descendants of Abram sojourned in Egypt, as shepherds still lived in tents, practised very little of the art of architecture till about eighty years before their Exodus, when by the overruling hand of providence they were trained up to the building with stone and brick, in order to make them expert Masons before they possessed the promised land;[22] after Abram left Charran 430 years, Moses marched out of Egypt at the head of 600,000 Hebrews, males, for whose sakes God divided the red sea to let them pass through Arabia to Canaan. God was pleased to inspire their grand master Moses, and Joshua his deputy, with wisdom of heart;[23] so the next year they raised the curious tabernacle or tent; God having called Moses up into the mount and gave him an exact pattern of it, and charges him to make it exactly to that pattern,[24] and withal gave him the two tables of stone; these he broke at the foot of the mount; God gave him orders to hew two more himself, after the likeness of the former. God did not only inspire Moses with wisdom to undertake the oversight of the great work, but he also inspired Bezaleel with knowledge to do all manner of cunning workmanship for it.[25] — Having entered upon the jewish dispensation, I must beg leave still to take a little notice of the Gentile nations, for we have but these two nations now to speak upon, namely, the Gentiles and the Jews, till I come to the Christian æra.

The Canaanites, Phenicians and Sidonians, were very expert in the sacred architecture of stone, who being a people of a happy genius and frame of mind, made many great discoveries and improvements of the sciences, as well as in point of learning. The glass of Sidon, the purple of Tyre, and the exceeding fine linnen they wove, were the product of their own country and their own invention; and for their extraordinary skill in working of metals, in hewing of timber and stone; in a word, for their perfect knowledge of what was solid in architecture, it need but be remembered that they had in erecting and decorating of the temple at Jerusalem, than which nothing can more redound to their honour, or give a clearer idea of what this one building must have been. — Their fame was such for their just taste, design, and ingenious inventions, that whatever was elegant, great or pleasing, was distinguished by way of excellence with the epithet of Sidonian.[26] — The famous temple of Jupiter Hammon, in Libian Africa, was erected, that stood till demolished by the first Christians in those parts;[27] but I must pass over many other cities and temples built by the Gentiles.

God having inspired Solomon with wisdom and understanding, he as grand master and undertaker, under God the great architect, sends to Hiram king of Tyre, and after acquainting him of his purpose of building a house unto the name of the Lord his God, he sends to him for some of his people to go with some of his, to Mount Lebanon, to cut down and hew cedar trees, as his servants understood it better than his own, and moreover he requested him to send him a man that was cunning, to work in gold and in silver, and in brass, iron, purple, crimson and in blue, and that had skill to engrave with the cunning men, and he sent him Hiram, his name-sake; this Hiram, God was pleased to inspire with wisdom and understanding to undertake, and strength to go through the most curious piece of workmanship that was ever done on earth.[28] — Thus Solomon as grand master, and Hiram as his deputy, carried on and finished that great work of the temple of the living God, the inside work of which, in many instances as well as the tabernacle, resembles men's bodies; but this is better explained in a well filled lodge; but this much I may venture to say, that our blessed Saviour compared his sacred body to a temple, when he said, John ii. 19. Destroy this temple and I will raise it up again in three days; and the Apostle, I Peter, i. 14 says, that shortly he should put off this tabernacle.[29] I could show also that one grand end and design of Masonry is to build up the temple that Adam destroyed in Paradise — but I forbear. Thus hath God honoured the Craft, or Masons, by inspiring men with wisdom to carry on his stupendous works.

It is worthy our notice to consider the number of Masons employed in the work of the Temple: Exclusive of the two Grand Masters, there were 300 princes, or rulers, 3300 overseers of the work, 80000 stone squarers, setters, layers or builders, being able and ingenious Crafts, and 30000 appointed to work in Lebanon, 10000 of which every month, under Adoniram, who was the Grand Warden;[30] all the free Masons employed in the work of the Temple was 119,600, besides 70,000 men who carried burdens, who were not numbered among Masons;[31] these were partitioned into certain Lodges, although they were of different nations and different colours, yet were they in perfect harmony among themselves, and strongly cemented in brotherly love and friendship, till the glorious Temple of Jehovah was finished, and the cape-stone[32] was celebrated with great joy—Having finished all that Solomon had to do, they departed unto their several homes, and carried with them the high taste of architecture to the different parts of the world, and built many other temples and cities in the Gentile nations, under the direction of many wise and learned and royal Grand Masters, as Nebuchadnezar over Babylon—Cyrus over the Medes and Persians—Alexander over the Macedonians—Julius Cæsar over Rome,[33] and a great number more I might mention of crowned heads of the Gentile nations who were of the Craft, but this may suffice.—I must just mention Herod the Great,[34] before I come to the state of Masonry from the birth of our Saviour Jesus Christ.—This Herod was the greatest builder of his day, the patron and Grand Master of many Lodges; he being in the full enjoyment of peace and plenty, formed a design of new building the Temple of Jerusalem. The Temple built by the Jews after the captivity was greatly decayed, being 500 years standing, he proposed to the people that he would not take it down till he had all the materials ready for the new, and accordingly he did so, then he took down the old one and built a new one.—Josephus describes this Temple as a most admirable and magnificent fabric of marble, and the finest building upon earth.—Tiberius having attained the imperial throne, became an encourager of the fraternity.[35]

Which brings me to consider their freedom, and that will appear not only from their being free when accepted, but they have a free intercourse with all Lodges over the whole terrestial globe; wherever arts flourish, a man hath a free right (having a recommendation) to visit his brethren, and they are bound to accept him;[36] these are the laudable bonds that unite Free Masons together in one indissoluble fraternity—thus in every nation he finds a friend, and in every climate he may find a house—this it is to be kindly affectioned one to another, with brotherly love, in honour preferring one another.

Which brings me to answer some objections which are raised against the Masons, and the first is the irregular lives of the professors of it.—It must be admitted there are some persons who, careless of their own reputation, will consequently disregard the most instructive lessons—Some, I am sorry to say, are sometimes to be found among us; many by

yielding to vice and intemperance, frequently not only disgrace themselves, but reflect dishonour on Masonry in general; but let it be known
that these apostates[37] are unworthy of their trust, and that whatever
name or designation they assume, they are in reality no Masons: But if
the wicked lives of men were admitted as an argument against the religion which they profess, Christianity itself, with all its divine beauties,
would be exposed to censure; but they say there can be no good in
Masonry because we keep it a secret, and at the same time these very
men themselves will not admit an apprentice into their craft whatever,
without enjoining secresy on him, before they receive him as an apprentice; and yet blame us for not revealing our's — Solomon says, Prov. xi.
12, 13.[38] He that is void of wisdom despiseth his neighbour, but a man
of understanding holdeth his peace; a tale-bearer revealeth secrets, but
he that is of a faithful spirit concealeth the matter. Thus I think I have
answered these objections. I shall conclude the whole by addressing the
Brethren of the African Lodge.

Dear and beloved brethren, I don't know how I can address you better than in the words of Nehemiah (who had just received liberty from
the king Artaxerxes, letters and a commission, or charter, to return to
Jerusalem) that thro the good hand of our God upon us we are here this
day to celebrate the festival of St. John[39] — as members of that honorable society of free and accepted Masons — as by charter we have a
right to do[40] — remember your obligations you are under to the great
God, and to the whole family of mankind in the world — do all that in you
lies to relieve the needy, support the weak, mourn with your fellow
men in distress, do good to all men as far as God shall give you ability,
for they are all your brethren, and stand in need of your help more or
less — for he that loves every body need fear nobody: But you must
remember you are under a double obligation to the brethren of the craft
of all nations on the face of the earth, for there is no party spirit in
Masonry;[41] let them make parties who will, and despise those they
would make, if they could, a species below them, and as not made of the
same clay with themselves; but if you study the holy book of God, you
will there find that you stand on the level not only with them, but with
the greatest kings on the earth, as Men and as Masons,[42] and these
truly great men are not ashamed of the meanest of their brethren.
Ancient history will produce some of the Africans who were truly good,
wise, and learned men, and as eloquent as any other nation whatever,[43]
though at present many of them in slavery, which is not a just cause of
our being despised; for if we search history, we shall not find a nation

on earth but has at some period or other of their existence been in slavery, from the Jews down to the English Nation, under many Emperors, Kings and Princes; for we find in the life of Gregory, about the year 580, a man famous for his charity, that on a time when many merchants were met to sell their commodities at Rome, it happened that he passing by saw many young boys with white bodies, fair faces, beautiful countenances and lovely hair, set forth for sale; he went to the merchant their owner and asked him from what country he brought them; he answered from Britain, where the inhabitants were generally so beautiful. Gregory (sighing) said, alas! for grief, that such fair faces should be under the power of the prince of darkness, and that such bodies should have their souls void of the grace of God.[44]

I shall endeavour to draw a few inferences on this discourse by way of application. —

My dear Brethren, let us pray to God for a benevolent heart, that we may be enabled to pass through the various stages of this life with reputation, and that great and infinite Jehovah, who overrules the grand fabric of nature, will enable us to look backward with pleasure, and forward with confidence — and in the hour of death, and in the day of judgment, the well grounded hope of meeting with that mercy from our Maker which we have ever been ready to shew to others, will refresh us with the most solid comfort, and fill us with the most unspeakable joy.

And should not this learn us that new and glorious commandment of our Lord Jesus Christ to his disciples, when he urges it to them in these words — Love the Lord thy God with all thy heart, and thy neighbour as thyself. — Our Lord repeats and recommends this as the most indispensable duty and necessary qualification of his disciples, saying, hereby shall all men know that ye are my disciples, if ye have love one to another. — And we are expressly told by the Apostle, that charity, or universal love and friendship, is the end of the commandment.[45]

Shall this noble and unparalleled example fail of its due influence upon us — shall it not animate our hearts with a like disposition of benevolence and mercy, shall it not raise our emulation and provoke our ambition — to go and do likewise.

Let us then beware of such a selfishness as pursues pleasure at the expence of our neighbour's happiness, and renders us indifferent to his peace and welfare; and such a self-love is the parent of disorder and the source of all those evils that divide the world and destroy the peace of mankind; whereas christian charity — universal love and friendship — benevolent affections and social feelings, unite and knit men together, render them happy in themselves and useful to one another, and recommend them to the esteem of a gracious God, through our Lord Jesus Christ.

The few inferences that have been made on this head must be to you, my worthy brethren, of great comfort, that every one may see the propriety of a discourse on brotherly love before a society of free Masons — who knows their engagements as men and as christians, have superadded the bonds of this ancient and honourable society — a society founded upon such friendly and comprehensive principles, that men of all nations and languages, or sects of religion, are and may be admitted and received as members, being recommended as persons of a virtuous character.[46]

Religion and virtue, and the continuance and standing of this excellent society in the world — its proof of the wisdom of its plan — and the force of its principles and conduct has, on many occasions, been not a little remarkable — as well among persons of this, as among those of different countries, who go down to the sea and occupy their business in the great waters, they know how readily people of this institution can open a passage to the heart of a brother; and in the midst of war, like a universal language, is understood by men of all countries — and no wonder. — If the foundation has been thus laid in wisdom by the great God, then let us go on with united hearts and hands to build and improve upon this noble foundation — let love and sincere friendship in necessity instruct our ignorance, conceal our infirmities, reprove our errors, reclaim us from our faults — let us rejoice with them that rejoice, and weep with those that weep[47] — share with each other in our joys, and sympathize in our troubles.

And let the character of our enemies be to resent affronts — but our's to generously remit and forgive the greatest; their's to blacken the reputation and blast the credit of their brethren — but our's to be tender of their good name, and to cast a vail over all their failings; their's to blow the coals of contention and sow the seeds of strife among men — but our's to compose their differences and heal up their breaches.

In a word, let us join with the words of the Apostle John in the 19th chapter of Revelations, and after these things I heard a great voice of much people in heaven, saying, Alleluia, salvation and glory, and honour, and power, unto the Lord our God; for true and righteous are his judgments — — and the four and twenty elders, and the four beasts, fell down and worshipped God that sat on the throne, saying, Amen; Alleluia; and a voice came out of the throne, saying, praise our God, all ye his servants, and ye that fear him, both small and great.[48]

To conclude the whole, let it be remembered, that all that is outward, whether opinions, rites or ceremonies, cannot be of importance in regard to eternal salvation, any further than they have a tendency to produce inward righteousness and goodness—pure, holy, spiritual and benevolent affections can only fit us for the kingdom of heaven; and therefore the cultivation of such must needs be the essence of Christ's religion—God of his infinite mercy grant that we may make this true use of it. Unhappily, too many Christians, so called, take their religion not from the declarations of Christ and his apostles, but from the writings of those they esteem learned.— —But I am to say, it is from the New-Testament only, not from any books whatsoever, however piously wrote, that we ought to seek what is the essence of Christ's religion; and it is from this fountain I have endeavoured to give my hearers the idea of Christianity in its spiritual dress, free from any human mixtures—if we have done this wisely we may expect to enjoy our God in the world that is above— —in which happy place, my dear brethren, we shall all, I hope, meet at that great day, when our great Grand Master shall sit at the head of the great and glorious Lodge in heaven—where we shall all meet to part no more for ever and ever—Amen.

NOTES

1. Marrant's two opening paragraphs are saturated with allusions to and quotations from Romans 12.
2. In Masonic lore, the Grand Architect of the Universe is God, the creator of Freemasonry. As Grand Master Henry Price of Boston's St. John's Grand Lodge said on 23 November 1768, God "incorporate[s] our Hearts with Unity, Love, Strength, and Wisdom, to Contrive, Conduct and Support the establishing in the three Grand Principles, Brotherly Love, Relief and Truth." See *The Proceedings of the Grand Lodge of Massachusetts Free and Accepted Masons 1733-1792* (Boston: Grand Lodge of Massachusetts, 1895), p. 153.
3. See Genesis 1:3, 16-17, 20-25.
4. Genesis 1:26.
5. Seneca "the Younger" or "the Philosopher" (ca. 4 B.C.–A.D. 65) wrote *Epistulae Morales*, which was approved and made use of by early Christian writers. St. Jerome and others believed that Seneca had corresponded with St. Paul.
6. The concept of man as a world within himself, reflective of God's outer cosmos, is a philosophical commonplace. Compare the first two lines of John Donne's *Holy Sonnet 5*: "I am a little world made cunningly / Of elements, and an angelic sprite."
7. Genesis 2:15-17, 10-11.
8. Petrus Galtruchius is the Latin name of Pierre Gautruche (1602-1681), author of *The Poetical History: Being a Compleat Collection of All the Stories Necessary for a Perfect Understanding of the Greek and Latin Poets and Other Ancient Authors* (pre-1669), a book of ancient mythology first translated into English from the French in 1671. Marrant may be referring to information in this volume or, alternatively,

in Gautruche's *L'Histoire Sainte, avec l'explication controversée de la religion* (pre-1668), a history of Biblical events that was reprinted throughout the late seventeenth and early eighteenth centuries.

9. Flavius Josephus was a Jewish historian (ca. A.D. 37–after A.D. 93). Eusebius was a Greek Christian writer and bishop in Palestine (ca. A.D. 260–ca. A.D. 340). Jerome was a Latin father of the Church (ca. A.D. 347–420).

10. Marrant refers to Genesis 2:11-14. Verse 14 identifies Hiddekel (the Tigris) and the Euphrates as the third and fourth rivers originating in the Garden of Eden. "Euphrates" is, according to William Smith's *Bible Dictionary* (New York, n.d.), "probably a word of Aryan origin, signifying 'the good and abounding river'": thus Marrant relates the river's name to "its fructifying quality."

11. See the introduction to this volume, p. 12.

12. That is, their father's slaying of Abel.

13. Either Marrant or the printer makes an error here; see instead I Kings 20:29-34.

14. See I Kings 20:32-34. In verse 34, Benhadad, king of Syria, and Ahab, king of Israel, make a peace treaty, which Benhadad seals by saying, "thou shall make streets for thee in Damascus" (the Syrian capital); it is presumably this line that Marrant interprets in a Masonic sense.

15. Genesis 2:7.

16. For the entire story of Noah and the Ark, see Genesis 6-9:17. In Genesis 11:2 the journey to Shinar is made, not by Noah and his immediate family, but by the peoples that spring from Noah's three sons.

17. For Nimrod, see Genesis 10:8-10.

18. Marrant is alluding to the Tower of Babel; see Genesis 11:1-9.

19. The second son of Ham is Mizraim (Genesis 10:6), which is also the usual name of Egypt in the Old Testament. The ancient city of Thebes in Upper Egypt became the religious and political capital of Egypt during the twelfth dynasty (ca. 2000 B.C.). Homer calls the city "hundred-gated" (*hecatompylos*) in the ninth book of the *Iliad* (verse 381). Heliopolis (the city of the sun) is the Greek name for the Egyptian city of On, located in the Nile Delta region of northern Egypt.

20. Marrant means Eber, the great-grandson of Shem (Genesis 10:24).

21. See Genesis 11:16-26, 31, 12:10.

22. Here Marrant alludes to the enslavement of the Jews, whom the Egyptians forced to make bricks and to build cities. See Exodus 1:8-14, 5:4-19.

23. According to eighteenth-century Masonic ritual, Moses is "the inspired Writer of Gods Commands, and Grand Master of the Lodge of Israel"; with the prophets and the apostles, he is responsible for delivering "the Grand Archive of Masonry"—the Bible (see *Proceedings*, p. 155).

24. See Exodus 25-27. The Tabernacle itself was an oblong rectangular structure, divided into two chambers: the first, with an altar of incense at its center, served as an antechamber to the second, called the "Holy of Holies," which contained the Ark of the Covenant, a chest that held the Two Tables of Law.

25. See Exodus 31:18, 32:19, 34:1, 35:30-35. See chapters 36-39 for the construction of the Ark.

26. In the third edition of *Lemprière's Classical Dictionary of Proper Names mentioned in Ancient Authors, Writ Large* (1788; rpt. London: Routledge and Kegan Paul, 1987), John Lemprière indicates that the "epithet of *Sidonius*" is "used to express the excellence of anything, especially embroidery or dyed garments" (pp. 583-84).

27. In ancient times Jupiter was worshipped in Libya under the name Ammon, or Hammon. The temple of Jupiter Ammon, located in the deserts of Libya nine days from Alexandria, boasted a famous oracle purportedly established 1,800 years before Augustus was born. Alexander the Great numbered among the oracle's most famous visitors.

Coincidentally, "Jupiter Hammon" is also the name of the earliest established African-American male poet (1711–ca. 1800). Hammon was named by his master, Henry Lloyd of Long Island, New York. Although it would become the usual American custom to name slaves after their masters, Lloyd here followed the British fashion of naming slaves after classical Greek or Roman figures.

28. See I Kings 4:29-34, 5:2-6, 7:13-14.

29. Marrant inverts the syntax of the King James version of John 2:19 (see John 2:19-21). Moreover, I Peter 1:14 is either an author's or a printer's error; instead see II Peter 1:13-14.

30. The two Grand Masters are Hiram and Solomon. I Kings 5:13-16 provides each of these first statistics except for the "300 princes, or rulers," for which we have not been able to find a Biblical reference.

31. Adding together the 300 princes, 3,300 overseers, 80,000 stone masons, and 30,000 workers in Lebanon results in a sum of 113,600 "free Masons," not the 119,600 quoted in the sermon. See I Kings 5:15 concerning the 70,000 "men who carried burdens." In the *Official History of Freemasonry Among the Colored People in North America* (1903; rpt. New York: Negro Universities Press, 1969), William H. Grimshaw states that Solomon's Temple cost "800,000,000 shekels, or in round numbers about four hundred million dollars." He even provides a monthly pay roll of the temple workers, from "Entered Apprentices" to "Super Excellent Masons," with columns of wages expended in both dollars and shekels (p. 11).

32. The capstone, or copestone (for which capestane is a Scottish variant), is the top stone, usually slanted, of a wall or structure. It also denotes the crowning or final stroke, as in the finishing touch of a project.

33. Under Nebuchadnezzar II, Babylon became the ruling power of the Near East. Nebuchadnezzar is (in)famous in Biblical history for his destruction of Jerusalem and the Temple of Solomon in 587 B.C., which led to the Babylonian captivity of the Jews chronicled in II Kings 24:10-25, 25:11-21; II Chronicles 26:6-21; and Jeremiah 37:1-10, 52:1-30.

Cyrus the Great of Persia seized Babylon in 539 B.C. and freed the Jews from their captivity in 538 B.C.

By his death at age thirty-three, Alexander of Macedonia, also known as Alexander the Great (356-323 B.C.), had conquered an immense geographical area that covered Greece, Mesopotamia, Persia (modern-day Iran), Afghanistan, western India, Palestine, and northern Africa.

Julius Caesar (100-44 B.C.), reknowned warrior, orator, and statesman, ruled the Roman Empire from 49 B.C. to his assassination in 44 B.C.

34. Herod the Great, appointed Tetrarch of Judaea in 41 B.C., began his restoration of the Temple of Jerusalem in 20 B.C.

35. Tiberius Claudius Nero Caesar (42 B.C.–A.D. 37) reluctantly succeeded his step-father Augustus as emperor of the Roman Empire between A.D. 14 and A.D. 37. During his reign he actively promoted building and restoration throughout the Empire. At his decree, masons restored crumbling or ruined works originally commissioned by Augustus and Pompey and built many new roads, linking the far-flung lands under Roman rule.

36. The philosophical laws guiding Freemasonry are known as the Twenty-Five Ancient Landmarks, which antedate and are incorporated within the official Thirty-Nine General Regulations adopted in 1721. Key to these guidelines is the right of visitation, which declares that all Freemasons can visit and sit in on the rituals of any regular Lodge in the world.

37. Apostates are people who have abandoned their religious faith, political beliefs, or ethical principles.

38. Solomon is traditionally regarded to be the author of the book of Proverbs.

39. St. John the Baptist and St. John the Evangelist are the two patron saints of the Freemasons. The Festival of St. John takes place on Midsummer Day (June 24), the celebration of the nativity of John the Baptist. Theories abound concerning the origin of St. John's importance to Masonry. One theory posits that Robert I of Scotland (1247-1329)—popularly known as Robert the Bruce, who ruled as Scotland's king from 1306 to 1329—revived Masonry after his army defeated the English in the St. John's Day Battle of Bannockburn in 1314.

40. The Ninth Landmark notes the Freemasons' right to assemble in Lodges. Since the formal institution of Freemasonry in 1717, the charter, or founding document of a Masonic Lodge, has become the primary instrument through which that body garners the authority to meet as an assemblage and freely practice the rituals and lessons of Masonry.

41. The General Regulations bid all Freemasons to refrain from expressing any partisan affiliation within the Lodge, since the factiousness of party spirit could irreparably damage the peace and harmony that the Lodge and Freemasonry are instituted to uphold.

42. The phrase "stand on the level" refers to the Masonic creed that all Masons are equal (despite societal ranking) and must pursue at a common level the same goals: knowledge and the respect accorded to virtue. Hence the level, an instrument used in masonry and carpentry to measure the straightness of a surface, is also an important Masonic symbol.

43. Marrant's note: "Such as Tertullian, Cyprian, Origen, Augustine, Chrysostrom, Gregory Nazianzen, Arnobius, and ma[n]y others."

Tertullian (ca. A.D. 160–ca. A.D. 225) was born in Carthage; he converted to Christianity before A.D. 197. He was the first Latin theologian and was noted for his asceticism.

Cyprian (ca. A.D. 200-258), a bishop of Carthage, was beheaded for refusing to sacrifice to Roman gods.

Origen (A.D. 185-254), the most prolific Biblical commentator, was born in Alexandria. His writings, in addition to those of Augustine, most influenced the development of Christian thought.

Augustine (A.D. 354-430) is better known today as St. Augustine, bishop of Hippo in northern Africa. He profoundly influenced Western Christian thought through both personal example and prolific writings, including *The City of God* and his autobiographical *Confessions.*

John Chrysostom (ca. A.D. 347-407), an archbishop of Constantinople reknowned for his eloquent preaching, was the most famous of the Greek Fathers of the Church.

Gregory of Nazianzus "the Divine" (A.D. 329-389) was a bishop of Constantinople known for his philosophical sermons. He was one of four great Greek doctors of the Church.

Arnobius (fl. A.D. 303-313) was an erudite Christian who wrote the treatise *De Rhetoricâ Institutione* (not extant), in which he satirizes non-Christian religious beliefs.

44. The life of Pope Gregory the Great (ca. A.D. 540-640), including this episode, is recounted by Bede (A.D. 673-735) in *The Ecclesiastical History of the English People,* Bk. 2, ch. 1.

45. See Matthew 22:37-39, John 13:35, I Corinthians 13:13.

46. Freemasons imposed strict qualifications on the admission of new members. Candidates had to be free adult males who lacked physical defect and were of virtuous character and good reputation. Historian Jeremy Belknap, friend and correspondent of Freemason St. George Tucker, inscribed a brief message about the African Lodge members' qualifications on the inside cover of Tucker's copy of Prince Hall's *A Charge Delivered to the Brethren of the African Lodge on the 25th of June, 1792:* "This Lodge consists of about thirty Brethren & great care is taken to admit none but persons of good moral Character—So saith the Grand master P. Hall—March 7. 1795."

47. Romans 12:15.

48. See Revelation 19:1-2, 4-5.

QUOBNA
OTTOBAH
CUGOANO

ABOUT
QUOBNA OTTOBAH CUGOANO

LIFE

Unlike the other authors in our volume, Quobna Ottobah Cugoano wrote a brief sketch of his life, which was included in various copies of the London, 1787, edition of *Thoughts and Sentiments* and published separately in *The Negro's Memorial, or Abolitionist's Catechism. By an Abolitionist* (London, [1824]). Here is Cugoano's story in his own voice:

> Since these Thoughts and Sentiments have been read by some, I find a general Approbation has been given, and that the things pointed out thereby might be more effectually taken into consideration, I was requested by some friends to add this information concerning myself: — When I was kidnapped and brought away from Africa, I was then about 13 years of age, in the year of the Christian æra 1770; and after being about nine or ten months in the slave-gang at Grenada, and about one year at different places in the West-Indies, with Alexander Campbell, Esq; who brought me to England in the end of the year 1772, I was advised by some good people to get myself baptized, that I might not be carried away and sold again. — I was called *Steuart* by my master, but in order that I might embrace this ordinance, I was called *John Steuart*, and I went several times to Dr. Skinner, who instructed me, and I was baptized by him, and registered at St. James's Church in the year 1773. Some of

my fellow-servants, who assisted me in this, got themselves turned away for it; I have only put my African
name to the title of the book. —When I was brought away
from Africa, my father and relations were then chief men
in the kingdom of Agimaque and Assinee; but what they
may be now, or whether dead or alive, I know not. I
wish to go back as soon as I can hear any proper security
and safe conveyance can be found; and I wait to hear how
it fares with the Black People sent to Sierra Leona. But
it is my highest wish and earnest prayer to God, that
some encouragement could be given to send able school
masters, and intelligent ministers, who would be faithful
and able to teach the Christian religion. This would be
doing great good to the Africans, and be a kind restitu-
tion for the great injuries that they have suffered. But still
I fear no good can be done near any of the European settlements, while such a horrible and infernal traffic of
slavery is carried on by them. Wherever the foot of man
can go, at the forts and garrisons it would seem to be
wrote with these words — —

O earth! O sea! cover not thou the blood of the poor negro slaves.

Born around 1757 in Ajumako, a stretch of Fanti tribal land located
along the coast of what is now Ghana, Quobna Ottobah Cugoano probably received his name from his father eight days after his birth, in accordance with tribal custom. One of his names would have been taken either
from a deceased ancestor or from a special family friend who would have
assisted Cugoano's father during the naming ceremony. Joining this fam-
ily/community name would be a personal name, derived from the day of
Cugoano's birth and celebratory of the moment Cugoano first drew breath.
That personal name could be either Quobna, derived from Quabino (the
masculine name for Tuesday), or Cugoano, derived from Cudjoe (the
masculine name for Monday).

Cugoano's life largely remains a mystery. He tells us that he visited various relations as he grew; he was staying with an uncle when black slave
traders kidnapped him along with approximately twenty other children.
After several days' delay, he traveled with a slaver to a coastal European
trade depot, where he was incarcerated for three days. He then boarded a
ship that carried him to Cape Coast Castle, where he caught his last
glimpse of Africa before sailing for the island of Grenada. Here the details

of Cugoano's life become even sketchier. He slaved in Grenada for nearly a year, apparently on or near a sugar plantation, before Alexander Campbell chose him to be his servant. Cugoano then traveled with Campbell to England.

Cugoano arrived in England in late 1772 and within a year had been both instructed and baptized in the Christian faith in St. James's Church, located in the Westminster section of London. We then lose track of him until 28 July 1786, when he was known to have associated with a man named Green (probably William Green, a black man who was among those dismissed with Olaudah Equiano from the Sierra Leone repatriation project). Cugoano and Green informed Granville Sharp about the plight of Harry Demane, a black slave who had been seized by his master and tied to the mast of a ship bound for the West Indies. Cugoano's and Green's timely assistance enabled Sharp to free Demane from the ship and thereby save his life. In the same year, 1786, Cugoano wrote to the Prince of Wales, urging the abolition of slavery and the slave trade. Cugoano continued his letter-writing campaign against slavery over the next three years. As part of the Sons of Africa, a group of at least twenty-four black men (including Olaudah Equiano) who fought to secure basic human rights for the black community, he included his signature on petitions to Granville Sharp; Prime Minister William Pitt; Parliament members Sir William Dolben and the Hon. Charles James Fox; and William Dixon, formerly private secretary to Edward Hay, governor of the island of Barbados. On his own he wrote again to the Prince of Wales, as well as to Edmund Burke and King George III. He juggled his epistolary efforts and the writing and publication of *Thoughts and Sentiments* with his work as a domestic servant for the artist Richard Cosway, now famous for a miniature he painted of the Prince of Wales. From 1784 to at least 1787, Cosway lived in Pall Mall, London, the address Cugoano lists on a letter that he wrote to Edmund Burke around 1787. Although we know Cugoano was in Cosway's employ about this time, it is uncertain when his employment commenced or how long it continued.

In 1791, Cugoano appears to have been working with the Sierra Leone Company, seeking volunteers to aid the black settlers in its ailing West African colony. His letter to Granville Sharp, probably written that year, mentioned that he would soon sail to New Brunswick, Nova Scotia. He might then have joined the Nova Scotia vessels on their journey to Sierra Leone. We do not know, however, for at this point Cugoano fades from sight.

BIBLIOGRAPHICAL NOTE

Thoughts and Sentiments on the Evil and Wicked Traffic of the Slavery and Commerce of the Human Species, humbly submitted to The Inhabitants of Great Britain by Ottobah Cugoano, A Native of Africa was first published in London in 1787; T. Becket published another London imprint that year. In 1788, Paris bookseller Royez sold a French translation. Three years later, Cugoano published a brief treatise in London that closely resembles portions of *Thoughts and Sentiments,* similarly titled *Thoughts and Sentiments on the Evil of Slavery, or, The Nature of Servitude as admitted by the Law of God Compared to the Modern Slavery of the Africans in the West Indies in an Answer to the Advocates for Slavery and Oppression.* The British Museum Library calls this 1791 work an abridged edition, a conclusion with which Paul Edwards disagrees. In his "Introduction" to the 1969 reprint of a London, 1787, imprint of *Thoughts and Sentiments* (London, Dawsons of Pall Mall), he contends that "the 1791 edition is not an abridgement of the earlier edition, but a text from which the 1787 edition was expanded" (p. xii).

Paul Edwards also argues that Equiano probably assisted Cugoano in crafting *Thoughts and Sentiments* ("Introduction," pp. x-xi), an idea that Folarin Shyllon seconds and expands upon in *Black People in Britain 1555-1833* (London: Oxford University Press, 1977). Shyllon remarks that "some of" Cugoano's work "is identical with Equiano's letters to the press between 1787 and 1789" (p. 173); we have discovered in *Thoughts and Sentiments* many phrases, sentences, paragraphs, and Biblical quotations that Equiano tended to employ both in his letters and in his *Narrative.* Since Equiano was the more prolific and accomplished of the two, frequently sending skillfully fashioned book reviews and letters of protest to the London newspapers, as well as personally publishing and continually revising his own *Narrative,* it seems likely that he did help his friend Cugoano.

In addition to the Dawsons 1969 reprint, an abridged version of a 1787 imprint of *Thoughts and Sentiments* appears in Francis D. Adams's and Barry Sanders's book, *Three Black Writers in Eighteenth Century England* (Belmont, CA: Wadsworth Publishing, 1971). The text of a London, 1787, imprint of *Thoughts and Sentiments* is also available in a mimeographed copy from the Institute of African Studies at the University of Ghana in Legon, Sources and Documents series (no. 5).

*Thoughts and Sentiments on the Evil and Wicked
Traffic of the Slavery and Commerce
of the Human Species, Humbly Submitted to
the Inhabitants of Great-Britain,
by Ottobah Cugoano, a Native of Africa*
(EXCERPTS)

THOUGHTS and SENTIMENTS on the EVIL of SLAVERY.

*One law, and one manner shall be for you, and for the stranger
that sojourneth with you; and therefore, all things whatsoever
ye would that men should do to you, do ye even so to them.*
Numb. xv. 16.—Math. vii. 12.

AS several learned gentlemen of distinguished abilities, as well as eminent for their great humanity, liberality and candour, have written various essays against that infamous traffic of the African Slave Trade, carried on with the West-India planters and merchants, to the great shame and disgrace of all Christian nations wherever it is admitted in any of their territories, or in any place or situation amongst them; it cannot be amiss that I should thankfully acknowledge these truly worthy and humane gentlemen with the warmest sense of gratitude, for their beneficent and laudable endeavours towards a total suppression of that infamous and iniquitous traffic of stealing, kid-napping, buying, selling, and cruelly enslaving men!

Those who have endeavoured to restore to their fellow-creatures the common rights of nature, of which especially the poor unfortunate Black People have been so unjustly deprived, cannot fail in meeting with the applause of all good men, and the approbation of that which will for ever redound to their honor; they have the warrant of that which is divine: *Open thy mouth, judge righteously, plead the cause of the poor and needy; for the liberal deviseth liberal things, and by liberal things shall stand.*[1] And they can say with the pious Job, *Did not I weep for him that was in trouble; was not my soul grieved for the poor?*[2]

The kind exertions of many benevolent and humane gentlemen, against the iniquitous traffic of slavery and oppression, has been attended with much good to many, and must redound with great honor to themselves, to humanity and their country; their laudable endeavours have been productive of the most beneficent effects in preventing that savage barbarity from taking place in free countries at home. In this, as well as in many other respects, there is one class of people (whose virtues of probity and humanity are well known) who are worthy of universal approbation and imitation, because, like men of honor and humanity, they have jointly agreed to carry on no slavery and savage barbarity among them; and, since the last war,[3] some mitigation of slavery has been obtained in some respective districts of America, though not in proportion to their own vaunted claims of freedom; but it is to be hoped, that they will yet go on to make a further and greater reformation. However, notwithstanding all that has been done and written against it, that brutish barbarity, and unparalelled injustice, is still carried on to a very great extent in the colonies, and with an avidity as insidious, cruel and oppressive as ever. The longer that men continue in the practice of evil and wickedness, they grow the more abandoned; for nothing in history can equal the barbarity and cruelty of the tortures and murders committed under various pretences in modern slavery, except the annals of the Inquisition and the bloody edicts of Popish massacres.

It is therefore manifest, that something else ought yet to be done; and what is required, is evidently the incumbent duty of all men of enlightened understanding, and of every man that has any claim or affinity to the name of Christian, that the base treatment which the African Slaves undergo, ought to be abolished; and it is moreover evident, that the whole, or any part of that iniquitous traffic of slavery, can no where, or in any degree, be admitted, but among those who must eventually resign their own claim to any degree of sensibility and humanity, for that of barbarians and ruffians.

But it would be needless to arrange an history of all the base treatment which the African Slaves are subjected to, in order to shew the exceeding wickedness and evil of that insidious traffic, as the whole may easily appear in every part, and at every view, to be wholly and totally inimical to every idea of justice, equity, reason and humanity. What I intend to advance against that evil, criminal and wicked traffic of enslaving men, are only some Thoughts and Sentiments which occur to me, as being obvious from the Scriptures of Divine Truth, or such arguments as are chiefly deduced from thence, with other such observations as I have been able to collect. Some of these observations may lead into a larger field of consideration, than that of the African Slave Trade alone; but those causes from wherever they originate, and become the production of slavery, the evil effects produced by it, must shew that its origin and source is of a wicked and criminal nature.

No necessity, or any situation of men, however poor, pitiful and wretched they may be, can warrant them to rob others, or oblige them to become thieves, because they are poor, miserable and wretched: But the robbers of men, the kid-nappers, ensnarers and slave-holders, who take away the common rights and privileges of others to support and enrich themselves, are universally those pitiful and detestable wretches; for the ensnaring of others, and taking away their liberty by slavery and oppression, is the worst kind of robbery, as most opposite to every precept and injunction of the Divine Law, and contrary to that command which enjoins that *all men should love their neighbours as themselves,*[4] and *that they should do unto others, as they would that men should do to them.* As to any other laws that slave-holders may make among themselves, as respecting slaves, they can be of no better kind, nor give them any better character, than what is implied in the common report—that there may be some honesty among thieves. This may seem a harsh comparison, but the parallel is so coincident that, I must say, I can find no other way of expressing my Thoughts and Sentiments, without making use of some harsh words and comparisons against the carriers on of such abandoned wickedness. But, in this little undertaking, I must humbly hope the impartial reader will excuse such defects as may arise from want of better education; and as to the resentment of those who can lay their cruel lash upon the backs of thousands, for a thousand times less crimes than writing against their enormous wickedness and brutal avarice, is what I may be sure to meet with.

However, it cannot but be very discouraging to a man of my complexion in such an attempt as this, to meet with the evil aspersions of some men, who say, "That an African is not entitled to any competent degree of knowledge, or capable of imbibing any sentiments of probity; and that nature designed him for some inferior link in the chain, fitted only to be a slave."[5] But when I meet with those who make no scruple to deal with the human species, as with the beasts of the earth, I must think them not only brutish, but wicked and base; and that their aspersions are insidious and false: And if such men can boast of greater degrees of knowledge, than any African is entitled to, I shall let them enjoy all the advantages of it unenvied, as I fear it consists only in a greater share of infidelity, and that of a blacker kind than only skin deep. And if their complexion be not what I may suppose, it is at least the nearest in resemblance to an infernal hue. A good man will neither speak nor do as a bad man will; but if a man is bad, it makes no difference whether he be a black or a white devil.

By some of such complexion, as whether black or white it matters not, I was early snatched away from my native country, with about eighteen or twenty more boys and girls, as we were playing in a field. We lived but a few days journey from the coast where we were kid-napped, and as we were decoyed and drove along, we were soon conducted to a factory,[6] and from thence, in the fashionable way of traffic, consigned to Grenada. Perhaps it may not be amiss to give a few remarks, as some account of myself, in this transposition of captivity.

I was born in the city of Agimaque, on the coast of Fantyn; my father was a companion to the chief in that part of the country of Fantee,[7] and when the old king died I was left in his house with his family; soon after I was sent for by his nephew, Ambro Accasa, who succeeded the old king in the chiefdom of that part of Fantee known by the name of Agimaque and Assinee.[8] I lived with his children, enjoying peace and tranquillity, about twenty moons, which, according to their way of reckoning time, is two years. I was sent for to visit an uncle, who lived at a considerable distance from Agimaque. The first day after we set out we arrived at Assinee, and the third day at my uncle's habitation, where I lived about three months, and was then thinking of returning to my father and young companion at Agimaque; but by this time I had got well acquainted with some of the children of my uncle's hundreds of relations, and we were some days too ventursome in going into the woods to gather fruit and catch birds, and such amusements as pleased us. One day I refused to go with the rest, being rather apprehensive that something might happen to us; till one of my play-fellows said to me, because you belong to the great men, you are afraid to venture your carcase, or else of the *bounsam*, which is the devil.[9] This enraged me so much, that I set a resolution to join the rest, and we went into the woods as usual; but we had not been above two hours before our troubles began, when several great ruffians came upon us suddenly, and said we had committed a fault against their lord, and we must go and answer for it ourselves before him.

Some of us attempted in vain to run away, but pistols and cutlasses were soon introduced, threatening, that if we offered to stir we should all lie dead on the spot. One of them pretended to be more friendly than the rest, and said, that he would speak to their lord to get us clear, and desired that we should follow him; we were then immediately divided into different parties, and drove after him. We were soon led out of the way which we knew, and towards the evening, as we came in sight of a town, they told us that this great man of theirs lived there, but pretended it was too late to go and see him that night. Next morning there came three other men, whose language differed from ours, and spoke to some of those who watched us all the night, but he that pretended to be our friend with the great man, and some others, were gone away. We asked our keepers what these men had been saying to them, and they answered, that they had been asking them, and us together, to go and feast with them that day, and that we must put off seeing the great man till after; little thinking that our doom was so nigh, or that these villains meant to feast on us as their prey. We went with them again about half a day's journey, and came to a great multitude of people, having different music playing; and all the day after we got there, we were very merry with the music, dancing and singing. Towards the evening, we were again persuaded that we could not get back to where the great man lived till next day; and when bed-time came, we were separated into different houses with different people. When the next morning came, I asked for the men that brought me there, and for the rest of my companions; and I was told that they were gone to the sea side to bring home some rum, guns and powder, and that some of my companions were gone with them, and that some were gone to the fields to do something or other. This gave me strong suspicion that there was some treachery in the case, and I began to think that my hopes of returning home again were all over. I soon became very uneasy, not knowing what to do, and refused to eat or drink for whole days together, till the man of the house told me that he would do all in his power to get me back to my uncle; then I eat a little fruit with him, and had some thoughts that I should be sought after, as I would be then missing at home about five or six days. I enquired every day if the men had come back, and for the rest of my companions, but could get no answer of any satisfaction. I was kept about six days at this man's house, and in the evening there was another

man came and talked with him a good while, and I heard the one say to
the other he must go, and the other said the sooner the better; that man
came out and told me that he knew my relations at Agimaque, and that
we must set out to-morrow morning, and he would convey me there.
Accordingly we set out next day, and travelled till dark, when we came
to a place where we had some supper and slept. He carried a large bag
with some gold dust, which he said he had to buy some goods at the sea
side to take with him to Agimaque. Next day we travelled on, and in the
evening came to a town, where I saw several white people, which made
me afraid that they would eat me, according to our notion as children
in the inland parts of the country.[10] This made me rest very uneasy all
the night, and next morning I had some victuals brought, desiring me
to eat and make haste, as my guide and kid-napper told me that he had
to go to the castle with some company that were going there, as he had
told me before, to get some goods. After I was ordered out, the horrors
I soon saw and felt, cannot be well described; I saw many of my miserable countrymen chained two and two, some hand-cuffed, and some
with their hands tied behind. We were conducted along by a guard, and
when we arrived at the castle, I asked my guide what I was brought
there for, he told me to learn the ways of the *browfow*, that is the white
faced people.[11] I saw him take a gun, a piece of cloth, and some lead for
me, and then he told me that he must now leave me there, and went off.
This made me cry bitterly, but I was soon conducted to a prison, for
three days, where I heard the groans and cries of many, and saw some
of my fellow-captives. But when a vessel arrived to conduct us away to
the ship, it was a most horrible scene; there was nothing to be heard but
rattling of chains, smacking of whips, and the groans and cries of our fellow-men. Some would not stir from the ground, when they were lashed
and beat in the most horrible manner. I have forgot the name of this
infernal fort; but we were taken in the ship that came for us, to another
that was ready to sail from Cape Coast.[12] When we were put into the
ship, we saw several black merchants coming on board, but we were all
drove into our holes, and not suffered to speak to any of them. In this
situation we continued several days in sight of our native land; but I
could find no good person to give any information of my situation to
Accasa at Agimaque. And when we found ourselves at last taken away,
death was more preferable than life, and a plan was concerted amongst
us, that we might burn and blow up the ship, and to perish all together
in the flames;[13] but we were betrayed by one of our own countrywomen,
who slept with some of the head men of the ship, for it was common for

the dirty filthy sailors to take the African women and lie upon their bodies; but the men were chained and pent up in holes. It was the women
and boys which were to burn the ship, with the approbation and groans
of the rest; though that was prevented, the discovery was likewise a cruel
bloody scene.

But it would be needless to give a description of all the horrible
scenes which we saw, and the base treatment which we met with in this
dreadful captive situation, as the similar cases of thousands, which suffer by this infernal traffic, are well known. Let it suffice to say, that I was
thus lost to my dear indulgent parents and relations, and they to me. All
my help was cries and tears, and these could not avail; nor suffered long,
till one succeeding woe, and dread, swelled up another. Brought from a
state of innocence and freedom, and, in a barbarous and cruel manner,
conveyed to a state of horror and slavery: This abandoned situation may
be easier conceived than described. From the time that I was kid napped
and conducted to a factory, and from thence in the brutish, base, but
fashionable way of traffic, consigned to Grenada, the grievous thoughts
which I then felt, still pant in my heart; though my fears and tears have
long since subsided. And yet it is still grievous to think that thousands
more have suffered in similar and greater distress, under the hands of
barbarous robbers, and merciless task-masters; and that many even
now are suffering in all the extreme bitterness of grief and woe, that no
language can describe[.] The cries of some, and the sight of their misery, may be seen and heard afar; but the deep sounding groans of thousands, and the great sadness of their misery and woe, under the heavy
load of oppressions and calamities inflicted upon them, are such as can
only be distinctly known to the ears of Jehovah Sabaoth.[14]

This Lord of Hosts, in his great Providence, and in great mercy to me,
made a way for my deliverance from Grenada. — Being in this dreadful
captivity and horrible slavery, without any hope of deliverance, for about
eight or nine months, beholding the most dreadful scenes of misery and
cruelty, and seeing my miserable companions often cruelly lashed, and
as it were cut to pieces, for the most trifling faults; this made me often
tremble and weep, but I escaped better than many of them. For eating a
piece of sugar-cane, some were cruelly lashed, or struck over the face to
knock their teeth out. Some of the stouter ones, I suppose often reproved,
and grown hardened and stupid with many cruel beatings and lashings,
or perhaps faint and pressed with hunger and hard labour, were often
committing trespasses of this kind, and when detected, they met with
exemplary punishment. Some told me they had their teeth pulled out to

deter others, and to prevent them from eating any cane in future. Thus seeing my miserable companions and countrymen in this pitiful, distressed and horrible situation, with all the brutish baseness and barbarity attending it, could not but fill my little mind with horror and indignation. But I must own, to the shame of my own countrymen, that I was first kid-napped and betrayed by some of my own complexion, who were the first cause of my exile and slavery; but if there were no buyers there would be no sellers. So far as I can remember, some of the Africans in my country keep slaves, which they take in war, or for debt; but those which they keep are well fed, and good care taken of them, and treated well; and, as to their cloathing, they differ according to the custom of the country. But I may safely say, that all the poverty and misery that any of the inhabitants of Africa meet with among themselves, is far inferior to those inhospitable regions of misery which they meet with in the West-Indies, where their hard-hearted overseers have neither regard to the laws of God, nor the life of their fellow-men.

Thanks be to God, I was delivered from Grenada, and that horrid brutal slavery.—A gentleman coming to England, took me for his servant, and brought me away, where I soon found my situation more agreeable.[15] After coming to England, and seeing others write and read, I had a strong desire to learn, and getting what assistance I could, I applied myself to learn reading and writing, which soon became my recreation, pleasure, and delight; and when my master perceived that I could write some, he sent me to a proper school for that purpose to learn. Since, I have endeavoured to improve my mind in reading, and have sought to get all the intelligence I could, in my situation of life, towards the state of my brethren and countrymen in complexion, and of the miserable situation of those who are barbarously sold into captivity, and unlawfully held in slavery.

But, among other observations, one great duty I owe to Almighty God, (the thankful acknowledgement I would not omit for any consideration) that, although I have been brought away from my native country, in that torrent of robbery and wickedness, thanks be to God fo[r] his good providence towards me; I have both obtained liberty, and acquired the great advantages of some little learning, in being able to read and write, and, what is still infinitely of greater advantage, I trust, to know something of HIM *who is that God whose providence rules over all, and who is the only Potent One that rules in the nations over the children of men. It is unto Him, who is the Prince of the Kings of the earth, that I would give all thanks.*[16] And, in some manner, I may say with Joseph, as he did with respect to the evil intention of his brethren, when they sold him into Egypt, that whatever evil intentions and bad motives those insidious robbers had in carrying me away from my native country and friends, I trust, was what the Lord intended for my good.[17] In this respect, I am highly indebted to many of the good people of England for learning and principles unknown to the people of my native country. But, above all, what have I obtained from the Lord God of Hosts, the God of the Christians! in that divine revelation of the only true God, and the Saviour of men, what a treasure of wisdom and blessings are involved? How wonderful is the divine goodness displayed in those invaluable books the Old and New Testaments, that inestimable compilation of books, the Bible? And, O what a treasure to have, and one of the greatest advantages to be able to read therein, and a divine blessing to understand!

✳ ✳ ✳

Here Cugoano refutes various pro-slavery positions that James Tobin outlines in his work *Cursory Remarks upon the Reverend Mr. Ramsay's Essay on the Treatment and Conversion of African Slaves in the Sugar Colonies. By a friend to the West India colonies, and their inhabitants* (London, 1785). To the proposition that the poor in Britain and Ireland suffer more acutely than the slaves in the West Indies, Cugoano replies that poor whites, unlike bartered and tortured slaves, retain their freedom. He also retorts that the advocates of slavery warp the "natural order" of life by refusing to treat humanity's welfare as their first priority.

"Some pretend that the Africans, in general, are a set of poor, ignorant, dispersed, unsociable people; and that they think it no crime to sell one another, and even their own wives and children; therefore they bring them away to a situation where many of them may arrive to a better state than ever they could obtain in their own native country." This specious pretence is without any shadow of justice and truth, and, if the argument was even true, it could afford no just and warrantable matter for any society of men to hold slaves. But the argument is false; there can be no ignorance, dispersion, or unsociableness so found among them, which can be made better by bringing them away to a state of a degree equal to that of a cow or a horse.

But let their ignorance in some things (in which the Europeans have greatly the advantage of them) be what it will, it is not the intention of those who bring them away to make them better by it; nor is the design of slave-holders of any other intention, but that they may serve them as a kind of engines and beasts of burden; that their own ease and profit may be advanced, by a set of poor helpless men and women, whom they despise and rank with brutes, and keep them in perpetual slavery, both themselves and children, and merciful death is the only release from their toil. By the benevolence of some, a few may get their liberty, and by their own industry and ingenuity, may acquire some learning, mechanical trades, or useful business; and some may be brought away by different gentlemen to free countries, where they get their liberty but no thanks to slave-holders for it. But amongst those who get their liberty, like all other ignorant men, are generally more corrupt in their morals, than they possibly could have been amongst their own people in Africa; for, being mostly amongst the wicked and apostate Christians,[18] they sooner learn their oaths and blasphemies, and their evil ways, than any thing else. Some few, indeed, may eventually arrive at some knowledge of the Christian religion, and the great advantages of it. Such was the case of Ukawsaw Groniosaw, an African prince, who lived in England. He was a long time in a state of great poverty and distress, and must have died at one time for want, if a good and charitable Attorney had not supported him. He was long after in a very poor state, but he would not have given his faith in the Christian religion, in exchange for all the kingdoms of Africa, if they could have been given to him, in place of his poverty, for it. And such was A. Morrant in America.[19] When a boy, he could stroll away into a desert, and prefer the society of wild beasts to the absurd Christianity of his mother's house. He was conducted to the king of the Cherokees, who, in a miraculous manner, was induced by him to embrace the Christian faith. This Morrant was in the British service last war, and his royal convert, the king of the Cherokee Indians, accompanied General Clinton at the siege of Charles-Town.[20]

❋ ❋ ❋

In this section, Cugoano points to corrupted Christianity as the root of the slave trade. He contrasts the great number of Christian lands infested with "ruffians, barbarians and slave-holders" with the few African nations that keep slaves. He suggests that European avarice has now infected African merchants and chieftains. Lured by the spectacle of European wealth, and lulled by the presence of gaudily dressed blacks in the Europeans' employ, some Africans are willing to sell their countrymen for financial gain. Chiefs and princes exploit the traditionally accepted African traffic in prisoners of war by waging war solely to capture saleable slaves. Still, Cugoano argues, Africans have not been entirely corrupted by the slave trade, as deep, natural feelings of familial affection as well as passionate belief in personal liberty keep Africans from selling their wives and children.

But the supporters and favourers of slavery make other things a pretence and an excuse in their own defence; such as, that they find that it was admitted under the Divine institution by Moses,[21] as well as the long continued practice of different nations for ages; and that the Africans are peculiarly marked out by some signal prediction in nature and complexion for that purpose.[22]

This seems to be the greatest bulwark of defence which the advocates and favourers of slavery can advance, and what is generally talked of in their favour by those who do not understand it. I shall consider it in that view, whereby it will appear, that they deceive themselves and mislead others. Men are never more liable to be drawn into error, than when truth is made use of in a guileful manner to seduce them. Those who do not believe the scriptures to be a Divine revelation, cannot, consistently with themselves, make the law of Moses, or any mark or prediction they can find respecting any particular set of men, as found in the sacred writings, any reason that one class of men should enslave another. In that respect, all that they have to enquire into should be, whether it be right, or wrong, that any part of the human species should enslave another; and when that is the case, the Africans, though not so learned, are just as wise as the Europeans; and when the matter is left to human wisdom, they are both liable to err. But what the light of nature, and the dictates of reason, when rightly considered, teach, is, that no man ought to enslave another; and some, who have been rightly guided thereby, have made noble defences for the universal natural rights and privileges of all men. But in this case, when the learned take neither revelation nor reason for their guide, they fall into as great, and worse errors, than the unlearned; for they only make use of that system of Divine wisdom, which should guide them into truth, when they can find or pick out any thing that will suit their purpose, or that they can pervert to such—the very means of leading themselves and others into error. And, in consequence thereof, the pretences that some men make use of for holding of slaves, must be evidently the grossest perversion of reason, as well as an inconsistent and diabolical use of the sacred writings. For it must be a strange perversion of reason, and a wrong use or disbelief of the sacred writings, when any thing found there is so perverted by them, and set up as a precedent and rule for men to commit wickedness. They had better have no reason, and no belief in the scriptures, and make no use of them at all, than only to believe, and make use of that which leads them into the most abominable evil and wickedness of dealing unjustly with their fellow men.

But this will appear evident to all men that believe the scriptures, that every reason necessary is given that they should be believed; and, in this case, that they afford us this information: "That all mankind did spring from one original, and that there are no different species among men. For God who made the world, hath made of one blood all the nations of men that dwell on all the face of the earth."[23] Wherefore we may justly infer, as there are no inferior species, but all of one blood and of one nature, that there does not an inferiority subsist, or depend, on their colour, features or form, whereby some men make a pretence to enslave others; and consequently, as they have all one creator, one original, made of one blood, and all brethren descended from one father, it never could be lawful and just for any nation, or people, to oppress and enslave another.

And again, as all the present inhabitants of the world sprang from the family of Noah, and were then all of one complexion, there is no doubt, but the difference which we now find, took its rise very rapidly after they became dispersed and settled on the different parts of the globe. There seems to be a tendency to this, in many instances, among children of the same parents, having different colour of hair and features from one another. And God alone who established the course of nature, can bring about and establish what variety he pleases; and it is not in the power of man to make one hair white or black.[24] But among the variety which it hath pleased God to establish and caused to take place, we may meet with some analogy in nature, that as the bodies of men are tempered with a different degree to enable them to endure the respective climates of their habitations, so their colours vary, in some degree, in a regular gradation from the equator towards either of the poles.[25] However, there are other incidental causes arising from time and place, which constitute the most distinguishing variety of colour, form, appearance and features, as peculiar to the inhabitants of one tract of country, and differing in something from those in another, even in the same latitudes, as well as from those in different climates. Long custom and the different way of living among the several inhabitants of the different parts of the earth, has a very great effect in distinguishing them by a difference of features and complexion. These effects are easy to be seen; as to the causes, it is sufficient for us to know, that all is the work of an Almighty hand. Therefore, as we find the distribution of the human species inhabiting the barren, as well as the most fruitful parts of the earth, and the cold as well as the most hot, differing from one another in complexion according to their situation; it may be reasonably, as well as religiously, inferred, that He who placed them in their various situations, hath extended equally his care and protection to all; and from thence, that it becometh unlawful to counteract his benignity, by reducing others of different complexions to undeserved bondage.

According, as we find that the difference of colour among men is only incidental, and equally natural to all, and agreeable to the place of their habitation; and that if nothing else be different or contrary among them, but that of features and complexion, in that respect, they are all equally alike entitled to the enjoyment of every mercy and blessing of God. But there are some men of that complexion, because they are not black, whose ignorance and insolence leads them to think, that those who are black, were marked out in that manner by some signal interdiction or curse, as originally descending from their progenitors. To those I must say, that the only mark which we read of, as generally alluded to, and by them applied wrongfully, is that mark or sign which God gave to Cain, to assure him that he should not be destroyed. Cain understood by the nature of the crime he had committed, that the law required death, or cutting off, as the punishment thereof. But God in his providence doth not always punish the wicked in this life according to their enormous crimes, (we are told, by a sacred poet, that he saw the wicked flourishing like a green bay tree)[26] though he generally marks them out by some signal token of his vengeance; and that is a sure token of it, when men become long hardened in their wickedness. The denunciation that passed upon Cain was, that he should be a fugitive and a vagabond on the earth,[27] bearing the curse and reproach of his iniquity; and the rest of men were prohibited as much from meddling with him, or defiling their hands by him, as it naturally is, not to pull down the dead carcase of an atrocious criminal, hung up in chains by the laws of his country. But allow the mark set upon Cain to have consisted in a black skin, still no conclusion can be drawn at all, that any of the black people are of that descent, as the whole posterity of Cain were destroyed in the universal deluge.

Only Noah, a righteous and just man, who found grace in the sight of God, and his three sons, Japheth, Shem and Ham, and their wives, eight persons, were preserved from the universal deluge, in the ark which Noah was directed to build.[28] The three sons of Noah had each children born after the flood, from whom all the present world of men descended. But it came to pass, in the days of Noah, that an interdiction, or curse, took place in the family of Ham, and that the descendants of one of his sons should become the servants of servants to their brethren, the descendants of Shem and Japheth.[29] This affords a grand pretence for the supporters of the African slavery to build a false notion upon, as it is found by history that Africa, in general, was peopled by the descendants of Ham; but they forget, that the prediction has already been fulfilled as far as it can go.

There can be no doubt, that there was a shameful misconduct in Ham himself, by what is related of him; but the fault, according to the prediction and curse, descended only to the families of the descendants of his youngest son, Canaan. The occasion was, that Noah, his father, had drank wine, and (perhaps unawares) became inebriated by it, and fell asleep in his tent. It seems that Ham was greatly deficient of that filial virtue as either becoming a father or a son, went into his father's tent, and, it may be supposed, in an undecent manner, he had suffered his own son, Canaan, so to meddle with, or uncover, his father, that he saw his nakedness; for which he did not check the audacious rudeness of Canaan, but went and told his brethren without in ridicule of his aged parent. This rude audacious behaviour of Canaan, and the obloquy of his father Ham, brought on him the curse of his grandfather, Noah, but he blessed Shem and Japheth for their decent and filial virtues, and denounced, in the spirit of prophecy, that Canaan should be their servant, and should serve them.

It may be observed, that it is a great misfortune for children, when their parents are not endowed with that wisdom and prudence which is necessary for the early initiation of their offspring in the paths of virtue and righteousness. Ham was guilty of the offence as well as his son; he did not pity the weakness of his father, who was overcome with wine in that day wherein, it is likely, he had some solemn work to do. But the prediction and curse rested wholly upon the offspring of Canaan, who settled in the land known by his name, in the west of Asia, as is evident from the sacred writings.[30] The Canaanites became an exceeding wicked people, and were visited with many calamities, according to the prediction of Noah, for their abominable wickedness and idolatry.

Chederluomer, a descendant of Shem, reduced the Canaanitish kingdoms to a tributary subjection; and some time after, upon their revolt, invaded and pillaged their country. Not long after Sodom, Gomorrah, Admah and Zeboim, four kingdoms of the Canaanites were overthrown for their great wickedness, and utterly destroyed by fire and brimstone from heaven.[31] The Hebrews, chiefly under Moses, Joshua and Barak, as they were directed by God, cut off most of the other Canaanitish kingdoms, and reduced many of them to subjection and vassalage.[32]

✳ ✳ ✳

Cugoano first explains where Ham's descendants settled in Africa. Like Equiano, he mentions that Africa derived its name from Aphra, a descendant of Abraham and Keturah. In acclimating to life in the Torrid Zone, the skin of Africans naturally achieved its dark color. Cugoano's "scientific" account of black skin serves to counter the superstitious view that a "sable complexion" is a mark of divine disfavor.

Cugoano then attacks the notion that the ancient custom of slavery is a precedent for modern slavery. In antiquity, lawful servants sometimes were forced into becoming bond servants in order to survive, or were tricked and sold into slavery, but these iniquitous practices were in no way as cruel and inhuman as contemporary racial slavery.

Now, in respect to that kind of servitude which was admitted into the law of Moses, that was not contrary to the natural liberties of men, but a state of equity and justice, according as the nature and circumstances of the times required. There was no more harm in entering into a covenant with another man as a bond-servant, than there is for two men to enter into partnership the one with the other; and sometimes the nature of the case may be, and their business require it, that the one may find money and live at a distance and ease, and the other manage the business for him: So a bond-servant was generally the steward in a man's house, and sometimes his heir. There was no harm in buying a man who was in a state of captivity and bondage by others, and keeping him in servitude till such time as his purchase was redeemed by his labour and service. And there could be no harm in paying a man's debts, and keeping him in servitude until such time as an equitable agreement of composition was paid by him. And so, in general, whether they had been bought or sold in order to pay their just debts when they became poor, or were bought from such as held them in an unlawful captivity, the state of bondage which they and their children fell under, among the Israelites, was into that of a vassalage state, which rather might be termed a deliverance from debt and captivity, than a state of slavery.

✳ ✳ ✳

Continuing his examination of bond servants, Cugoano stresses that the plight of the ancient Canaanites is analogous to that of the laboring poor in any free country because they were allowed to observe their civil and religious customs; as such, their servitude was not contrary to their natural rights. He underscores the necessity of reading scriptural evidence allegorically: in the Bible, literal bondage typically serves as a *figure* for humanity's bondage to sin and iniquity.

_____

Nothing but heavenly wisdom, and heavenly grace, can teach men to understand. The most deplorable of all things is, that the dreadful situation of our universal depraved state, which all mankind lyeth under, is such, that those who are not redeemed in time, must for ever continue to be the subjects of eternal bondage and misery. Blessed be God! he hath appointed and set up a deliverance, and the Saviour of Men is an Almighty Redeemer. When God, the Almighty Redeemer and Saviour of his people, brought his Israel out of Egypt and temporal bondage, it was intended and designed thereby, to set up an emblematical representation of their deliverance from the power and captivity of sin, and from the dominion of that evil and malignant spirit, who had with exquisite subtilty and guile at first seduced the original progenitors of mankind. And when they were brought to the promised land, and had gotten deliverance, and subdued their enemies under them, they were to reign over them; and their laws respecting bond-servants, and other things of that nature, were to denote, that they were to keep under and in subjection the whole body of their evil affections and lusts. This is so declared by the Apostle, that the law is spiritual, and intended for spiritual uses.[33]

❋ ❋ ❋

According to Cugoano, throughout Europe's age of discovery the arbitrary laws of conquerors and despoilers have superseded the laws of God. Citing Europe's history of barbarity to the Indian nations, he reveals and deplores the bloody foundations of European colonialism in the example of Spanish explorer Francisco Pizarro. In the name of Christianity and in pursuit of gold and land, Pizarro killed Atahualpa, the Inca emperor, and destroyed the Inca civilization. Cugoano likens Pizarro and his men, along with slave traders and their complacent governments, to the Antichrist.

_____

. . . But should it be asked, what advantages Great-Britain has gained by all its extensive territories abroad, the devastations committed, and the abominable slavery and oppression carried on in its colonies? It may be answered according to the old proverb,

> *It seldom is the grand-child's lot,*
> *To share of wealth unjustly got.*[34]

This seems to be verified too much in their present situation: for however wide they have extended their territories abroad, they have sunk into a world of debt at home, which must ever remain an impending burden upon the inhabitants.[35] And it is not likely, by any plan as yet adopted, to be ever paid, or any part of it, without a long continued heavy annual load of taxes. Perhaps, great as it is some other plan, more equitable for the good of the whole community, if it was wanted to be done, and without any additional taxes, might be so made use of to pay it all off in twenty or thirty years time, and in such manner as whatever emergencies might happen, as never to need to borrow any money at interest. The national debt casts a sluggish deadness over the whole realm, greatly stops ingenuity and improvements, promotes idleness and wickedness, clogs all the wheels of commerce, and drains the money out of the nation. If a foreigner buys stock,[36] in the course of years that the interest amounts to the principal, he gets it all back; and in an equitable time the same sum ever after, and in course must take that money to foreign parts. And those who hold stock at home, are a kind of idle drones, as a burden to the rest of the community: whereas if there were no funds, those who have money would be obliged to occupy it in some improvements themselves, or lend it to other manufacturers or merchants, and by that means useful employments, ingenuity and commerce would flourish. But all stock-jobbing, lotteries, and useless business, has a tendency to slavery and oppression; for as the greater any idle part of the community is, there must be the greater labour and hardships resting upon the industrious part who support the rest; as all men are allotted in some degree to eat their bread with the sweat of their brow; *but it is evil with any people when the rich grind the face of the poor.*[37] Lotteries must be nearly as bad a way of getting money for the good of a nation, as it is for an individual when he is poor, and obliged to pawn his goods to increase his poverty, already poor. On the reverse, if a nation was to keep a bank to lend money to merchants and others, that nation might flourish, and its support to those in need might be attended with advantage to the whole; but that nation which is obliged to borrow money from others, must be in a poor and wretched situation, and the inhabitants, who have to bear the load of its taxes, must be greatly burdened, and perhaps many of those employed in its service (as soldiers and others) poorly paid. It was otherwise with *the people of Israel of old;* it was the promise and blessing of God to them, *That they should lend unto many nations, but should not borrow.*[38]

✳ ✳ ✳

Here Cugoano describes the insidious role slavery plays in Britain's economy. Supported as a venture that will decrease the national debt incurred by wars with foreign nations, slavery merely increases debt because its proceeds are converted to government stock. Aided and abetted by profligate men in power—he points to half the legislature—slavery stands as a significant example of abuse in and of British government.

Cugoano then outlines the history of the African slave trade in Europe, an economic pursuit that Britain first entered into under Charles II with the Royal African Company. Drawing on authorities such as Anthony Benezet, Thomas Clarkson, and Granville Sharp, Cugoano sharply reproaches Britain for its role in the slave trade—a stain that leaves no Briton untouched—and prophesies Divine punishment. Switching tactics, he then proffers a three-point outline for "general reformation" throughout the nation. First, the government must appoint days of fasting and atonement for national depravity; next, it must totally abolish the slave trade and immediately commence universal emancipation. The third point calls for sending a fleet of war ships to the African coast to intercept all slave ships and intercede on behalf of the captives on board. Repeopling the British forts and factories in Africa with Africans newly trained in true Christian and democratic ideals, Britain could eventually establish a legitimate trade relationship with Africa.

Particular thanks is due to every one of that humane society of worthy and respectful gentlemen, whose liberality hath supported many of the Black poor about London.[39] *Those that honor their Maker have mercy on the poor; and many blessings are upon the head of the just: may the fear of the Lord prolong their days, and cause their memory to be blessed, and may their number be encreased to fill their expectation with gladness;* for they have not only commiserated the poor in general, *but even those which are accounted as beasts, and imputed as vile in the sight of others.*[40] The part that the British government has taken, to co-operate with them, has certainly a flattering and laudable apppearance of doing some good; and the fitting out ships to supply a company of Black People with clothes and provisions, and to carry them to settle at Sierra Leona, in the West coast of Africa, as a free colony to Great-Britain, in a peaceable alliance with the inhabitants, has every appearance of honour, and the approbation of friends.[41] According to the plan, humanity hath made its appearance in a more honorable way of colonization, than any Christian nation have ever done before, and may be productive of much good, if they continue to encourage and support them. But after all, there is some doubt whether their own flattering expectation in the manner as set forth to them, and the hope of their friends may not be defeated and rendered abortive; and there is some reason to fear, that they never will be settled as intended, in any permanent and peaceable way at Sierra Leona.

This prospect of settling a free colony to Great-Britain in a peaceable alliance with the inhabitants of Africa at Sierra Leona, has neither altogether met with the credulous approbation of the Africans here, nor yet been sought after with any prudent and right plan by the promoters of it. Had a treaty of agreement been first made with the inhabitants of Africa, and the terms and nature of such a settlement fixed·upon, and its situation and boundary pointed out; then might the Africans, and others here, have embarked with a good prospect of enjoying happiness and prosperity themselves, and have gone with a hope of being able to render their services, in return, of some advantage to their friends and benefactors of Great-Britain.[42] But as this was not done, and as they were to be hurried away at all events, come of them after what would; and yet, after all, to be delayed in the ships before they were set out from the coast, until many of them have perished with cold, and other disorders, and several of the most intelligent among them are dead, and others that, in all probability, would have been most useful for them were hindered from going, by means of some disagreeable jealousy of those who were appointed as governors,[43] the great prospect of doing good seems all to be blown away. And so it appeared to some of those who are now gone, and at last, hap hazard, were obliged to go; who endeavoured in vain to get away by plunging into the water, that they might, if possible wade ashore, as dreading the prospect of their wretched fate,[44] and as beholding their perilous situation, having every prospect of difficulty and surrounding danger.

What with the death of some of the original promoters and proposers of this charitable undertaking,[45] and the death and deprivation of others that were to share the benefit of it, and by the adverse motives of those employed to be the conductors thereof, we think it will be more than what can be well expected, if we ever hear of any good in proportion to so great, well-designed, laudable and expensive charity. Many more of the Black People still in this country would have, with great gladness, embraced the opportunity, longing to reach their native land; but as the old saying is, A burnt child dreads the fire, some of these unfortunate sons and daughters of Africa have been severally unlawfully dragged

away from their native abodes, under various pretences, by the insidious treachery of others, and have been brought into the hands of barbarous robbers and pirates, and, like sheep to the market, have been sold
into captivity and slavery, and thereby have been deprived of their natural liberty and property, and every connection that they held dear and
valuable, and subjected to the cruel service of the hard-hearted brutes
called planters. But some of them, by various services either to the public or to individuals, as more particularly in the course of last war, have
gotten their liberty again in this free country.[46] They are thankful for the
respite, but afraid of being ensnared again; for the European seafaring
people in general, who trade to foreign parts, have such a prejudice
against Black People, that they use them more like asses than men, so
that a Black Man is scarcely ever safe among them. Much assiduity was
made use to perswade the Black People in general to embrace the opportunity of going with this company of transports; but the wiser sort
declined from all thoughts of it, unless they could hear of some better
plan taking place for their security and safety.[47] For as it seemed prudent
and obvious to many of them taking heed to that sacred enquiry, *Doth a
fountain send forth at the same place sweet water and bitter?*[48] They were afraid
that their doom would be to drink of the bitter water. For can it be readily conceived that government would establish a free colony for them
nearly on the spot, while it supports its forts and garrisons, to ensnare,
merchandize, and to carry others into captivity and slavery.

✳ ✳ ✳

Cugoano supports a detailed program of theological instruction for blacks.
Key to this plan are wise and learned instructors who use the apostle Paul
as their role model, and the translation of the Bible into many languages
to facilitate the spread of the Gospel. Although he feels encouraged by the
rainbow, which he views as God's covenant with humanity, Cugoano
admits to a distinct lack of enthusiasm for organized religion and the role
it has played in slavery. Citing the Protestants as "the most barbarous
slave-holders," he offers only the cynical hope that in the wake of a "sinking" Roman Catholic church, Catholics will feel increasingly merciful and
temper the severity of slavery in their lands.

But I shall add another observation, which I am sorry to find among
Christians, and I think it is a great deficiency among the clergy in general, when covetous and profligate men are admitted amongst them, who
either do not know, or dare not speak the truth, but neglect their duty

much, or do it with such supineness, that it becomes good for nothing. Sometimes an old woman selling matches, will preach a better, and a more orthodox sermon, than some of the clergy, who are only decked out (as Mr. Turnbul[49] calls it) with the external trappings of religion. Much of the great wickedness of others lieth at their door, and these words of the Prophet are applicable to them: *And first, saith the Lord, I will recompence their iniquity, and their sin double; because they have defiled my land, they have filled mine inheritance with the carcases of their detestable and abominable things.*[50] Such are the errors of men. Church, signifies an assembly of people; but a building of wood, brick or stone, where the people meet together, is generally called so; and should the people be frightened away by the many abominable dead carcases which they meet with, they should follow the multitudes to the fields, to the vallies, to the mountains, to the islands, to the rivers, and to the ships, and compel them to come in, that the house of the Lord may be filled. But when we find some of the covetous connivers with slave-holders, in the West-Indies, so ignorant as to dispute whether a Pagan can be baptized without giving him a Christian name, we cannot expect much from them, or think that they will follow after much good. No name, whether Christian or Pagan, has any thing to do with baptism; if the requisite qualities of knowledge and faith be found in a man, he may be baptized let his name be what it will. And Christianity does not require that we should be deprived of our own personal name, or the name of our ancestors; but it may very fitly add another name unto us, Christian, or one anointed. And it might as well be answered so to that question in the English liturgy, *What is your name?* — A Christian.[51]

> "*A Christian is the highest stile of man!*
> *And is there, who the blessed cross wipes off*
> *As a foul blot, from his dishonor'd brow?*
> *If angels tremble, 'tis at such a sight:*
> *The wretch they quit disponding of their charge,*
> *More struck with grief or wonder who can tell?*"[52]

And let me now hope that you will pardon me in all that I have been thus telling you, O ye inhabitants of Great-Britain! to whom I owe the greatest respect; to your king! to yourselves! and to your government! And tho' many things which I have written may seem harsh, it cannot be otherwise evaded when such horible iniquity is transacted; and tho' to some what I have said may appear as the rattling leaves of autumn, that may soon be blown away and whirled in a vortex where few can hear and know: I must yet say, although it is not for me to determine the manner, that the voice of our complaint implies a vengeance, because of the great iniquity that you have done, and because of the cruel injustice done unto us Africans; and it ought to sound in your ears as the rolling waves around your circum-ambient shores; and if it is not hearkened unto, it may yet arise with a louder voice, as the rolling thunder, and it may encrease in the force of its volubility, not only to shake the leaves of the most stout in heart, but to rend the mountains before them, and to cleave in pieces the rocks under them, and to go on with fury to smite the stoutest oaks in the forest; and even to make that which is strong, and wherein you think that your strength lieth, to become as stubble, and as the fibres of rotten wood, that will do you no good, and your trust in it will become a snare of infatuation to you!

FINIS.

NOTES

1. Isaiah 32:8.
2. Job 30:25. These joined quotations from Isaiah and Job are also found in Olaudah Equiano's letter to the Senate of Great Britain in the *Public Advertiser* of 13 February 1788 and his letter to the "Humanity" poet Samuel Jackson Pratt in the 27 June 1788 edition of the *Morning Chronicle and London Advertiser.* Furthermore, these quotations appear together again in Equiano's *Narrative* (see p. 248 of this volume).
3. The American Revolution, 1775-1783.
4. The New Testament is filled with exhortations to love one's neighbor. See Matthew 19:19 and 22:39, Mark 12:31, 33, Romans 13:9, Galatians 5:14, and James 2:8.
5. The "chain" referred to here is the Great Chain of Being, the widespread Western notion that all of God's creatures had been assigned hierarchical ranks in the cosmos. Between God and man there intervened a hierarchy of angels and other "spiritous beings"; of all creatures on the earth, man occupied the highest link. See Milton, *Paradise Lost*, Bk. V, ll. 470-505; Alexander Pope, *An Essay on Man*, Epistle I, ll. 233-46. Beginning in the eighteenth century, certain thinkers sought to establish a graduated scale of perfection within the category of "Man." The concept of racial hierarchy may be found in the classification work of Carl Linné (Linnaeus), who regarded white skin as characteristic of preëminent members of the human species. In a similar manner, in their respective studies of human skulls, Johann Friedrich Blumenbach, Pieter Camper, John Hunter, and Samuel Thomas von Soemmerring gave the cranial characteristics of Caucasian skulls a preferential

ranking over those from Ethiopia. Blumenbach, in fact, coined the now-familiar term *Caucasian*, after the Caucasus Mountains in southern Russia, the provenance of those skulls in his collection that he inferred to be European. For more information, see William Stanton, *The Leopard's Spots: Scientific Attitudes toward Race in America 1815-59* (Chicago: University of Chicago Press, 1965); and Winthrop D. Jordan's "Introduction" to his critical edition of Samuel Stanhope Smith's *An Essay on the Causes of the Variety of Complexion and Figure in the Human Species* (Cambridge, MA: Harvard University Press, 1965), pp. vii-liii.

6. The word *factory* derives from the Portuguese *feitorias,* land-based European trade depots, which were thickly clustered along the West African coast by the eighteenth century. In his second edition of *An Essay on the Slavery and Commerce of the Human Species, Particularly the African* (enlarged and revised, London, 1788; rpt. New York: AMS Press, 1972), Thomas Clarkson notes the addition of "a new kind of factory established by the British merchants" in African waters: "It consists of a large ship, stationed along the coast, and is called a factory ship. Slaves are brought down and put on board, where they remain as in the factories upon land, till the ships from Europe come along-side, receive them, and carry them off" (p. 26n.). He appends this statement to his discussion of the usual methods through which Europeans procured slaves, to wit, "by sending their boats to the villages situated up the creeks and rivers, or upon the sea shore; by dispatching tenders to different parts: or by an application to the factories, either publickly or privately, established there" (pp. 25-26).

7. Cugoano hails from the Fanti (Fante) tribal region of West Africa, located in modern Ghana. His birthplace, "the city of Agimaque," is the town or district of Ajumako. Fantyn may be a reference to Infantin, which, according to Albert van Dantzig and Adam Jones, was "the nucleus of what later became the 'Fantin' or 'Fante' confederacy." The present-day port of Biriwa (earlier known as Anishan) covers an area believed to correspond with the former Infantin, where the Fante chiefs would often meet. See Van Dantzig's and Jones's reprint of Pieter de Marees, *Description and Historical Account of the Gold Kingdom of Guinea (1602)* (rpt. Oxford: Oxford University Press, 1987), pp. 94 n. 1, 84 n. 22.

8. "Agimaque and Assinee," where Cugoano lived with Ambro Accasa, are the districts or towns of Ajumako and Assin. In 1853 Brodie Cruickshank noted that the people from Fanti and Assin, as well as those from Wassaw, Tufel, Denkera, Akim, Aquapim, and Ashantee—areas immediately surrounding or relatively close to Fanti—"all speak dialects of the same language." See *Eighteen Years on the Gold Coast of Africa including an account of the native tribes, and their intercourse with the Europeans*, 2nd ed., 2 vols. (1853; rpt. New York: Barnes & Noble, 1966), vol. 1, p. 46.

9. Paul Edwards notes that *bounsam* in modern Fanti is *abunsam*, "a devil or any other evil or dangerous creature." See his introduction to the reprint of Cugoano's *Thoughts and Sentiments on the Evil of Slavery* (London: Dawsons of Pall Mall, 1969), p. xiv.

10. John Matthews reveals in *A Voyage to the River Sierra-Leone* (London, 1788; rpt. London: Frank Cass, 1966) that Europeans were quite familiar with the Africans'

fears about the white man's plans for them: once enslaved, an African "imagines the white man buys him either to offer him as a sacrifice to his God, or to devour him as food." Matthews adds that the natives tended to respond to these fears either by falling into a catatonic state, refusing all nourishment, or by laughing—presumably at the white man's foreign, and therefore strange and absurd, appearance (p. 152). Both Cugoano and Olaudah Equiano refused to eat when they were captured; see pp. 133, 179, and 186 of this volume.

11. According to Paul Edwards ("Introduction," 1969), *browfow* corresponds with the plural modern Fanti word *abrofo,* which means "white men" (p. xiv).

12. The words *castle* and *fort* appear to be relatively synonymous in Cugoano's text, and not without reason. Cape Coast Castle, for example, was both a major European town and fort in which the slave trade was vigorously practiced, so much so that the town and the fort became virtually indistinguishable from each other in ordinary speech. Cugoano tells us that he sailed to Grenada from Cape Coast Castle, but it is virtually impossible to determine which castle or fort the slavers took him to first; approximately forty European forts dotted the Gold Coast landscape in the latter half of the eighteenth century.

13. Slave revolts aboard ship were not uncommon. In *Sketches Taken during Ten Voyages to Africa, Between the Years 1786 and 1800* (n.d.; rpt. New York: Johnson Reprint, 1970) English captain John Adams states, "Whenever insurrections have occurred on board of slave ships on the Gold Coast, as the Fantees and Ashantees were invariably the promoters of them, the Chambas [a people who lived north of the Ashante], as if to be revenged on them, always assisted the crews in suppressing these mutinies, and keeping them in subjection" (p. 9). Compare note 53 in the Equiano section of this volume.

14. Sabaoth is the Greek form of the Hebrew *tsebâóth,* "armies"; to the ancient Hebrews, Yahweh-*tsebâóth* was God as the leader of the Israelite armies, who "went forth with them" (Psalms 44:9). In the KJV New Testament, the phrase "Lord of Sabaoth" appears in Romans 9:29 and James 5:4.

15. Cugoano's account of his rescue from the island of Grenada differs from that of Henri Grégoire in *An Enquiry concerning the Intellectual and Moral Faculties, and Literature of Negroes; Followed with an Account of the Life and Works of Fifteen Negroes & Mulattoes, Distinguished in Science, Literature and the Arts* (Paris, 1808; Eng. trans. D. B. Warden [Brooklyn, New York: Printed by Thomas Kirk, 1810]), pp. 188-96. In a brief biographical passage gummed into the front matter of *Thoughts and Sentiments,* Cugoano writes that Alexander Campbell brought him to England; Grégoire avers that one "Lord Hoth" had done so. These conflicting reports may have arisen (at least in part) because Cugoano's short biography was not inserted in all copies of his work; therefore, distribution of his biography would not have been widespread. Apparently Grégoire was not aware of it. Where or how he discovered his own version of events remains unknown to us; compounding the problem is Grégoire's noted proclivity for error. Lord Hoth could possibly be a title belonging to Alexander Campbell; we have not been able, however, to uncover any information about either "Hoth" or Campbell.

16. See 1 Timothy 6:15 and Revelation 1:5.

17. See Genesis 45:5-7.
18. An apostate is a person who has abandoned his or her religious faith, political beliefs, or ethical principles.
19. Cugoano means John Marrant.
20. For General Clinton and the siege of Charleston, South Carolina, see Marrant's *Narrative*, note 60.
21. Exodus 21:2-6.
22. See the introduction to this volume, p. 12.
23. Acts 17:24, 26. Equiano favored this verse.
24. Matthew 5:36.
25. Cugoano refers to a scientific theory propounded by eighteenth-century intellectuals such as Samuel Stanhope Smith, Johann Friedrich Blumenbach, and George Louis Leclerc, le Comte de Buffon, who attributed human skin color to the combined effect of geographic location, climactic variables (especially sustained temperature), and daily regimen. Cugoano probably takes his information from Thomas Clarkson, who devoted over ten pages of the second edition of his *Essay on the Slavery and Commerce of the Human Species* to the relationship between climate and skin color.
26. Psalms 37:35.
27. Genesis 4:12.
28. See Genesis 6-9:17.
29. See Genesis 9:18-27.
30. Genesis 10:15-19.
31. Genesis 14, 19.
32. The invasion of Canaan referred to takes place in the books of Numbers 31-36, Joshua 1-12, and Judges 4-5.
33. See Romans 7-8, especially verse 7:14.
34. This couplet may be derived from Proverbs 13:22: "A good man leaveth an inheritance to his children's children: and the wealth of the sinner is laid up for the just."
35. Cugoano's point here is that for all the wealth derived from Britain's expanding empire, the nation had sunk deeper and deeper into debt over the course of the century. Indeed, nothing hastened the growth of the national debt more than the Seven Years' War with France (1756-1763), fought primarily to acquire new territories in North America, the West Indies, and West Africa. Britain's debt rose from £14.2 million in 1700 to £130 million in 1763; it climbed to £456 million by 1800.
36. That is, stock in one of the joint-stock companies that financed Britain's national debt. Cugoano's complaint is against stockholders (or, derisively, "stockjobbers") who, without actually *producing* anything, prospered through one of the financial institutions that serviced the debt (among them, the British East India Company and the Bank of England). Diatribes against stockjobbing, typically moralistic in tone, were common throughout the eighteenth century; see David Hume's influential essay, "Of Public Credit" (1752).
37. A conflation of verses 11 and 15 in the third chapter of Isaiah.

38. Deuteronomy 15:6.
39. Cugoano refers to the Committee for the Relief of the Black Poor, established in January 1786. Its original members included Henry and Samuel Thornton of the evangelical Clapham sect; Jonas Hanway; Sir Joseph Andrews, Bart.; George Peter; John Osborn; Samuel Hoare; John Julius Angerstein; James Pettitt Andrews; William Ward; John Cornwall; Montague Burgoyne (original chair); George Drake; F. Matthews; Richard Shaw; B. Johnson; and Thomas Boddington. With proceeds donated from the public, the committee provided food, clothing, shelter, medical care, and, in some cases, employment for London's impoverished blacks.
40. The text *"Those that honor . . . in the sight of others"* appears almost verbatim in Equiano's letters of 13 February and 27 June 1788 (discussed in note 2 above). This text is saturated with allusions to and quotations from Proverbs 14:31 and 10:6, 27, 7.
41. To reduce the number of destitute blacks in London, the Committee for the Relief of the Black Poor and the British government agreed in 1786 upon a plan, initiated by amateur botanist Henry Smeathman, to relocate blacks in Sierra Leone. (Smeathman seems not to have recalled his 1785 testimony before a government prisoner relocation committee in which he described the fatal dangers of West Africa.) Hundreds of blacks initially contracted to relocate, but the death of key project officials, fears for personal safety, allegations of fraud among project handlers, dismissals of black leaders, and outbreaks of disease aboard ship caused many to abandon the idea before the ships set sail. Upon reaching Sierra Leone, the 424 colonists—whittled down from 459 due to thirty-five deaths at sea during the month-long voyage—faced severe hardship, intensified by the commencement of the rainy season. Building permanent structures and planting food were imperative but nearly impossible; British seeds wouldn't grow in the African climate; disease killed and crippled hundreds; and nearby Europeans and Africans constantly raided the colony for saleable slaves. Not until 1792, when the Sierra Leone Company sent 1,900 blacks from Nova Scotia to join the beleaguered remnant who managed to survive, did the newly named colony of Freetown take root and flourish. Paul Edwards and David Dabydeen reprint "The Sierra Leone Settlers' Letters" (1791-1800) in *Black Writers in Britain 1760-1890* (Edinburgh: Edinburgh University Press, 1991), pp. 83-98.
42. No arrangements were made with African governments before the colonists sailed for Sierra Leone. In June 1787, Captain Thompson, the naval officer in charge of settling the colonists in Africa, made a treaty with King Tom and his subchiefs Pa Bongee and Queen Yamacouba for ownership of a stretch of land for the new settlement. Over the next two years, however, local Europeans and African chiefs—including King Tom—harassed the colony and raided it for saleable slaves as its defenses weakened through death, desertion, and loss of ammunition.
43. Olaudah Equiano had planned to accompany the colonists to Sierra Leone as part of his duties as Commissary of Provisions and Stores for the Black Poor to Sierra Leone. Yet when he discovered and spoke out against rampant fraud among pro-

ject officials, including Superintendent Joseph Irwin, Reverend Patrick Fraser (Frazer), and Dr. Currie, a surgeon (all of whom he castigates in a letter to Cugoano dated 24 March 1787 and printed in the 4 April 1787 issue of *The Public Advertiser*), Samuel Hoare, the new chair of the Committee for the Relief of the Black Poor, dismissed Equiano and twenty-three of his associates. These twenty-four people did not go to Sierra Leone. See also p. 247 of this volume.

44. The Africans who jumped ship in Plymouth to escape resettlement in Sierra Leone did so after Equiano had been replaced.

45. Henry Smeathman, the originator of the Sierra Leone repatriation plan, died on 1 July 1786, only one-and-a-half months after the Committee for the Relief of the Black Poor first informed the black community about Smeathman's idea. Jonas Hanway, the chair of the Committee, died soon thereafter, on 5 September. Shortly after the new colonists reached Sierra Leone on 9 May 1787, Joseph Irwin, Smeathman's associate and replacement as superintendent of the colony, numbered among the many people who died of disease.

46. Many blacks, enslaved and free, fought for the British during the Revolutionary War. In return, blacks from the American colonies were promised freedom at the end of the war, when many moved to Nova Scotia and other British colonies or to Britain itself. Financial assistance, however, was usually withheld. In London, relocated white Loyalists were often reimbursed for property lost during the war, a privilege that rarely extended to blacks, who lacked the necessary paperwork to prove their claims. On 20 April 1786 the government began offering destitute blacks a slight stipend of 6d. per day, but the sum was well below subsistence level.

47. *The Morning Herald* of 15 December 1786 (and three days later, *The Public Advertiser*) announced that several leaders of the Black Poor consulted political agitator and working-class hero Lord George Gordon, who advised them not to go to Sierra Leone.

48. James 3:11.

49. Gordon Turnbull (fl. eighteenth century), a British planter in the West Indies, wrote the pro-slavery and slave trade tracts *Letters to a Young Planter; or Observations on the Management of a Sugar-Plantation. To which is added, The planter's kalendar. Written on the island of Grenada, by an old Planter* (London, 1785) and *An Apology for Negro Slavery: or, The West-India planters vindicated from the charge of inhumanity* (London, 1786). Equiano's review of Turnbull's *Apology* appears in the 5 February 1788 issue of *The Public Advertiser*, in which Equiano decries Turnbull's support of fellow pro-slavery writer James Tobin, and the "hissing zeal and impotent malevolence" of both men against abolitionist James Ramsay and the African people. The letter is reprinted in Folarin Shyllon, *Black People in Britain 1555-1833* (London: Oxford University Press, 1977), pp. 251-53.

50. Jeremiah 16:18.

51. In the Catechism found within the Anglican *Book of Common Prayer*, the priest's initial question to the catechumen is "What is your name?" The catechumen then responds with his or her baptismal name. Cugoano's point here is that a baptismal name, bestowed upon a person by godparents during the baptismal

ceremony, does not signify an abiding Christian faith and character; therefore, a baptized non-European should not be required to replace his or her personal name with a baptismal name as a sign of Christian faith. Rather, Cugoano advocates that the Anglican Church rewrite the Catechism to embrace a multicultural congregation by changing the answer to "What is your name?" to "A Christian," a response that constitutes a spiritual commitment. John Stuart (Stewart) was probably Cugoano's baptismal name; likewise, James Albert may have been Ukawsaw Gronniosaw's baptismal name.

52. Here Cugoano quotes lines 788-93 from Night IV, "The Christian Triumph" (1743), of Edward Young's *Night Thoughts* (1742-1745). According to Stephen Cornford, the poem became "a standard devotional work, reinforcing conversion as the central metaphor of Christian believing," during "the years of the Methodist and Evangelical revivals and through the early nineteenth century." See Cornford's critical edition of *Night Thoughts* (Cambridge, England: Cambridge University Press, 1989), p. ix.

OLAUDAH EQUIANO

ABOUT
OLAUDAH EQUIANO

LIFE

Olaudah Equiano was born in 1745 to a family of high social standing in the Igbo agricultural society of Essaka, a village or town in what is known today as Igboland, Nigeria. According to Nigerian scholar Catherine Obianuju Acholonu, Equiano's real name is Adipuoerie Olaude Ekwealuo, an ancestor of the Ekwealuo family of the village Isseke, Ihiala Local Government Area, Anambra State, Nigeria. Equiano, as he called himself in English, grew up in a family of six other children, but he often preferred the company of his mother as he learned the traditions and rituals of his culture. At the age of ten, Equiano and his sister were stolen from their home by slavers who quickly separated the two. The terrified and lonely boy was forced to embark on a long journey through and beyond Igboland, enduring many different masters and a final, agonizingly brief glimpse of his sister, before being trundled aboard a slave ship bound for Barbados.

After a horrifying middle passage and a two-week stay in Barbados, Equiano was shipped to the North American colonies aboard a slave ship. On this ship he was renamed Michael. He was then sold to a Mr. Campbell, who changed the boy's name to Jacob and set him to work on a Virginia plantation until late 1756 or early 1757. At this time, Equiano was purchased by British navy lieutenant Michael Henry Pascal, who was briefly serving on leave as captain of a West Indies merchant vessel. Pascal renamed him Gustavus Vassa, after a sixteenth-century Swedish patriot, and took him to England, where they arrived in the early spring of 1757. At first Equiano lodged with different families in Falmouth and Guernsey as Pascal returned to naval duty at sea; by summer, however, the boy chose to accompany his master aboard ship, a decision coinciding with Prime

Minister William Pitt's intensification of the British war effort against France and her allies during the Seven Years' War (1756-1763).

As a servant, a powder boy, and a gunmate in the Royal Navy over the next five and a half years, Equiano fought in several of Britain's most crucial battles against the French. Aboard Vice-Admiral Edmund Boscawen's flagship, the *Namur*, the youth was part of the naval force in the successful British siege of the French fort at Louisburg on 26 July 1758. A year later, he sailed to victory with Boscawen in the Mediterranean theatre when the British fleet routed the French in the Battle of Lagos on 18 August 1759. He also served throughout the naval assault on the citadel of Belle Isle, which the British finally captured in early June of 1761.

During these war years, 1757 to 1762, Equiano strove in his spare time to improve his skills in reading, writing, and arithmetic. He also read the Bible, and was baptized in February 1759 at St. Margaret's Church in the Westminster section of London. He chose the baptismal name of Gustavus Vassa, perhaps as a sign of his own determination to fight for his people who had long suffered in bondage.

Equiano would need massive inner strength to survive what befell him after military hostilities lapsed in late 1762. On 10 December, Pascal abruptly sold him to Captain James Doran, who sailed with him twenty days later for the island of Montserrat in the West Indies. On this island— where blacks outnumbered whites at least 8 to 1—Doran sold Equiano to Quaker merchant Robert King in May of 1763. For the next few years, Equiano sailed with Captain Thomas Farmer throughout the West Indies, working both as a small-goods trader among the islands and as a slaver and small-goods trader between the West Indies and the North American ports of Savannah, Charleston, and Philadelphia. He also witnessed and, at times, personally experienced the atrocities enacted on slaves and "freemen." On 11 July 1766, Equiano bought his freedom from King with his own money. He then continued to work for King as a free man, encountering yet more racism and violence. Still, not until he was shipwrecked three times during the first six months of 1767 did Equiano decide to leave the West Indies. He moved to England in the latter part of July.

Although he briefly settled in the Haymarket section of London and learned the hairdressing trade, Equiano was incessantly drawn—by desire as well as necessity—to the seafaring life. He intermittently worked in London as a hairdresser for Dr. Charles Irving, the inventor of water desalination, but he spent the better part of the 1770s sailing all over the world as a personal servant to various ship captains. In May 1773, he even took part in Constantine Phipps's four-month expedition toward the

North Pole to find a northeast passage to India. Equiano traveled to Spain in 1775 before accompanying Dr. Irving to Central America's Mosquito Coast, where he managed a plantation until 15 June 1776. After avoiding several attempts to sell him into slavery, Equiano returned to England on 7 January 1777.

In the midst of these adventures, Equiano started to take serious interest in spiritual matters, beginning the long process of introspection that would culminate in his evangelical conversion. One of the London churches he regularly attended in 1774 was St. James's, where he probably first met Quobna Ottobah Cugoano, a man destined to become his good friend. It was aboard ship, however, either in late 1774 or early 1775, that Equiano experienced his rebirth in Christ.

While sea ventures remained his focus over the next several years, Equiano nonetheless found time to begin his humanitarian efforts on behalf of both the Afro-English and his native African countrymen. In 1779 he experienced bitter disappointment when the Bishop of London rejected his application to serve as a missionary in Africa. His personal visit with Granville Sharp in March of 1783 was much more successful, for the abolitionist agreed to work toward exposing the governmental corruption at work in the case of the slave ship *Zong*.[1]

In the late 1780s, Equiano turned his full energies to obtaining justice and opportunity for the black community. In November of 1786, the Committee for the Relief of the Black Poor appointed Equiano the Commissary of Provisions and Stores for the London blacks who had agreed to relocate to a new colony in Sierra Leone, West Africa. When his discovery of and protests against widespread misuse of project funds resulted in his dismissal on 24 March 1787, he campaigned still more ardently for black rights. He devoted himself to the cause, attending Parliamentary debates on the slave trade, writing letters to key government officials as well as the queen, joining the letter campaign launched by the Sons of Africa (see p. 127 of this volume), sending scathing book reviews of pro-slave-trade works to London newspapers, and penning his own *Narrative*, which was first published on 1 March 1789. Buoyed by the patronage of subscribers, including members of John Thornton's evangelical Clapham sect and the Countess of Huntingdon's Methodist Connexion, Equiano traveled throughout England, Ireland, and Scotland pressing for abolition—despite a virulent pro-slave-trade backlash—and selling copies of his book to the gentry and working class alike.

We do not know much about Equiano's life in his later years. After listening to Parliament's debate on the slave trade on 2-3 April 1792, he married Susannah Cullen a few days later (7 April) in Soham, Cambridgeshire. He and Susannah had two daughters: Anna Maria died in childhood, but Joanna, born in 1795, survived to adulthood and received an inheritance of £950 on her twenty-first birthday in 1816. In 1793 Equiano published the sixth "edition" of his *Narrative*, which includes updated biographical material through 1792. Although Equiano died in 1797, his *Narrative* continued—and continues—to be published. It is an eloquent testimony to the horrors of slavery, the spirit of freedom, and the courage of faith.

BIBLIOGRAPHICAL NOTE

Of all the works in this collection, *The Interesting Narrative of the Life of Olaudah Equiano, or Gustavus Vassa, the African. Written by Himself* has occupied the literary marketplace in the widest variety of forms over the longest period of time. Originally appearing in 1789, the work was frequently republished during the next thirty years, but virtually disappears after 1837; upon resurfacing in the 1960s, however, its popularity has continued to grow as interest flourishes in African literature and culture, African-American studies, and Black Atlantic history and culture. As a testament to its broad appeal, Equiano's *Narrative* can now be found in classroom textbooks, adult trade books, children's books, and even in comic books. Accordingly, the book's publishing history is lengthy—and snarled in spots where references fail to furnish complete information. Some of the "editions," for example, may represent conflations or multiple copies of one issue. The following list is intended to provide a preliminary guide to the *Narrative*'s presence in the world of letters. The titles are arranged chronologically by year of publication. Imprints that claim to be a particular edition are grouped together; English language imprints, listed alphabetically by place of publication, are followed by foreign language imprints. When several sources appear to cite the same imprint or "edition," the most authoritative sources are listed first. Parenthetical information is taken from title pages and from sources. Asterisks mark those texts we have seen.

London, 1789 . . . . BM
London: Author, [1789] (1st London ed.) . . . . NUC, P
London: Author, 1789 . . . . J, JD
London: Author, by T. Wilkins, [1789] (2nd ed.) . . . . . . NUC, P
London, 1790 (3rd ed.) . . . . BM

London: Author, 1790 (3rd ed., enlarged) . . . . *NUC, P*
1790 (3rd ed., enlarged) . . . . *J, JD*
Rotterdam: Bij Pieter Holsteyn, 1790 . . . . *NUC, J, JD*
Dublin: Author, 1791 (4th ed., enlarged) . . . . *NUC, P, J, JD*
New York, 1791 (1st American ed.) . . . . *BM*
*New York: W. Durell, 1791 (1st American ed.) . . . *NUC, P, J, JD*
Edinburgh: Author; London: G. G. J. & J. Robinson,
   1792 (5th ed., enlarged) . . . . *NUC, P*
Edinburgh: Author, 1792 (5th ed., enlarged) . . . . *J, JD*
Göttingen: Johann Christian Dietrich, 1792 . . . . *J, JD*
London, 1793 (6th ed., enlarged) . . . . *BM, NUC, JD*
*London: Author; and G. G. J. & J. Robinson,
   and Charles Stalker, 1793 (6th ed., enlarged) . . . . *P*
London, 1793 (7th ed., enlarged) . . . . *BM*
London: Author, 1793 (7th ed., enlarged) . . . . *NUC, P*
1793 (7th ed.) . . . . *J, JD*
Norwich, 1794 (8th ed., enlarged) . . . . *BM*
Norwich: Author, 1794 (8th ed., enlarged) . . . . *NUC*
Norwich, 1794 (8th ed.) . . . . *J, JD*
London: Author, 1794 (9th ed., enlarged) . . . . *P*
[n.p.]: [n.s.], 1794 . . . . *P*
Moscow: Selivanovski, 1794
   (Russian trans. from the German) . . . . *NUC*
Belper, [England]: S. Mason, 1809 (new ed.;
   w/Phillis Wheatley's *Poems on Various Subjects*) . . . . . *BM, J, JD*
Belper, [England]: S. Mason, 1809 (new ed.) . . . . *NUC*
Halifax: J. Nicholson & Co., 1813 (w/Phillis Wheatley's
   Poems on Various Subjects) . . . . *NUC, P, J, JD*
Halifax: J. Nicholson & Co., 1814 (w/Phillis Wheatley's
   Poems on Various Subjects) . . . . *BM, P, J, JD*
Leeds: James Nichols, 1814 (new ed., corrected) . . . . *BM*
*Leeds: James Nichols; London: Cradock and Joy;
   Darlington: W. H. Blackburn, 1814
   (new ed., corrected) . . . . *NUC, P*
Penryn, [England]: W. Cook, 1815 . . . . *NUC, P, J, JD*
Halifax: M. Garlick, 1819 (w/Phillis Wheatley's
   Poems on Various Subjects) . . . . *J, JD*
Halifax: M. Garlick, 1819 . . . . *OCLC*
[London: Bagster, 182-?] . . . . *NUC*
*New York: Samuel Wood & Sons, 1829
   (abridged by A. Mott) . . . . *NUC, P, J, JD*
[London]: Harvey & Darton et al., [1830?] . . . . *NUC*
Boston: I. Knapp, 1837 . . . . *NUC*
Boston: J. Knapp, 1837 . . . . *J, JD*
London: Heinemann, 1964 . . . . *J*

Stockholm: Tiden, 1964 (Swedish trans.) . . . . *JD*
London: Heinemann, 1967 (abridged) . . . . *NUC, JD*
London, Ibadan: Heinemann, 1967
  (African Writers Series, no. 10) . . . . *JD*
*New York: Praeger, 1967 (American rpt. of Heinemann,
  1967, ed.) . . . . *JD*
Madison: University of Wisconsin Press, 1967
  (excerpt) . . . . *NUC*
London: Dawsons of Pall Mall, 1969
  (two-volume facsimile rpt. of London,
  1789, ed.; the Colonial History series) . . . . *NUC*
*London: Heinemann, 1969 (abridged; 2nd ed.) . . . . *OCLC*
New York: Negro Universities Press, 1969
  (rpt. of 1837 ed.) . . . .*NUC*
*Belmont, CA: Wadsworth Publishing, 1971
  (selections) . . . . *NUC*
*New York: Dutton, 1971 (juvenile book) . . . . *NUC*
Haarlem, [Netherlands], 1977 (Dutch trans.) . . . . *AC*
Sacramento, CA: Press of Arden Park, 1983
  (excerpt from 1791 ed.) . . . . *OCLC*
*New York: Penguin, 1987
  (rpt. Leeds and London, 1814) . . . . *OCLC*
Paris: Editions Caribéennes, 1987 . . . . *OCLC*
*Braamfontein Ravan Press; Johannesburg,
  [South Africa]: Sached Trust, 1988 (comic book) . . . . . . *OCLC*
*Coral Gables, FL: Mnemosyne, 1989
  (rpt. of 1 March 1789 ed.) . . . . *OCLC*
*Harlow, [England]: Longman, 1989 (rpt. of 1789 ed.) . . . *OCLC*
*New York: Knopf, 1994 (juvenile book) . . . . *OCLC*

We have chosen the "new edition, corrected" of Leeds, London, and Darlington (1814) for our diplomatic reprint because it includes additional material on Equiano's experiences up to and including 1792. (We have not, however, included the nineteenth-century editorial notes that decry Equiano's "indiscreet" choice of language.) Unlike the texts of Ukawsaw Gronniosaw or John Marrant, Equiano's text remains remarkably consistent over time. Still, several important differences exist among imprints. Thus, we include textual glosses on significant alterations made in the *Narrative* among the following major imprints: Coral Gables, FL: Mnemosyne, 1989 (rpt. of 1 March 1789 ed.); New York: W. Durrell, 1791 (rpt. of 2nd London ed.); London: Author, and G. G. J. & J. Robinson, and Charles Stalker, 1793 (6th ed., enlarged).

NOTE

1. In 1781, a debilitating illness killed or severely disabled a significant percentage of the slaves aboard the slave ship *Zong* during the ship's return to England. Because the sale of the remaining healthy slaves would not recover the slavers' initial investment, the ship's captain dumped 133 slaves overboard. Casting blacks overboard regularly occurred aboard some ships at sea, according to preacher Thomas Fuller (*The Holy State* [Cambridge, England, 1642]), because perpetrators could rationalize that "dumbe fishes will tell no tales" (p. 129). British law underwrote this practice by making legal provision for slaves "irretrievably" lost at sea; courts could order maritime insurers to absorb the cost of any property—including slaves—that had been disposed of as an immediate danger to a ship's safety. Such was the purported case of the *Zong*. At court the *Zong*'s owners pled, despite evidence to the contrary, that the slaves' presence endangered the ship's insufficient water supply; they won the case. This result so angered Olaudah Equiano that he requested Granville Sharp on 19 March 1783 to, in Sharp's words, "avenge the blood of his murdered countrymen." Sharp's ensuing campaign effected only a brief burst of public outrage. Peter Fryer, however, credits it with aiding the passage of the Dolben Act in 1788, which regulated overcrowding aboard slavers. See Prince Hoare, *Memoirs of Granville Sharp, Esq.* (London: Printed for Henry Colburn and Co., 1820), pp. 236, 242; Peter Fryer, *Staying Power: The History of Black People in Britain* (London: Pluto Press, 1984), p. 129.

The Interesting Narrative of the Life of Olaudah Equiano, or Gustavus Vassa, the African. Written by Himself

(ABRIDGED)

CHAPTER 1

I BELIEVE it is difficult for those who publish their own memoirs to escape the imputation of vanity. Nor is this the only disadvantage under which they labour: it is also their misfortune, that whatever is uncommon is rarely, if ever, believed, and from what is obvious we are apt to turn with disgust, and to charge the writer of it with impertinence. People generally think those memoirs only worthy to be read or remembered which abound in great or striking events; those in short, which, in a high degree, excite either admiration or pity: all others they consign to contempt and oblivion. It is therefore, I confess, not a little hazardous in a private and obscure individual, and a stranger too, thus to solicit the indulgent attention of the public; especially when I own I offer here the history of neither a saint, a hero, nor a tyrant. I believe there are a few events in my life which have not happened to many. It is true the incidents of it are numerous; and did I consider myself an European, I might say my sufferings were great: but when I compare my lot with that of most of my countrymen, I regard myself as a *particular favourite of Heaven,* and acknowledge the mercies of Providence in every occurrence of my life. If, then, the following narrative does not appear sufficiently interesting to engage general attention, let my motive be some excuse for its publication. I am not so foolishly vain as to expect from it either immortality or literary reputation. If it affords any satisfaction to my numerous friends, at whose request it has been written, or in the smallest degree promotes the interests of humanity, the ends for which

it was undertaken will be fully attained, and every wish of my heart grat-
ified. Let it therefore be remembered that, in wishing to avoid censure,
I do not aspire to praise.

That part of Africa, known by the name of Guinea, to which the
trade for slaves is carried on, extends along the coast above 3,400 miles,
from Senegal to Angola, and includes a variety of kingdoms.[1] Of these
the most considerable is the kingdom of Benin, both as to extent and
wealth, the richness and culture of the soil, the power of its king, and the
number and warlike disposition of its inhabitants. It is situated nearly
under the line,[2] and extends along the coast about 170 miles, but runs
back into the interior of Africa to a distance hitherto, I believe, unex-
plored by any traveller; and seems only terminated at length by the
empire of Abyssinia, near 1,500 miles from its beginning. This kingdom
is divided into many provinces or districts; in one of the most remote and
fertile of which, named Essaka, situated in a charming fruitful vale, I was
born, in the year 1745.[3] The distance of this province from the capital
of Benin and the sea coast must be very considerable: for I had never
heard of white men or Europeans, nor of the sea; and our subjection to
the king of Benin was little more than nominal. Every transaction of the
government, as far as my slender observation extended, was conducted
by the chiefs or elders of the place. The manners and government of a
people who have little commerce with other countries, are generally very
simple; and the history of what passes in one family or village, may serve
as a specimen of the whole nation. My father was one of those elders or
chiefs of whom I have spoken, and was stiled Embrenche;[4] a term, as I
remember, importing the highest distinction, and signifying in our language "a mark of grandeur." This mark is conferred on the person entitled to it by cutting the skin across at the top of the forehead, and
drawing it down to the eyebrows; and applying a warm hand to it,
while in this situation, and rubbing it until it shrinks up into a thick wale
across the lower part of the forehead.[5] Most of the judges and senators
were thus marked; my father had long borne this badge: I had seen it
conferred on one of my brothers, and I also was destined to receive it by
my parents. Those Embrenche, or chief men, decided disputes, and
punished crimes; for which purpose they always assembled together.
The proceedings were generally short; and in most cases the law of
retaliation prevailed. I remember a man was brought before my father,
and the other judges, for kidnapping a boy; and, although he was the son
of a chief, or senator, he was condemned to make recompense by a man
or woman slave. Adultery, however, was sometimes punished by slavery

or death; a punishment which, I believe, is inflicted on it throughout most of the nations of Africa;[6] so sacred among them is the honour of the marriage bed, and so jealous are they of the fidelity of their wives. Of this I recollect an instance; — A woman was convicted, before the judges, of adultery, and delivered over, as the custom was, to her husband to be punished. Accordingly he determined to put her to death; but it being found, just before her execution, that she had an infant at her breast; and no woman being prevailed on to perform the part of a nurse, she was spared on account of the child. The men, however, do not preserve the same constancy to their wives, which they expect from them; for they indulge in a plurality, though seldom in more than two. Their mode of marriage is this: — Both parties are usually betrothed when young by their parents, though I have known the males betroth themselves. On this occasion a feast is prepared, and the bride and bridegroom stand up in the midst of all their friends, who are assembled for the purpose, while he declares she is henceforth to be looked upon as his wife, and that no person is to pay any addresses to her. This is also immediately proclaimed in the vicinity, on which the bride retires from the assembly. Some time after she is brought home to her husband, and then another feast is made, to which the relations of both parties are invited. Her parents then deliver her to the bridegroom, accompanied with a number of blessings, and at the same time they tie round her waist a cotton string of the thickness of a goose-quill, which none but married women are permitted to wear. She is now considered as completely his wife; and at this time the dowry is given to the new-married pair, which generally consists of *portions of land, slaves and cattle, household goods, and implements of husbandry.* These are offered by the friends of both parties: besides which the parents of the bridegroom present gifts to those of the bride, whose property she is looked upon before marriage; but after it she is esteemed the sole property of the husband. The ceremony being now ended, the festival begins, which is celebrated with bonfires, and loud acclamations of joy, accompanied with music and dancing.

We are almost a nation of dancers, musicians, and poets. Every great event, such as a triumphant return from battle, or other cause of public rejoicing, is celebrated in public dances, which are accompanied with songs and music suited to the occasion. The assembly is separated into four divisions, which dance either apart or in succession, and each with a character peculiar to itself. The first division contains the married men, who in their dances frequently exhibit feats of arms, and the representation of a battle. To these succeed the married women, who dance in the second division. The young men occupy the third; and the maidens the fourth. Each represents some interesting scene of real life, such as a great achievement, domestic employment, a pathetic story, or some rural sport. And as the subject is generally founded on some recent event, it is therefore ever new. This gives our dances a spirit and variety which I have scarcely seen elsewhere.[7] We have many musical instruments, particularly drums of different kinds, a piece of music which resembles a guitar, and another much like a sticcado.[8] These last are chiefly used by betrothed virgins, who play on them on all grand festivals.

As our manners are simple, our luxuries are few. The dress of both sexes is nearly the same. It generally consists of a long piece of calico or muslin, wrapped loosely round the body, somewhat in the form of a Highland plaid. This is usually dyed blue, which is our favourite colour. It is extracted from a berry, and is brighter and richer than any I have seen in Europe. Besides this, our women of distinction wear golden ornaments, which they dispose with some profusion on their arms and legs. When our women are not employed with the men in tillage, their usual occupation is spinning and weaving cotton, which they afterwards dye, and make into garments. They also manufacture earthen vessels, of which we have many kinds; among the rest, tobacco pipes, made after the same fashion, and used in the same manner, as those in Turkey.[9]

Our manner of living is entirely plain; for as yet the natives are unacquainted with those refinements in cookery which debauch the taste. Bullocks, goats, and poultry, supply the greatest part of their food. These constitute likewise the principal wealth of the country, and the chief articles of its commerce. The flesh is usually stewed in a pan; to make it savory we sometimes use also pepper, and other spices, and we have salt made of wood ashes. Our vegetables are mostly plantains, eadas,[10] yams, beans, and Indian corn. The head of the family usually eats alone; his wives and slaves have also their separate tables. Before we taste food we always wash our hands: indeed our cleanliness on all occasions is extreme; but on this it is an indispensable ceremony. After washing, libation is made, by pouring out a small portion of the drink on the floor, and by tossing a small quantity of the food in a certain place, for the spirits of departed relations, which the natives suppose to preside over their conduct, and to guard them from evil. They are totally unacquainted with strong or spirituous liquors; and their principal beverage is palm wine. This is got from a tree of that name, by tapping it at the top, and fastening a large gourd to it; and sometimes one tree will yield three or four gallons in a night. When just drawn it is of a delicious sweetness; but in a few days it acquires a spirituous flavour: though I never saw any one intoxicated by it. The same tree also produces nuts and oil. Our principal luxury is in perfumes; one sort of these is an odoriferous wood of delicious fragrance: the other a kind of earth, a small portion of which thrown into the fire diffuses a most powerful odour.[11] We beat this wood into powder, and mix it with palm oil; with which both men and women perfume themselves.

In our buildings we study convenience rather than ornament. Each master of a family has a large square piece of ground, surrounded with a moat or fence, or enclosed with a wall, made of red earth tempered: which, when dry, is as hard as brick. Within this are his houses to accommodate his family and slaves; which, if numerous, frequently cause these tenements to present the appearance of a village. In the middle stands the principal building, appropriated to the sole use of the master, and consisting of two apartments;[12] in one of which he sits in the day with his family, the other is left apart for the reception of his friends. He has besides these a distinct apartment in which he sleeps, together with his male children. On each side are the apartments of his wives, who have also their separate day and night houses.[13] The habitations of the slaves and their families are distributed throughout the rest of the enclosure. These houses never exceed one story in height: they are always built of wood, or stakes driven into the ground, crossed with wattles, and neatly plastered within and without. The roof is thatched with reeds. Our day houses are left open at the sides; but those in which we sleep are always covered, and plastered in the inside with a composition mixed with cow dung, to keep off the different insects, which annoy us during the night.[14] The walls and floors also of these are generally covered with mats. Our beds consist of a platform, raised three or four feet from the ground, on which are laid skins, and different parts of a spungy tree called plantain. Our covering is calico, or muslin, the same as our dress. The usual seats are a few logs of wood; but we have benches, which are generally perfumed, to accommodate strangers: these compose the greater part of our household furniture. Houses so constructed and furnished require but little skill to erect them. Every man is a sufficient architect for the purpose. The whole neighbourhood afford their unanimous assistance in building them, and in return receive, and expect no other recompense than a feast.

As we live in a country where nature is prodigal of her favours, our wants are few, and easily supplied; of course we have few manufactures. They consist, for the most part, of calicoes, earthenware, ornaments, and

instruments of war and husbandry. But these make no part of our commerce, the principal articles of which, as I have observed, are provisions.
In such a state money is of little use; however we have some small pieces
of coin, if I may call them such. They are made something like an anchor;
but I do not remember either their value or denomination. We have also
markets, at which I have been frequently with my mother. These are
sometimes visited by stout mahogany-coloured men from the south-west
of us. We call them Oye-Eboe,[15] which term signifies "red men living at
a distance." They generally bring us fire-arms, gunpowder, hats, beads,
and dried fish. The last we esteemed a great rarity, as our waters were
only brooks and springs. These articles they barter with us for odoriferous woods and earth, and our salt of wood ashes.[16] They always carry
slaves through our land; but the strictest account is exacted of their
manner of procuring them, before they are suffered to pass. Sometimes,
indeed, we sold slaves to them, but they were only prisoners of war, or
such among us as had been convicted of kidnapping, or adultery, and
some other crimes, which we esteemed heinous. This practice of kidnapping induces me to think, that, notwithstanding all our strictness,
their principal business among us was to trepan our people. I remember,
too, they carried great sacks along with them, which not long after, I had
an opportunity of fatally seeing applied to that infamous purpose.

Our land is uncommonly rich and fruitful, and produces all kinds of
vegetables in great abundance. We have plenty of Indian corn, and vast
quantities of cotton and tobacco. Pine-apples grow without culture;
they are about the size of the largest sugar loaf, and finely flavoured. We
have also spices of different kinds, particularly pepper; and a variety of
delicious fruits which I have never seen in Europe; together with gums
of various kinds, and honey in abundance. All our industry is exerted to
improve those blessings of nature. Agriculture is our chief employment;
and every one, even to children and women, is engaged in it. Thus we
are habituated to labour from our earliest years. Every one contributes
something to the common stock: and as we are unacquainted with idleness, we have no beggars.[17] The benefits of such a mode of living are
obvious. — The West India planters prefer the slaves of Benin or Eboe,
to those of any other part of Guinea, for their hardiness, intelligence,
integrity and zeal. — Those benefits are felt by us in the general health-
iness of the people, and in their vigour and activity; I might have added,
too, in their comeliness. Deformity is indeed unknown amongst us, I
mean that of shape. Numbers of the natives of Eboe, now in London,
might be brought in support of this assertion: for, in regard to complexion,

ideas of beauty are wholly relative.[18] I remember while in Africa to
have seen three negro children, who were tawny, and another quite
white, who were universally regarded as deformed by myself and the
natives in general, as far as related to their complexions.[19] Our women
too, were, in my eyes at least, uncommonly graceful, alert, and modest
to a degree of bashfulness; nor do I remember to have ever heard of an
instance of incontinence amongst them before marriage. They are also
remarkably cheerful. Indeed cheerfulness and affability are two of the
leading characteristics of our nation.

Our tillage is exercised in a large plain or common, some hours' walk
from our dwellings, and all the neighbours resort thither in a body.
They use no beasts of husbandry; and their only instruments are hoes,
axes, shovels, and beaks, or pointed iron to dig with. Sometimes we are
visited by locusts, which come in large clouds, so as to darken the air,
and destroy our harvest. This, however, happens rarely, but when it
does, a famine is produced by it. I remember an instance or two of this
happening. This common is often the theatre of war; and therefore,
when our people go out to till their land, they not only go in a body, but
generally take their arms with them for fear of a surprise: and when they
apprehend an invasion, they guard the avenues to their dwellings by
striking sticks into the ground, which are so sharp at one end as to pierce
the foot, and are generally dipped in poison. From what I can recollect
of these battles, they appear to have been irruptions of one little state or
district into another, to obtain prisoners or booty. Perhaps they were
incited to this by those traders, who brought amongst us the European
goods which I mentioned. Such a mode of obtaining slaves in Africa is
common; and I believe more are procured in this way, and by kidnapping, than in any other.[20] When a trader wants slaves, he applies to a
chief for them, and tempts him with his wares. It is not extraordinary,
if on this occasion he yields to the temptation with as little firmness, and
accepts the price of his fellow-creature's liberty with as little reluctance
as the enlightened merchant. Accordingly he falls on his neighbours, and
a desperate battle ensues. If he prevails and takes prisoners, he gratifies
his avarice by selling them; but if his party be vanquished, and he falls
into the hands of the enemy, he is put to death: for, as he has been
known to foment their quarrels, it is thought dangerous to let him survive, and no ransom can save him, though all other prisoners may be
redeemed. We have fire-arms, bows and arrows, broad two-edged
swords, and javelins, also shields which will cover a man from head to
foot. All are taught the use of these weapons; even our women are war-

riors, and march boldly out to fight along with the men.[21] Our whole district is a kind of militia: on a certain signal given, such as the firing of a gun at night, they all rise in arms and rush upon their enemy. It is, perhaps, something remarkable, that when our people march to the field, a red flag or banner is borne before them. I was once a witness to a battle on our common. We had all been at work in it one day, as usual, when our people were suddenly attacked. I climbed a tree at some distance, from which I beheld the fight. There were many women, as well as men, on both sides; among others my mother was there, and armed with a broad sword. After fighting for a considerable time with great fury, when many had been killed, our people obtained the victory, and took their enemy's chief prisoner. He was carried off in great triumph, and though he offered a large ransom for his life, he was put to death. A virgin of note among our enemies had been slain in the battle, and her arm was exposed in our marketplace, where our trophies were always exhibited. The spoils were divided according to the merit of the warriors. Those prisoners which were not sold or redeemed we kept as slaves: but how different was their condition from that of the slaves in the West Indies! With us they do no more work than other members of the community, than even their master; their food, clothing, and lodging, were nearly the same as theirs, except that they were not permitted to eat with those who were free-born; and there was scarcely any other difference between them than a superior degree of importance, which the head of a family possesses in our state, and that authority which, as such, he exercises over every part of his household. Some of these slaves have even slaves under them, as their own property, and for their own use.

As to religion, the natives believe that there is one Creator of all things, and that he lives in the sun, and is girded round with a belt that he may never eat or drink;[22] but, according to some, he smokes a pipe, which is our own favourite luxury. They believe he governs events, especially our deaths or captivity; but as for the doctrine of eternity, I do not remember to have ever heard of it: some, however, believe in the transmigration of souls in a certain degree.[23] — Those spirits, which are not transmigrated, such as their dear friends or relations, they believe always attend them, and guard them from the bad spirits, or their foes. For this reason they always before eating, as I have observed, put some small portion of the meat, and pour some of the drink, on the ground for them; and they often make oblations of the blood of beasts, or of fowls at their graves. I was very fond of my mother, and was almost constantly with her. When she went to make these oblations at her mother's tomb, which was a kind of small solitary thatched house, I sometimes attended her. There she made her libations, and spent most of the night in cries and lamentations. I have been often extremely terrified on these occasions. The loneliness of the place, the darkness of the night, and the ceremony of libation, naturally awful and gloomy, were heightened by my mother's lamentations; and these concurring with the doleful cries of birds, by which these places were frequented, gave an inexpressible terror to the scene.

We compute the year from the day on which the sun crosses the line, and, on its setting that evening, there is a general shout throughout the land; at least I can speak from my own knowledge, throughout our vicinity. The people, at the same time, make a great noise with rattles, not unlike the basket rattles used by children here, though much larger, and hold up their hands to heaven for a blessing. It is then the greatest offerings are made, and those children who, our wise men foretel, will be fortunate, are then presented to different people. I remember many used to come to see me, and I was carried about to others for that purpose. They have many offerings, particularly at full moons; generally two at harvest, before the fruits are taken out of the ground: and when any young animals are killed, they sometimes offer up a part of them as a sacrifice. These offerings, when made by one of the heads of a family, serve for the whole. I remember we often had them at my father's and my uncle's, and their families have been present. Some of our offerings are eaten with bitter herbs. We had a saying among us to any one of a cross temper, "that if they were to be eaten, they should be eaten with bitter herbs."

We practised circumcision like the Jews, and made offerings and feasts on that occasion in the same manner as they did. Like them also, our children were named from some event, some circumstance, or fancied foreboding at the time of their birth. I was named Olaudah, which, in our language, signifies "vicissitude or fortunate," also, "one favoured, and having a loud voice and well spoken." I remember we never polluted the name of the object of our adoration; on the contrary, it was always mentioned with the greatest reverence; and we are totally unacquainted with swearing, and all those terms of abuse and reproach which find their way so readily and copiously into the language of more civilized people. The only expressions of that kind I remember were, "May you rot!" or "may you swell!" or "may a beast take you!"

I have before remarked that the natives of this part of Africa are extremely cleanly. This necessary habit of decency was with us a part of religion, and therefore we had many purifications and washings; indeed almost as many, and used on the same occasions, if my recollection does not fail me, as the Jews. Those that touched the dead, at any time, were obliged to wash and purify themselves before they could enter a dwelling-house, or touch any person or any thing we eat.[24] I was so fond of my mother I could not keep from her, or avoid touching her at some of those periods, in consequence of which I was obliged to be kept out with her, in a little house made for that purpose, till offering was made, and then we were purified.[25]

Though we had no places of public worship, we had priests and magicians, or wise men. I do not remember whether they had different offices, or whether they were united in the same persons, but they were held in great reverence by the people. They calculated our time, and foretold events, as their name imported, for we called them Ah-affoe-way-cah, which signifies "calculators or yearly men," our year being called Ah-affoe. They wore their beards; and when they died they were succeeded by their sons. Most of their implements and things of value were interred with them. Pipes and tobacco were also put into the graves with the corpse, which was always perfumed and ornamented, and animals were offered in sacrifice to them. None accompanied their funerals but those of the same profession or tribe. These buried them after sunset, and always returned from the grave by a different way from that by which they went.[26]

These magicians were also our doctors or physicians. They practised bleeding by cupping: and were very successful in healing wounds and expelling poisons. They had likewise some extraordinary method of discovering jealousy, theft, and poisoning; the success of which, no doubt, they derived from their unbounded influence over the credulity and superstition of the people. I do not remember what those methods were, except that, as to poisoning, I recollect an instance or two, which I hope it will not be deemed impertinent here to insert, as it may serve as a kind of specimen of the rest, and is still used by the negroes in the West Indies. A young woman had been poisoned, but it was not known by whom. The doctors ordered the corpse to be taken up by some persons and carried to the grave. As soon as the bearers had raised it on their shoulders, they seemed seized with some[27] sudden impulse, and ran to and fro unable to stop themselves. At last, after having passed through a number of thorns and prickly bushes unhurt, the corpse fell from them close to a house, and defaced it in the fall; and the owner being taken up, he immediately confessed the poisoning.[28]

The natives are extremely cautious about poison. When they buy any eatable, the seller kisses it all round before the buyer, to shew him it is not poisoned; and the same is done when meat and drink are presented, particularly to a stranger. We have serpents of different kinds, some of which are esteemed ominous when they appear in our houses, and these we never molest. I remember two of those ominous snakes, each of which was as thick as the calf of a man's leg, and in colour resembling a dolphin in the water, crept into my mother's night house, where I always lay with her, and coiled themselves into folds, and each time they crowed like a cock. I was desired by some of our wise men to touch these, that I might be interested in the good omens, which I did, for they were quite harmless, and would tamely suffer themselves to be handled; and then were put into a large open earthen pan, and set on one side of the highway. Some of our snakes, however, were poisonous: one of them crossed the road one day, as I was standing on it, and passed between my feet without offering to touch me, to the great surprise of many who saw it; and these incidents were accounted by the wise men, and likewise by my mother and the rest of the people, as remarkable omens in my favour.

Such is the imperfect sketch, with which my memory has furnished me, of the manners and customs of a people among whom I first drew my breath. And here I cannot forbear suggesting what has long struck me very forcibly, namely, the strong analogy, which, even by this sketch, imperfect as it is, appears to prevail in the manners and customs of my countrymen and those of the Jews, before they reached the Land of Promise, and particularly the Patriarchs,[29] while they were yet in that pastoral state which is described in Genesis — an analogy which alone would induce me to think that the one people had sprung from the other.[30] Indeed this is the opinion of Dr. Gill, who, in his commentary on Genesis, very ably deduces the pedigree of the Africans from Afer and Afra, the descendants of Abraham by Keturah his wife and concubine (for both these titles are applied to her).[31] It is also conformable to the sentiments of Dr. John Clarke, formerly Dean of Sarum, in his "Truth of the Christian Religion."[32] Both these authors concur in ascribing to us this original. The reasonings of those gentlemen are still further confirmed by the scripture chronology of the Rev. Arthur Bedford;[33] and if any further corroboration were required, this resemblance in so many respects is a strong evidence in support of the opinion. — Like the Israelites in their primitive state, our government was conducted by our chiefs or judges, our wisemen, and elders; and the head of a family, with us, enjoyed a similar authority over his household with that which is ascribed to Abraham and the other Patriarchs. The law of retaliation prevailed almost universally with us as with them:[34] and even their religion appeared to have shed upon us a ray of its glory, though broken and spent in its passage, or eclipsed by the cloud with which time, tradition, and ignorance might have enveloped it. For we had our circumcision (a rite, I believe, peculiar to that people):[35] we had also our sacrifices and burnt-offerings, our washings and purifications, on the same occasions as they had.

As to the difference of colour between the Eboan Africans and the modern Jews, I shall not presume to account for it. It is a subject which has engaged the pens of men both of genius and learning, and is far above my strength. The most able and Rev. Mr. T. Clarkson, however, in his much admired "Essay on the Slavery and Commerce of the Human Species"[36] has ascertained the cause in a manner that at once solves every objection on that account, and, on my mind at least, has produced the fullest conviction. I shall therefore refer to that performance for the theory,[37] contenting myself with extracting a fact as related by Dr. Mitchell.[38] "The Spaniards, who have inhabited America under the torrid zone, for any time, are become as dark coloured as our native Indians of Virginia; of which I myself have been a witness." There is also another instance[39] of a Portuguese settlement at Mitomba, a river in Sierra Leona, where the inhabitants are bred from a mixture of the first Portuguese discoverers with the natives, and are now become in their complexion, and in the woolly quality of their hair, perfect negroes, retaining, however, a smattering of the Portuguese language.

These instances, and a great many more which might be adduced, while they shew how the complexions of the same persons vary in different climates, it is hoped may tend also to remove the prejudice that some conceive against the natives of Africa on account of their colour. Surely the minds of the Spaniards did not change with their complexions! Are there not causes enough to which the apparent inferiority of an African may be ascribed, without limiting the goodness of God, and supposing He forebore to stamp understanding on what is certainly his own image, because "carved in ebony?"[40] Might it not naturally be ascribed to their situation? When they come among Europeans, they are ignorant of their language, religion, manners, and customs. Are any pains taken to teach them these? Are they treated as men? Does not slavery itself depress the mind, and extinguish all its fire, and every noble sentiment? But above all, what advantages do not a refined people possess over those who are rude and uncultivated! Let the polished and haughty European recollect that his ancestors were once like the

Africans, uncivilized and even barbarous. Did Nature make them infe-rior to their sons? And should they too have been made slaves? Every rational mind answers, "No." Let such reflections as these melt the pride of their superiority into sympathy for the wants and miseries of their sable brethren, and compel them to acknowledge, that under-standing is not confined to feature or colour. If, when they look round the world, they feel exultation, let it be tempered with benevolence to others and gratitude to God, "who hath made of one blood all nations of men for to dwell on all the face of the earth;" (Acts xvii. 26.) and whose wisdom is not our wisdom, neither are our ways his ways.[41]

☩ ☩ ☩

CHAPTER 2

I HOPE the reader will not think I have trespassed on his patience, in introducing myself to him with some account of the manners and cus-toms of my country. They had been implanted in me with great care, and made an impression on my mind, which time could not erase, and which all the adversity and variety of fortune I have since experienced, served only to rivet and record; for, whether the love of one's country be real or imaginary, a lesson of reason or an instinct of nature, I still look back with pleasure on the first scenes of my life, though that pleasure has been for the most part mingled with sorrow.

I have already acquainted the reader with the time and place of my birth. My father, besides many slaves, had a numerous family, of which seven lived to grow up, including myself and a sister, who was the only daughter. As I was the youngest of the sons, I became, of course, the greatest favourite with my mother, and was always with her, and she used to take particular pains to form my mind. I was trained up from my earliest years in the art of war: my daily exercise was shooting and throwing javelins; and my mother adorned me with emblems, after the manner of our greatest warriors. In this way I grew up till I was turned the age of eleven, when an end was put to my happiness in the follow-ing manner: — When the grown people in the neighbourhood were gone far in the fields to labour, the children generally assembled together in some of the neighbours' premises to play; and some of us often used to get up into a tree to look out for any assailant, or kidnapper, that might come upon us. For they sometimes took those opportunities of our parents' absence, to attack and carry off as many as they could seize. One day, as I was watching at the top of a tree in our yard, I saw one of those people come into the yard of our next neighbour but one, to kidnap, there being many stout young people in it. Immediately on this I gave the alarm of the rogue, and he was surrounded by the stoutest of them, who entangled him with cords, so that he could not escape till some of the grown people came and secured him.

But alas! ere long it was my fate to be thus attacked, and to be carried off, when none of the grown people were nigh. One day, when all our people were gone out to their work as usual, and only I and my sister were left to mind the house, two men and a woman got over our walls, and in a moment seized us both; and without giving us time to cry out, or to make any resistance, they stopped our mouths and ran off with us into the nearest wood. Here they tied our hands, and continued to carry us as far as they could, till night came on, when we reached a small house, where the robbers halted for refreshment and spent the night. We were then unbound, but were unable to take any food; and being quite over-powered by fatigue and grief, our only relief was some sleep, which allayed our misfortune for a short time. The next morning we left the house, and continued travelling all the day. For a long time we had kept the woods, but at last we came into a road which I believed I knew. I had now some hopes of being delivered; for we had advanced but a little way before I discovered some people at a distance, on which I began to cry out for their assistance; but my cries had no other effect than to make them tie me faster and stop my mouth; they then put me into a large sack. They also stopped my sister's mouth, and tied her hands; and in this man-ner we proceeded till we were out of sight of these people.

When we went to rest the following night, they offered us some vict-uals; but we refused it; and the only comfort we had was in being in one another's arms all that night, and bathing each other with tears. But alas! we were soon deprived of even the small comfort of weeping together. The next day proved one of greater soroow than I had yet experienced; for my sister and I were then separated, while we lay clasped in each other's arms. It was in vain that we besought them not to part us; she was torn from me, and immediately carried away, while I was left in a state of distraction not to be described. I cried and grieved continually; and for several days did not eat any thing but what they forced into my mouth. At length, after many days' travelling, during which I had often changed masters, I got into the hands of a chieftain, in a pleasant coun-try. This man had two wives and some children, and they all used me extremely well, and did all they could to comfort me; particularly the first wife, who was something like my mother. Although I was a great many days' journey from my father's house, yet these people spoke exactly the same language with us. This first master of mine, as I may call him, was a smith, and my principal employment was working his bellows, which were the same kind as I had seen in my vicinity. They were in some respects not unlike the stoves here in gentlemen's kitchens; and were covered over with leather, and in the middle of that leather a stick was fixed, and a person stood up and worked it, in the same manner as is done to pump water out of a cask with a hand pump. I believe it was gold he worked, for it was of a lovely bright yellow colour, and was worn by the women on their wrists and ancles.

I was there, I suppose, about a month, and they at length used to trust me some little distance from the house. I employed this liberty in embracing every opportunity to inquire the way to my own home: and I also sometimes, for the same purpose, went with the maidens, in the cool of the evenings, to bring pitchers of water from the springs for the use of the house. I had also remarked where the sun rose in the morning, and set in the evening, as I had travelled along: and had observed that my father's house was towards the rising of the sun. I therefore determined to seize the first opportunity of making my escape, and to shape my course for that quarter; for I was quite oppressed and weighed down by grief after my mother and friends; and my love of liberty, ever great, was strengthened by the mortifying circumstance of not daring to eat with the free-born children, although I was mostly their companion.

While I was projecting my escape, one day an unlucky event happened, which quite disconcerted my plan, and put an end to my hopes. I used to be sometimes employed in assisting an elderly woman slave to cook and take care of the poultry: and one morning, while I was feeding some chickens, I happened to toss a small pebble at one of them, which hit it on the middle, and directly killed it. The old slave having soon after missed the chicken, inquired after it; and on my relating the accident (for I told her the truth, because my mother would never suffer me to tell a lie) she flew into a violent passion, threatened that I should suffer for it; and, my master being out, she immediately went and told her mistress what I had done. This alarmed me very much, and I expected an instant flogging, which to me was uncommonly dreadful; for I had seldom been beaten at home. I therefore resolved to fly; and accordingly I ran into a thicket that was hard by, and hid myself in the bushes. Soon afterwards my mistress and the slave returned, and, not seeing me, they searched all the house, but not finding me, and I not making answer when they called me, they thought I had run away, and the whole neighbourhood was raised in the pursuit of me.

In that part of the country, as well as in ours, the houses and villages were skirted with woods, or shrubberies, and the bushes were so thick that a man could readily conceal himself in them, so as to elude the strictest search. The neighbours continued the whole day looking for me, and several times many of them came within a few yards of the place where I lay hid. I expected every moment, when I heard a rustling among the trees, to be found out, and punished by my master. But they never discovered me, though they often were so near that I even heard their conjectures, as they were looking about for me; and I now learned from them, that any attempt to return home would be hopeless. Most of them supposed I had fled towards home; but the distance was so great, and the way so intricate, that they thought I could never reach it, and that I should be lost in the woods. When I heard this I was seized with a violent panic, and abandoned myself to despair. Night too began to approach, and aggravated all my fears. I had before entertained hopes of getting home and had determined when it should be dark to make the attempt; but I was now convinced it was fruitless, and began to consider that, if possibly I could escape all other animals, I could not those of the human kind; and that, not knowing the way, I must perish in the woods. Thus was I like the hunted deer:

"Ev'ry leaf, and ev'ry whisp'ring breath
Convey'd a foe, and ev'ry foe a death."[42]

I heard frequent rustlings among the leaves, and being pretty sure they were snakes, I expected every instant to be stung by them. This increased my anguish, and the horror of my situation became now quite insupportable. I at length quitted the thicket, very faint and hungry, for I had not eaten nor drunk any thing all the day. I crept to my master's kitchen, from whence I set out at first, which was an open shed, and laid myself down in the ashes with an anxious wish for death to relieve me from all my pains. I was scarcely awake in the morning, when the old woman slave, who was the first up, came to light the fire, and saw me in the fire place. She was very much surprised to see me, and could scarcely believe her own eyes. She now promised to intercede for me, and went for her master, who soon after came, and, having slightly reprimanded me, ordered me to be taken care of, and not ill treated.

Soon after this my master's only daughter and child by his first wife, sickened and died, which affected him so much that for some time he was almost frantic, and really would have killed himself, had he not been watched and prevented. However, in a small time afterwards he recovered, and I was again sold. I was now carried to the left of the sun's rising, through many dreary wastes and dismal woods, amidst the hideous roaring of wild beasts.[43] The people I was sold to used to carry me very often, when I was tired, either on their shoulders or on their backs. I saw many convenient well-built sheds along the road, at proper distances, to accommodate the merchants and travellers. They lie in those buildings along with their wives, who often accompany them: and they always go well armed.

From the time I left my own nation I always found somebody that understood me till I came to the sea coast. The languages of different nations did not totally differ, nor were they so copious as those of the Europeans, particularly the English. They were therefore easily learned; and, while I was journeying thus through Africa, I acquired two or three different tongues. In this manner I had been travelling for a considerable time, when one evening, to my great surprise, whom should I see brought to the house where I was, but my dear sister? As soon as she saw me she gave a loud shriek, and ran into my arms. I was quite overpowered: neither of us could speak; but for a considerable time, clung to each other in mutual embraces, unable to do any thing but weep. Our meeting affected all who saw us; and indeed I must acknowledge, in honour of those sable destroyers of human rights, that I never met with any ill treatment, or saw any offered to their slaves, except tying them, when necessary, to keep them from running away.

When these people knew we were brother and sister, they indulged us to be together; and the man, to whom I supposed we belonged, lay with us, he in the middle, while she and I held one another by the hands across his breast all night; and thus for a while we forgot our misfortunes in the joy of being together. But even this small comfort was soon to have an end, for scarcely had the fatal morning appeared, when she was again torn from me for ever! I was now more miserable, if possible, than before. The small relief which her presence gave me from pain was gone, and the wretchedness of my situation was redoubled by my anxiety after her fate, and my apprehensions lest her sufferings should be greater than mine, when I could not be with her to alleviate them.

Yes, dear partner of all my childish sports! Sharer of my joys and sorrows; happy should I have ever esteemed myself to encounter every misery for you, and to procure your freedom by the sacrifice of my own! Though you were early forced from my arms, your image has been always rivetted in my heart, from which neither time nor fortune has been able to remove it: so that, while the thoughts of your sufferings have damped my prosperity, they have mingled with adversity and increased its bitterness. To that Heaven, which protects the weak from the strong, I commit the care of your innocence and virtues, if they have not already received their full reward, and if your youth and delicacy have not long since fallen victims to the violence of the African trader, the pestilential stench of a Guinea ship, the seasoning in the European colonies,[44] or the lash and lust of a brutal and unrelenting overseer.

I did not long remain after my sister. I was again sold, and carried through a number of places, till, after travelling a considerable time, I came to a town called Tinmah, in the most beautiful country I had yet seen in Africa. It was extremely rich, and there were many rivulets which flowed through it, and supplied a large pond in the centre of the town, where the people washed. Here I first saw and tasted cocoa nuts, which I thought superior to any nuts I had ever tasted before; and the trees which were loaded, were also interspersed among the houses, which had commodious shades adjoining, and were in the same manner as ours, the insides being neatly plastered and whitewashed. Here I also saw and tasted, for the first time, sugar-cane. Their money consisted of little white shells, the size of the finger nail.[45] I was sold for one hundred and seventy-two of these, by a merchant who lived at this place. I had been about two or three days at his house, when a wealthy widow, a neighbour of his came there one evening, and brought with her an only son, a young gentleman about my own age and size. Here they saw me; and, having taken a fancy to me, I was bought of the merchant, and went home with them. Her house and premises were situated close to one of those rivulets I have mentioned, and were the finest I ever saw in Africa: they were very extensive, and she had a number of slaves to attend her. The next day I was washed and perfumed, and when meal-time came, I was led into the presence of my mistress, and ate and drank before her with her son. This filled me with astonishment; and I could scarcely avoid expressing my surprise that the young gentleman should suffer me, who was bound, to eat with him who was free; and not only so, but that he would not at any time either eat or drink till I had taken first, because I was the eldest, which was agreeable to our custom. Indeed every thing here, and their treatment of me, made me forget that I was a slave. The language of these people resembled ours so nearly, that we

understood each other perfectly. They had also the very same customs
as we. There were likewise slaves daily to attend us, while my young
master and I, with other boys, sported with our darts, and bows and
arrows, as I had been used to do at home. In this resemblance to my former happy state, I passed about two months; and now I began to think
I was to be adopted into the family, and was beginning to be reconciled
to my situation,[46] and to forget by degrees my misfortunes, when all at
once the delusion vanished; for, without the least previous knowledge,
one morning, early, while my dear master and companion was still
asleep, I was awakened out of my reverie to fresh sorrow, and hurried
away even amongst the uncircumcised.

Thus, at the very moment I dreamed of the greatest happiness, I
found myself most miserable; and it seemed as if fortune wished to give
me this taste of joy, only to render the reverse more poignant. The
change I now experienced was as painful as it was sudden and unex-
pected. It was a change indeed from a state of bliss to a scene which is
unexpressible by me, as it discovered to me an element I had never
before beheld, and of which till then had no idea; and wherein such
instances of hardship and cruelty continually occurred, as I can never
reflect on but with horror.

All the nations and people I had hitherto passed through resembled
our own in their manners, customs, and language: but I came at length
to a country, the inhabitants of which differed from us in all these particulars. I was very much struck with this difference, especially when I
came among a people who did not circumcise, and who ate without
washing their hands. They cooked their provisions also in iron pots, and
had European cutlasses and cross bows, which were unknown to us; and
fought with their fists among themselves. Their women were not so
modest as ours, for they ate, drank, and slept with their men. But, above
all, I was amazed to see no sacrifices or offerings among them. In some
of those places the people ornamented themselves with scars, and likewise filed their teeth very sharp.[47] They sometimes wanted to ornament
me in the same manner, but I would not suffer them; hoping that I
might sometime be among a people who did not thus disfigure themselves, as I thought they did. At last I came to the banks of a large river,
covered with canoes, in which the people appeared to live, with their
household utensils, and provisions of all kinds. I was beyond measure
astonished at this, as I had never before seen any water larger than a
pond or a rivulet: and my surprise was mingled with no small fear when
I was put into one of these canoes, and we began to paddle and move

along the river. We continued going on thus till night; and when we came to land, and made fires on the banks, each family by themselves, some dragged their canoes on shore, others cooked in theirs, and laid in them all night. Those on the land had mats, of which they made tents, some in the shape of little houses: in these we slept: and after the morning meal, we embarked again, and proceeded as before. I was often very much astonished to see some of the women as well as the men, jump into the water, dive to the bottom, come up again, and swim about.[48] Thus I continued to travel, both by land and by water, through different countries and various nations, till at the end of six or seven months after I had been kidnapped, I arrived at the sea coast.

It would be tedious and uninteresting to relate all the incidents which befell me during this journey, and which I have not yet forgotten, or to mention the various lands I passed through, and the manners and customs of the different people among whom I lived: I shall therefore only observe, that in all the places where I was, the soil was exceedingly rich; the pomkins, aedas, plantains, yams, &c. &c. were in great abundance, and of incredible size. There were also large quantities of different gums, though not used for any purpose; and every where a great deal of tobacco. The cotton even grew quite wild; and there was plenty of red wood. I saw no mechanics whatever in all the way, except such as I have mentioned. The chief employment in all these countries was agriculture, and both the males and females, as with us, were brought up to it, and trained in the arts of war.

The first object that saluted my eyes when I arrived on the coast was the sea, and a slave ship, which was then riding at anchor, and waiting for its cargo.[49] These filled me with astonishment, that was soon converted into terror, which I am yet at a loss to describe, and much more the then feelings of my mind when I was carried on board. I was immediately handled and tossed up to see if I was sound, by some of the crew; and I was now persuaded that I had got into a world of bad spirits, and that they were going to kill me. Their complexions too, differing so much from ours, their long hair, and the language they spoke, which was very different from any I had ever heard, united to confirm me in this belief. Indeed such were the horrors of my views and fears at the moment, that if ten thousand worlds had been my own, I would have freely parted with them all to have exchanged my condition with the meanest slave in my own country. When I looked round the ship too, and saw a large furnace or copper boiling, and a multitude of black people, of every description, chained together, every one of their countenances expressing dejection and sorrow, I no longer doubted of my fate; and, quite overpowered with horror and anguish, I fell motionless on the deck, and fainted. When I recovered a little, I found some black people about me, who I believed were some of those who brought me on board, and had been receiving their pay: they talked to me in order to cheer me, but all in vain. I asked them if we were not to be eaten by those white men with horrible looks, red faces, and long hair.[50] They told me I was not: and one of the crew brought me a small portion of spirituous liquor in a wine glass; but, being afraid of him, I would not take it out of his hand. One of the blacks therefore took it from him and gave it to me, and I took a little down my palate, which, instead of reviving me, as they thought it would, threw me into the greatest consternation at the strange feeling it produced, having never tasted any such liquor before.

Soon after this the blacks who brought me on board went off, and left me abandoned to despair. I now saw myself deprived of all chance of returning to my native country, or even the least glimpse of gaining the shore, which I now considered as friendly; and I even wished for my former slavery, in preference to my present situation, which was filled with horrors of every kind, still heightened by my ignorance of what I was to undergo. I was not long suffered to indulge my grief. I was soon put down under the decks, and there I received such a salutation in my nostrils as I had never experienced in my life: so that, with the loathsomeness of the stench, and with my crying together, I became so sick and low that I was not able to eat, nor had I the least desire to taste any thing. I now wished for the last friend, death, to relieve me;[51] but soon, to my grief, two of the white men offered me eatables; and, on my refusing to eat, one of them held me fast by the hands, and laid me across, I think, the windlass,[52] and tied my feet, while the other flogged me severely. I had never experienced any thing of this kind before, and although, not being used to the water, I naturally feared that element the first time I saw it, yet nevertheless, could I have got over the nettings, I would have jumped over the side, but I could not; and besides the crew used to watch us very closely, who were not chained down to the decks, lest we should leap into the water. I have seen some of these poor African prisoners most severely cut for attempting to do so, and hourly whipped for not eating. This indeed was often the case with myself.[53] In a little time after, amongst the poor chained men, I found some of my own nation, which in a small degree gave ease to my mind. I inquired of these what was to be done with us. They gave me to understand we were to be carried to these white people's country to work for them. I was then a little revived, and thought if it were no worse than working, my situation was not so desperate. But still I feared I should be put to death, the white people looked and acted, as I thought, in so savage a manner; for I had never seen among any people such instances of brutal cruelty: and this is not only shewn towards us blacks, but also to some of the whites themselves. One white man in particular I saw, when we were permitted to be on deck, flogged so unmercifully with a large rope near the foremast,[54] that he died in consequence of it; and they tossed him over the side as they would have done a brute. This made me fear these people the more; and I expected nothing less than to be treated in the same manner. I could not help expressing my fearful apprehensions to some of my countrymen; I asked them if these people had no country, but lived in this hollow place, the ship. They told me they did not, but came from a distant one. 'Then,' said I, 'how comes it, that in all our country we never heard of them?' They told me, because they lived so very far off. I then asked, where their women were: had they any like themselves. I was told they had. 'And why,' said I, 'do we not see them?' They answered, because they were left behind. I asked how the vessel could go. They told me they could not tell; but that there was cloth put upon the masts by the help of the ropes I saw, and then the vessel went on; and the white men had some spell or magic they put in the water, when they liked, in order to stop the vessel. I was exceedingly amazed at this account, and really thought they were spirits. I therefore wished much to be from amongst them, for I expected they would sacrifice me; but my wishes were in vain, for we were so quartered that it was impossible for any of us to make our escape.

While we stayed on the coast I was mostly on deck; and one day, to my great astonishment, I saw one of these vessels coming in with the sails up. As soon as the whites saw it, they gave a great shout, at which we were amazed; and the more so as the vessel appeared larger by approaching nearer. At last she came to an anchor in my sight, and when the anchor was let go, I and my countrymen who saw it, were lost in astonishment to observe the vessel stop, and were now convinced it was done by magic. Soon after this the other ship got her boats out, and they came on board of us, and the people of both ships seemed very glad to see each other. Several of the strangers also shook hands with us black people, and made motions with their hands, signifying, I suppose, we were to go to their country; but we did not understand them. At last, when the ship, in which we were, had got in all her cargo, they made ready with many fearful noises, and we were all put under deck, so that we could not see how they managed the vessel.

But this disappointment was the least of my grief. The stench of the hold, while we were on the coast, was so intolerably loathsome, that it was dangerous to remain there for any time, and some of us had been permitted to stay on the deck for the fresh air; but now that the whole ship's cargo were confined together, it became absolutely pestilential. The closeness of the place, and the heat of the climate, added to the number in the ship, being so crowded that each had scarcely room to turn himself, almost suffocated us. This produced copious perspirations, so that the air soon became unfit for respiration, from a variety of loathsome smells, and brought on a sickness among the slaves, of which many died, thus falling victims to the improvident avarice, as I may call it, of their purchasers. This deplorable situation was again aggravated by the galling of the chains, now become insupportable; and the filth of necessary tubs, into which the children often fell, and were almost suffocated. The shrieks of the women, and the groans of the dying, rendered it a scene of horror almost inconceivable. Happily, perhaps, for myself, I was soon reduced so low here that it was thought necessary to keep me almost continually on deck; and from my extreme youth, I was not put in fetters. In this situation I expected every hour to share the fate of my companions, some of whom were almost daily brought upon deck at the point of death, and I began to hope that death would soon put an end to my miseries. Often did I think many of the inhabitans of the deep much more happy than myself; I envied them the freedom they enjoyed, and as often wished I could change my condition for theirs. Every circumstance I met with served only to render my state more painful, and heighten my apprehensions and my opinion of the cruelty of the whites. One day they had taken a number of fishes; and when they had killed and satisfied themselves with as many as they thought fit, to our astonishment who were on the deck, rather than give any of them to us to eat, as we expected, they tossed the remaining fish into the sea again, although we begged and prayed for some as well as we could, but in vain; and some of my countrymen, being pressed by hunger, took an opportunity, when they thought no one saw them, of trying to get a little privately; but were discovered, and the attempt procured for them some very severe floggings.

One day, when we had a smooth sea and moderate wind, two of my wearied countrymen, who were chained together, (I was near them at the time) preferring death to such a life of misery, somehow made through the nettings and jumped into the sea: immediately another quite dejected fellow, who on account of his illness was suffered to be out of irons, also followed their example; and I believe many more would very soon have done the same, if they had not been prevented by the ship's crew, who were instantly alarmed. Those of us who were the most active were in a moment put down under the deck; and there was such a noise and confusion amongst the people of the ship as I never heard before, to stop her and get the boat out to go after the slaves. However, two of the wretches were drowned; but they got the other, and afterwards flogged him unmercifully, for thus attempting to prefer death to slavery. In this manner we continued to undergo more hardships than I can now relate; hardships which are inseparable from this accursed trade. Many a time we were near suffocation from the want of fresh air, being deprived thereof for days together. This, and the stench of the necessary tubs, carried off many.

During our passage I first saw flying fishes, which surprised me very much: they used frequently to fly across the ship, and many of them fell on the deck. I also now first saw the use of the quadrant.[55] I had often with astonishment seen the mariners make observations with it, and I could not think what it meant. They at last took notice of my surprise: and one of them, willing to increase it, as well as to gratify my curiosity, made me one day look through it. The clouds appeared to me to be land, which disappeared as they passed along. This heightened my wonder; and I was now more persuaded than ever that I was in another world, and that every thing about me was magic. At last we came in sight of the island of Barbadoes, at which the whites on board gave a great shout, and made many signs of joy to us. We did not know what to think of this, but as the vessel drew nearer we plainly saw the harbour, and other ships of different kinds and sizes; and we soon anchored amongst them off Bridge Town. Many merchants and planters now came on board, though it was in the evening. They put us in separate parcels, and examined us attentively. They also made us jump, and pointed to the land, signifying we were to go there. We thought by this we should be eaten by these ugly men, as they appeared to us; and, when soon after we were all put down under the deck again, there was much dread and trembling among us, and nothing but bitter cries to be heard all the night from these apprehensions, insomuch that at last the white people got some old slaves from the land to pacify us. They told us we were not to be eaten, but to work, and were soon to go on land, where we should see many of our country people. This report eased us much; and, sure enough, soon after we landed, there came to us Africans of all languages.

We were conducted immediately to the merchant's yard, where we were all pent up together like so many sheep in a fold, without regard to sex or age. As every object was new to me, every thing I saw filled me with surprise. What struck me first was that the houses were built with bricks in stories, and were in every other respect different from those I had seen in Africa; but I was still more astonished at seeing people on horseback. I did not know what this could mean; and indeed I thought these people full of nothing but magical arts. While I was in this astonishment one of my fellow prisoners spoke to a countryman of his about the horses, who said they were the same kind they had in their country. I understood them, though they were from a distant part of Africa, and I thought it odd I had not seen any horses there; but afterwards, when I came to converse with different Africans, I found they had many horses amongst them, and much larger than those I then saw.[56]

We were not many days in the merchants' custody before we were sold after the usual manner, which is this:—On a signal given, such as the beat of a drum, the buyers rush at once into the yard where the slaves are confined, and make choice of that parcel they like best. The noise and clamour with which this is attended, and the eagerness visible in the countenances of the buyers, serve not a little to increase the apprehensions of the terrified Africans, who may well be supposed to consider them the ministers of that destruction to which they think themselves devoted. In this manner, without scruple, are relations and friends separated, most of them never to see each other again. I remember in the vessel in which I was brought over, in the man's apartment, there were several brothers, who, in the sale, were sold in different lots; and it was very moving on this occasion to see their distress and hear their cries at parting. O, ye nominal Christians! might not an African ask you, "learned you this from your God, who says unto you, Do unto all men as you would men should do unto you?[57] Is it not enough that we are torn from our country and friends, to toil for your luxury and lust of gain? Must every tender feeling be likewise sacrificed to your avarice? Are the dearest friends and relations now rendered more dear by their separation from the rest of their kindred, still to be parted from each other, and thus prevented from cheering the gloom of slavery, with the small comfort of being together, and mingling their sufferings and sorrows? Why are parents to lose their children, brothers their sisters, or husbands their wives? Surely this is a new refinement in cruelty, which, while it has no advantage to atone for it, thus aggravates distress, and adds fresh horrors even to the wretchedness of slavery."

✠ ✠ ✠

CHAPTER 3

I NOW totally lost the small remains of comfort I had enjoyed in conversing with my countrymen; the women, too, who used to wash and take care of me, were all gone different ways, and I never saw one of them afterwards.

I stayed in this island for a few days; I believe it could not be above a fortnight; when I and some few more slaves, who from very much fretting were not saleable among the rest, were shipped off in a sloop for North America. On the Passage we were better treated than when coming from Africa, and we had plenty of rice and fat pork. We were landed up a river a good way from the sea, about Virginia county, where we saw few of our native Africans, and not one soul who could talk to me. I was a few weeks weeding grass and gathering stones in a plantation; and at last all my companions were distributed different ways, and only myself was left. I was now exceedingly miserable, and thought myself worse off than any of the rest of my companions; for they could talk to each other, but I had no person to speak to that I could understand. In this state I was constantly grieving and pining, and wishing for death rather than any thing else. While I was in this plantation the gentleman to whom I supposed the estate belonged being unwell, I was one day sent for to his dwelling-house to fan him. When I came into the room where he was, I was very much affrighted at some things I saw, and the more so, as I had seen a black woman slave as I came through the house, who was cooking the dinner, and the poor creature was cruelly loaded with various kinds of iron machines; she had one particularly on her head, which locked her mouth so fast that she could scarcely speak, and could not eat nor drink. I much astonished and shocked at this contrivance, which I afterwards learned was called the iron muzzle. Soon after I had a fan put into my hand, to fan the gentleman while he slept; and so I did indeed with great fear. While he was fast asleep I indulged myself a great deal in looking about the room, which to me appeared very fine and curious. The first object that engaged my attention was a watch, which hung on the chimney, and was going. I was quite surprised at the noise it made, and was afraid it would tell the gentleman any thing I might do amiss: and when I immediately after observed a picture hanging in the room, which appeared constantly to look at me, I was still more affrighted, having never seen such things as these before. At one time I thought it was something relative to magic; and not seeing it move, I thought it might be some way the whites had to keep their great men when they died, and offer them libations, as we used to do to our friendly spirits. In this state of anxiety I remained till my master awoke, when I was dismissed out of the room, to my no small satisfaction and relief; for I thought that these people were all made up of wonders. In this place I was called JACOB; but on board the African Snow[58] I was called MICHAEL.

I had been some time in this miserable, forlorn, and much dejected state, without any one to talk to, which made my life a burden, when the kind and unknown hand of the Creator, who in every deed leads the blind in a way they know not,[59] now began to appear to my comfort; for one day the captain of a merchant ship, called the "Industrious Bee," came on some business to my master's house. This gentleman, whose name was Michael Henry Pascal, was a lieutenant in the royal navy, but now commanded this trading ship, which was somewhere in the confines of the county many miles off.[60] While he was at my master's house it happened that he saw me, and liked me so well that he made a purchase of me. I think I have often heard him say he gave thirty or forty pounds sterling for me; the exact sum I do not now remember. However he meant me for a present to some of his friends in England: and I was sent accordingly from the house of my then master, one Mr. Campbell, to the place where the ship lay. I was conducted on horseback by an elderly black man, a mode of travelling which appeared very odd to me. When I arrived, I was carried on board a fine large ship, loaded with tobacco, &c. and just ready to sail for England. I now thought my condition much mended; having sails to lie on, and plenty of good victuals to eat; and every body on board used me very kindly, quite contrary to what I had seen of any white people before; I therefore began to think that they were not all of the same disposition. A few days after I was on board we sailed for England. I was still at a loss to conjecture my destiny. By this time, however I could smatter a little imperfect English, and I wanted to know as well I could where we were going. Some of the people of the ship used to tell me they were going to carry me back to my own country, and this made me very happy. I was quite rejoiced at the idea of going back; and thought if I should get home what wonders I should have to tell. But I was reserved for another fate, and was soon undeceived when we came within sight of the English coast.

While I was on board of this ship my captain and master named me GUSTAVUS VASSA.[61] I at that time began to understand him a little, and refused to be called so, and told him, as well as I could, that I would be called JACOB; but he said I should not, and still called me Gustavus. And when I refused to answer to my new name, which at first I did, it gained me many a cuff; so at length I submitted, and by it I have been known ever since. The ship had a very long passage; and on that account we had very short allowance of provisions; having towards the last only one pound and a half of bread per week, and about the same quantity of meat, and one quart of water a-day. We spoke with only one vessel during the voyage, and but once caught a few fishes. In our extremity the captain and people told me in jest they would kill and eat me, but I thought them in earnest, and was depressed beyond measure, expecting every moment to be my last. While I was in this situation one evening they caught a large shark, and got it on board. This rejoiced my heart exceedingly, as I thought it would serve the people to eat instead of their eating me; but very soon, to my astonishment, they cut off a small part of the tail, and tossed the rest over the side. This increased my consternation; and I did not know what to think of these white people, though I very much feared they intended to kill and eat me.

There was on board the ship a young lad, who had never been at sea before, about four or five years older than myself; his name was Richard Baker. He was a native of America, had received an excellent education, and was of a most amiable temper. Soon after I went on board he shewed me a great deal of partiality and attention, and in return I grew very fond of him. We at length became inseparable; and, for the space of two years, he was of great use to me, and was my constant companion and instructor. Although this dear youth had many slaves of his own, yet he and I have gone through many sufferings together on shipboard; and have many nights lain in each other's bosoms, when in great distress. Thus such a friendship was cemented between us, as we cherished till his death, which, to my very grief, happened in the year 1759, when he was up the Archipelago, on board his Majesty's ship the Preston: an event which I never ceased to regret, as I lost at once a kind interpreter, an agreeable companion, and a faithful friend; who at the age of fifteen, discovered a mind superior to prejudice, being not ashamed to notice, to associate with, and to be the friend and instructor of one who was ignorant, a stranger, and a slave! My master had lodged in his mother's house in America: he respected him very much, and made him always eat with him in the cabin. He used often to tell him jocularly that he would kill and eat me. Sometimes he used to say to me—the black people were not good to eat, and ask me if we did not eat people in my country. I said "No:" then he said he would first kill Dick, as he always called him, and afterwards me. Though this hearing relieved my mind a little as to myself, I was alarmed for Dick, and whenever he was called I used to be very much afraid he was to be killed; and I would peep and watch to see if they were going to kill him; nor was I free from this consternation till we made the land.

One night we lost a man overboard; and the cries and noise were so great and confused, in stopping the ship, that I, who did not know what was the matter, began, as usual, to be very much afraid, and to think they were going to make an offering with me, and perform some magic; in which I still believed that they dealt. As the waves were very high, I thought the Ruler of the seas was angry, and I expected to be offered up to appease him. This filled my mind with agony, and I could not any more, that night, close my eyes again to rest. However, when daylight appeared, I was a little eased in my mind; but still, when called, I thought it was that I might be killed. Some time after this we saw some very large fishes, which I afterwards found were called grampusses. They looked to me extremely terrible, and made their appearance just at dusk. They were so near as to blow the water on the ship's deck. I believed them to be the rulers of the sea: and as the white people did not make any offerings at any time, I thought they were angry at them: and, at last, what confirmed my belief, the wind just then died away, and a calm ensued, and in consequence of it the ship ceased from going. I supposed that the fishes had performed this, and hid myself in the forepart of the ship, through fear of being offered up to appease them, every minute peeping and quaking; but my good friend Dick came shortly to me, and I took an opportunity to ask him, as well as I could, what these fishes were. Not being able to talk much English, I could but just make him understand my question; and not at all, when I asked him if any offerings were to be made to them: however he told me these fishes would devour any body, which sufficiently alarmed me. Here he was called away by the captain, who was leaning over the quarter-deck railing,[62] and looking at the fishes; and most of the people were busied in getting a barrel of pitch to light, for them to play with. The Captain now called me, having learned some of my apprehensions from Dick; and having diverted himself and others, for some time, with my fears, which appeared ludicrous enough in my crying and trembling, he dismissed me. The barrel of pitch was then lighted and put over the side into the water: by this time it was just dark, and the fishes went after it; and to my great joy, I saw them no more.

However, all my alarms began to subside when we got sight of land; and at last the ship reached Falmouth, after a passage of thirteen weeks. Every heart on board seemed gladdened on our reaching the shore, and none more than mine. The captain immediately went on shore, and sent on board some fresh provisions, which we wanted very much: we made good use of them, and our famine was soon turned into feasting, almost without ending. It was about the beginning of spring 1757, when I arrived in England, and I was nearly twelve years of age at that time. I was very much struck with the buildings and the pavement of the streets in Falmouth; and, indeed, every object I saw filled me with fresh surprise.

One morning, when I got upon deck, I perceived it covered all over with the snow that fell over-night. As I had never seen any thing of the kind before, I thought it was salt; so I immediately ran down to the mate and desired him, as well as I could, to come and see how somebody in the night had thrown salt all over the deck. He, knowing what it was, desired me to bring some of it down to him: accordingly I took up a handful of it, which I found very cold indeed; and when I brought it to him he desired me to taste it. I did so, and was surprised above measure. I then asked him what it was; he told me it was snow; but I could not by any means understand him. He asked me if we had no such thing in our country; and I told him "No." I then asked him the use of it, and who made it: he told me a great man in the heavens, called God: but here again I was to all intents and purposes at a loss to understand him; and the more so, when a little after I saw the air filled with it, in a heavy shower, which fell down on the same day.

After this I went to church; and having never been at such a place before, I was again amazed at seeing and hearing the service. I asked all I could about it; and they gave me to understand it was "worshiping God, who made us and all things." I was still at a loss, and soon got into an endless field of inquiries, as well as I was able to speak and ask about things. However, my dear little friend Dick used to be my best interpreter; for I could make free with him and he always instructed me with pleasure. And from what I could understand by him of this God, and in seeing that these white people did not sell one another as we did, I was much pleased: and in this I thought they were much happier than we Africans. I was astonished at the wisdom of the white people in all things which I beheld; but I was greatly amazed at their not sacrificing, nor making any offerings, and at their eating with unwashen hands, and touching the dead. I also could not help remarking the particular slenderness of their women, which I did not at first like, and I thought them not so modest and shamefaced as the African women.

I had often seen my master and Dick employed in reading; and I had a great curiosity to talk to the books, as I thought they did; and so to learn how all things had a beginning. For that purpose I have often taken up a book, and talked to it, and then put my ears to it, when alone, in hopes it would answer me; and I have been very much concerned when I found it remaining silent.[63]

My master lodged at the house of a gentleman in Falmouth, who had a fine little daughter, about six or seven years of age, and she grew prodigiously fond of me; insomuch that we used to eat together, and had servants to wait on us. I was so much caressed by this family, that it often reminded me of the treatment I had received from my little noble African master. After I had been here a few days, I was sent on board of the ship; but the child cried so much after me, that nothing could pacify her till I was sent for again. It is ludicrous enough, that I began to fear I should be betrothed to this young lady; and when my master asked me if I would stay there with her behind him, as he was going away with the ship, having taken in the tobacco again, I cried immediately, and said I would not leave him.[64] At last, by stealth, one night I was sent on board the ship again; and in a little time sailed for Guernsey, where she was in part owned by a merchant, one Nicholas Doberry.

As I was now amongst a people who had not their faces scarred, like some of the African nations where I had been, I was very glad at my not having permitted them to ornament me in that manner. When we arrived at Guernsey, my master placed me to board and lodge with one of his mates, who had a wife and family there; and some months afterwards he returned to England, and left me in care of this mate, together with my friend Dick. This mate had a little daughter, aged about five or six years, with her I used to be much delighted. I had often observed that when her mother washed her face it looked very rosy; but when she washed mine it did not look so: I therefore tried oftentimes myself if I could not by washing make my face of the same colour as my little play-mate, Mary, but it was all in vain; and I then began to be mortified at the difference in our complexions. This woman behaved to me with great kindness and attention. She taught me every thing in the same manner as she did her own child, and indeed in every respect treated me as such.

※　※　※

Equiano remains in Guernsey until the summer of 1757, when Pascal is appointed first lieutenant of the *Roebuck,* a 44-gun warship. During this time, British prime minister William Pitt intensified his country's war against France and her allies; the war, formally declared between England and France in the late spring of 1756, was already well under way in Canada. While Equiano serves aboard the *Roebuck* the ship ferries several eminent passengers from Holland to England, escorts a huge fleet of transport ships carrying soldiers to England from Scotland and the Orkneys, and seizes seventeen French vessels off the coast of France. Once the tour is over, Equiano arrives in London, where he meets Pascal's relative Mr. Guerin and his two sisters, known hereafter as the Miss Guerins. He has little time to explore the city, however, before he is hospitalized with a severe case of chilblains followed immediately by a bout with smallpox. His health regained, he rejoins Pascal and Dick aboard the *Preston* 50-gun man o'war, which ferries the Duke of Cumberland to England. When Pascal is appointed to the *Royal George* (at 100 guns, one of the largest warships in the British navy), he leaves Dick aboard the *Preston.* Equiano chooses to follow Pascal, who does not remain with the *Royal George* for long; after a few weeks the ship's entire crew is transferred to the *Namur,* a 90-gun battleship that includes in its complement both the flag officer, Vice-Admiral Edmund Boscawen, and Brigadier General James Wolfe. The *Namur* leads the naval fleet in the land-and-sea attack against Louisburg, a French fortification on the southern shore of Cape Breton Island off the Canadian coast. Landing in Cape Breton in June of 1758, Equiano witnesses the decisive British victory at Louisburg on 26 July and returns to London with Boscawen by 1759.

CHAPTER 4

IT was now between two and three years since I first came to England,[65] a great part of which I had spent at sea; so that I became inured to that service, and began to consider myself as happily situated; for my master treated me always extremely well; and my attachment and gratitude to him were very great. From the various scenes I had beheld on shipboard, I soon grew a stranger to terror of every kind, and was, in that respect at least, almost an Englishman. I have often reflected with surprise that I never felt half the alarm, at any of the numerous dangers in which I have been, that I was filled with at the first sight of the Europeans, and at every act of theirs, even the most trifling, when I first came among them, and for some time afterwards. That fear, however, the effect of my ignorance, wore away as I began to know them.

I could now speak English tolerably well, and perfectly understood every thing that was said. I not only felt myself quite easy with these new countrymen, but relished their society and manners. I no longer looked upon them as spirits, but as men superior to us; and therefore I had the stronger desire to resemble them, to imbibe their spirit, and imitate their manners. I therefore embraced every occasion of improvement; and every new thing that I observed I treasured up in my memory. I had long wished to be able to read and write; and for this purpose I took every opportunity to gain instruction, but had made as yet but very little progress. However, when I went to London with my master, I had soon an opportunity of improving myself, which I gladly embraced. Shortly after my arrival, he sent me to wait upon the Miss Guerins, who had treated me with so much kindness when I was there before, and they sent me to school.

While I was attending these ladies, their servants told me I could not go to Heaven, unless I was baptized. This made me very uneasy; for I had now some faint idea of a future state: accordingly I communicated my anxiety to the eldest Miss Guerin, with whom I was become a favourite, and pressed her to have me baptized; when, to my great joy, she told me I should. She had formerly asked my master to let me be baptized, but he had refused; however she now insisted on it; and he, being under some obligation to her brother, complied with her request; so I was baptized at St. Margaret's church, Westminster, in February 1759, by my present name. The clergyman, at the same time, gave me a book, called "a Guide to the Indians," written by the Bishop of Sodor and Man.[66] On this occasion, Miss Guerin did me the honour to stand as godmother, and afterwards gave me a treat.

I used to attend these ladies about the town, in which service I was extremely happy, as I had thus very many opportunities of seeing London, which I desired of all things. I was sometimes, however, with my master at his rendezvous-house, at the foot of Westminster-bridge. Here I used to enjoy myself in playing about the bridge stairs, and often in the watermen's wherries, with other boys.[67] On one of these occasions there was another boy with me in a wherry, and we went out into the current of the river; while there, two more stout boys came to us in another wherry, and, abusing us for taking the boat, desired me to get into the other wherry-boat. Accordingly I went to get out of the wherry I was in; but just as I had got one of my feet into the other boat, the boys shoved it off, so that I fell into the Thames, and not being able to swim, I should unavoidably have been drowned, but for the assistance of some watermen, who providentially came to my relief.

✳ ✳ ✳

By the spring of 1759 Equiano is off to Gibraltar with Pascal aboard the *Namur* as Boscawen takes up his command post in the Mediterranean. While docked at Gibraltar, Equiano discovers with the arrival of the *Preston* the sad news that his friend Dick had died in Turkey. When a *Preston* crew member turns over Dick's belongings to Pascal, the latter, in turn, gives them to Equiano for remembrance. Soon afterward, Boscawen's fleet commences a blockade of the French navy at its southeastern base in Toulon. Boscawen's concern for the health of his crew eventually causes him to break this maneuver and sail back to nearby Gibraltar to procure fresh supplies for the fleet. In the absence of the British, the French fleet will slip away from Toulon and head for Cadiz, only to be spied off Gibraltar by a British watch patrol. These events will set the stage for the Battle of Lagos Bay on 18 August—a battle that Equiano vividly describes in the following pages.

After this [the blockade of Toulon and a brief spat with two French frigates] we sailed for Gibraltar, and arrived there about August, 1759. We remained here with all our sails unbent, while the fleet was watering and doing other necessary things. While we were in this situation, one day the admiral,[68] together with most of the principal officers, and many people of all stations, being on shore, about seven o'clock in the evening we were alarmed by signals from the frigates stationed for that purpose, and in an instant there was a general cry that the French fleet was out, and just passing through the streights.[69] The admiral immediately came on board with some other officers; and it is impossible to describe the noise, hurry, and confusion, throughout the fleet, in bending their sails and slipping their cables;[70] many people and ship's boats were left on shore in the bustle. We had two captains on board of our ship, who came away in the hurry and left their ships to follow. We shewed lights from the gun-wales to the main-top-mast-head;[71] and all

our lieutenants were employed amongst the fleet to tell the ships not to
wait for their captains, but to put the sails to the yards, slip their cables,
and follow us; and, in this confusion of making ready for fighting, we set
out for sea in the dark after the French fleet. Here I could have
exclaimed with Ajax,

> "O Jove! O father! if it be thy will
> That we must perish, we thy will obey,
> But let us perish by the light of day."[72]

They had got the start of us so far that we were not able to come up
with them that night; but at day-light we saw seven sail of the line some
miles ahead. We immediately chased them till four o'clock in the
evening, our ships then came up with them; and though we were about
fifteen large ships, our gallant admiral only fought them with his own
division, consisting of seven, so that we were just ship for ship.[73] We
passed by the whole of the enemy's fleet in order to come at their commander, Mons. Le Clue,[74] who was in the Ocean, an eighty-four gun
ship. As we passed they all fired at us; and at one time three of them fired
together, continuing to do so for some time. Notwithstanding which our
admiral, to my astonishment, would not suffer a gun to be fired at any
of them, but made us lie on our bellies on the deck till we came quite
close to the Ocean,[75] which was ahead of them all, when we had orders
to pour the whole three tiers into her at once.[76]

The engagement now commenced with great fury on both sides: the
Ocean immediately returned our fire, and we continued engaged with
each other for some time; during which I was frequently stunned with
the thundering of the great guns, whose dreadful contents hurried many
of my companions into eternity. At last the French line was entirely broken, and we obtained the victory, which was immediately proclaimed
with loud huzzas and acclamations. We took three prizes, La Modeste,
of sixty-four guns, and Le Temeraire and Centaur, of seventy-four guns
each. The rest of the French ships took to flight, with all the sail they
could crowd. Our ship being very much damaged, and quite disabled
from pursuing the enemy, the admiral immediately quitted her, and
went in a broken boat, the only one we had left, on board the Newark,
with which, and some other ships, he went after the French. The Ocean,
and another large French ship, called the Redoubtable, endeavouring to
escape, ran ashore at Cape Logas,[77] on the coast of Portugal, and the
French admiral and some of the crew got ashore; but we, finding it
impossible to get the ships off, set fire to them both.[78] About midnight I

saw the Ocean blew up with a most dreadful explosion. I never beheld a more awful scene. About the space of a minute, the midnight seemed turned into day by the blaze, attended with a noise louder and more terrible than thunder, that seemed to rend every element around us.

My station during the engagement was on the middle deck, where I was quartered with another boy, to bring powder to the aftermost Gun.[79] And here I was witness of the dreadful fate of many of my companions, who, in the twinkling of an eye, were dashed to pieces, and launched into eternity. Happily I escaped unhurt, though the shot and splinters flew thick about me during the night. Towards the latter part of it my master was wounded, and I saw him carried down to the surgeon; but though I was much alarmed for him, and longed to assist him, I durst not quit my post.

At this station my gun-mate[80] and I ran a very great risk, for more than half an hour, of blowing up the ship. For when we had taken the cartridges out of the boxes, the bottoms of many of them proving rotten, the powder ran all about the deck, near the match tub: we scarcely had water enough at the last to throw on it. We were also, from our employment, very much exposed to the enemy's shots; for we had to go through nearly the whole length of the ship to bring the powder. I expected therefore every minute to be my last; especially when I saw our men fall so thick about me. But, wishing to guard as much against the dangers as possible, at first I thought it would be the safest not to go for the powder till the Frenchmen had fired their broadside; and then, while they were charging, I could go and come with my powder. But immediately afterwards I thought this caution was fruitless; and, cheering myself with the reflection that there was a time allotted for me to die as well as to be born,[81] I instantly cast off all fear or thought whatever of death, and went through the whole of my duty with alacrity; pleasing myself with the hope, if I survived the battle, of relating it and the dangers I had escaped, to the Miss Guerins, and others, when I should return to London.[82]

Our ship suffered very much in this engagement; for, besides the number of our killed and wounded, she was almost torn to pieces, and our rigging so much shattered, that our mizen-mast, main-yard, &c. hung over the side of the ship;[83] so that we were obliged to get many carpenters and others, from some of the ships of the fleet, to assist in setting us in some tolerable order. Notwithstanding which, it took us some time before we were completely refitted; after which we left Admiral Broderick[84] to command, and we, with the prizes, steered for England.

On the passage, and as soon as my master recovered of his wounds, the admiral appointed him captain of the Ætna fire-ship,[85] on which he and I left the Namur, and went on board of her at sea. I liked this small ship very much. I now became the captain's steward, in which situation I was very happy: for I was extremely well treated by all on board; and had leisure to improve myself in reading and writing. Of the latter I had learned a little before I left the Namur, there being a school on board. When we arrived at Spithead, the Ætna went into Portsmouth harbour to refit,[86] which being done, we returned to Spithead, and joined a large fleet that was thought to be intended against Havannah. But about that time the king died;[87] whether that prevented the expedition I know not; but it caused our ship to be stationed at Cowes, in the isle of Wight, till the beginning of the year 1761.[88] Here I spent my time very pleasantly: I was much on shore all about this delightful island, and found the inhabitants very civil.

While I was here, I met with a trifling incident, which surprised me agreeably. I was one day in a field belonging to a gentleman, who had a black boy about my own size; this boy having observed me from his master's house, was transported at the sight of one of his own countrymen, and ran to meet me with the utmost haste. I, not knowing what he was about, turned a little out of his way at first, but to no purpose: he soon came close to me, and caught me in his arms as if I had been his brother, though we had never seen each other before. After we had talked together for some time, he took me to his master's house, where I was treated very kindly. This benevolent boy and I were very happy in frequently seeing each other, till about the month of March 1761, when our ship had orders to fit again for another expedition. When we got ready, we joined a very large fleet at Spithead, commanded by Commodore Keppel, destined against Belleisle;[89] and having a number of transport ships in company, with troops on board, to make a descent on the place, we sailed once more in quest of fame. I longed to engage in new adventures, and to see fresh wonders.

I had a mind, on which every thing uncommon, and every thing which I considered marvellous, made their full impression. Every extraordinary escape, or signal deliverance, either of myself or others, I looked upon to be effected by the interposition of Providence. We had not been above ten days at sea before an incident of this kind happened, which, whatever credit it may obtain from the reader, made no small impression upon my mind.

We had on board a gunner, whose name was John Mondle, a man of very indifferent morals. This man's cabin was between the decks, exactly over where I lay, a-breast of the quarter-deck ladder. One night, the 5th of April, being terrified in a dream, he awoke in so great a fright that he could not rest in his bed any longer, nor even remain in his cabin; and he went upon deck about four o'clock in the morning extremely agitated. He immediately told those upon the deck of the agonies of his mind, and the dream which occasioned them: in which he said he had seen many things very awful, and had been warned by St. Peter to repent, who told him time was short. This he said had greatly alarmed him, and he was determined to alter his life. People generally mock the fears of others when they are themselves in safety; and some of his shipmates, who heard him, only laughed at him. However, he made a vow that he never would drink strong liquors again; and he immediately got a light, and gave away his sea-store of liquor. After which his agitation still continuing, he began to read the Scriptures, hoping to find some relief; and soon afterwards he laid himself down again on his bed, and endeavoured to compose himself to sleep, but to no purpose; his mind still continuing in a state of agony. By this time it was exactly half after seven in the morning: I was then under the half deck at the great cabin door; and all at once I heard the people in the waist[90] cry out most fearfully—"The Lord have mercy upon us! We are all lost! The Lord have mercy upon us!"—Mr. Mondle, hearing the cries, immediately ran out of his cabin; and we were instantly struck by the Lynne, a forty gun ship, Captain Clark, which nearly ran us down. This ship had just put about, and was by the wind, but had not got full head-way, or we must all have perished: for the wind was brisk. However, before Mr. Mondle had got four steps from his cabin door, she struck our ship, with her cutwater, right in the middle of his bed and cabin, and ran it up to the combings of the quarter-deck-hatchway, and above three feet below water;[91] and in a minute there was not a bit of wood to be seen where Mr. Mondle's cabin stood; and he was so near being killed that some of the splinters tore his face. As Mr. Mondle must inevitably have perished from this accident, had he not been alarmed in the very extraordinary way I have related, I could not help regarding this as an awful interposition of Providence for his preservation.

The two ships for some time swinged alongside of each other: for ours being a fire-ship, our grappling-irons caught the Lynne every way, and the yards and rigging went at an astonishing rate. Our ship was in such a shocking condition that we all thought she would instantly go down, and every one ran for their lives, and got as well as they could on board the Lynne; but our lieutenant being the aggressor, he never quitted the ship. However, on finding she did not sink immediately, the captain came on board again, and encouraged our people to return and try to save her. Many of them came back, but some would not venture. Some of the ships in the fleet, seeing our situation, immediately sent their boats to our assistance; but it took us the whole day to save the ship with all their help. And by using every possible means, particularly frapping[92] her together with many hawsers, and putting a great quantity of tallow below water where she was damaged, she was kept together; but had we met with any gale of wind she must have gone to pieces, being in such a crazy condition that we had ships to attend us till we arrived at Belleisle, the place of our destination; and then we had all things taken out of the ship, and she was properly repaired. This escape of Mr. Mondle, which he, as well as myself, always considered as a singular act of Providence, I believe had a great influence on his life and conduct ever afterwards.

Now that I am on this subject, I beg leave to relate another instance or two which strongly raised my belief of the particular interposition of Heaven, and which might not otherwise have found a place here, from their insignificance. I belonged for a few days, in the year 1758, to the Jason, of fifty-four guns, at Plymouth.[93] One night, when I was on board, a woman, with a child at her breast, fell from the upper-deck down into the hold, near the keel. Every one thought that the mother and child must be both dashed to pieces; but, to our great surprise, neither of them was hurt. I myself one day fell headlong from the upper-deck of the Ætna down the after-hold, when the ballast was out; and all who saw me fall called out I was killed; but I received not the least injury. And in the same ship a man fell from the mast-head on the deck without being hurt. In these, and in many more instances, I thought I could very plainly trace the hand of God; without whose permission a sparrow cannot fall.[94] I began to raise my fear from man to Him alone, and to call daily on his holy name, with fear and reverence: and I trust He heard my supplications, and graciously condescended to answer me according to his holy word; and to implant the seeds of piety in me, even one of the meanest of his creatures.

❊ ❊ ❊

While crews busily repair and resupply the Ætna, British troops in the fleet ready themselves to land at Belle Isle off the west coast of France and the north coast of Spain. Largest of all French-owned European islands, Belle Isle and its dependencies, the smaller islands Houac and Hedic, are heavily fortified both to guard valuable fisheries and to ward off British privateers from Jersey and Guernsey. On 12 April 1761, British troops are ordered to disembark; as a junior captain and commander of the *Ætna*, Pascal assists in directing the landing. The land forces initially face stiff French resistance on shore, but they are finally able to land successfully and force back the French on 21 April. Equiano then assists Pascal in landing the supplies necessary to storm the citadel, a castle garrisoned with French troops. The siege soon commences; well over a month later the French capitulate on 7 June and formally surrender on 12 June. Thereafter Equiano accompanies Commodore Sir Thomas Stanhope's squadron to Basque Road, a large stretch of anchorage among the islands of Ré, Oléron, and Aix, to block the French fleet at nearby Rochefort, a major French naval arsenal. The two fleets battle each other through the end of the year. Before England and Spain formally declare war in January 1762, Stanhope sends the *Wasp* sloop and Equiano's ship from Basque Road to St. Sebastian in northern Spain. In late January Equiano is part of a cartel of ships that travel to Bayonne, France, to exchange prisoners of war. He then reconnoiters at Belle Isle for a few months, finally sailing that summer to the British naval base in Portsmouth. Equiano visits in Guernsey with his former hostess and her daughter between September and October of 1762; he then returns to duty at Portsmouth.

Our ship having arrived at Portsmouth, we went into the harbour and remained there till the end of November, when we heard great talk about a peace; and, to our very great joy, in the beginning of December, we had orders to go up to London with our ship, to be paid off.[95] We received this news with loud huzzas, and every other demonstration of gladness: and nothing but mirth was to be seen through every part of the ship. I too was not without my share of the general joy on this occasion. I thought now of nothing but being freed, and working for myself, and thereby getting money to enable me to get a good education. For I always had a great desire to be able at least to read and write; and while I was on shipboard I had endeavoured to improve myself in both. While in the *Ætna*, particularly, the captain's clerk taught me to write, and gave me a smattering of arithmetic, as far as the Rule of Three.[96]

There was also one Daniel Queen, about forty years of age, a man very well educated, who messed with me on board this ship, and he likewise dressed and attended the captain. Fortunately this man soon became very much attached to me, and took great pains to instruct me in many things. He taught me to shave, and dress hair a little, and also to read in the Bible, explaining many passages to me, which I did not comprehend. I was wonderfully surprised to see the laws and rules of my own country written almost exactly here; a circumstance which, I believe, tended to impress our manners and customs more deeply on my memory. I used to tell him of this resemblance; and many a time we have sat up the whole night together at this employment. In short, he was like a father to me; and some used even to call me after his name: they also styled me "the black Christian." Indeed I almost loved him with the affection of a son. Many things I have denied myself, that he might have them; and when I used to play at marbles or any other game, and won a few halfpence, or got some money for shaving any one, I used to buy him a little sugar or tobacco, as far as my stock of money would go. He used to say that he and I never should part, and that when our ship was paid off, as I was as free as himself or any other man on board, he would instruct me in his business, by which I might gain a good livelihood. This gave me new life and spirits; and my heart burned within me, while I thought the time long till I obtained my freedom. For though my master had not promised it to me, yet, besides the assurances I had often received that he had no right to detain me, he always treated me with the greatest kindness, and reposed in me an unbounded confidence. He even paid attention to my morals; and would never suffer me to deceive him, or tell lies, of which he used to tell me the consequences; and that if I did so, God would not love me. So that from all this tenderness I had never once supposed, in all my dreams of freedom, that he would think of detaining me any longer than I wished.

In pursuance of our orders we sailed from Portsmouth for the Thames, and arrived at Deptford the 10th of December, where we cast anchor just as it was high water. The ship was up about half an hour, when my master ordered the barge to be manned; and, all in an instant, without having before given me the least reason to suspect any thing of the matter, he forced me into the barge, saying, I was going to leave him, but he would take care that I did not. I was so struck with the unexpectedness of this proceeding, that for some time I did not make a reply; only I made an offer to go for my books and chest of clothes, but he swore I should not move out of his sight; and if I did, he would cut my throat, at the same time taking out his hanger.[97] I began, however, to collect myself; and, plucking up courage, I told him that I was free, and he could not by law serve me so. But this only enraged him the more; and he continued to swear, and said he would soon let me know whether he would or not; and at that instant sprung himself into the barge, from the ship, to the astonishment and sorrow of all on board.

The tide, rather unluckily for me, had just turned downward, so that we quickly fell down the river along with it, till we came among some outwardbound West Indiamen; for he was resolved to put me on board the first vessel he could get to receive me. The boat's crew, who pulled against their will, became quite faint at different times, and would have gone ashore, but he would not let them. Some of them strove then to cheer me, and told me he could not sell me, and that they would stand by me, which revived me a little, and I still entertained hopes; for as they pulled me along he asked some vessels to receive me, and they refused.

But, just as we had got a little below Gravesend, we came alongside of a ship going away the next tide for the West-Indies; her name was the Charming Sally, Captain James Doran. My master went on board and agreed with him for me; and in a little time I was sent for into the cabin. When I came there Captain Doran asked me if I knew him: I answered I did not; 'Then,' said he, 'you are now my slave.' I told him my master could not sell me to him nor to any one else. 'Why,' said he, 'did not your master buy you?' I confessed he did. 'But I have served him,' said I, 'many years, and he has taken all my wages and prize-money,[98] for I only got one sixpence during the war. Besides this I have been baptized; and, by the laws of the land, no man has a right to sell me:' And I added, that I had heard a lawyer, and others, at different times, tell my master so.[99] They both then said, that those people who told me so, were not my friends: but I replied—it was very extraordinary that other people did not know the law as well as they. Upon this, Captain Doran said I talked too much English, and if I did not behave myself well and be quiet, he had a method on board to make me. I was too well convinced of his power over me to doubt what he said; and my former sufferings in the slave-ship presenting themselves to my mind, the recollection of them made me shudder. However, before I retired I told them, that as I could not get any right among men here, I hoped I should hereafter in Heaven, and I immediately left the cabin, filled with resentment and sorrow.

The only coat I had with me my master took away with him, and said, 'if your prize-money had been £10,000, I had a right to it all, and would have taken it.' I had about nine guineas, which, during my long sea-faring life, I had scraped together from trifling perquisites and little ventures; and I hid it that instant, lest my master should take that from me likewise, still hoping that, by some means or other, I should make my escape to the shore. Indeed some of my old shipmates told me not to despair, for they would get me back again; and that, as soon as they could get their pay, they would immediately come to Portsmouth to me, where this ship was going. But, alas! all my hopes were baffled, and the hour of my deliverance was, as yet, far off. My master, having soon concluded his bargain with the captain, came out of the cabin, and he and his people got into the boat and put off. I followed them with aching eyes as long as I could, and when they were out of sight I threw myself on the deck, with a heart ready to burst with sorrow and anguish.

✠ ✠ ✠

CHAPTER 5

THUS, at the moment I expected all my toils to end, was I plunged, as I supposed, in a new slavery; in comparison of which all my service hitherto had been perfect freedom; and whose horrors, always present to my mind, now rushed on it with tenfold aggravation. I wept very bitterly for some time; and began to think that I must have done something to displease the Lord, that he thus punished me so severely. This filled me with painful reflections on my past conduct. I recollected that, on the morning of our arrival at Deptford, I had very rashly sworn that as soon as we reached London, I would spend the day in rambling and sport. My conscience smote me for this unguarded expression: I felt that the Lord was able to disappoint me in all things, and immediately considered my present situation as a judgment of Heaven, on account of my presumption in swearing. I therefore, with contrition of heart, acknowledged my transgression to God, and poured out my soul before Him with unfeigned repentance, and with earnest supplications I besought Him not to abandon me in my distress, nor cast me from his mercy for ever. In a little time my grief, spent with its own violence, began to subside; and after the first confusion of my thoughts was over, I reflected with more calmness on my present condition. I considered that trials and disappointments are sometimes for our good; and I thought God might perhaps have permitted this, in order to teach me wisdom and resignation. For he had hitherto shadowed me with the wings of his mercy and by his invisible, but powerful hand, had brought me the way I knew not.[100] These reflections gave me a little comfort, and I arose at last from the deck with dejection and sorrow in my countenance, yet mixed with some faint hope that the *Lord would appear* for my deliverance.

Soon afterwards, as my new master was going on shore, he called me to him, and told me to behave myself well, and do the business of the ship the same as any of the rest of the boys, and that I should fare the better for it; but I made him no answer. I was then asked if I could swim, and I said, "No." However, I was made to go under the deck, and was carefully watched. The next tide the ship got under way, and soon arrived at the Mother Bank, Portsmouth; where she waited few days for some of the West-India convoy. While here I tried every means I could devise amongst the people of the ship to get me a boat from the shore, as there was none suffered to come alongside of the ship; and their own, whenever it was used, was hoisted in again immediately. A sailor on board took a guinea[101] from me, on pretence of getting me a boat; and promised me, time after time, that it was hourly to come off. When he had the watch upon deck I watched also, and looked long enough, but all in vain; I could never see either the boat or my guinea again. And, what I thought was still the worst of all, the fellow gave information, as I afterwards found, all the while to the mates of my intention to go off if possible; but, rogue-like, he never told them he had got a guinea from me to procure my escape. However, after we had sailed, and his trick was made known to the ship's crew, I had some satisfaction in seeing him detested and despised by them all for his behaviour to me.

I was still in hopes that my old shipmates would not forget their promise to come for me to Portsmouth; and, indeed, at last, but not till the day before we sailed, some of them did come there, and sent me off some oranges,[102] and other tokens of their regard. They also sent me word they would come off to me themselves the next day, or the day after: and a lady also who lived in Gosport, wrote to me that she would come and take me out of the ship at the same time. This lady had been once very intimate with my former master. I used to sell and take care of a great deal of property for her, in different ships; and in return she always shewed great friendship for me, and used to tell my master she would take me away to live with her. But, unfortunately for me, a disagreement soon afterwards took place between them; and she was succeeded in my master's good graces by another lady, who appeared sole mistress of the Ætna, and mostly lodged on board. I was not so great a favourite with this lady as with the former; she had conceived a pique against me, on some occasion when she was on board, and she did not fail to instigate my master to treat me in the manner he did.[103]

However, the next morning, the 30th of December, the wind being brisk and easterly, the Æolus frigate,[104] which was to escort the convoy, made a signal for sailing. All the ships then got up their anchors; and before any of my friends had an opportunity to come off to my relief, to my inexpressible anguish, our ship had got under way. What tumultuous emotions agitated my soul when the convoy got under sail, and I a prisoner on board, now without hope! I kept my swimming eyes upon the land in a state of unutterable grief; not knowing what to do, and despairing how to help myself. While my mind was in this situation, the fleet sailed on, and in one day's time I lost sight of the wished-for land. In the first expressions of my grief, I reproached my fate, and wished I had never been born. I was ready to curse the tide that bore us, the gale that wafted my prison, and even the ship that conducted us; and, in the despair of the moment, I called on death to relieve me from the horrors I felt and dreaded, that I might be in that place.

> 'Where slaves are free, and men oppress no more.
> Fool that I was, inur'd so long to pain,
> To trust to hope, or dream of joy again!
>   ❋ ❋ ❋ ❋ ❋ ❋ ❋ ❋ ❋ ❋ ❋ ❋
> Now dragg'd once more beyond the western main,
> To groan beneath some dastard planter's chain;
> Where my poor countrymen in bondage wait
> The long enfranchisement of ling'ring fate:
> Hard ling'ring fate! while, ere the dawn of day,
> Rous'd by the lash they go their cheerless way;
> And as their souls with shame and anguish burn,
> Salute with groans unwelcome morn's return,
> And, chiding ev'ry hour the slow-pac'd sun,
> Pursue their toils till all his race is run.
> No eye to mark their suff'rings with a tear;
> No friend to comfort, and no hope to cheer:
> Then, like the dull unpity'd brutes, repair
> To stalls as wretched, and as coarse a fare;
> Thank heaven one day of mis'ry was o'er,
> Then sink to sleep, and wish to wake no more.'[105]

The turbulence of my emotions, however, naturally gave way to calmer thoughts, and I soon perceived what fate had decreed no mortal on earth could prevent. The convoy sailed on without any accident, with a pleasant gale and smooth sea, for six weeks, till February, when one morning the Æolus ran down a brig, one of the convoy, and she instantly went down and was engulfed in the dark recesses of the ocean. The convoy was immediately thrown into great confusion till it was day-light; and the Æolus illuminated with lights to prevent farther mischief. On the 13th of February 1763, from the mast-head, we descried our destined island, Montserrat, and soon after I beheld those

'Regions of sorrow, doleful shades, where peace
And rest can rarely dwell. Hope never comes
That comes to all, but torture without end
Still urges.'[106]

At the sight of this land of bondage, a fresh horror ran through all my
frame, and chilled me to the heart. My former slavery now rose in
dreadful review to my mind, and displayed nothing but misery, stripes,
and chains; and in the first paroxysm of my grief, I called upon God's
thunder, and his avenging power, to direct the stroke of death to me,
rather than permit me to become a slave, and to be sold from lord to lord.

In this state of my mind our ship came to an anchor, and soon after
discharged her cargo. I now knew what it was to work hard; I was made
to help to unload and load the ship. And to comfort me in my distress,
at that time two of the sailors robbed me of all my money, and ran away
from the ship. I had been so long used to an European climate, that at
first I felt the scorching West-India sun very painful, while the dashing
surf would toss the boat and the people in it, frequently above high-
water-mark. Sometimes our limbs were broken with this, or even
attended with instant death, and I was day by day mangled and torn.

About the middle of May, when the ship was got ready to sail for
England, I all the time believing that fate's blackest clouds were gathering over my head, and expecting that their bursting would mix me with
the dead, Captain Doran sent for me on shore one morning, and I was
told by the messenger that my fate was determined. With trembling
steps and a fluttering heart I came to the captain, and found with him one
Mr. Robert King, a quaker, and the first merchant in the place. The captain then told me my former master had sent me there to be sold; but that
he had desired him to get me the best master he could, as he told him I
was a very deserving boy, which Captain Doran said he found to be true,
and if he were to stay in the West-Indies he would be glad to keep me
himself; but he could not venture to take me to London, for he was very
sure that when I came there, I would leave him. I at that instant burst out
a crying, and begged much of him to take me with him to England, but
all to no purpose. He told me he had got me the very best master in the
whole island, with whom I should be as happy as if I were in England,
and for that reason he chose to let him have me, though he could sell me
to his own brother-in-law for a great deal more money than what he got
from that gentleman. My new master, Mr. King, then made a reply, and
said the reason he had bought me was on account of my good character;
and, as he had not the least doubt of my good behaviour, I should be very

well off with him. He also told me he did not live in the West-Indies, but at Philadelphia, where he was soon going; and, as I understood something of the rules of arithmetic, when we got there he would put me to school, and fit me for a clerk. This conversation relieved my mind a little, and I left those gentlemen considerably more at ease in myself than when I came to them; and I was very thankful to Captain Doran, and even to my old master, for the character they had given me; a character which I afterwards found of infinite service to me.

I went on board again, and took leave of all my shipmates, and the next day the ship sailed. When she weighed anchor I went to the water-side, and looked at her with a very wishful and aching heart, following her with my eyes until she was totally out of sight. I was so bowed down with grief, that I could not hold up my head for many months; and if my new master had not been kind to me, I believe I should have died under it at last. And indeed I soon found that he fully deserved the good character which Capt. Doran had given me of him; for he possessed a most amiable disposition and temper, and was very charitable and humane. If any of his slaves behaved amiss, he did not beat or use them ill, but parted with them. This made them afraid of disobliging him; and as he treated his slaves better than any other man on the island, so he was better and more faithfully served by them in return. By this kind treatment I did at last endeavour to compose myself; and with fortitude, though moneyless, determined to face whatever fate had decreed for me. Mr. King soon asked me what I could do; and at the same time said he did not mean to treat me as a common slave. I told him I knew something of sea-manship, and could shave and dress hair pretty well; I could refine wines, which I had learned on shipboard, where I had often done it; and that I could write, and understood arithmetic tolerably well as far as the Rule of Three. He then asked me if I knew any thing of gauging;[107] and, on my answering that I did not, he said one of his clerks should teach me to gauge.

Mr. King dealt in all manner of merchandize, and kept from one to six clerks. He loaded many vessels in a year; particularly to Philadelphia, where he was born, and was connected with a great mercantile house in that city. He had besides many vessels and doggers,[108] of different sizes, which used to go about the island; and others to collect rum, sugar, and other goods. I understood pulling and managing those boats very well; and this hard work, which was the first that he set me to, in the sugar seasons used to be my constant employment. I have rowed the boat and slaved at the oars, from one hour to sixteen in the twenty-four; during which I had fifteen pence sterling per day to live on, though sometimes only ten pence. However, this was much more than was allowed to other slaves that used to work often with me, and belonged to other gentlemen on the island: these poor souls had never more than ninepence a day, and seldom more than sixpence, from their masters or owners, though they earned them three or four pisterines.[109] For it is a common practice in the West-Indies for men to purchase slaves, though they have not plantations themselves, in order to let them out to planters and merchants, at so much a piece by the day, and they give what they choose, out of this produce of their daily work; to their slaves for subsistence. This allowance is often very scanty.

My master often gave the owners of these slaves two and a half of these pieces per day, and found the poor fellows in victuals himself, because he thought their owners did not feed them well enough, according to the work they did. The slaves used to like this very well; and, as they knew my master to be a man of feeling, they were always glad to work for him in preference to any other gentleman; some of whom, after they had been paid for these poor people's labours, would not give them their allowance out of it. Many times have I seen these unfortunate wretches beaten for asking for their pay; and often severely flogged by their owners, if they did not bring them their daily or weekly money exactly to the time; though the poor creatures were obliged to wait on the gentlemen they had worked for, sometimes more than half the day before they could get their pay, and this generally on Sundays, when they wanted the time for themselves. In particular, I knew a countryman of mine, who once did not bring the weekly money directly that it was earned; and though he brought it the same day to his master, yet he was staked to the ground for his pretended negligence, and was just going to receive a hundred lashes, but for a gentleman who begged him off fifty.

This poor man was very industrious, and by his frugality had saved so much money, by working on shipboard, that he had got a white man to buy him a boat, unknown to his master. Some time after he had this little estate, the governor wanted a boat to bring his sugar from different parts of the island; and, knowing this to be a negro-man's boat, he seized upon it for himself, and would not pay the owner a farthing. The man on this went to his master, and complained to him of this act of the governor; but the only satisfaction he received was to be damned very heartily by his master, who asked him how dared any of his negroes to have a boat. If the justly-merited ruin of the governor's fortune could be any gratification to the poor man he had thus robbed, he was not without consolation. Extortion and rapine are poor providers; and some time after this, the governor died in the King's Bench,[110] in England, as I was told, in great poverty. The last war favoured this poor negro-man, and he found some means to escape from his christian master: he came to England, where I saw him afterwards several times. Such treatment as this often drives these miserable wretches to despair, and they run away from their masters at the hazard of their lives. Many of them, in this place, unable to get their pay when they have earned it, and fearing to be flogged, as usual, if they return home without it, run away where they can for shelter, and a reward is often offered to bring them in dead or alive. My master used sometimes, in these cases, to agree with their owners, and to settle with them himself; and thereby he saved many of them a flogging.

Once, for a few days, I was let out to fit a vessel, and I had no victuals allowed me by either party; at last I told my master of this treatment, and he took me away from it. In many of the estates, on the different islands where I used to be sent for rum or sugar, they would not deliver it to me, or to any other negro; he was therefore obliged to send a white man along with me to those places; and then he used to pay him from six to ten pisterines a day. From being thus employed, during the time I served Mr. King, in going about the different estates on the island, I had all the opportunity I could wish for to see the dreadful usage of the poor men—usage that reconciled me to my situation, and made me bless God for the hands into which I had fallen.

I had the good fortune to please my master in every department in which he employed me; and there was scarcely any part of his business, or household affairs, in which I was not occasionally engaged. I often supplied the place of a clerk, in receiving and delivering cargoes to the ships, in tending stores, and delivering goods; and, besides this, I used to shave and dress my master, when convenient, and take care of his horse; and when it was necessary, which was very often, I worked likewise on board of his different vessels. By these means I became very useful to my master, and saved him, as he used to acknowledge, above a hundred pounds a year. Nor did he scruple to say I was of more advantage to him than any of his clerks; tho' their usual wages in the West-Indies are from sixty to a hundred pounds current a year.

I have sometimes heard it asserted that a negro cannot earn his master the first cost; but nothing can be further from the truth. I suppose nine tenths of the mechanics throughout the West-Indies are negro slaves; and I well know the coopers among them earn two dollars a-day;

the carpenters the same, and oftentimes more; also the masons, smiths, and fishermen, &c. and I have known many slaves whose masters would not take a thousand pounds current for them. But surely this assertion refutes itself: for, if it be true, why do the planters and merchants pay such a price for slaves? And, above all, why do those, who make this assertion, exclaim the most loudly against the abolition of the slave trade? So much are men blinded, and to such inconsistent arguments are they driven by mistaken interest! I grant, indeed, that slaves are sometimes, by half-feeding, half-clothing, over-working, and stripes, reduced so low, that they are turned out as unfit for service, and left to perish in the woods, or to expire on a dunghill.

My master was several times offered by different gentlemen one hundred guineas for me; but he always told them he would not sell me, to my great joy: and I used to double my diligence and care for fear of getting into the hands of these men, who did not allow a valuable slave the common support of life. Many of them used to find fault with my master for feeding his slaves so well as he did; although I often went hungry, and an Englishman might think my fare very indifferent: but he used to tell them he always would do it, because the slaves thereby looked better and did more work.

While I was thus employed by my master, I was often a witness to cruelties of every kind, which were exercised on my unhappy fellowslaves. I used frequently to have different cargoes of new negroes in my care for sale; and it was almost a constant practice with our clerks, and other whites, to commit violent depredations on the chastity of the female slaves; and to these atrocities I was, though with reluctance, obliged to submit at all times, being unable to help them. When we have had some of these slaves on board my master's vessels to carry them to other islands, or to America, I have known our mates commit these acts most shamefully, to the disgrace not of christians only, but of men. I have even known them gratify their brutal passion with females not ten years old; and these abominations some of them practised to such a scandalous excess, that one of our captains discharged the mate and others on that account. And yet in Montserrat I have seen a negro-man staked to the ground, and cut most shockingly, and then his ears cut off, bit by bit, because he had been connected with a white woman, who was a common prostitute! As if it were no crime in the whites to rob an innocent African girl of her virtue; but most heinous in a black man only to gratify a passion of nature, where the temptation was offered by one of a different colour, though the most abandoned woman of her species.

One Mr. D— —, told me he had sold 41,000 negroes, and he once cut off a negroman's leg for running away. I asked him if the man had died in the operation, how he, as a christian, could answer, for the horrid act, before God. And he told me, answering was a thing of another world; what he thought and did were policy. I told him that the christian doctrine taught us "to do unto others as we would that others should do unto us." He then said that his scheme had the desired effect—it cured that man and some others of running away.[111]

Another negro-man was half hanged, and then burnt, for attempting to poison a cruel overseer. Thus, by repeated cruelties, are the wretched first urged to despair, and then murdered, because they still retain so much of human nature about them as to wish to put an end to their misery, and to retaliate on their tyrants! These overseers are, indeed, for the most part, persons of the worst character of any denomination of men in the West-Indies. Unfortunately, many humane gentlemen, by not residing on their estates, are obliged to leave the management of them in the hands of these human butchers, who cut and mangle the slaves in a shocking manner, on the most trivial occasions, and altogether treat them, in every respect, like brutes. They pay no regard to the situation of pregnant women, nor the least attention to the lodging of the field negroes. Their huts, which ought to be well covered, and the place dry where they take their short repose, are often open sheds, built in damp places; so that, when the poor creatures return tired from the toils of the field, they contract many disorders, from being exposed to the damp air in this uncomfortable state, while they are heated, and their pores are open.

The neglect certainly conspires with many others to cause a decrease in the births, as well as in the lives of the grown negroes. I can quote many instances of gentlemen who reside on their own estates in the West-Indies, and then the scene is quite changed; the negroes are treated with lenity and proper care, by which their lives are prolonged, and their masters profited. To the honour of humanity, I know several gentlemen who managed their estates in this manner, and found that benevolence was their true interest. And, among many I could mention in Montserrat,[112] whose slaves looked remarkably well, and never needed any fresh supplies of negroes, (and there are many other estates, especially in Barbadoes, which, from such judicious treatment, need no fresh stock of negroes at any time) I have the honour of knowing a most worthy and humane gentleman, who is a native of Barbadoes, and has estates there.[113] This gentleman has written a treatise on the usage of his own slaves. He allows them two hours for refreshment at mid-day, and many other indulgences and comforts, particularly in their lying; and, besides this, he raises more provisions on his estate than they can destroy; so that by these attentions he saves the lives of his negroes, and keeps them healthy, and as happy as the condition of slavery can admit. I myself, as shall appear in the sequel, managed an estate, where, by such attentions, the negroes were uncommonly cheerful and healthy, and did more work by half than by the common mode of treatment they usually do. For want, therefore, of such care and attention to the poor negroes, and otherwise oppressed as they are, it is no wonder that the decrease should require 20,000 new negroes annually to fill up the vacant places of the dead.

Even in Barbadoes, notwithstanding those humane exceptions which I have mentioned and others with which I am acquainted that justly make it quoted as a place where slaves meet with the best treatment, and need fewest recruits of any in the West-Indies; yet this island requires 1,000 negroes annually to keep up the original stock, which is only 80,000. So that the whole term of a negro's life may be said to be there but sixteen years![114] And yet the climate here is in every respect the same as that from which they are taken, except in being more wholesome. Do the British colonies decrease in this manner? And yet what a prodigious difference is there between an English and West-India climate?

While I was in Montserrat I knew a negro-man, one Emanuel Sankey, who endeavoured to escape from his miserable bondage, by concealing himself on board of a London ship. But fate did not favour the poor oppressed man; for, being discovered when the vessel was under sail, he was delivered up again to his master. This christian master immediately pinned the wretch to the ground, at each wrist and ancle, and then took some sticks of sealing wax, lighted them, and dropped it all over his back. There was another master noted for cruelty: — I believe he had not a slave but had been cut, and pieces fairly taken out of the flesh: and after they had been punished thus, he used to make them get into a long wooden box, or case, he had for that purpose, and shut them up during pleasure. It was just about the height and breadth of a man; and the poor wretches had no room when in the case to move.

It was very common in several of the islands, particularly in St. Kitt's, for the slaves to be branded with the initial letters of their master's name, and a load of heavy iron hooks hung about their necks. Indeed on the most trivial occasions they were loaded with chains, and often instruments of torture were added. The iron muzzle, thumb-screws, &c. are so well known as not to need a description, and were sometimes applied for the slightest faults. I have seen a negro beaten till some of his bones were broken, for only letting a pot boil over. It is not uncommon, after a flogging, to make slaves go on their knees and thank their owners, and pray, or rather say, "God bless you." I have often asked many of the men slaves (who used to go several miles to their wives, and late in the night, after having been wearied with a hard day's labour) why they went so far for wives, and did not take them of their own master's negro-women, and particularly those who lived together as household slaves. Their answers have ever been — "Because when the master or mistress choose to punish the women, they make the husbands flog their own wives, and that we could not bear to do."[115] Is it surprising such usage should drive the poor creatures to despair, and make them seek a refuge in death, from those evils which render their lives intolerable — while

> 'With shudd'ring horror pale, and eyes aghast,
> They view their lamentable lot, and find
> No rest?'[116]

This they frequently do. A negro-man, on board a vessel of my master's, while I belonged to her, having been put in irons for some trifling misdemeanour, and kept in that state some days, being weary of life, took an opportunity of jumping overboard into the sea; however he was picked up without being drowned. Another, whose life was also a burden to him, resolved to starve himself to death, and refused to eat any victuals: this procured him a severe flogging; and he also on the first occasion that offered, jumped overboard at Charles Town, but was saved.

Nor is there any greater reward shewn to the little property than there is to the persons and lives of the negroes. I have already related an instance or two of particular oppression, out of many which I have witnessed; but the following is frequent in all the islands: — The wretched field-slaves, after toiling all the day for an unfeeling owner, who gives them but little victuals, steal sometimes a few moments from rest or refreshment to gather some small portion of grass, according as their time will admit. This they commonly tie up in a parcel; either a bits worth (sixpence) or half a bit's worth, and bring it to town, or to the market to sell. Nothing is more common than for the white people, on this occasion, to take the grass from them without paying for it; and not only so, but too often also, to my knowledge, our clerks and many others, at the same time have committed acts of violence on the poor, wretched, and helpless females; whom I have seen for hours stand crying to no purpose, and get no redress or pay of any kind. Is not this one common and crying sin enough to bring down God's judgment on the islands? He tells us the oppressor and the oppressed are both in his hands; and if these are not the poor, the broken-hearted, the blind, the captive, the bruised, of which our Saviour speaks, who are they?[117]

One of these depredators once, in St. Eustatia, came on board of our vessel, and bought some fowls and pigs of me; and a whole day after his departure with the things, he returned and wanted his money back:—I refused to give it; and, he not seeing my captain on board, began the common pranks with me; and swore he would even break open my chest and take my money. I therefore expected, as my captain was absent, that he would be as good as his word: and he was just proceeding to strike me, when fortunately a British seaman on board, whose heart had not been debauched by a West-India climate, interposed and prevented him. But had the cruel man struck me, I certainly should have defended myself, at the hazard of my life. For what is life to a man thus oppressed? He went away, however, swearing; and threatened that whenever he caught me a-shore he would shoot me, and pay for me afterwards.

The small account, in which the life of a negro is held in the West-Indies, is so universally known, that it might seem impertinent to quote the following extract, if some people had not been hardy enough of late to assert, that negroes are on the same footing in that respect as Europeans. By the 329th Act, page 125, of the Assembly of Barbadoes, it is enacted 'That if any negro, or other slave, under punishment by his master, or his order, for running away, or any other crime or misdemeanour towards his said master, unfortunately shall suffer in life or member, no person whatsoever shall be liable to a fine; but if any man shall out of *wantonness, or only of bloody-mindedness, or cruel intention, wilfully kill a negro, or other slave, of his own, he shall pay into the public treasury £15. sterling.'* And it is the same in most, if not all, of the West India islands. Is not this one of the many acts of the islands which call loudly for redress? And do not the Assembly, which enacted it, deserve the appellation of savages and brutes rather than of christians and men? It is an act at once unmerciful, unjust, and unwise; which for cruelty would disgrace an assembly of those who are called barbarians; and for its injustice and insanity would shock the morality and common sense of a Samaide or Hottentot.[118]

Shocking as this and many other acts of the bloody West-India code at first appear, how is the iniquity of it heightened when we consider to whom it may be extended! Mr. James Tobin, a zealous labourer in the vineyard of slavery, gives an account[119] of a French planter, of his

acquaintance, in the island of Martinico, who shewed him many mulattoes working in the fields like beasts of burden; and he told Mr. Tobin
these *were all the produce of his own loins!* And I myself have known similar instances. Pray, reader, are these sons and daughters of the French
planter less his children by being begotten on black women? And what
must be the virtue of those legislators, and the feelings of those fathers,
who estimate the lives of their sons, however begotten, at no more than
fifteen pounds; though they should be murdered, as the act says, *out of
wantonness and bloody-mindedness?* But is not the slave-trade entirely a
war with the heart of man? And surely that which is begun by break-
ing down the barriers of virtue, involves in its continuance destruction
to every principle, and buries all sentiments in ruin!

I have often seen slaves, particularly those who were meagre, in different islands, put into scales and weighed; and then sold from three-
pence to six-pence or nine-pence a pound. My master, however, whose
humanity was shocked at this mode, used to sell such by the lump. And
at or after a sale, even those negroes born in the islands it is not uncommon to see taken from their wives, wives from their husbands, and children from their parents, and sent off to other islands, and wherever else
their merciless lords choose; and, probably, never more, during life, see
each other! Oftentimes my heart has bled at these partings; when the
friends of the departed have been at the water-side, and, with sighs and
tears, have kept their eyes fixed on the vessel till it went out of sight.

A poor Creole negro I knew well, who, after having been often thus
transported from island to island, at last resided in Montserrat. This
man used to tell me many melancholy tales of himself. Generally, after he
had done working for his master, he used to employ his few leisure
moments to go a fishing. When he had caught any fish, his master would
frequently take them from him without paying him; and at other times
some other white people would serve him in the same manner. One day
he said to me very movingly, 'Sometimes when a white man take away
my fish I go to my maser, and he get me my right; and when my maser,
by strength, take away my fishes, what me must do? I can't go to any
body to be righted; then,' said the poor man, looking up above, 'I must
look up to God Mighty in the top for right.' This artless tale moved me
much, and I could not help feeling the just cause Moses had in redress-
ing his brother against the Egyptian.[120] I exhorted the man to look up still
to the God in the top, since there was no redress below. Though I little
thought then that I myself should more than once experience such imposition, and need the same exhortation hereafter, in my own transactions

in the islands; and that even this poor man and I should, some time after, suffer together in the same manner, as shall be related hereafter.

Nor was such usage as this confined to particular places or individuals; for, in all the different islands in which I have been (and I have visited no less than fifteen) the treatment of the slaves was nearly the same; so nearly, indeed, that the history of an island, or even a plantation, with a few such exceptions as I have mentioned, might serve for a history of the whole. Such a tendency has the slave-trade to debauch men's minds, and harden them to every feeling of humanity! For I will not suppose that the dealers in slaves are born worse than other men. No; it is the fatality of this mistaken avarice, that it corrupts the milk of human kindness and turns it into gall.[121] And, had the pursuits of those men been different, they might have been as generous, as tender-hearted, and just, as they are unfeeling, rapacious and cruel. Surely this traffic cannot be good, which spreads like a pestilence, and taints what it touches! Which violates that first natural right of mankind, equality, and independency; and gives one man a dominion over his fellows which God could never intend! For it raises the owner to a state as far above man as it depresses the slave below it; and, with all the presumption of human pride, sets a distinction between them, immeasurable in extent, and endless in duration! Yet how mistaken is the avarice even of the planters. Are slaves more useful by being thus humbled to the condition of brutes, than they would be if suffered to enjoy the privileges of men? The freedom which diffuses health and prosperity throughout Britain answers you—"No." When you make men slaves, you deprive them of half their virtue, you set them, in your own conduct, an example of fraud, rapine, and cruelty, and compel them to live with you in a state of war; and yet you complain that they are not honest or faithful! You stupify them with stripes, and think it necessary to keep them in a state of ignorance; and yet you assert that they are incapable of learning; that their minds are such a barren soil or moor that culture would be lost on them; and that they come from a climate, where nature, though prodigal of her bounties in a degree unknown to yourselves, has left man alone scant and unfinished, and incapable of enjoying the treasures she has poured out for him!—An assertion at once impious and absurd. Why do you use those instruments of torture? Are they fit to be applied by one rational being to another? And are ye not struck with shame and mortification, to see the partakers of your nature reduced so low? But, above all, are there no dangers attending this mode of treatment? Are you not hourly in dread of an insurrection? Nor would it be surprising: for when

> No peace is given
> To us enslav'd, but custody severe;
> And stripes and arbitrary punishment
> Inflicted—What peace can we return?
> But to our power, hostility and hate,
> Untam'd reluctance, and revenge, tho' slow,
> Yet ever plotting how the conqueror least
> May reap his conquest, and may least rejoice
> In doing what we most in suff'ring feel? MILTON[122]

But by changing your conduct, and treating your slaves as men, every cause of fear would be banished. They would be faithful, honest, intelligent and vigorous; and peace, prosperity, and happiness, would attend you.

✠ ✠ ✠

CHAPTER 6

❋ ❋ ❋

Earthquakes are only one of the shocks Equiano experiences as 1763 draws to a close. Already busy as a jack-of-all-trades for his master, Equiano nevertheless must increase his workload by crewing occasionally for Captain Thomas Farmer on an inter-island passenger ship, until Mr. King finally assigns Equiano to a permanent post on Farmer's sloop. During the four years that he sails among the islands he also becomes an entrepreneur in his own right, a small-goods trader dealing in glass tumblers, gin, limes, oranges, and so forth. As he gradually deepens his investments he discovers that chicanery and corruption lie even in the course of small trade routes; he is especially pained when two white men rob him of his goods.

At one of our trips to St. Kitt's, I had eleven bits[123] of my own; and my friendly captain lent me five more, with which I bought a Bible. I was very glad to get this book, which I could scarcely meet with any where. I think there were none sold in Montserrat; and, much to my grief, from being forced out of the Ætna, in the manner I have related, my Bible, and the "Guide to the Indians,"[124] the two books I loved above all others, were left behind.

While I was in St. Kitt's, a very curious imposition on human nature took place:—A white man wanted to marry, in the church, a free black woman that had land and slaves in Montserrat: but the clergyman told him it was against the law of the place to marry a white and a black in the church. The man then asked to be married on the water, to which the parson consented, and the lovers went in one boat, and the parson and clerk in another, and thus the ceremony was performed. After this the loving pair came on board our vessel, and my captain treated them extremely well, and brought them safe to Montserrat.

The reader cannot but judge of the irksomeness of this situation to a mind like mine, in being daily exposed to new hardships and impositions, after having seen many better days, and been, as it were, in a state of freedom and plenty; added to which, every part of the world in which I had hitherto been, seemed to me a paradise in comparison of the West-Indies. My mind was therefore hourly replete with inventions and thoughts of being freed, and, if possible, by honest and honourable means; for I always remembered the old adage, and I trust that it has ever been my ruling principle, that *Honesty is the best policy;* and likewise that other golden precept—*To do unto all men as I would they should do unto me.* However, as I was from early years a predestinarian,[125] I thought whatever fate had determined must ever come to pass; and therefore, if ever it were my lot to be freed, nothing could prevent me, although I should at present see no means or hope to obtain my freedom; on the other hand, if it were my fate not to be freed, I never should be so; and all my endeavours for that purpose would be fruitless. In the midst of these thoughts I therefore looked up with prayers anxiously to God for my liberty; and at the same time used every honest means, and did all that was possible on my part, to obtain it.

❋ ❋ ❋

Throughout 1764 and 1765, Captain Farmer and Equiano ship slaves to Savannah and Charleston, and rum and sugar to Philadelphia; Equiano also continues to widen his own small-goods trade. One stop in Savannah in 1765 nearly proves fatal to him, however, when a white doctor and his servant beat and imprison him. Deliverance comes in the form of a physician named Dr. Brady, who diligently nurses him back to health. After several weeks he is well enough to return to Montserrat.

CHAPTER 7

Every day now brought me nearer my freedom, and I was impatient till we proceeded again to sea, that I might have an opportunity of getting a sum large enough to purchase it. I was not long ungratified; for in the beginning of the year 1766, my master bought another sloop, named the Nancy, the largest I had ever seen. She was partly laden, and was to proceed to Philadelphia. Our captain had his choice of three, and I was well pleased he chose this, which was the largest; for, from his having a large vessel, I had more room, and could carry a larger quantity of goods with me. Accordingly, when we had delivered our old vessel, the Prudence, and completed the lading of the Nancy, having made near three hundred per cent. by four barrels of pork I brought from Charlestown, I laid in as large a cargo as I could, trusting to God's Providence to prosper my undertaking. With these views I sailed for Philadelphia. On our passage, when we drew near the land, I was for the first time surprised at the sight of some whales, having never seen any such large sea-monsters before; and, as we sailed by the land, one morning I saw a puppy whale close by the vessel; it was about the length of a wherry-boat, and it followed us all the day until we got within the Capes. We arrived safe and in good time at Philadelphia, and I sold my goods there chiefly to the quakers. They always appeared to be a very honest and discreet sort of people, and never attempted to impose on me; I therefore liked them, and ever after chose to deal with them in preference to any others.

One Sunday morning while I was here, as I was going to church, I chanced to pass a meeting-house. The doors being open, and the house full of people, it excited my curiosity to go in. When I entered the house, to my great surprise, I saw a very tall woman standing in the midst of them, speaking in an audible voice something which I could not understand. Having never seen any thing of this kind before, I stood and stared about me for some time, wondering at this odd scene. As soon as it was over, I took an opportunity to make enquiry about the place and people, when I was informed they were called Quakers. I particularly asked what that woman I saw in the midst of them had said, but none of them were pleased to satisfy me; so I quitted them, and soon after, as I was returning, I came to a church crowded with people; the church-yard was full likewise, and a number of people were even mounted on ladders, looking in at the windows. I thought this a strange sight, as I had never seen churches, either in England or the West-Indies, crowded in this manner before. I therefore made bold to ask some people the meaning of all this, and they told me the Rev. George Whitfield[126] was preaching. I had often heard of this gentleman, and had wished to see and hear him; but I had never before had an opportunity. I now therefore resolved to gratify myself with the sight, and pressed in amidst the multitude. When I got into the church I saw this pious man exhorting the people with the greatest fervour and earnestness, and sweating as much as ever I did while in slavery on Montserrat-beach. I was very much struck and impressed with this; I thought it strange I had never seen divines exert themselves in this manner before; and was no longer at a loss to account for the thin congregations they preached to. When we had discharged our cargo here, and were loaded again, we left this fruitful land once more, and set sail for Montserrat. My traffic had hitherto succeeded so well with me, that I thought, by selling my goods when we arrived at Montserrat, I should have enough to purchase my freedom. But as soon as our vessel arrived there, my master came on board, and gave orders for us to go to St. Eustatia, and discharge our cargo there, and from thence to proceed for Georgia. I was much disappointed at this; but thinking, as usual, it was of no use to murmur at the decrees of fate, I submitted without repining, and we went to St. Eustatia.

After we had discharged our cargo there, we took in a live cargo, as we call a cargo of slaves. Here I sold my goods tolerably well; but not being able to lay out all my money in this small island to as much advantage as in many other places, I laid out only part, and the remainder I brought away with me neat. We sailed from hence to Georgia, and I was glad when we got there, though I had not much reason to like the place from my last adventure in Savannah; but I longed to get back to Montserrat and procure my freedom, which I expected to be able to purchase when I returned. As soon as we had arrived here I waited on my careful doctor, Mr. Brady, to whom I made the most grateful acknowledgments in my power, for his former kindness and attention during my illness.

While we remained here, an odd circumstance happened to the Captain and me, which disappointed us both a great deal. A silversmith, whom we had brought to this place some voyages before, agreed with the Captain to return to the West-Indies, and promised at the same time to give the Captain a great deal of money, having pretended to take a liking to him, and being, as we thought, very rich. But while we stayed to load our vessel this man was taken ill, in a house where he worked, and in a week's time became very bad. The worse he grew the more he used to speak of giving the Captain what he had promised him, so that he expected something considerable from the death of this man, who had no wife or child, and he attended him day and night.

I used also to go with the Captain, at his own desire, to attend him; especially when we saw there was no appearance of his recovery: and in order to recompence me for my trouble, the Captain promised me ten pounds, when he should get the man's property. I thought this would be of great service to me, although I had nearly money enough to purchase my freedom, if I should get safe this voyage to Montserrat. In this expectation I laid out above eight pounds of my money for a suit of superfine clothes to dance in at my freedom, which I hoped was then at hand. We still continued to attend this man, and were with him even on the last day he lived, till very late at night when we went on board. After we were got to bed, about one or two o'clock in the morning, the Captain was sent for, and was informed the man was dead. On this he came to my bed, and, waking me, informed me of it, and desired me to get up, procure a light, and to go immediately with him. I told him I was very sleepy, and wished he would take somebody else with him; or else, as the man was dead, and could want no further attendance, to let all things remain as they were till the next morning. 'No, no,' said he, 'we will have the money to-night. I cannot wait till to-morrow; so let us go.' Accordingly I got up and struck a light, and away we both went, and saw the man as dead as we could wish. The Captain said he would give him a grand burial, in gratitude for the promised treasure; and desired that all the things belonging to the deceased might be brought forth. Amongst others there was a nest of trunks, of which he had kept the keys whilst the man was ill; and when they were produced, we opened them with no small eagerness and expectation;—as there were a great number within one another, with much impatience we took them out of each other. At last, when we came to the smallest, and had opened it, we saw it was full of papers, which we supposed to be notes; at the sight of which our hearts leapt for joy; and that instant the Captain, clapping his hands, cried out—'Thank God! here it is!'

But when we began to examine the supposed treasure and long-looked-for bounty, alas! alas! how uncertain and deceitful are all human affairs! what had we found? While we thought we were embracing a substance, we grasped an empty nothing. The whole amount in the nest of trunks was only a dollar and a half; and all that the man possessed would not pay for his coffin! Our sudden and exquisite joy was now suc-ceeded by as sudden and exquisite pain; and my captain and I exhibited, for some time, most ridiculous figures—pictures of chagrin and disappointment! We went away greatly mortified, and left the deceased to do as well as he could for himself, as we had taken so good care of him when alive for nothing.

We set sail once more for Montserrat, and arrived there safe; but much out of humour with our friend, the silversmith. When we had unladen the vessel, and I had sold my venture, finding myself master of about forty-seven pounds, I consulted my true friend, the Captain, how I should proceed in offering my master the money for my freedom. He told me to come on a certain morning, when he and my master would be at breakfast together. Accordingly, on that morning I went, and met the Captain there, as he had appointed. When I went in I made my obeisance to my master, and with my money in my hand, and many fears in my heart, I prayed him to be as good as his offer to me, when he was pleased to promise me my freedom as soon as I could purchase it. This speech seemed to confound him; he began to recoil; and my heart that instant sunk within me. 'What,' said he, 'give you your freedom? Why, where did you get the money? Have you got forty pounds sterling?' 'Yes, sir,' I answered. 'How did you get it?' replied he. I told him, 'very honestly.' The Captain then said he knew I got the money very honestly and with much industry, and that I was particularly careful. On which my master replied, I got money much faster than he did; and said he would not have made me the promise which he did, had he thought I should have got the money so soon. 'Come, come,' said my worthy Captain, clapping my master on the back, 'Come, Robert, (which was his name) I think you must let him have his freedom. You have laid your money out very well; you have received good interest for it all this time, and here is now the principal at last. I know GUSTAVUS has earned you more than a hundred a year, and he will still save you money, as he will not leave you. Come, Robert, take the money.' My master then said, he would not be worse than his promise; and, taking the money, told me to go to the Secretary at the Register Office, and get my manumission drawn up.

These words of my master were like a voice from heaven to me: in an instant all my trepidation was turned into unutterable bliss, and I most reverently bowed myself with gratitude, unable to express my feelings, but by the overflowing of my eyes, and a heart replete with thanks to God; while my true and worthy friend, the Captain, congratulated us both with a peculiar degree of heartfelt pleasure. As soon as the first transports of my joy were over, and that I had expressed my thanks to these my worthy friends in the best manner I was able, I rose with a heart full of affection and reverence, and left the room, in order to obey my master's joyful mandate of going to the Register Office. As I was leaving the house I called to mind the words of the Psalmist, in the 126th Psalm, and like him, 'I glorified God in my heart, in whom I trusted.'[127] These words had been impressed on my mind from the very day I was forced from Deptford to the present hour, and I now saw them, as I thought, fulfilled and verified.

My imagination was all rapture as I flew to the Register Office; and in this respect, like the apostle Peter[128] (whose deliverance from prison was so sudden and extraordinary, that he thought he was in a vision) I could scarcely believe I was awake. Heavens! who could do justice to my feelings at this moment? Not conquering heroes themselves, in the midst of a triumph—Not the tender mother who has just regained her long-lost infant, and presses it to her heart—Not the weary, hungry mariner, at the sight of the desired friendly port—Not the lover, when he once more embraces his beloved mistress, after she has been ravished from his arms!—All within my breast was tumult, wildness, and delirium! My feet scarcely touched the ground; for they were winged with joy, and, like Elijah, as he rose to Heaven, they 'were with lightning sped as I went on.'[129] Every one I met I told of my happiness, and blazed about the virtue of my amiable master and Captain.

When I got to the office and acquainted the Register with my errand, he congratulated me on the occasion, and told me he would draw up my manumission for half-price, which was a guinea. I thanked him for his kindness; and, having received it and paid him, I hastened to my master to get him to sign it, that I might be fully released. Accordingly he signed the manumission that day; so that, before night, I, who had been a slave in the morning, trembling at the will of another, was become my own master, and completely free. I thought this was the happiest day I had ever experienced; and my joy was still heightened by the blessings and prayers of many of the sable race, particularly the aged, to whom my heart had ever been attached with reverence.

❋ ❋ ❋

Here Equiano adverts to the document of his legal manumission; this document is not reproduced in the present edition.

In short, the fair as well as black people immediately styled me by a new appellation,—to me the most desirable in the world,—which was "Freeman," and, at the dances I gave, my Georgia superfine blue clothes made no indifferent appearance, as I thought. Some of the sable females, who formerly stood aloof, now began to relax and appear less coy; but my heart was still fixed on London, where I hoped to be ere long. So that my worthy Captain, and his owner, my late master, finding that the bent of my mind was towards London, said to me, 'We hope you won't leave us, but that you will still be with the vessels.' Here gratitude bowed me down; and none but the generous mind can judge of my feelings, struggling between inclination and duty. However, notwithstanding my wish to be in London, I obediently answered my benefactors that I would go in the vessel, and not leave them; and from that day I was entered on board as an able-bodied seaman, at thirty-six shillings per month, besides what perquisites I could make. My intention was to make a voyage or two, entirely to please these my honoured patrons; but I determined that the year following, if it pleased God, I would see Old England once more, and surprise my old master, Captain Pascal, who was hourly in my mind; for I still loved him, notwithstanding his usage to me, and I pleased myself with thinking of what he would say when he saw what the Lord had done for me in so short a time, instead of being, as he might perhaps suppose, under the cruel yoke of some planter.

With such reveries I used often to entertain myself, and shorten the time till my return; and now, being as in my original free African state,[130] I embarked on board the Nancy, after having got all things ready for our voyage. In this state of serenity we sailed for St. Eustatia; and having smooth seas and calm weather, we soon arrived there; after taking our cargo on board, we proceeded to Savannah in Georgia, in August, 1766. While we were there, as usual, I used to go for the cargo up the rivers in boats; and, when on this business, I have been frequently beset by Alligators, which were very numerous on that coast and river. I have shot many of them when they have been near getting into our boats; which we have with great difficulty sometimes prevented, and have been very much frightened at them. I have seen a young one sold in Georgia alive for sixpence.

During our stay at this place, one evening a slave belonging to Mr. Read, a merchant of Savannah, came near our vessel, and began to use me very ill. I entreated him, with all the patience of which I was master, to desist, as I knew there was little or no law for a free negro here. But the fellow, instead of taking my advice, persevered in his insults, and even struck me. At this I lost all temper, and fell on him, and beat him soundly. The next morning his master came to our vessel, as we lay alongside the wharf, and desired me to come ashore that he might have me flogged all round the town, for beating his negro slave! I told him he had insulted me, and had given the provocation by first striking me. I had also told my Captain the whole affair that morning, and desired him to go along with me to Mr. Read, to prevent bad consequences; but he said that it did not signify, and if Mr. Read said any thing he would make matters up, and desired me to go to work, which I accordingly did.

The Captain being on board when Mr. Read came and applied to him to deliver me up, he said he knew nothing of the matter, I was a free man. I was astonished and frightened at this, and thought I had better keep where I was, than go ashore and be flogged round the town, without judge or jury. I therefore refused to stir; and Mr. Read went away, swearing he would bring all the constables in the town, for he would have me out of the vessel. When he was gone, I thought his threat might prove too true to my sorrow; and I was confirmed in this belief, as well by the many instances I had seen of the treatment of free negroes, as from a fact that had happened within my own knowledge here a short time before.

There was a free black man, a carpenter, that I knew, who for asking a gentleman that he had worked for, for the money he had earned, was put into gaol; and afterwards this oppressed man was sent from Georgia, with false accusations, of an intention to set the gentleman's house on fire, and run away with his slaves. I was therefore much embarrassed, and very apprehensive of a flogging at least. I dreaded, of all things, the thoughts of being stripped, as I never in my life had the marks of any violence of that kind. At that instant a rage seized my soul, and for a little I determined to resist the first man that should attempt to lay violent hands on me, or basely use me without a trial; for I would sooner die like a free man, than suffer myself to be scourged, by the hands of ruffians, and my blood drawn like a slave.

The Captain and others, more cautious, advised me to make haste and conceal myself; for they said Mr. Read was a very spiteful man, and he would soon come on board with constables and take me. At first I refused this counsel, being determined to stand my ground; but at length, by the prevailing entreaties of the Captain and Mr. Dixon, with whom we lodged, I went to Mr. Dixon's house, which was a little out of the town, at a place called Yea-ma-chra.[131] I was but just gone when Mr. Read, and the constables, came for me, and searched the vessel; but, not finding me there, he swore he would have me dead or alive. I was secreted about five days; however the good character which my Captain always gave me, as well as some other gentlemen, who also knew me, procured me some friends. At last some of them told my Captain that he did not use me well, in suffering me thus to be imposed upon, and said they would see me redressed, and get me on board some other vessel. My Captain, on this, immediately went to Mr. Read, and told him, that ever since I eloped from the vessel his work had been neglected, and he could not go on with her loading, himself and mate not being well; and as I had managed things on board for them, my absence must have retarded his voyage, and consequently hurt the owner. He therefore begged of him to forgive me, as he said he never heard any complaint of me before, during the several years I had been with him. After repeated entreaties, Mr. Read said I might go to hell; and that he would not meddle with me; on which my Captain came immediately to me at his lodging, and telling me how pleasantly matters had gone on, desired me to go on board.

Some of my other friends then asked him if he had got the constable's warrant from them; the Captain said, "No." On this I was desired by them to stay in the house; and they said they would get me on board of some other vessel before the evening. When the Captain heard this he became almost distracted. He went immediately for the warrant, and, after using every exertion in his power, he at last got it from my hunters; but I had all the expences to pay.

After I had thanked all my friends for their kindness, I went on board again to my work, of which I had always plenty. We were in haste to complete our lading, and were to carry twenty head of cattle with us to the West-Indies, where they are a very profitable article. In order to encourage me in working, and to make up for the time I had lost, my Captain promised me the privilege of carrying two bullocks of my own with me; this made me work with redoubled ardour. As soon as I had got the vessel loaded, in doing which I was obliged to perform the duty of the mate as well as my own work, and when the bullocks were near coming on board, I asked the Captain leave to bring my two, according to his promise; but, to my great surprise, he told me there was no room for them. I then asked him to permit me to take one; but he said he could not. I was a good deal mortified at this usage, and told him I had no notion that he intended thus to impose on me; nor could I think well of any man that was so much worse than his word. On this we had some disagreement, and I gave him to understand that I intended to leave the vessel. At this he appeared to be very much dejected; and our mate, who had been very sickly, and whose duty had long devolved upon me, advised him to persuade me to stay. In consequence of which he spoke very kindly to me, making many fair promises, telling me that, as the mate was so sickly, he could not do without me; and that, as the safety of the vessel and cargo depended greatly upon me, he therefore hoped that I would not be offended at what had passed between us, and swore he would make up all matters when we arrived in the West-Indies; so I consented to slave on as before.

Soon after this, as the bullocks were coming on board, one of them ran at the Captain, and butted him so furiously in the breast, that he never recovered of the blow. In order to make me some amends for his treatment about the bullocks, the Captain now pressed me very much to take some turkeys, and other fowls, with me, and gave me liberty to take as many as I could find room for; but I told him he knew very well I had never carried any turkeys before, as I always thought they were such tender birds as were not fit to cross the seas. However, he continued to press me to buy them for once; and, what seemed very surprising to me, the more I was against it, the more he urged my taking them, insomuch that he insured me from all losses that might happen by them, and I was prevailed on to take them. But I thought this very strange, as he had never acted so with me before. This, and not being able to dispose of my paper-money in any other way, induced me at length to take four dozen. The turkeys, however, I was so dissatisfied about that I determined to make no more voyages to this quarter, nor with this Captain; and was very apprehensive that my free voyage would be the worst I had ever made.

We set sail for Montserrat. The Captain and mate had been both complaining of sickness when we sailed, and as we proceeded on our voyage they grew worse. This was about November, and we had not been long at sea before we began to meet with strong northerly gales and rough seas; and in about seven or eight days all the bullocks were near being drowned, and four or five of them died. Our vessel, which had not been tight at first, was much less so now: and, though we were but nine in the whole, including five sailors and myself, yet we were obliged to attend to the pumps, every half or three quarters of an hour. The Captain and mate came on deck as often as they were able, which was now but seldom; for they declined so fast, that they were not well enough to make observations above four or five times the whole passage. The whole care of the vessel rested therefore upon me, and I was obliged to direct her by mere dint of reason, not being able to work a traverse.[132]

The Captain was now very sorry he had not taught me navigation, and protested, if ever he should get well again, he would not fail to do so. But in about seventeen days his illness increased so much, that he was obliged to keep his bed, continuing sensible, however, until the last, constantly having the owner's interest at heart; for this just and benevolent man ever appeared much concerned about the welfare of what he was intrusted with. When this dear friend found the symptoms of death approaching, he called me by my name; and, when I came to him, he asked (with almost his last breath) if he had ever done me any harm. 'God forbid I should think so!' I replied, 'I should then be the most ungrateful of wretches to the best of benefactors.' While I was thus expressing my affection and sorrow by his bedside, he expired without saying another word, and the day following we committed his body to the deep. Every man on board loved him, and regretted his death; but I was exceedingly affected at it, and found that I did not know, till he was gone, the strength of my regard for him. Indeed I had every reason in the world to be attached to him; for, besides that he was in general mild, affable, generous, faithful, benevolent, and just, he was to me a friend and father; and had it pleased Providence that he had died but five months before, I verily believe I should not have obtained my freedom when I did; and it is not improbable that I might not have been able to get it at any rate afterwards.

The Captain being dead, the mate came on the deck, and made such observations as he was able, but to no purpose. In the course of a few days more, the few bullocks that remained were found dead; but the turkeys I had, though on the deck, and exposed to so much wet and bad weather, did well, and I afterwards gained near three hundred per cent. on the sale of them. So that in the event it proved a happy circumstance for me that I had not bought the bullocks I intended, for they must have perished with the rest. I could not help looking upon this, otherwise trifling, circumstance, as a particular providence of God; and was accordingly thankful. The care of the vessel took up all my time, and engaged my attention entirely. As we were now out of the variable winds, I thought I should not be much puzzled to hit the islands. I was persuaded I steered right for Antigua, which I wished to reach, as the nearest to us; and in the course of nine or ten days we made that island to our great joy, and the day after we came safe to Montserrat.

Many were surprised when they heard of my conducting the sloop into the port; and I now obtained a new appellation, and was called "Captain." This elated me not a little, and it was quite flattering to my vanity to be thus styled by as high a title as any sable freeman in this place possessed. When the death of the Captain became known, he was much regretted by all who knew him; for he was a man universally respected. At the same time the sable Captain lost no fame; for the success I had met with increased the affection of my friends in no small measure; and I was offered, by a gentleman of the place, the command of his sloop, to go amongst the islands, but I refused.

❊ ❊ ❊

In January of 1767, Captain William Phillips and Equiano take a cargo of slaves to Georgia. Equiano's daily routines are interrupted, however, after he dreams on three consecutive nights about being shipwrecked: life mirrors his dream, and he finds himself stranded in the Bahamas. Two more shipwrecks and many weeks and struggles later he returns to Georgia only to have a Savannah night patrol attempt to flog him for having a light on after nine o'clock at night. Dr. Brady's intervention saves him again, an act of kindness that Equiano is able to repay to someone else when he performs a funeral service for a black child. He then sails for Montserrat via Martinique.

Equiano sets foot in Montserrat by 23 July 1767 solely to bid farewell to Mr. King and his friends and return to London. Settling down in Haymarket, he learns both the French horn and the hairdressing trade, and he studies arithmetic. After a three-month stint as a hairdresser to Dr. Charles Irving, the inventor of water desalination, he finds himself in need of better wages. He thus becomes a ship captain's personal servant for a few years and travels throughout Europe, the Mediterranean, and the West Indies. By August of 1772, he returns to London to work for Dr. Irving again until he follows his wanderlust toward the North Pole in May of 1773 on Constantine Phipps's four-month expedition to find a northeast passage to India.

CHAPTER 10

Our voyage to the North Pole being ended, I returned to London with Dr. Irving; with whom I continued for some time, during which I began seriously to reflect on the dangers I had escaped, particularly those of my last voyage, which made a lasting impression on my mind, and, by the grace of God, proved afterwards a mercy to me; it caused me to reflect deeply on my eternal state, and to seek the Lord with full purpose of heart ere it was too late. I rejoiced greatly; and heartily thanked the Lord for directing me to London, where I was determined to work out my own salvation, and, in so doing, procure a title to heaven; this being the result of a mind blinded by ignorance and sin.

In process of time I left my master, Dr. Irving, the purifier of waters. I lodged in Coventry Court, Haymarket, where I was continually oppressed and much concerned about the salvation of my soul, and was determined in my own strength to be a first-rate Christian. I used every means for this purpose; and not being able to find any person amongst those with whom I was then acquainted, that acquiesced with me in point of religion, or, in scripture language, that *would shew me any good*, I was much dejected, and knew not where to seek relief; however, I first frequented the neighbouring churches, St. James's and others, two or three times a day for many weeks. Still I came away dissatisfied; something was wanting that I could not obtain, and I really found more heart-felt relief in reading my Bible at home than in attending the church; and, being resolved to be saved, I pursued other methods. First I went among the people called Quakers, whose meeting at times was held in silence, and I remained as much in the dark as ever. I then searched into the Roman Catholic principles; but was not in the least edified. I at length had recourse to the Jews, which availed me nothing, as the fear of eternity daily harassed my mind, and I knew not where to seek shelter from the wrath to come.

However, this was my conclusion, at all events, to read the Four Evangelists,[133] and whatever sect or party I found adhering thereto, such I would join. Thus I went on heavily without any guide to direct me the way that leadeth to eternal life.[134] I asked different people questions about the manner of going to heaven, and was told different ways. Here I was much staggered, and could not find any at that time more righteous than myself, or indeed so much inclined to devotion. I thought we should not all be saved, (this is agreeable to the scriptures,) nor would all be damned. I found none among the circle of my acquaintance that kept wholly the Ten Commandments.[135] So righteous was I in my own eyes, that I was convinced I excelled many of them in that point, by keeping eight out of ten; and finding those, who in general termed themselves Christians, not so honest nor so good in their morals as the Turks, I really thought the Turks were in a safer way of salvation than my neighbours; so that between hopes and fears I went on, and the chief comforts I enjoyed were in the musical French-horn, which I then practised, and also dressing of hair. Such was my situation some months, experiencing the dishonesty of many people here. I determined at last to set out for Turkey, and there to end my days.

It was now early in the spring 1774. I sought for a master, and found a captain John Hughes, commander of a ship called the Anglicania, fitting out in the river Thames, and bound to Smyrna in Turkey. I shipped myself with him as steward; at the same time I recommended to him a very clever black man, John Annis, as a cook. This man was on board the ship near two months doing his duty: he had formerly lived many years with Mr. William Kirkpatrick, a gentleman of the island of St. Kitt's, from whom he parted by consent, though he afterwards tried many schemes to inveigle the poor man. He had applied to many Captains, who traded to St. Kitt's, to trepan him; and when all their attempts and schemes of kidnapping proved abortive, Mr. Kirkpatrick came to our ship at Union Stairs, on Easter Monday, April the 4th, with two wherry-boats and six men, having learned that the man was on board; and tied, and forcibly took him away from the ship, in the presence of the crew and the chief mate, who had detained him after he had information to come away. I believe this was a combined piece of business: but be that as it may, it certainly reflected great disgrace on the mate and Captain also; who, although they had desired the oppressed man to stay on board, yet notwithstanding this vile act on the man who had served him, he did not in the least assist to recover him, or pay me a farthing of his wages, which was about Five Pounds. I proved the only friend he had who attempted to regain him his liberty, if possible, having known the want of liberty myself. I sent, as soon as I could, to Gravesend, and got knowledge of the ship in which he was; but, unluckily, she had sailed the first tide after he was put on board. My intention was then immediately to apprehend Mr. Kirkpatrick, who was about setting off for Scotland; and having obtained a *habeas corpus* for him, and got a tipstaff[136] to go with me to St. Paul's church-yard, where he lived, he, suspecting something of this kind, set a watch to look out. My being known to them obliged me to use the following deception: I whitened my face, that they might not know me; and this had the desired effect. He did not go out of his house that night, and next morning I contrived a well plotted stratagem, notwithstanding he had a gentleman in his house to personate him. My direction to the tipstaff had the desired effect; he got admittance into the house, and conducted him to a judge, according to the writ. When he came there, his plea was, that he had not the body in custody, on which he was admitted to bail. I proceeded immediately to that well-known philanthropist, Granville Sharp, Esq.[137] who received me with the utmost kindness, and gave me every instruction that was needful on the occasion. I left him in full hope that I should gain the unhappy man his liberty, with the warmest sense of gratitude towards Mr. Sharp for his kindness. But, alas! my attorney proved unfaithful: he took my money, lost me many months' employ, and did not the least good in the cause. When the poor man arrived at St. Kitt's, he was, according to custom, staked to the ground with four pins through a cord, two on his wrists, and two on his ancles; was cut and flogged most unmercifully, and afterwards loaded cruelly with irons about his neck. I had two very moving letters from him, while he was in this situation; and I made attempts to go after him at a great hazard, but was sadly disappointed: I also was told of it by some very respectable families, now in London, who saw him in St. Kitt's, in the same state, in which he remained till kind death released him out of the hands of his tyrants.

During this disagreeable business I was under strong convictions of sin, and thought that my state was worse than any man's; my mind was unaccountably disturbed; I often wished for death, though at the same time convinced that I was altogether unprepared for that awful summons. Suffering much by villains in the late cause, and being much concerned about the state of my soul, these things (but particularly the latter) brought me very low; so that I became a burden to myself, and viewed all things around me as emptiness and vanity, which could give no satisfaction to a troubled conscience. I was again determined to go to Turkey, and resolved, at that time, never more to return to England. I engaged as steward on board a Turkeyman, the Wester Hall, Captain Lina; but was prevented by means of my late Captain, Mr. Hughes, and others. All this appeared to be against me, and the only comfort I then experienced was in reading the holy scriptures, where I saw that 'there is no new thing under the sun.' (Eccles. i. 9.) And what was appointed for me I must submit to. Thus I continued to travel in much heaviness, and frequently murmured against the Almighty, particularly in his providential dealings; and, awful to think! I began to blaspheme, and wished often to be any thing but a human being.

In these severe conflicts the Lord answered me by awful 'visions of the night, when deep sleep falleth upon men, in slumbering upon the bed.' (Job xxxiii. 15.) He was pleased, in much mercy, to give me to see, and in some measure understand, the great and awful scene of the judgment-day, that 'no unclean person, no unholy thing, can enter into the kingdom of God.' (Eph. v. 5.) I would then, if it had been possible, have changed my nature with the meanest worm on the earth; and was ready to say to the mountains and rocks, 'fall on me.' (Rev. vi. 16.)[138] But all in vain! I then in the greatest agony requested the Divine Creator, that he would grant me a small space of time to repent of my follies and vile iniquities, which I felt to be grievous. The Lord, in his manifold mercies, was pleased to grant my request; and being yet in a state of time, the sense of God's mercies was so great on my mind when I awoke, that my strength entirely failed me for many minutes, and I was exceedingly weak. This was the first spiritual mercy I ever was sensible of; and being on praying ground, as soon as I recovered a little strength, and got out of bed and dressed myself, I invoked Heaven from my inmost soul, and fervently begged that God would never again permit me to blaspheme his most holy name. The Lord, who is long-suffering, and full of compassion[139] to such poor rebels as we are, condescended to hear and answer. I felt that I was altogether unholy, and saw clearly what a bad use I had made of the faculties I was endowed with; they were given me to glorify God with; I thought, therefore, I had better want them here, and enter into life eternal, than abuse them and be cast into hell-fire.

I prayed to be directed, if there were any holier persons than those with whom I was acquainted, that the Lord would point them out to me. I appealed to the Searcher of hearts, whether I did not wish to love him more, and serve him better. Notwithstanding all this, the reader may easily discern, if a believer, that I was still in nature's darkness.[140] At length I hated the house in which I lodged, because God's most holy name was blasphemed in it; then I saw the word of God verified, viz. 'Before they call, I will answer; and while they are yet speaking, I will hear.'[141]

I had a great desire to read the Bible the whole day at home; but not having a convenient place for retirement, I left the house in the day, rather than stay amongst the wicked ones; and that day, as I was walking, it pleased God to direct me to a house where there was an old seafaring man, who experienced much of the love of God shed abroad in his heart. He began to discourse with me, and, as I desired to love the Lord, his conversation rejoiced me greatly; and indeed I had never heard before the love of Christ to believers set forth in such a manner, and in so clear a point of view. Here I had more questions to put to the man, than his time would permit him to answer; and in that memorable hour there came in a dissenting minister; he joined our discourse, and asked me some few questions; among others, *where I heard the gospel preached.* I knew not what he meant by "hearing the gospel;" I told him I had read the gospel; and he asked me, *where I went to church, or whether I went at all or not.* To which I replied 'I attend St. James's, St. Martin's, and St. Ann's Soho.'—'So,' said he, 'you are a churchman?' I answered, I was. He then invited me to a love-feast[142] at his chapel that evening. I accepted the offer, and thanked him; and soon after he went away, I had some further discourse with the old Christian, added to some profitable reading, which made me exceedingly happy. When I left him he reminded me of coming to the feast; I assured him I would be there. Thus we parted, and I weighed over the heavenly conversation that had passed between these two men, which cheered my then heavy and drooping spirit more than any thing I had met with for many months.

However, I thought the time long in going to my supposed banquet. I also wished much for the company of these friendly men; their company pleased me much: and I thought the gentleman very kind in asking me, a stranger, to a feast; but how singular did it appear to me, to have it in a chapel! When the wished-for hour came I went, and happily the old man was there, who kindly seated me, as he belonged to the place. I was much astonished to see the place filled with people, and no signs of eating and drinking. There were many ministers in the company. At last they began by giving out hymns, and, between the singing, the ministers engaged in prayer: in short, I knew not what to make of this sight, having never seen any thing of the kind in my life before now. Some of the guests began to speak their experience, agreeably to what I read in the Scriptures: much was said by every speaker of the providence of God, and his unspeakable mercies to each of them. This I knew in a great measure, and could most heartily join them. But when they spoke of a future state, they seemed to be altogether certain of their calling and election of God;[143] and that no one could ever separate them from the love of Christ, or pluck them out of his hands. This filled me with utter consternation, intermingled with admiration. I was so amazed as not to know what to think of the company; my heart was attracted, and my affections were enlarged; I wished to be as happy as they, and was persuaded in my mind that they were different from the world, that lieth in wickedness. (I John v. 19.) Their language and singing, &c. did well harmonize; I was entirely overcome, and wished to live and die thus. Lastly, some persons produced some neat baskets full of buns, which they distributed about; and each person communicated with his neighbour, and sipped water out of different mugs, which they handed about to all who were present.

This kind of Christian fellowship I had never seen, nor ever thought of seeing on earth. It fully reminded me of what I had read in the holy Scriptures, of the primitive Christians, who loved each other and broke bread, in partaking of it, even from house to house.[144] This entertainment (which lasted about four hours) ended in singing and prayer. It was the first soul-feast I ever was present at. These last twenty-four hours produced me things spiritual and temporal, sleeping and waking, judgment and mercy, that I could not but admire the goodness of God, in directing the blind, blasphemous sinner in the path that he knew not of, even among the just; and instead of judgment he hath shewed mercy, and will hear and answer the prayers and supplications of every returning prodigal.

> O! to grace how great a debtor
> Daily I'm constrain'd to be![145]

After this I was resolved to win heaven, if possible; and if I perished I thought it should be at the feet of Jesus, in praying to him for salvation. After having been an eye-witness to some of the happiness which attended those who feared God, I knew not how, with any propriety, to return to my lodgings, where the name of God was continually profaned, at which I felt the greatest horror; I paused in my mind for some time, not knowing what to do; whether to hire a bed elsewhere, or go home again. At last, fearing an evil report might arise, I went home, with a farewell to card-playing and vain jesting, &c. I saw that time was very short, eternity long, and very near; and I viewed those persons alone blessed, who were found ready at midnight call, or when the judge of all, both quick and dead, cometh.[146]

The next day I took courage, and went to Holborn, to see my new and worthy acquaintance, the old man, Mr. C— —. He and his wife, a gracious woman, were at work in silk-weaving; they seemed mutually happy, and both quite glad to see me, and I more to see them. I sat down and we conversed much about soul matters, &c. Their discourse was amazingly delightful, edifying, and pleasant. I knew not at last how to leave this agreeable pair, till time summoned me away. As I was departing, they lent me a little book, entitled "The Conversion of an Indian."[147] It was in questions and answers. The poor man came over the sea to London, to enquire after the Christian's God whom, through rich mercy, he found, and had not his journey in vain. The above book was of great use to me, and at that time was a means of strengthening my faith; in parting, they both invited me to call on them when I pleased. This delighted me, and I took care to make all the improvement from it I could; and so far I thanked God for such company and desires. I prayed that the many evils I felt within might be done away, and that I might be weaned from my former carnal acquaintances. This was quickly heard and answered, and I was soon connected with those whom the scripture calls "the excellent of the earth."[148] I heard the gospel preached, and the thoughts of my heart and actions were laid open by the preachers, and the way of salvation by Christ alone was evidently set forth.

Thus I went on happily for near two months: and I once heard, during this period, a reverend gentleman, Mr. G— —, speak of a man who had departed this life in full assurance of his going to glory. I was much astonished at the assertion; and did very deliberately inquire how he could get at this knowledge. I was answered fully, agreeably to what I read in the oracles of truth: and was told also, that if I did not experience the new birth, and the pardon of my sins, through the blood of Christ, before I died, I could not enter the kingdom of heaven.[149]

I knew not what to think of this report, as I thought I kept eight commandments out of ten: then my worthy interpreter told me I did not do it, nor could I; and he added, that no man ever did or could keep the commandments, without offending in one point. I thought this sounded very strangely; it puzzled me much for many weeks; for I thought it a hard saying. I then asked my friend Mr. L— —d, who was clerk in a chapel, *why the commandments of God were given, if we could not be saved by them.* To which he replied, 'The law is a school-master to bring us to Christ,'[150] who alone could, and did keep the commandments, and fulfilled all their requirements for his elect people, even those to whom he had given a living faith, and the sins of those chosen vessels *were already* atoned for, and forgiven them whilst living;[151] and if I did not experience the same before my exit, the Lord would say at that great day to me, "Go, ye cursed," &c. &c.[152] for God would appear faithful in his judgments to the wicked, as he would be faithful in shewing mercy to those who were ordained to it before the world was; therefore Christ Jesus seemed to be all in all to that man's soul.[153]

I was much wounded at this discourse, and brought into such a dilemma as I never expected. I asked him, if *he* was to die that moment, whether he was sure to enter the kingdom of God: and added, 'Do you *know* that your sins are forgiven you?' He answered in the affirmative. Then confusion, anger, and discontent seized me, and I staggered much at this sort of doctrine: it brought me to a stand, not knowing which to believe, whether salvation by works, or by faith only in Christ. I requested him to tell me how I might know when my sins were forgiven me. He assured me he could not, and that none but God alone could do this. I told him it was very mysterious; but he said it was really matter of fact, and quoted many portions of scripture immediately to the point, to which I could make no reply. He then desired me to pray to God to

shew me these things. I answered I prayed to God every day. He said,
'I perceive you are a churchman.' I answered I was. He then entreated
me to beg of God *to shew me what I was, and the true state of my soul.* I
thought the prayer very short and odd; so we parted for that time.

I weighed all these things over, and could not help thinking how it
was possible for a man to know his sins were forgiven him in this life.
I wished that God would reveal this self-same thing to me. In a short
time after this, I went to Westminster chapel: The Rev. Mr. P— —
preached from Lam. iii. 39.[154] It was a wonderful sermon; he clearly
shewed that a living man had no cause to complain for the punishments
of his sins; he evidently justified the Lord in all his dealings with the
sons of men; he also shewed the justice of God in the eternal punishment of the wicked and impenitent. The discourse seemed to me like
a two-edged sword cutting all ways.[155] It afforded me much joy, intermingled with many fears about my soul; and when it was ended he
gave it out that he intended, the ensuing week, to examine all those
who meant to attend the Lord's table.[156] Now I thought much of my
good works, and at the same time was doubtful of my being a proper
object to receive the sacrament; I was full of meditation till the day
of examining.

However I went to the chapel; and, though much distressed, I
addressed the reverend gentleman, thinking if I was not right, he would
endeavour to convince me of it. When I conversed with him, the first
thing he asked me was, *What I knew of Christ.* I told him I believed in him,
and had been baptized in his name. 'Then,' said he, 'when were you
brought to the knowledge of God? and how were you convinced of sin?'
I knew not what he meant by these questions. I told him I kept eight
commandments out of ten; but that I sometimes swore on board of ship,
and sometimes when on shore, and broke the sabbath. He then asked
me if I could read. I answered 'Yes.' 'Then,' said he, 'do you read in the
Bible, *He that offends in one point is guilty of all?'*[157] I said, 'Yes.' Then he
assured me, that one sin, unatoned for, was as sufficient to damn a soul,
as one leak was to sink a ship. Here I was struck with awe; for the minister exhorted me much, and reminded me of the shortness of time, and
the length of eternity; and that no unregenerate soul, or any thing
unclean, could enter the kingdom of Heaven.[158]

He did not admit me as a communicant;[159] but recommended me to
read the scriptures, and hear the word preached; not to neglect fervent
prayer to God, who has promised to hear the supplications of those who
seek him in godly sincerity; so I took my leave of him with many thanks,

and resolved to follow his advice, so far as the Lord would condescend to enable me.

During this time I was out of employ; nor was likely to get a situation suitable for me: which obliged me to go once more to sea. I engaged as steward of a ship called the Hope, Captain Richard Strange, bound from London to Cadiz in Spain. In a short time after I was on board I heard the name of God much blasphemed, and I feared greatly least I should catch the horrible infection. I thought if I sinned again, after having life and death set evidently before me, I should certainly go to hell. My mind was uncommonly chagrined, and I murmured much at God's providential dealings with me, and was discontented with the commandments, that I could not be saved by what I had done. I hated all things, and wished I had never been born: confusion seized me, and I wished to be annihilated.

One day I was standing on the very edge of the stern of the ship, thinking to drown myself, but this scripture was instantaneously impressed on my mind — 'That no murderer hath eternal life abiding in him.' (1 John iii. 15.) Then I paused, and thought myself the unhappiest man living. Again I was convinced that the Lord was better to me than I deserved, and I was better off in the world than many. After this I began to fear death; I fretted, mourned, and prayed, till I became a burthen to others but more so to myself. At length I concluded to beg my bread on shore, rather than go again to sea amongst a people who feared not God, and I entreated the Captain three different times to discharge me; he would not, but each time gave me greater and greater encouragement to continue with him, and all on board shewed me very great civility: notwithstanding all this, I was unwilling to embark again. At last some of my religious friends advised me, by saying it was my lawful calling, consequently it was my duty to obey, and that God was not confined to place, &c. &c. particularly Mr. G. the governor of Tothillfields, Bridewell, who pitied my case, and read the eleventh chapter of the Hebrews to me, with exhortations.[160] He prayed for me, and I believe that he prevailed on my behalf, as my burden was then greatly removed, and I found a heart-felt resignation to the will of God.

The good man gave me a pocket Bible, and Alleine's "Alarm to the unconverted."[161] We parted, and the next day I went on board again. We sailed for Spain, and I found favour with the Captain. It was the fourth of September when we sailed from London, and we had a delightful voyage to Cadiz, where we arrived the twenty-third of the same month. The place is strong, commands a fine prospect, and is very rich. The

Spanish galloons frequent that port, and some arrived whilst we were there. I had many opportunities of reading the scriptures. I wrestled hard with God in fervent prayers, who had declared in his word that he would hear the groanings and deep sighs of the poor in spirit. This I found verified, to my utter astonishment and comfort, in the following manner: — On the morning of the sixth of October, (I pray you to attend,) all that day, I thought I should see or hear something supernatural. I had a secret impulse on my mind of something that was to take place, which drove me, for all that time, to a throne of grace. It pleased God to enable me to wrestle with him as Jacob did:[162] I prayed that if sudden death were to happen, and I perished, it might be at Christ's feet.

In the evening of the same day, as I was reading and meditating on the fourth chapter of the Acts, twelfth verse, under the solemn apprehensions of eternity, and reflecting on my past actions, I began to think I had lived a moral life, and that I had a proper ground to believe I had an interest in the divine favour; but still meditating on the subject, not knowing whether salvation was to be had partly for our own good deeds, or solely as the sovereign gift of God. In this deep consternation the Lord was pleased to break in upon my soul with his bright beams of heavenly light; and in an instant, as it were, removing the veil, and letting light into a dark place. (Isa. xxv. 7.) I saw clearly, with the eye of faith, the crucified Saviour bleeding on the cross on Mount Calvary: the Scriptures became an unsealed book; I saw myself a condemned criminal under the law, which came with its full force to my conscience, and when 'the commandment came, sin revived, and I died.'[163] I saw the Lord Jesus Christ in his humiliation, loaded, and bearing my reproach, sin, and shame.

I then clearly perceived, that *by the deeds of the law no flesh living could be justified*. I was then convinced, that by the first Adam sin came, and by the second Adam, the Lord Jesus Christ, all that are saved must be made alive.[164] It was given me at that time to know what it was to be born again. (John iii. 5.) I saw the eighth chapter to the Romans, and the doctrines of God's decrees verified, agreeably to his eternal, everlasting, and unchangeable purposes. The word of God was sweet to my taste, yea, sweeter than honey and the honey-comb.[165] Christ was revealed to my soul as the chiefest among ten thousand.[166] — These heavenly moments were really as life to the dead, and what John calls an earnest of the Spirit. (John xvi. 13, 14, &c.)[167] This was indeed unspeakable, and, I firmly believe, undeniable to many.

Now every leading providential circumstance that happened to me, from the day I was taken from my parents to that hour, was then, in my view, as if it had but just then occurred. I was sensible of the invisible hand of God, which guided and protected me, when in truth I knew it not: still the Lord pursued me, although I slighted and disregarded it; this mercy melted me down. When I considered my poor wretched state, I wept, seeing what a great debtor I was to sovereign free grace. Now the Ethiopian was willing to be saved by Jesus Christ,[168] the sinner's only surety, and also to rely on none other person or thing for salvation. Self was obnoxious, and good works I had none; for it is God that worketh in us both to will and to do.[169] Oh! the amazing things of that hour can never be told! It was joy in the Holy Ghost! I felt an astonishing change; the burden of sin, the gaping jaws of hell, and the fears of death, that weighed me down before, now lost their horror; indeed I thought death would now be the best earthly friend I ever had. Such were my grief and joy as I believe are seldom experienced. I was bathed in tears, and said, "What am I, that God should thus look on me, the vilest of sinners?" I felt a deep concern for my mother and friends, which occasioned me to pray with fresh ardour; and in the abyss of thought, I viewed the unconverted people of the world in a very awful state, being without God and without hope.

It pleased God to pour out on me the spirit of prayer and the grace of supplication, so that in loud acclamations I was enabled to praise and glorify his most holy name. When I got out of the cabin, and told some of the people what the Lord had done for me, alas! who could understand me or believe my report! — None but to whom the arm of the Lord was revealed. I became a barbarian to them in talking of the love of Christ: his name was to me as ointment poured forth; indeed it was sweet to my soul, but to them a rock of offence.[170] I thought my case singular, and every hour a day until I came to London; for I much longed to be with some to whom I could tell of the wonders of God's love towards me, and join in prayer to him whom my soul loved and thirsted after. I had uncommon commotions within, such as few can tell aught about. Now the Bible was my only companion and comfort; I prized it much, with many thanks to God that I could read it for myself, and was not left to be tossed about or led by man's devices and notions. The worth of a soul cannot be told. — May the Lord give the reader an understanding in this!

Whenever I looked in the Bible I saw things new, and many texts were immediately applied to me with great comfort, for I knew that to me was the word of salvation sent. Sure I was, that the Spirit, which indited the word, opened my heart to receive the truth of it as it is in Jesus, that the same Spirit enabled me to act with faith upon the promises which were precious to me, and enabled me to believe, to the salvation of my soul. By free grace I was persuaded that I had a part in the first resurrection, and was enlightened with the "light of the living." (Job xxxiii. 30.) I wished for a man of God, with whom I might converse: my soul was like the chariots of Aminadab. (Canticles vi. 12.)[171] These, among others, were the precious promises that were so powerfully applied to me: "All things whatsoever ye shall ask in prayer, believing, ye shall receive." (Matt. xxi. 22.) "Peace I leave with you, my peace I give unto you." (John xiv. 27.) I saw the blessed Redeemer to be the fountain of life, and the well of salvation.[172] I experienced him to be all in all. He had brought me by a way that I knew not, and he had made crooked paths straight.[173] Then in his name I set up my Ebenezer, saying, "Hitherto He hath helped me:"[174] and could say to the sinners about me, "Behold what a Saviour I have!" Thus I was, by the teaching of that all-glorious Deity, the great One in Three and Three in One,[175] confirmed in the truths of the Bible, those oracles of everlasting truth, on which every soul living must stand or fall eternally, agreeably to Acts iv. 12: "Neither is there salvation in any other: for there is none other name under heaven given among men whereby we must be saved, but only Jesus Christ."[176] May God give the reader a right understanding in these facts! "To him that believeth all things are possible, but to them that are unbelieving nothing is pure." (Titus i. 15.)

During this period we remained at Cadiz until our ship got laden. We sailed about the fourth of November; and, having a good passage, we arrived in London the month following, to my comfort, with heart-felt gratitude to God for his rich and unspeakable mercies.

On my return I had but one text which puzzled me, or that the devil endeavoured to buffet me with, viz. Rom. xi. 6. and, as I had heard of the Rev. Mr. Romaine,[177] and his great knowledge in the scriptures, I wished much to hear him preach. One day I went to Blackfriars church, and, to my great satisfaction and surprise, he preached from that very text. He very clearly shewed the difference between human works and free election, which is according to God's sovereign will and pleasure. These glad tidings set me entirely at liberty, and I went out of the church rejoicing, seeing my spots were those of God's children.[178] I went to Westminster chapel, and saw some of my old friends, who were glad when they perceived the wonderful change that the Lord had wrought in me, particularly Mr. G. Smith, my worthy acquaintance, who was a man of a choice spirit, and had great zeal for the Lord's service. I enjoyed his correspondence till he died in the year 1784. I was again examined in that same chapel, and was received into church-fellowship amongst them; I rejoiced in spirit, making melody in my heart to the God of all my mercies. Now my whole wish was to be dissolved, and to be with Christ. But, alas! I must wait my appointed time.

✳ ✳ ✳

After traveling once more to Spain, Equiano accompanies Dr. Irving to the Mosquito Coast in Central America to establish and manage a plantation, a post he holds until 15 June 1776. On his way back to England he encounters a series of deceptive ship captains eager to sell him into slavery. Equiano foils their schemes, however, and steps on English soil on 7 January 1777.

Sea ventures remain his focus for the next several years, especially after the Bishop of London rejects his application in 1779 to serve as a missionary in Africa. On three separate occasions between the spring of 1784 and August of 1786 Equiano travels to the United States; during one stay he visits the Quaker free school for blacks that Anthony Benezet established in Philadelphia. Back in London he learns of the Sierra Leone project co-sponsored by the British government and the Committee for the Black Poor. The Committee requests that he accompany a group of London blacks to a resettlement site on the west coast of Africa. Although he objects to the idea of resettling in an area rife with slave dealers, he does accept the Committee's appointment in November 1786 as Commissary of Provisions and Store for the Black Poor bound for Sierra Leone. While on the job he discovers—and protests against—rampant corruption in the use of the project's funds. The Committee for the Black Poor thereupon dismisses Equiano, who takes only bittersweet comfort in the letter from the government commissioners expressing their personal satisfaction with his service.

FROM CHAPTER 12

From that period to the present, my life has passed in an even tenour, and great part of my study and attention has been to assist in the cause of my much injured countrymen.

March the 21st, 1788, I had the honour of presenting the Queen with a petition on behalf of my African brethren, which was received most graciously by her Majesty.[179]

The negro consolidated act, made by the assembly of Jamaica last year, and the new act of amendment now in agitation there, contain a proof of the existance of those charges that have been made against the planters relative to the treatment of their slaves.

I hope to have the satisfaction of seeing the renovation of liberty and justice, resting on the British government, to vindicate the honour of our common nature. These are concerns which do not, perhaps, belong to any particular office: but to speak more seriously, to every man of sentiment actions like these are the just and sure foundation of future fame; a reversion, though remote, is coveted by some noble minds as a substantial good. It is upon these grounds that I hope and expect the attention of gentlemen in power. These are designs consonant to the elevation of their rank, and the dignity of their stations; they are ends suitable to the nature of a free and generous government; and connected with views of empire and dominion, suited to the benevolence and solid merit of the legislature. It is a pursuit of substantial greatness. May the time come—at least the speculation to me is pleasing—when the sable people shall gratefully commemorate the auspicious æra of extensive freedom! Then shall those persons[180] particularly be named with praise and honour who generously proposed, and stood forth in the cause of humanity, liberty, and good policy, and brought to the ear of the legislature designs worthy of a royal patronage and adoption. May Heaven make the British senators the dispersers of light, liberty, and science, to the uttermost parts of the earth! Then will be *Glory to God in the highest; on earth peace and good-will to men. —Glory, honour, peace, &c. to every soul of man that worketh good: to the* Britons *first,* (because to them the gospel is preached,) *and also to the nations. Those that honour their Maker have mercy on the poor. It is righteousness exalteth a nation, but sin is a reproach to any people; destruction shall be to the workers of iniquity, and the wicked shall fall by their own wickedness.* May the blessings of the Lord be upon the heads of all those who commiserated the cases of the oppressed negroes, and the fear of God prolong their days; and may their expectations be filled with gladness! "The liberal devise liberal things, and by liberal things shall stand." Isaiah xxxii. 8. They can say with pious Job, "Did not I weep for him that was in trouble? Was not my soul grieved for the poor?" Job xxx. 25.[181]

As the inhuman traffic of slavery is to be taken into the consideration of the British legislature,[182] I doubt not, if a system of commerce was established in Africa, the demand for manufactures will most rapidly augment, as the native inhabitants will insensibly adopt the British fashions, manners, customs, &c. In proportion to the civilization, so will be the consumption of British manufactures.

The wear and tear of a continent, nearly twice as large as Europe, and rich in vegetable and mineral productions, is much easier conceived than calculated.

A case in point. It cost the Aborigines of Britain little or nothing in clothing, &c. The difference between their forefathers and the present generation, in point of consumption, is literally infinite. The supposition is most obvious. — It will be equally immense in Africa. — The same cause, viz. civilization, will ever have the same effect.

It is trading upon safe grounds. A commercial intercourse with Africa opens an inexhaustible source of wealth to the manufacturing interests of Great Britain;[183] and to all which the slave-trade is an objection.[184]

If I am not misinformed, the manufacturing interest is equal, if not superior, to the landed interest, as to the value, for reasons which will soon appear. The abolition of slavery, so diabolical, will give a most rapid extension of manufactures, which is totally and diametrically opposite to what some interested people assert.

The manufactures of this country must and will, in the nature and reason of things, have a full and constant employ, by supplying the African markets.

Population, the bowels, and surface of Africa, abound in valuable and useful returns; the hidden treasures of centuries will be brought to light and into circulation. Industry, enterprise, and mining, will have their full scope, proportionably as they civilize. In a word, it lays open an endless field of commerce to the British manufacturers and merchant adventurers. The manufacturing interest and the general interests are synonimous. The abolition of slavery would be in reality an universal good.[185]

Tortures, murder, and every other imaginable barbarity and iniquity, are practised upon the poor slaves with impunity. I hope the slave trade will be abolished. I pray it may be an event at hand. The great body of manufacturers, uniting in the cause, will considerably facilitate and expedite it; and as I have already stated, it is most substantially their interest and advantage, and as such the nation's at large, except those persons concerned in manufacturing neck-yokes, collars, chains, hand-cuffs, leg-bolts, drags,[186] thumb-screws, iron muzzles, and coffins; cats,[187] scourges, and other instruments of torture used in the slave-trade. In a short time one sentiment will alone prevail, from motives of interest as well as justice and humanity. Europe contains one hundred and twenty millions of inhabitants. Query — How many millions doth Africa contain?

Supposing the Africans, collectively and individually, to expend £5. a head in raiment and furniture yearly, when civilized, &c. an immensity beyond the reach of imagination!

This I conceive to be a theory founded upon facts, and therefore an infallible one. If the blacks were permitted to remain in their own country, they would double themselves every fifteen years. In proportion to such increase will be the demand for manufactures. Cotton and indigo grow spontaneously in most parts of Africa; a consideration this of no small consequence to the manufacturing towns of Great Britain. It opens a most immense, glorious, and happy prospect; the clothing, &c. of a continent ten thousand miles in circumference, and immensely rich in productions of every denomination in return for manufactures.

Since the first publication of my narrative,[188] I have been in a great variety of scenes[189] in many parts of Great-Britain, Ireland, and Scotland, an account of which might well be added here; but as this would swell the volume too much, I shall only observe in general, that in May 1791, I sailed from Liverpool to Dublin, where I was very kindly received, and from thence to Cork, and then travelled over many counties in Ireland. I was every where exceedingly well treated, by persons of all ranks. I found the people extremely hospitable, particularly in Belfast, where I took my passage on board of a vessel for Clyde, on the 29th of January, and arrived at Greenock on the 30th. — Soon after I returned to London, where I found persons of note from Holland and Germany, who requested me to go there; and I was glad to hear that an edition of my Narrative had been printed in both places, also in New York. I remained in London till I heard the debate in the house of Commons on the slave-trade, April the 2d and 3d. I then went to Soham in Cambridgeshire, and was married on the 7th of April to Miss Cullen, daughter of James and Ann Cullen, late of Ely.[190]

I have only therefore to request the reader's indulgence, and conclude. I am far from the vanity of thinking there is any merit in this narrative: I hope censure will be suspended, when it is considered that it was written by one who was as unwilling as unable to adorn the plainness of truth by the colouring of imagination. My life and fortune have been extremely chequered, and my adventures various. Even those I have related are considerably abridged. If any incident in this little work should appear uninteresting and trifling to most readers, I can only say, as my excuse for mentioning it, that almost every event of my life made an impression on my mind, and influenced my conduct. I early accustomed myself to look at the hand of God in the minutest occurrence, and to learn from it a lesson of morality and religion; and in this light every circumstance I have related was, to me, of importance. After all, what makes any event important, unless by its observation we become better and wiser, and learn *to do justly, to love mercy, and to walk humbly before God?*[191] To those who are possessed of this spirit, there is scarcely any book or incident so trifling that does not afford some profit, while to others the experience of ages seems of no use; and even to pour out to them the treasures of wisdom is throwing the jewels of instruction away.

NOTES

1. Paul Edwards notes in his introduction to *The Life of Olaudah Equiano, or Gustavus Vassa the African* (Harlow, England: Longman, 1989, p. xxi) that Equiano's source here is Anthony Benezet's *Some Historical Account of Guinea, Its Situation, Produce and the General Disposition of Its Inhabitants* (1788): "That part of Africa from which the Negroes are said to be carried into slavery, commonly known by the name of Guinea, extends along the coast for three or four thousand miles." Equiano, however, conflates "three or four thousand miles" into "3,400 miles." See note 4 in the Gronniosaw section of this volume.

2. The line is the equator. Edwards limits the boundaries of Benin's empire to Idah in the north and "beyond Lagos" to the west, contending that east of the Niger River its influence waned considerably. He believes travel literature like Benezet's may have exaggerated Equiano's sense of Benin's size (*The Life*, p. 171, n. 1).

3. This convoluted sentence differs drastically from the sentence originally published in the 1789 edition: "This kingdom is divided into many provinces or districts: in one of the most remote and fertile of which, called Eboe, I was born, in the year 1745, in a charming fruitful vale, named Essaka." Here Equiano eloquently relates that he is of the Igbo people, born in Igboland ("Eboe"), a fairly large region in modern-day Nigeria that includes the Niger River Delta. The cumbersome sentence in our diplomatic reprint suggests that an editor, lacking the vital phrase "called Eboe," rearranged the syntax to improve the clarity of the text (perhaps in the 1809 Leeds imprint), but only succeeded in skewing the original meaning.

4. Commentators across the centuries have recorded their impressions of the "Embrenche." In *Sketches Taken during Ten Voyages to Africa, Between the Years 1786 and 1800* (n.d.; rpt. New York: Johnson Reprint, 1970), John Adams indicates that "Breeché, in the Heebo [Igbo] language, signifies gentleman, or the oldest son of one." Much to their chagrin, slavers discovered that this proud social class loved freedom too dearly to withstand meekly the chains of bondage; thus "masters of slave-ships" nourished "a strong aversion to purchase [them]" because they were "thought to have a very unfavourable influence on their shipmates and countrymen in misfortune" (p. 41). See note 53 below. Catherine Obianuju Acholonu's book *The Igbo Roots of Olaudah Equiano: An Anthropological*

Research (Owerri, Nigeria: AFA Publications, 1989) provides detailed linguistic information about "Embrenche." Acholonu, a member of the Igbo people and a lifelong resident of Igboland in Nigeria, says, "'Embrenche' is a combination of the words *Igbu ichi* and *Mgburichi*. *Igbu ichi* is the act of scarification of the face, while *mgburichi* [sic] is the term used for the generality of men who bear the scarification. The singular form is *nwichi*" (p. 12). Since the Igbo language had not been transcribed into written form while Equiano was alive, he had to use English letters to stand for their phonetic equivalents in Igbo as he remembered it spoken when he was a child. Acholonu also observes that the *Igbu ichi* carries a singular ethnic significance, for the "Igbo people are the *only* Africans who are associated with facial (forehead) marks, not as tribal identification marks, but as a mark of grandeur and greatness" (p. 29).

5. The words following "eyebrows" generally read as follows in the first edition, the New York imprint of 1791, and the London "sixth edition" (1793): "and while it is in this situation, applying a warm hand, and rubbing it until it shrinks up into a thick *weal* across the lower part of the forehead." The rearrangement of the syntax and the substitution of *wale* for *weal* may have been the result of either editorial idiosyncrasy or transcriptional error.

6. Equiano's note: "See Benezet's 'Account of Guinea' throughout."

7. Equiano's note: "When I was in Smyrna I frequently saw the Greeks dance after this manner."

8. According to Paul Edwards, modern Igbo still play the *obo,* which is similar to a guitar, and the *ngelenge,* or sticcado, a type of xylophone (*The Life*, p. 171, n. 5).

9. Equiano's note: "The bowl is earthen, curiously figured, to which a long reed is fixed as a tube. This tube is sometimes so long as to be borne by one, and frequently, out of grandeur, by two boys."

10. *Eadas* is an African name for an indigenous root vegetable; it is also spelled *eddoes, edoes,* and *eddas.* Paul Edwards notes in *Equiano's Travels: His Autobiography "The Interesting Narrative of the Life of Olaudah Equiano or Gustavus Vassa the African"* that the Igbo word is **edo** (New York: Frederick A. Praeger, 1967, p. 177, n. 5).

11. Equiano's note: "When I was in Smyrna I saw the same kind of earth, and brought some of it with me to England; it resembles musk in strength, but is more delicious in scent, and is not unlike the smell of a rose." Catherine Acholonu learned that the people in Isseke "frequently burned a kind of fruit which looked like a piece of wood (six inches or more in length) for its delicious odour. They called it *Uhighihi*. It was thrown into the fire and the smoke diffused a powerful but delicious perfume in the compound. The *Uhie,* cam wood, which to a child might appear like red earth, was mixed with palm oil and rubbed on the skin" (*Igbo Roots*, p. 21).

12. Herbert M. Cole and Chike C. Aniakor, authors of *Igbo Arts: Community and Cosmos* (Los Angeles: Museum of Cultural History, UCLA, 1984), incorporate Equiano's description of the *obi,* or "male meeting house," in their discussion of Igbo compounds. The *obi* of an extended family is "the conceptual and often physical center of a domestic compound in the heartland region. . . . Because

the compound head lives and entertains guests there and is the priest of ancestral, personal, and title-related shrines located there, and because children are often conceived there, and because every important family matter is discussed there, the *obi* is the foremost material and ideological family symbol. It is evidence of wealth and prestige and the hub of daily life, referring equally to revered ancestors and family members yet-to-be-born" (p. 64).

13. Separate living and sleeping arrangements for men and women is an important aspect of Igbo culture. According to Cole and Aniakor, "the spatial separation and balance of the sexes express basic notions of Igbo dualism . . . as well as male domination" (Ibid., p. 65).

14. John Adams found the practice of smearing interior walls "with fresh cowdung" to be "a useful practice, for it dries quickly, has by no means an unpleasant smell, and fills up crevices, which would otherwise be tenanted by noxious and troublesome insects" (*Sketches*, pp. 20-21).

15. Paul Edwards proffers Chinua Achebe's suggestion that the *Oye-Eboe* are the *onye Aboh*, the light-skinned riverain people of Aboh located south of Onitsha (*The Life*, p. xxii). Catherine Acholonu disagrees, asserting that *Oye-Eboe* is "Equiano's transcription of the Igbo word *Oyibo*," which signifies either an albino or "a very lightly coloured person" of non-European extraction ("The word existed before the Europeans appeared" [*Igbo Roots*, p. 14]). She contends that Equiano appears to be referring to the Aros, a fair-colored African people so heavily involved in the European slave trade that their name became synonymous with *Oyibo*, especially among children.

16. The Igbo word for this salt is *Ngu*, "a type of salty substance derived from burnt palm sponge" and still used today to cook breadfruit and make soap (Acholonu, *Igbo Roots*, pp. 21-22). Salt was a familiar and valuable item of exchange in Africa as early as the first century B.C. In *A Voyage to the River Sierra-Leone* (1788; rpt. London: Frank Cass, 1966), John Matthews declares that salt "always makes a part of the merchandize for the purchase of slaves in the interior country; yet, notwithstanding salt is in such great demand, the natives of the sea coast will not permit the import of it in European vessels, because it would interfere with the only article of their own manufacture, which they have for inland trade" (p. 146). For more information on *Voyage*, see note 27 below.

17. Pieter de Marees, an early seventeenth-century Dutchman, was surprised to find "no poor people (I mean people who beg for their bread)" among the lands close to Benin. One of the king's responsibilities was to appoint the infirm to various trades—for example, working the bellows or grinding ingredients for paint— that would benefit the individual and the community. See *Description and Historical Account of the Gold Kingdom of Guinea (1602)*, trans. and ed. Albert van Dantzig and Adam Jones (Oxford: Oxford University Press, 1987), p. 177.

18. The cultural relativity of beauty is a commonplace of classical and neoclassical aesthetics. As Sir Thomas Browne notes in *Pseudodoxia Epidemica* (1646), Bk. 6, ch. 11, Aristotle and Galen did not mention any skin color as being requisite to beauty; he concludes, "Beauty is determined by opinion." Sir Joshua Reynolds expands upon this idea in *The Idler*, no. 82 (10 November 1759): "Among the

various reasons why we prefer one part of [nature's] works to another, the most general, I believe, is habit and custom; custom makes, in a certain sense, white black, and black white; it is custom alone determines our preference of the colour of the Europeans to the Aethiopians, and they, for the same reason, prefer their own colour to ours." See Samuel Johnson, *The Idler and the Adventurer,* ed. W. J. Bate, John M. Bullitt, and L. F. Powell (New Haven: Yale University Press, 1963), pp. 254-58; the quotation is on p. 257.

19. See notes 11 and 12 in the Gronniosaw section of this volume.

20. Equiano's note: "See Benezet's 'Account of Africa' throughout."

21. According to James Africanus Beale Horton, the Igbo women "hold a very superior rank in the social scale" and thus do not feel "doomed to perpetual degradation" (*West African Countries and Peoples* [London, 1868; rpt. Edinburgh: Edinburgh University Press, 1969], p. 156). He contends that the women removed the wounded and the dead during battle (p. 161). Acholonu, attributing a still more active role to the Igbo women of Isseke, claims that they defended their homesteads with handy household items such as knives, machetes, and wooden pestles. They posed an effective military threat to marauding males from other places, who did not expect to find women taking active part in combat. Isseke village even boasts a famous woman warrior named Nwibe Ezike, who is said to have lived during Equiano's lifetime (*Igbo Roots,* pp. 18, 31-32, 49, 60, 71-72, 103).

22. Edwards observes: "Equiano's 'one creator' who lives in the sun is Chukwu, who is often said to live in the sun, or identified with the Sun, Anyanwu. The wearing of a belt 'that he may never eat or drink' may reflect the comparative rarity of sacrifices to Chukwu in parts of Ibo" (*The Life,* p. xxii).

23. The transmigration of souls is the passing of the individual soul at death into a new body or new form of life, typically animal or human.

24. As it originally appeared in Equiano's 1789 text, this sentence contained a reference to the unclean state of menstruating women: "Those that touched the dead, at any time, were obliged to wash and purify themselves before they could enter a dwelling-house. Every woman too, at certain times, was forbidden to come into a dwelling-house, or touch any person, or any thing we ate." "Ate" becomes "eat" in the 1791 New York imprint, a transcriptional error that persists in succeeding imprints; otherwise, the text above remains the same and appears again in the sixth London "edition" (1793). In all likelihood, a nineteenth-century editor deleted Equiano's oblique reference to menstruating women, retaining only the phrase "or touch any person or any thing we eat."

25. The separation and balance of the sexes is a crucial part of the Igbo worldview (see note 13 above). For Equiano to dote so heavily on his mother that he could not refrain from being with or touching her while she was menstruating in seclusion would have been an issue of concern to his family, especially since he was nearing the age to undergo the *Igbu ichi*. As the mature Equiano recognized, Igbo cleanliness codes resemble those found in the Hebrew Bible. Numbers 19:11-22 describes the unclean state of those who touch the dead and outlines the appropriate purification rites. Leviticus 15 discusses the unclean issues of the body

(that is, various bodily fluids); verses 19-30 focus on the uncleanness of menstruating women or of any who touch them, and the means of purification.

26. Contemporary African-American Freemasons have been known to perform the Masonic burial rites after sunset, a practice that may very well have stemmed from African secret societies (see the introduction to this volume, p. 15).

27. Equiano's note: "See also Lieutenant Matthew's 'Voyage,' p. 123." Equiano refers to John Matthews's book, *A Voyage to the River Sierra-Leone Containing an Account of the Trade and Productions of the Country and of the Civil and Religious Customs and Manners of the People during his Residence in that Country in the Years 1785, 1786 and 1787. With an Additional Letter on the Slave Trade* (London: Printed for B. White and Son, at Horace's Head Fleet-Street; and J. Sewell, Cornhill, 1788). Pages 121-24 contain Matthews's discussion of African burial rites.

28. Equiano's note: "An instance of this kind happened at Montserrat in the West Indies, in the year 1763. I then belonged to the Charming Sally, Capt. Doran.— The chief mate, Mr. Mansfield, and some of the crew being one day on shore, were present at the burying of a poisoned negro girl. Though they had often heard of the circumstance of the running in such cases, and had even seen it, they imagined it to be a trick of the corpse bearers. The mate therefore desired two of the sailors to take up the coffin, and carry it to the grave. The sailors, who were all of the same opinion, readily obeyed; but they had scarcely raised it to their shoulders, before they began to run furiously about, quite unable to direct themselves, till, at last, without intention, they came to the hut of him who had poisoned the girl. The coffin then immediately fell from their shoulders against the hut, and damaged part of the wall. The owner of the hut was taken into custody on this, and confessed the poisoning. I give this story as it was related by the mate and crew on their return to the ship. The credit which is due to it, I leave with the reader."

29. That is, Abraham, Isaac, and Jacob. (Jacob is renamed "Israel" in Genesis 32.)

30. This note appears in the 1793 "sixth edition": "See I Chron i. 33. Also John Brown's Dictionary of the Bible on the same verse." This verse in Chronicles is essentially the same as Genesis 25:4; both list Keturah's grandchildren, called variously "the sons" (Chronicles) or "the children" (Genesis) of Keturah. See note 31 below.

31. Keturah is called "wife" in Genesis 25:1 and "concubine" in I Chronicles 1:32. John Gill (1697-1771), among his many works, wrote the four-volume commentary *An Exposition of the Old Testament in which are Recorded the Original of Mankind, of the Several Nations of the World, and of the Jewish Nation in Particular* (London, 1763-1766). Equiano refers to Gill's discussion of Genesis 25:4, found in Volume I, *Genesis-Joshua*. Gill explains that Cleodemus refers to Abraham and Keturah's grandsons Ephah and Epher as Aphra and Apher, from whom the city of Aphra and the entirety of Africa took their names.

32. The Reverend Dr. John Clarke (1682-1757) translated into English Hugo Grotius's six-volume Latin opus *De veritate religionis Christianae,* known to us as *The Truth of the Christian Religion* (London, 1711), a popular work issued in sixteen imprints by 1823.

33. Equiano refers to Arthur Bedford (1668-1745), *The Scripture Chronology Demonstrated by Astronomical Calculations, and Also by the Year of Jubilee, and the Sabbatical Year among the Jews, or, An Account of Time from the Creation of the World to the Destruction of Jerusalem, as It May Be Proved from the Writings of the Old and New Testament Together with the History of the World, from the Creation, to the Time when Dr. Prideaux Began his Connexion* (London, 1730).

34. The law of retaliation is found in Exodus 21:23-25: "And if any mischief follow, then thou shalt give life for life, / Eye for eye, tooth for tooth, hand for hand, foot for foot, / Burning for burning, wound for wound, stripe for stripe."

35. Modern Biblical scholars tend to believe that circumcision was actually an ancient Egyptian and Canaanite practice.
    Equiano originally uses "rule," not "rite," in the first edition, the 1791 New York imprint, and the London "sixth edition" (1793).

36. The Reverend Thomas Clarkson (1760-1846) was a zealous and highly respected abolitionist integral to the success of the Society for the Abolition of Slavery. Best known among his voluminous oeuvre of anti-slavery treatises is *An Essay on the Slavery and Commerce of the Human Species, Particularly the African,* which won first prize at Cambridge University in 1785 for the best Latin dissertation upon the question, "Is it right to make slaves of others against their will?" Quaker bookseller James Phillips published the essay in London in 1786 and then issued an enlarged and revised second edition in 1788; Phillips also introduced Clarkson to Granville Sharp, James Ramsay, and the other abolitionists who labored to suppress the slave trade. See notes 119, 137, 180 below.

37. Equiano's note: "Page 178 to 216."

38. Equiano's note: "Philos. Trans. No. 476, Sect. 4, cited by the Rev. Mr. Clarkson, p. 205." This quotation appears on p. 205 of the 1786 edition of Clarkson's essay (mentioned above); Equiano (or the printer) makes only minor changes in the punctuation and appearance of the text, using Roman instead of italics for "Spaniards," "Indians," "Virginia," and "I myself have been a witness."

39. Equiano's note: "Same page." Equiano found this information in Clarkson's essay immediately following Dr. Mitchell's quotation. This section appears on p. 206 in the 1786 edition. Equiano's text from "now become in their complexion" to "the Portuguese language" is quoted from Clarkson's book with only slight variations.

40. In his book *The Holy State* (Cambridge, England, 1642), Thomas Fuller, a preacher to various noble families, writes that the good sea captain "counts the image of God neverthelesse *his image cut in ebony as if done in ivory,* and in the blackest Moores he sees the representation of the King of heaven" (p. 129; our emphasis).

41. See Isaiah 55:8.

42. We have not been able to locate the source of this quotation.

43. Equiano originally describes the African landscape "to the left of the sun's rising" as a route "through many different countries, and a number of large woods." By the "second edition" he incorporates the more vivid description reproduced in this volume.

44. "Seasoning" was a process of preparing Africans for the routine rigors of slavery. Slavers often took newly enslaved Africans to the West Indies, where they were initiated through on-the-job experience, harsh punishment, and, not infrequently, torture to the habits thought suitable to their new position in life. After a period of acclimatization, the seasoned slaves would be shipped to Europe and to the American colonies for sale.

45. The following sentence appears in the "sixth edition" (1793): "they are known in this country by the name of *core*." "Core" is probably the English transcription of "cowrie," for the cowrie shells used in African nations as mediums of exchange.

46. Lieutenant John Matthews remarks that the assimilation of house slaves into African families was common; these slaves customarily took their master's name and called him "Father" (*Voyage*, p. 150).

47. Captain Adams observes that the "Ibbibby or Quaw" (that is, the Ibibio) tribe living east of the Igbo had "their teeth filed so as to resemble those of a saw" (*Sketches*, pp. 40-41). "To this nation the Heebos express a strong aversion, and call them cannibals" (p. 40). See also notes 49 and 53 below.

48. De Marees appears to have been as surprised as Equiano to see women swimming, for he wrote a one-and-a-half-page chapter on the West Africans entitled "About their swimming and the fact that their Women swim quite nicely too" (*Description and Historical Account*, pp. 186-87).

49. Adams estimates that Bonny, a major slave port in the Niger Delta, sold no fewer than 20,000 slaves per year, 16,000 of whom were Igbo. He further calculates that "this single nation [the Igbo] has not exported a less number of its people, during the last twenty years, than 320,000; and those of the same nation sold at New and Old Calabar, probably amounted, in the same period of time, to 50,000 more, making an aggregate amount of 370,000 Heebos. The remaining part of the above 20,000 is composed of the natives of the brass country, called Allakoos, and also of Ibbibbys or Quaws" (p. 38). Slaves brought to Bonny tended to be "sold to Europeans the evening after their arrival, and taken on board the ships" (*Sketches*, p. 39). On "Ibbibbys," see notes 47 and 53.

50. See note 10 in the Cugoano section of this volume.

51. Equiano may be alluding here to lines 81-82 of Robert Burns's poem "Man Was Made to Mourn, A Dirge," first published in *Poems, Chiefly in the Scottish Dialect* (Kilmarnock, 1786): "O Death! the poor man's dearest friend, / The kindest and the best!" Equiano would have been attracted to the poem's theme of "Man's inhumanity to Man" (l. 55), especially as it is expressed in the ninth stanza: "If I'm design'd yon lordling's slave, / By Nature's law design'd, / Why was an independent wish / E'er planted in my mind? / If not, why am I subject to / His cruelty, or scorn? / Or why has Man the will and pow'r / To make his fellow mourn?" (ll. 65-72).

52. The windlass was part of the machinery (located in the ship's forward section) that raised and lowered the anchor and attached it to the ship.

53. Adams states that the "Ibbibby or Quaw" nation (see notes 47 and 49 above) was particularly infamous for retaliation aboard slavers: "Whenever insurrection has

taken place on board of a slave ship at Bonny, they [the "Ibbibby"] have always been found to be the ringleaders, and often the only slaves concerned in it, the Heebos remaining passive spectators" (*Sketches*, p. 40). Equiano's testimony about his experience aboard a slaver considerably qualifies Adams's blandly contemptuous remark about the Igbos. See note 13 in the Cugoano section of this volume.

54. One of two or three vertical poles (the masts) that support the sails and their auxiliary apparatus (the yards and the rigging), the foremast is located nearest the front or bow of a ship. Masts are crucial to the balance and the locomotion of a sailing ship.

55. A quadrant is an instrument for measuring the angular height of a planet or star above the horizon; it consists of a graduated arc of ninety degrees with a moveable index and a sight. By means of a quadrant, a skillful mariner on a clear night could determine a ship's latitude within ten miles or less.

56. According to editors Van Dantzig and Jones, "horses were (and are) rare near the coast of West Africa" because of the prevalence of the tsetse fly, which transmits a serious disease called sleeping sickness (*Description and Historical Account*, p. 129, n. 8; compare with p. 228, n. 8).

57. Adapted from Matthew 7:12, popularly known as the Golden Rule.

58. Equiano's note: "A large two-masted Ship." The snow was chiefly a merchant vessel, popular between the sixteenth and nineteenth centuries for its holding capacity (up to 1,000 tons). Snows were often used in the slave trade.

59. See Isaiah 42:16.

60. Naval historian N. A. M. Rodger explains that during peacetime British naval strength was not extensive; in the years leading up to the Seven Years' War, the Royal Navy had only 10,000 men. "This was far too few to provide employment for every officer who wished to serve and needed to earn a living, or every young gentleman who needed to get his sea-time [that is, accumulate experience]. Consequently they went to sea in merchantmen [merchant ships] in large numbers." As captain of the merchantman *Industrious Bee,* Pascal traded goods throughout the West Indies (*The Wooden World: An Anatomy of the Georgian Navy* [London: Collins, 1986], p. 269).

61. Gustavus Vasa, the sixteenth-century Swedish patriot who liberated his country from Danish tyranny, was a well-known name in eighteenth-century Britain. In 1738, Henry Brooke wrote his popular play, *Gustavus Vasa, the Deliverer of His Country;* in the early 1800s William Wordsworth considered writing an epic poem on Vasa (*The Prelude,* Bk. I, ll. 212-13).

62. The quarterdeck was a captain's special domain, located above the main deck and stretching from the rear (stern) of the ship to the ship's midpoint. To have gained the status—not necessarily the rank—to walk the quarterdeck was an honor coveted by potential career men in either the merchant navy or Royal Navy.

63. On the trope of the talking book, see note 15 in the Gronniosaw section of this volume.

64. Equiano remarks earlier that the Igbo "are usually betrothed when young by their parents, though I have known the males betroth themselves" (see p. 168 of this volume). Given this custom and the warm relationship between Equiano and the

daughter, it is reasonable for Equiano to assume that Pascal and the daughter's father may arrange a betrothal between the two young people, especially once Pascal asks Equiano if he would like to remain with her.

65. The London "sixth edition" (1793) is the only one we have seen that states, alternatively, "between three and four years."

66. *The Knowledge and Practice of Christianity made Easy to the Meanest Capacities; or, an Essay towards an Instruction for the Indians* (London, 1740), by Thomas Wilson (1663-1755), Bishop of Sodor and Man from 1697 to 1755, was quite popular in the eighteenth and nineteenth centuries among proselytizing groups such as the Society for Promoting Christian Knowledge and the Society for Propagating the Gospel among the Indians and Others in North America. So inextricably linked was the author to this work that, over twenty imprints later, *Bp. Wilson's Indians* was still being printed on the spines of volumes.

67. Wherries were open boats, propelled by oars, used in the seventeenth and eighteenth centuries to carry passengers on the tidal areas of the Thames River in England. Ranging in size from fourteen to twenty-five feet, they could accommodate anywhere from one to four rowers.

68. Admiral Edward Boscawen (1711-1761), nicknamed "Old Dreadnought," had a distinguished battle record throughout his naval career. Promoted to Admiral in 1758, he commanded the naval fleet at the siege of Louisburg (see p. 197 of this volume) and, at Prime Minister William Pitt's insistence, was appointed to command in the Mediterranean in 1759. He was known especially for his deep interest in the health and welfare of his crew.

69. Equiano is referring to the Straits of Gibraltar. While Boscawen's fleet was obtaining fresh supplies in Gibraltar, the French fleet slipped away from Toulon, through the Straits, and into the Atlantic Ocean—the only sea route to Brest, the French navy's largest anchorage.

70. In nautical lingo, to bend is to fasten something; to slip is to let go of something intentionally. Thus here the crew is scrambling frantically to ready their ships for the chase by fastening the huge sails to their riggings and letting loose the massive mooring ropes.

71. Paul Edwards provides a clear explanation in *Equiano's Travels:* "The gunwale is the barrier surrounding the deck, and the main topmast head is the top of the highest mast"—hence, the ship's lights are blazing "'from bottom to top'" (p. 187, n. 46).

72. Equiano adapts Pope's translation of Homer's *Iliad,* Bk. XVII, ll. 728-32.

73. Not all warships fought. Therefore, when Boscawen saw only seven French ships of the line—that is, seven man o' wars with sufficient armament to engage in the traditional battle lineup—he waged against them only seven of his own ships of the line.

74. Jean-François de Bertet, Marquis de la Clue (ca. 1703-1759), usually called La Clue, was an eminent French admiral. In battle formation, the commanders—here, Boscawen and La Clue—always fought each other.

75. Illustrated here is a key difference between the British navy's gunning strategy and that of most other nations. The British preferred to take their ships to

"half-musket shot" range (about 100 yards from the enemy; a musket shot could kill within 200 yards) before firing their cannons at the hull, where they wreaked immediate visible damage, or definite "killing" shots. The French, like many others, fired from a further distance at the British masts and rigging, hoping to disable the ships before they came within firing range.

76. The *Namur* was a 90-gun ship, one of the biggest man o' wars in the British navy. It was called a "three-decker" because its main armament was located on three decks. Here, Boscawen calls for the gunners to fire simultaneously from all three tiers, or decks, into the hull of the *Ocean,* La Clue's flagship.

77. That is, Cape Lagos.

78. La Clue was safe on shore while his ships burned. He later died there of his wounds.

79. A "quarter" is a war station, allocated to all members of the ship's company on a quarter bill posted within the ship. "The boys [aboard ship] were attached to the guns' crews, one or two to each, to fetch powder from the magazines" (Rodger, *The Wooden World,* pp. 60-61). The new 74-gun ships being built during the war were approximately 165 feet long; on the 90-gun *Namur,* Equiano would have run at least that far from his gun to the magazine.

80. Equiano's note: "A Partner in bringing powder to the same gun." This information is incorporated within the texts of the first edition, the 1791 New York imprint, and the London "sixth edition" (1793).

81. From Ecclesiastes 3:2: "To every thing there is a season, and a time to every purpose under the heaven: A time to be born, and a time to die."

82. Only the 1789 edition offers the singular form, "to the dear Miss Guerin" (vol. 1, p. 150). Wilfred D. Samuels notes of this scene, "Equiano in the final analysis emerges as one who had risen to the status that would have been his in Essaka, where the male youth's self-understanding was firmly grounded in the conceptual metaphor 'man is a warrior' and 'warrior is a person of honour, action, and bravery.'" See "Disguised Voice in *The Interesting Narrative of Olaudah Equiano,*" *Black American Literary Forum* 19, no. 2 (Summer 1985): 68.

83. The mizzenmast is located nearest the rear (stern) of the ship. A main yard is the wooden spar that supports the principal sail on the highest mast (or main mast) of a vessel.

84. Thomas Broderick (d. 1769), second in command in the Mediterranean. Once Boscawen returned to England with the captured ships, Broderick remained to blockade the French ships at Cadiz. He maintained the blockade until inclement weather forced the British fleet to seek shelter in Gibraltar.

85. A fire ship was originally a small warship containing explosives that would try to set the enemy on fire by igniting itself and sailing next to enemy craft. According to Rodger, by the mid-eighteenth century this practice "was obsolete, and fireships usually served as small cruisers" (*The Wooden World,* p. 425).

86. Spithead is a stretch of water by the Portsmouth British naval base, an important assembly point for the British fleet during the seventeenth- and eighteenth-century wars against France and Holland.

87. England's King George II, who reigned from 1727, died on 25 October 1760.

88. A suit was brought against Pascal for falsely imprisoning on Cowes a group of seamen carrying papers of exemption from impressment. This incident may have occurred during this layover.

89. Admiral Augustus Keppel (1725-1786). In the following year, 1762, Keppel would join the fleets at the conquests of Martinique and Havana (see note 57 in the Gronniosaw section of this volume).

90. The waist comprises the slightly sunken central section of a ship's upper deck. The people Equiano heard were probably "waisters," those members of the watch assigned to patrol the waist.

91. The cutwater is the forward part of the ship's prow. The coaming is a raised rim built around and designed to keep water out of an opening in the deck (in this case the quarterdeck) leading to a hold, compartment, or lower deck.

92. Equiano's note: "Giving a brace or tightening to the tackle, by a complication of ropes." To frap is to bind something together; a hawser is a heavy rope at least five or more inches in circumference. Here the crew is binding the broken hull with thick, heavy ropes to keep the ship afloat and protected from the battering force of the sea until it can reach a safe port.

93. The British captured the *Jason* from the French and refitted it for active duty as a 44-gun ship. Equiano's recollection of "fifty-four guns" may reflect a temporary change in firing power aboard ship. Alternatively, it may simply be a miscalculation or a misprint carried over from the first edition.

Plymouth is a British port and naval base at the western end of the English Channel in Devon County. John Marrant was hospitalized in Plymouth while he was in the British navy (see p. 95 of this volume).

94. See Matthew 10:29: "Are not two sparrows sold for a farthing? and one of them shall not fall on the ground without your Father."

95. The preliminary peace documents were signed during the early months of 1763, although military hostilities ceased in late 1762.

96. The "Rule of Three" is a way of determining whether a large number is divisible by three: if the sum of its digits is divisible by 3, then the original number is also divisible by 3. So, for example, one could determine that 171 is divisible by 3 by adding 1 + 7 + 1 = 9, and knowing that 3 x 3 = 9. The anonymous author of the following Elizabethan jingle (1570) expresses what may have been a popular view of this rule: "Multiplication is vexation, / Division is as bad; / The Rule of three doth puzzle me, / And Practice drives me mad."

97. A hanger is a short sword worn at the belt.

98. The "prize money" Equiano refers to was his share of the net proceeds from the sale of enemy ships and goods seized during battle by the warships he crewed (see note 47 in the Gronniosaw section of this volume). Originally all such "prizes" captured at sea and their value at sale were the sole property of the Crown, but in 1708 Queen Anne issued the Cruisers Act, which bestowed the proceeds upon the original captors, in an attempt to lure more men into the navy. Prize money was divided into eight portions: the captain received three; the commander-in-chief, one; the officers, one; the warrant officers, one; and the crew,

two. Any unclaimed money went into a fund for Greenwich Royal Hospital, chartered by William and Mary in 1695 for injured or elderly navy men and supported by the monthly sixpence taken from all mariners' pay.

99. Although this belief was prevalent among Christian groups and the black community in the eighteenth century—Cugoano, for example, writes upon his arrival in London, "I was advised by some good people to get myself baptized, that I might not be carried away and sold again" (see p. 125 of this volume)—no such law existed in Britain at this time. While the York and Talbot opinion of 1729 held that baptism could not confer freedom upon a slave because it did not change one's *temporal* condition, the confusing legal history of the slavery issue allowed the general public to believe and act upon whatever decision(s) best suited it, an imbroglio that the legal community assiduously avoided resolving in the face of Britain's heavy mercantile and governmental investment in slavery and the slave trade. On any given day in London, slaves and "free" blacks could be sold on city streets or advertised as missing from their masters in city newspapers; conversely, they could be supported in Christian fellowship in one of the city's many prayer meetings or left in relative peace to earn a living, visit friends, or gather with comrades at a local tavern for wine and song. How they were treated was always subject to the alternating winds of public opinion.

100. See Psalms 36:7, 91:4; also Isaiah 42:16, which appears as an epigraph on the title page of Gronniosaw's *Narrative*.

101. The guinea (worth one pound and one shilling) was first created and minted in 1663 to commemorate the Royal Adventurers into Africa, the first English company chartered specifically to procure slaves. The coin was discontinued after 1813.

102. Eating oranges and lemons to ward off scurvy had long been a common practice among seamen on ocean voyages.

103. Equiano's note: "Thus was I sacrificed to the envy and resentment of this woman, for knowing that the other lady designed to take me into her service; which, had I got once on shore, she would not have been able to prevent. She felt her pride alarmed at the superiority of her rival in being attended by a black servant: it was not less to prevent this, than to be revenged on me, that she caused the captain to treat me thus cruelly."

104. Equiano may be referring to the 32-gun ship fit for harbor duty or, possibly, to the slave ship *Æolus* of Liverpool. Traders from Liverpool—along with those from London and Bristol—"ranked among the world's foremost slavers" according to David Eltis (*Africans in the Americas: A History of the Black Diaspora*, ed. Michael L. Conniff and Thomas J. Davis [New York: St. Martin's Press, 1994], pp. 163-64)—not surprising given the massive industrial investments of these towns in products crucial to the slave trade. Textiles, copper, brass, and iron poured from mines and factories in Manchester, Liverpool, Birmingham, and Bristol and traveled to Africa both aboard ship—in the form of guns, cloth, and copper goods for slave bartering—and on the ships themselves: copper sheathing from Liverpool, for example, protected wooden hulls from decomposition and streamlined their bulk, significantly enhancing sailing speed. Lured by fan-

tastic profits, many industrial mercantilists traded in slaves as well; in 1752, eighty-eight Liverpool ships carried 24,730 slaves. So successful were these merchants that a saying soon circulated "in pleasantry, that at Liverpool, where many owners of vessels are enriched by this traffic, they pray God daily not to change the colour of negroes." See Henri Grégoire, *An Enquiry concerning the Intellectual and Moral Faculties, and Literature of Negroes; Followed with an Account of the Life and Works of Fifteen Negroes & Mulattoes, Distinguished in Science, Literature and the Arts* (Paris, 1808; Eng. trans. D. B. Warden [Brooklyn, NY: Printed by Thomas Kirk, 1810]), p. 28n.

105. Equiano's note: "'The Dying Negro,' a poem [written by Thomas Day and John Bicknell] originally published in 1773. Perhaps it may not be deemed impertinent here to add, that this elegant and pathetic little poem, was occasioned by the following incident, as appears from the advertisement prefixed to it:—'A black who, a few days before, had run away from his master, and got himself christened, with intent to marry a white woman, his fellow-servant, being taken and sent on board a ship in the Thames, took an opportunity of shooting himself through the head.'"

106. Equiano quotes Milton's *Paradise Lost,* Bk. I, ll. 65-68.

107. Generally, "gauging" means measuring. Gauging a ship, for example, means to measure how much water a ship draws when it is afloat.

108. The first edition and the 1791 New York imprint say "droggers," which are West Indian coasting vessels. By the London "sixth edition" (1793), the word becomes "doggers." The word may have been deliberately or inadvertently changed; if the former, then the printer may have thought "droggers" was itself a misprint of "doggers," the two-masted fishing vessels used in North Sea deep-sea fisheries, especially those along Dogger Bank.

109. Equiano's note: "These pisterines are of the value of a shilling."

110. Equiano refers to King's Bench Prison, located in the Southwark section of London.

111. Equiano added this paragraph in the London "second edition."

112. Equiano's note: "Mr. Dubury, and many others, in Montserrat."

113. Equiano's note: "Sir Philip Gibbes, Bart. Barbadoes."

114. Equiano's note: "Benezet's 'Account of Guinea,' p. 16."

115. The sentence "I have seen a negro beaten till some of his bones were broken, for only letting a pot boil over" appears in the first edition (there "even" takes the place of "only"). The text from "It is not uncommon, after a flogging" to "'that we could not bear to do'" first appears by the London "sixth edition" (1793); it varies slightly from that reprinted in this volume.

116. Equiano's citation of Milton's *Paradise Lost,* Bk. II, ll. 616-18, differs only slightly in wording from modern editions.

117. Luke 4:18.

118. The Samoyeds are a Mongolian race in Siberia. Hottentot is the Dutch name for the Khoi-khoin, an indigenous people of South Africa who originally inhabited an area near the Cape of Good Hope before the Dutch forced them into the south and southwestern interior of Africa. Peter Fryer explains that Hottentot is "a

derogatory reference to the 'clicks' in their language" (*Staying Power: The History of Black People in Britain* [London: Pluto Press, 1984], p. 12).

119. Equiano's note: "In his 'Cursory Remarks.'" Equiano refers to James Tobin's *Cursory Remarks upon the Reverend Mr. Ramsay's Essay on the Treatment and Conversion of African Slaves in the Sugar Colonies. By a friend to the West India colonies, and their inhabitants* (London, Salisbury, and Bristol, 1785), pp. 37-38. See note 180 below.

120. See Exodus 2.

121. Here Equiano adapts a line from *Macbeth*: Lady Macbeth, praying for steely resolution, implores, "And take my milk for gall, you murth'ring ministers" (I, v., l. 48). Earlier in the scene, Lady Macbeth claims that her husband's nature "is too full o' th' milk of human kindness" (l. 17).

122. Equiano's quotation from *Paradise Lost*, Bk. II, ll. 332-40, incorporates a few minor changes. The word "Milton" does not appear in the first edition, the 1791 New York imprint, or the London "sixth edition" (1793).

123. In the West Indies and North America's southern colonies during the eighteenth century, bits were small silver coins valued at one-eighth of a dollar or roughly 6½d. sterling.

124. See note 66 above.

125. Paul Edwards and Rosalind Shaw note that Equiano's belief in predestination has roots in his native Igbo conception of *chi*, "an entity sometimes described as a 'personal god' responsible for the individual's destiny" (see the introduction to this volume, p. 3).

126. On Whitefield, see the introduction to this volume, p. 5ff.

127. Psalm 126 concerns freedom from captivity, but this phrase does not appear in it. It seems to be a conflation of Psalms 28:7, 33:21, and 86:12.

128. Equiano's note: "Acts xii. 9."

129. Elijah rises to Heaven in II Kings 2:11. We have not been able to locate the source of "were with lightning sped as I went on."

130. The 1814 Leeds and London imprint used in Henry Louis Gates, Jr.'s book *The Classic Slave Narratives* (New York: Penguin, Mentor, 1987) lists "my original free African *style*" (our emphasis), a significant change from the stronger "state." Since the first edition, the 1791 New York imprint, the London "sixth edition" (1793), and the 1814 Leeds and London imprint we consulted use "state," a transcriptional error may have occurred either in 1814 or in the preparation of Gates's volume; alternatively, it may be a nineteenth-century editorial alteration.

131. Yeamachra, a Native American name for Savannah, derives from the Yammacraw, who inhabited Georgia before it became a colony. Here Equiano uses the name to refer to an outlying region of Savannah.

132. "To work a traverse" is to follow a zigzag course.

133. That is, the first four books in the New Testament.

134. See John 3:15, 36.

135. See Exodus 20:1-17.

136. A *habeas corpus ad subjiciendum* is an order requiring a restrained person to be brought before a judge, who will then determine the legality of the restraint.

"Tipstaff," originally an official who carries a staff with a metal tip as a badge of authority, is another word for constable, bailiff, or sheriff's deputy.

137. Granville Sharp (1735-1813) was a philanthropist and scholar who chaired the Society for the Abolition of Slavery, founded in 1787. He is best known for his advocacy of justice for blacks in England's legal system, especially in the landmark cases of Jonathan Strong, James Somerset, and the Zong slave ship. See the introduction, p. 4, and pp. 236-37 in the Equiano section of this volume.

138. Equiano slightly adapts the verses from Job and Revelation to fit his syntax. Ephesians 5:5 differs somewhat from Equiano's version but retains the same sense: "For this ye know, that no whoremonger, nor unclean person, nor covetous man, who is an idolater, hath any inheritance in the kingdom of Christ and of God."

139. From Ecclesiasticus 2:11: "For the Lord is full of compassion and mercy, long-suffering, and very pitiful, and forgiveth sins, and saveth in time of affliction."

140. Equiano refers to the belief that human perception, unassisted by the light of Christian revelation, operates within a spiritual darkness that is the lot of merely "natural" man. Through belief in Christ, man leaves the state of nature and enters a state of grace.

141. Isaiah 65:24.

142. The "love feast" was an informal method of group worship that Whitefield and John Wesley first encountered at London's "Fetter Lane Society" of Moravians in the 1730s. Whitefield writes in his *Journal* for Sunday, 10 December 1738: "In the evening I went to Fetter Lane Society, where we had (what might not improperly be called) a love feast—eating a little bread and water, and spending about two hours in singing and prayers. . . . Surely a primitive spirit is reviving amongst us." By the later eighteenth century, love feasts had become a common practice among a variety of evangelical societies.

143. On the Calvinist doctrine of election and reprobation, see the introduction to this volume, pp. 6-7.

144. Acts 2:46.

145. Equiano is quoting a common Methodist hymn influenced by Romans 8. The Methodist preacher Freeborn Garrettson wrote in his journal: "O! to grace, how great a debtor / Daily I am constrained to be / Let that grace now like a fetter / Bind my wandering soul to thee." See *American Methodist Pioneer: The Life and Journals of The Rev. Freeborn Garrettson 1752-1827,* ed. Robert Drew Simpson (Rutland, VT: Academy Books; Madison, NJ: Drew University Library, 1984), p. 238.

146. See II Timothy 4:1, I Peter 4:5, and the Apostles' Creed.

147. Probably Lawrence Harlow's *The Conversion of an Indian, in a Letter to a Friend* (London, 1774), published several times during the late eighteenth century.

148. A derivative of Psalms 16:3: "But to the saints that are in the earth, and to the excellent, in whom is all my delight."

149. On the "new birth" see John 3:3 and our commentary in the introduction to this volume, pp. 5-6.

150. Galatians 3:24.

151. A note in the "sixth edition" (1793): "Romans, chapter viii. verses 1, 2, 3."
152. Matthew 25:41.
153. See Colossians 3:11, Ephesians 1:23, and I Corinthians 12:6, 15:28.
154. Westminster Chapel was, according to Paul Edwards and Rosalind Shaw, a Congregationalist establishment that favored Calvinistic theology ("The Invisible Chi in Equiano's *Interesting Narrative,*" *Journal of Religion in Africa* 19, no. 2 [1989]: 154).
155. See Hebrews 4:12.
156. The phrase "meant to attend the Lord's table" presumably refers here to the hope of eternal salvation. The book of Revelation culminates in an apocalyptic banquet that celebrates the marriage of Christ as Lamb and His bride the Church: "Blessed are they which are called unto the marriage supper of the Lamb" (Revelation 19:9).
157. James 2:10.
158. Ephesians 5:5.
159. That is, a full member of the church, entitled to receive Holy Communion.
160. The basic lesson of Hebrews 11 is that although the righteous must often undergo severe trials and persecutions, God is ever "a rewarder of them that diligently seek him" (verse 6).
161. *An Alarme to Unconverted Sinners, in a Serious Treatise* by Joseph Alleine (1634-1668), published with a preface by Richard Baxter in 1672, was the most popular seventeenth-century conversion treatise next to Baxter's *Call to the Unconverted* (see note 28 in the Gronniosaw section of this volume). Twenty thousand copies were sold upon its first publication, a figure bested only three years later when a second imprint, newly entitled *The True Way to Happiness,* cleared 50,000 copies. By 1691 Alleine's text was also available under the title *A Sure Guide to Heaven.* Over three hundred years later, it is still being published.
162. See Genesis 32:24-28.
163. Luke 23:33, Revelation 5:5, and Romans 7:9.
164. Jesus is the "second Adam" according to the method of Biblical interpretation known as typology, in which Old Testament characters and events are said to foreshadow or prefigure details in the life of Christ. Thus, Adam, the Old Man, is said to be a type of Christ, the New Man; and the tree that bore the fruit occasioning Adam's original sin becomes a prefiguration of the cross that bore redemption as its fruit.
165. Psalms 19:9-10.
166. Song of Solomon 5:10; compare I Samuel 18:7.
167. An "earnest" is a pledge; in John 16, Jesus speaks of "the Spirit" (the *Paraclete,* also known as "The Holy Ghost") that will abide in the Christian community after his death and serve as a comforting pledge or guarantee of eternal life in God the Father.
168. "Ethiopian" is used here in its ancient Greek sense to mean "black African"; this usage prevailed through the nineteenth century. Compare Psalms 68:31: "Princes shall come out of Egypt; Ethiopia shall soon stretch out her hands unto God."
169. Philippians 2:13.

170. Song of Solomon 1:3 and Isaiah 8:14.
171. *Canticles* (from the Latin *canticum*, "song") is another title for the Song of Solomon.
172. Zechariah 13:1 and John 4:14.
173. Isaiah 40:4.
174. Ebenezer, "the stone of help," is a stone that Samuel sets in place, after defeating the Philistines, to commemorate Yahweh's help in battle (I Samuel 7:12).
175. I John 5:7.
176. The phrase "but only Jesus Christ" does not appear in Acts 4:12.
177. Reverend William Romaine (1714-1795) was an Anglican preacher and author who was pastor of St. Anne's, Blackfriars, London. Included among his theological treatises are *An Alarm to a Careless World* (1755) and *A Treatise upon the Life of Faith* (1764). Romaine was a close associate of the Countess of Huntingdon.
178. Compare Jeremiah 13:23: "Can the Ethiopian change his skin, or the leopard his spots? then may ye also do good, that are accustomed to do evil."
179. The following footnote appears here in the first edition, the 1791 New York imprint, and the London "sixth edition" (1793): "At the request of some of my most particular friends, I take the liberty of inserting it here." By the nineteenth century, Equiano's petition (not reprinted in this volume) had been moved from the main text and placed in an appendix.
180. Equiano's note: "Granville Sharp, Esq. the Rev. Thomas Clarkson; the Rev. James Ramsay; our approved friends, men of virtue, are an honour to their country, ornamental to human nature, happy in themselves, and benefactors to mankind!" See notes 36-39, 119, 137 above.
181. The text from "May Heaven make the British senators" to the quotation from Job 30:25 reappears frequently in various versions throughout Equiano's oeuvre: see his letter to the Senate of Great Britain in the *Public Advertiser*, 13 February 1788; his letter to the author of the "Humanity" poem, Samuel Jackson Pratt, in the 27 June 1788 issue of the *Morning Chronicle and London Advertiser;* and Cugoano's *Thoughts and Sentiments* (pp. 129-30 of this volume).
182. Equiano reprints here a near exact copy of his 13 March 1788 letter to Lord Hawkesbury, the late Commissary for the African Settlement. The text begins with "As the inhuman traffic" and stretches for nine paragraphs to "in return for manufactures."
183. Equiano's note: "In the ship Trusty, lately for the new Settlement of Sierra Leona, in Africa, were 1,300 pair of shoes (an article hitherto scarcely known to be exported to that country) with several others equally new, as articles of export. Thus will it not become the interest, as well as the duty, of every artificer, mechanic, and tradesman, publicly to enter their protest against this traffic of the human species?— What a striking, what a beautiful contrast is here presented to view, when compared with the cargo of a slave ship! Every feeling heart, indeed, sensibly participates of the joy, and with a degree of rapture reads of barrels of *flour* instead of *gunpowder*— *biscuits and bread* instead of *horse beans*—*implements of husbandry* instead of *guns* for destruction, rapine, and murder—and various articles of *usefulness* are the pleasing substitutes for the *torturing thumbscrew,* and the *galling chain,* &c."

184. The argument that free trade with Africa would be more advantageous to Britain than slavery and the slave trade is also made, among others, by Ignatius Sancho in his *Letters* and Cugoano in a section of *Thoughts and Sentiments* not reprinted in this volume.

185. Here Equiano omits this key phrase from the letter: "and for which a partial Ill must be supported." See the introduction to this volume, note 35.

186. A drag is a hook with which a person is forcibly pulled.

187. A cat is slang for cat-o'-nine-tails, a whip made of nine knotted thongs used by the British army and navy until 1881 to punish offenders.

188. This paragraph appears for the first time in the London "sixth edition" (1793) as a footnote to the text.

189. Equiano's note: "Viz. Some curious adventures beneath the earth, in a river in Manchester,—and a most astonishing one under the Peak of Derbyshire—and in September 1792, I went 90 fathoms down St. Anthony's Colliery, at Newcastle, under the river Tyne, some hundreds of yards on the Durham side." Equiano visited these towns to advertise and sell his *Narrative* among an increasingly politicized working class.

190. Equiano's note: "See Gentleman's Magazine for April 1792, Literary and Biographical Magazine and British Review for May 1792, and the Edinburgh Historical Register or Monthly Intelligencer for April 1792."

191. Micah 6:8.